MW00609178

The Seven Thunders Of God

Revelation Revealed

Hope of Glory Ministries
www.hopeofglory.us
vtanner@kohm.net
(336) 286-6400

By Van Tanner

NOTICE OF RIGHTS:

All rights reserved. No part of this publication may be stored, transmitted, reproduced in any way, including but not limited to photocopy, photograph, electronic, magnetic or other record, without prior agreement and written permission of the publisher.

Copyright © 2001
Van Tanner
Kingdom of Heaven Ministries
4747 Lake Brandt Road
Greensboro, North Carolina, 27455
336-286-6400

Table of Contents

Acknowledgements:

Jesus, Jesus, Jesus, Jesus, Jesus, Jesus, and Jesus. All Glory and honor to Him First!!

I want to give special thanks to my beloved partner and wife, Gina. You endured untold hardship as the Lord kept me from you. Without you, Gina, this work would have never become a reality. You deserve full recognition for the completion of this book.

To my daughters: Bree, Cassie, and Summer. Thank you for understanding the importance of this work and enduring all the hardship of over 4000 hours away from you.

Blessings to everyone at Hope of Glory Ministries. Your encouragement through the tribulation enabled me to continue to the end. You shared not only the hardship but also the vision of the end-time manifestation of Christ.

Finally, to Karen, "Thank you, I can only pray the Lord return a hundred-fold into your life."

Special acknowledgement to artist Sandi O'Reilly, whose painting was used for the cover. I thank God for giving you such a prophetic vision. Special thanks to Sharen for your help.

To order more books or make contact with Van Tanner...

Hope of Glory Ministries - www.hopeofglory.us

Greensboro, NC

336 286-6400

Email: vtanner@kohm.net

Color Separations: DTP, Inc.
Printing: M Press, Inc.
Greensboro, NC 27409
(336) 855-0400

Revelation

Blessed is he that <u>readeth</u>, and they that hear *the words of this prophecy, and* keep *those things, which are written therein: for the time is at hand. (Rev. 1:3)*

Preface...   The trumpet call?

You are about to partake in the fulfillment of a promise given two thousand years ago and anticipated by countless men and women of God for generations. This promise is that the mystery of Jesus Christ, hidden for generations, is revealed as He comes again to reign in the hearts of men. This book is a trumpet call for those who have cried out to know the fullness of Christ, whose hearts have ached with desire for the intimacy of a consuming relationship with God, whose spirits have hungered for living water to flood through them as a river of righteousness. God has been waiting since the Garden for a generation of people who would lose themselves utterly in a relationship with Him, so that they could be restored unto Him as sons and daughters. David was called a "man after God's own heart" not because he was without sin, but because of his steadfast desire to know and please his Lord. Like David, this chosen generation of sold out Christians, consumed by a desire to follow Him, is being called to fulfill God's plan to bring His people back into intimate fellowship with Him. He is beginning to gather His Bride without spot or blemish!

The evidence of this end-time calling of God is not to be found in the recent resurgence of interest by many in attending church. It is not to be found in millennial stories that have captured the popular imagination in fiction, movies, and even the Christian media. It is not to be found in the attitudes of many believers who feel that since they have been saved by grace, they need only to patiently endure the tribulations of this world until they can escape through death or the rapture to a place of eternal bliss. The testimony that Christ's appearing is nigh is manifest in the coming together of a people who have heard the voice of God speaking in their hearts and minds; He is beckoning them to enter in at the narrow gate. They have heard His call to separate themselves from the things of this world, to lay down their lives and die to self so that Christ can live in them, and that they can keep His commandment to be "perfect" in Him. His Spirit has flooded them with an overwhelming and all-consuming desire to know Him intimately. They are diligently seeking Him out in prayer and through His Word. Their spirits burn with a hunger no longer able to be satisfied with the things of this world and only relieved by drinking deeply of the Water of Life.

This message is for those who have been asking the question, "Isn't there MORE to my walk with Christ than just waiting to be with Him in Heaven?" This message is for those whose hearts are - at this moment - being stirred by God that there is a deeper truth waiting to be revealed by His Spirit. They are the ones whom He has chosen to receive the revelation of Jesus Christ and are ordained to a great end-day ministry. This revelation is not imparted to all Christians. If you believe there is still more to God's plan, then you are a candidate to receive the revelation of Jesus Christ; just because you are a Christian does not mean that you have this Revelation. You may believe in Jesus and even profess Him, but has He revealed Himself in and through you? How can you be certain? Read this introduction and ask God to reveal the truth to you. The book of Revelation is a deeply spiritual book, one that must become a part of the reader ("eaten" Rev. 10:9) if it is to be understood, and its precious promises are to be fulfilled. It is a book created for a special time. It will <u>profoundly</u> change the lives of a generation of people.

Revelation is the only book in the Bible that begins with a promise of blessing. **"Blessed is he that <u>readeth</u>, and they that <u>hear</u> the words of this prophecy, and <u>keep</u> those things, which are written therein: for the time is at hand." Rev. 1:3.** *However, this promise of blessing is given only to a <u>people</u> who have "eyes to see and ears to hear." Those who refuse to open their hearts to the 'fresh manna of heaven' will miss the "blessings" of God in these last days. Sadder still will be those who receive this revelation but refuse to "keep" or take to heart what they hear. They will hear the trumpet of Zion but refuse to ascend together into a holy assembly. These people are not able to separate themselves from the preoccupation of their own lives; thus the sound of His voice will be lost in the strife, concerns, ambitions, and dreams of daily living.*

Two thousand years ago Israel was crying out for a messiah; yet when He came, they did not recognize Him. He appeared among them in a way that they had not anticipated and were unwilling to see; thus they were blind to the Truth and missed the blessings of the kingdom. They wanted a "king" on a white stallion riding in to claim His kingdom; instead, they got a suffering Christ riding a donkey, with no-name followers, declaring the way of the kingdom. Being offended they struck down their very blessing. Could this happen again? Are we prepared to hear the truth about Christ's return, or will the veil of traditions deny us the true 'blessed hope' as it did the Sadducees and Pharisees? Do not let that happen to you. Open your hearts to the revelation of Christ and watch as the book of Revelation in your understanding changes from a book of hopeless despair into a book of life and love. You will discover a book that blesses those who rise to the call of the Trumpet and partake in the greatest Harvest of souls the world has ever seen.

INTRODUCTION

The word **Revelation** in 1:1, "The *Revelation* (apokalupsis) of Jesus Christ…" gives us insight into the contents of this powerful book. According to Thayer's dictionary, 'apokalupsis' means; a disclosure of truth and instruction. It comes from the Greek words "apo", *to remove* and "kalupto", *veil*.

'Revelation' is the removing of the veil that we may receive the truth designed to instruct us.

This book will open the book of Revelation to God's true meaning for the events surrounding Christ's return. Yet, in Rev. 5: 4-5, John declares that only Jesus Christ can open the book. Therefore, for us to understand the book of Revelation, we must hunger and thirst for more of Christ. Our relationship with Him must be so sold out that we can say with Paul that "it is no longer I that live but Christ that lives in me"(Gal.2: 20). It is only Christ, living in us, who can open the book to our understanding. Total surrender to His will is the test that each of us must pass if we are to be able to receive the true revelation of Christ!

This does not mean that only perfect Christians can receive the revelation, but rather that it is the receiving of the revelation that opens us to more of the life of Christ. Those who have hearts that are truly open to His fullness will find that each step taken on this journey through the book of Revelation will bring forth an awakening in their spirits. Each new revelation will resound like thunder in their hearts and manifest as a life-changing event, bringing them ever closer to knowledge of the Father through consummate unity with the Son. For the book of Revelation is the revelation of Jesus Christ given by Jesus Christ to his sold out bondservants. The words of Revelation may be read and studied with diligence, they may be meditated on day and night, they may even be memorized; but if Christ does not reveal them through His Spirit, then they will remain a mystery – they CANNOT BE UNDERSTOOD WITH A CARNAL MIND!

The understanding of the truths of Revelation will only be unlocked as you open the door of your heart and let Jesus come in. As you walk with Him through this book, He will take you by the Spirit into the kingdom of heaven, to the tabernacle of the living God, which is in your heart. If you allow the Lamb who was slain to sit upon the throne of your heart, He will be established as the Lord of your life. If you bow down your 'will' before Him, you will be recognized as His true bondservant. As you begin to worship Him in Spirit and in Truth, He will offer you the revelation of Jesus Christ and ask that you consume it. The joy of the revelation will be sweet to the taste. But as you consume it, it will consume you; thus it will become bitter to your belly as you realize that what the Lord has really offered you is the death of self. For only by dying can you unloose the seven seals of the revelation that release the trumpets of God to sound in your spirit. As each seal is loosed and the trumpets begin to sound, carnality is revealed and purified. Burned by the fire of His righteous

judgment, we become vessels for His appearing. To increase in understanding of the revelation of Jesus Christ, you will be required to offer even more of yourself as a living sacrifice, until all of you is finally crucified, poured out, refined by His love, and cleansed of all unrighteousness. As part of His purified Bride without spot or blemish, you will become one with Him to fulfill the remainder of His ministry here on earth as a Harvester of the lost before reigning with Him eternally.

The work of this revelation is deeply personal and uncovered in a uniquely individual way by each disciple of Christ. However, the book should also be read and understood as an end-time instruction manual for His chosen generation. It is an outline of the events that will occur in the latter days as Christ appears again on earth through a corporate manifestation through a unified body of believers. It is this dynamic aspect of the revelation that will be the primary focus of this text.

Pattern of the Study

This study is laid out in seven sections. Sections 1-4 lay a foundation for the understanding of Christ's appearing. Sections 5 and 6 reveal the story of Christ' return and ministry. These two sections in particular constitute the heart of this study; but without Sections 1-4, you will not be able to understand their truth. Section 7, as the last section, will act as an epilogue to the Revelation.

Section 1 begins by laying the foundation, where the Word will be revealed to us in the language of Jesus Christ. Jesus spoke in parables using **types** and shadows as a form of communicating the truth of the kingdom. Without an understanding of these types, we will be as the Sadducees and Pharisees who could not "hear" the words of Jesus. He said that His words were "life", because the types bring life to our heart. Then we will look to the prophetic words of Joel and Daniel as they describe the **chosen generation** who will be called forth by the trumpet of revelation as the army of God during the last days. We will proceed in Section 2 to study how, through obedience unto the death of self, the **mystery of Christ-in-us is revealed** in the second coming or 'appearing' of Christ in a corporate body of believers. This end-day army of God will join together to usher in the Greatest Harvest of lost souls ever known. Section 3 begins the study of the actual Revelation scriptures describing how the book is opened in our own spirits and how, through a vision of the throne room, we can learn to grow in Glory until Christ becomes manifest in us. Section

4 heralds Christ's message to the churches in the latter days (Chapter 3) and also reveals the 'pattern of Sevens'. In this pattern we find that there are five groups of seven, each having its own piece of the seven Thunders of God – the 7 seals, 7 angels, 7 trumpets, 7 vials, and 7 vial angels.

The primary focus of our study and the actual story of the end-time appearance of Christ begins in Section 5 and is continued in Section 6. Section 5 discusses the First Dispensation, covering the first three-and-one-half years during which Christ gathers His Bride out of dead religion. Section 6 discusses the Second Dispensation where over the remaining three-and-one-half years of Christ's ministry, He appears in a corporate body of believers to restore His kingdom. The final section, which covers the last chapter, is the Epilogue to both the book of Revelation and this study and delivers His promise of blessing to all who will keep this prophecy. The seven sections are followed by ten parentheticals which are supplementary scriptural studies designed to enhance the understanding of Revelation.

These parentheticals, which amplify or explain the events and types of Revelation, are taken from chapters and verses of Revelation not covered in the previous seven sections. The parentheticals are followed by ten Commentaries, which are similar to the parentheticals, but they are **subject studies** using supporting scriptures from other books of the Bible. They are designed to give greater background to types and doctrines associated with this study. A comprehensive annotated dictionary of the terms and types portrayed throughout the book of Revelation concludes the study.

Final note: All the scriptures should be in King James unless otherwise noted. There also many references to Strong's, it was the primary source of Greek and Hebrew definitions. Since many words have been defined with a cultural or doctrinal bias, several secular lexicons were utilized as well. Any questions should be addressed to Van Tanner at vtanner@kohm.net.

May God bless the reading of this book and the study of His Holy Bible.

Reference Notes

Section I   Laying the Foundation

Be patient with this study. The study of the book of Revelation is not to be taken lightly. It will not be understood if foundations are not first laid that will enable your eyes to be open to truths that will change your life and your eternal relationship with Jesus Christ. Revelation is a book written in the language of Jesus Christ, and we must first learn that language. There is a dictionary in the back of the book that you can refer to as needed to help you learn this new language. We must also understand the mysteries of God, which have now been opened to the Saints. Much of the foundation that we will lay in the first two chapters of this study will be directed toward demonstrating that Col. 1:25 (the mystery of God) is both the key to understanding Revelation and the goal of every Christian's life. With these foundations laid in your spirit, it is guaranteed that the whole Bible will become alive with deeper life-giving truth.

Chapter 1

The Method of Interpretation of Revelation

How it began

This study was undertaken with great reverence because God had directed it. All who were part of this study were directed by God to open their hearts and souls to "thus says the Lord." Many were initially reluctant to pursue any study concerning Revelation, reasoning that mortal man was not able to unlock the deep mysteries of this book. Our desire to please God, however, overcame our concerns, and we joined to hear what God wanted to say. We had no idea what was soon to be revealed. Most of us believed in the traditional Pre-tribulation Rapture doctrine and were very surprised at what the Lord showed us. We fasted, prayed, and set ourselves apart to seek God. As we opened our hearts and focused our desires on the Lord, He began to direct our path and unlock truths none of us had ever known before.

Days turned into months of inspired study that was closer to worship than it was to scholarship. God seemed to fill every moment of our time, opening verse after verse with inspired truth. This truth was not conceived in the mind of man, but wholly inspired by the Spirit of Christ. Scriptures began to support one another so quickly and with such strength, we marveled that we had never seen the connections. As we continued to fellowship the Lord and His Revelation, the Spirit of Peace seemed to reveal truth to us all. In this way we learned that the Lord wanted to *reveal* Revelation to our spirits, not to have us approach Revelation as a scholarly endeavor.

On one such occasion, we found ourselves puzzled by Chapter Four of Revelation. Try as we might, nothing seemed to become clear, and we entertained thoughts of skipping this chapter until later. Finally, the Lord spoke through one of the pastors and told us to stop for the night and go to bed. That night everyone heard the same thing from the Lord: do not skip Chapter Four because it is the foundation of the whole book. In prayer the next morning a wonderful picture of the throne room appeared to one of the pastors, illuminating the images in Chapter Four like pictures in a slide show. As that pastor began to draw what he saw, another pastor was moved to add scripture to the

pictures. Still another pastor received a vision of a time line that connected images and scripture together to form a cohesive outline of the message God was speaking to us. When it was all brought together, we were amazed to see Chapter Four in a completely new light: it was the throne room of our heart in which Christ was to sit as Lord. We will discuss this in greater depth in a later chapter.

Being inspired and hearing from God is not by itself a unique way to approach God's word. What God also did was to show us **from His Word** the definitions to the imagery used throughout Revelation. As one image was revealed, then that image would work in conjunction with other known definitions to unlock the meaning of yet others. The Lord built this study line by line, here a little there a little, until the picture was complete. It has been there all along, yet we had seen it only in pieces and never as a living whole. The final picture is not one of a series of Middle East conflicts with Israel fulfilling God's plan, but a wonderful appearing of Jesus Christ…the risen Lord. Revelation is penned, after all, as the 'revelation of Jesus' Christ, not the Battle of the antichrist. Christ has used this study to put together a puzzle in which each piece adds to the whole; and when He is finished, we find ourselves looking into the glorious face of Jesus.

Isaiah prophesied about the day of Christ's appearing and the revealing of Revelation in Isaiah 28. We know that he was speaking of the end time because in verse 22, he spoke of 'a destruction' for the whole earth proclaiming that great Day of the Lord when he returns to claim His kingdom …Judgment Day. What an awesome feeling to hear God's word spoken by His prophet Isaiah thousands of years ago directly to us today! The power and relevance of Isaiah's prophecy for today brings destiny to our doorstep. This is the time even the prophets of old desired to see!

God, through Isaiah, has spoken through the ages to us today, pray that you have ears to hear…

Line upon line, here a little there a little is the way Revelation is opened.
Isaiah 28:8-22

8 *For all tables are full of vomit and filth; no place is clean.*

These are the spots that must be removed; worldliness mixed with His body makes the Lord sick. Lukewarm Christians are spewed out of His mouth in Rev. 3:16.

---

9 *"Whom will he teach knowledge? And whom will he make to understand the message? Those just weaned from milk? Those just drawn from the breasts?*

This is a revelation of meat; only those mature enough in the Spirit will be able to receive this revelation. It will be meaningless to all others.

---

10 *For precept must be upon precept, precept upon precept, line upon line, line upon line, here a little, there a little."*

This is exactly the way the book has to be opened. As stated earlier, it takes time to understand the language that Jesus uses.

---

11 *For with stammering lips and another tongue he will speak to this people,*

This is the language of Jesus Christ, a spiritual tongue. You must open your heart fully to Christ before you will understand His language. It is the carnal mind that veils types and parables.

---

12 *To whom He said, "This is the rest with which you may cause the weary to rest," and, "This is the refreshing"; yet they would not hear.*

He is pointing out that this revelation will bring the Lord's Day, a day of refreshing and rest.

---

13 *But the word of the LORD was to them, "Precept upon precept, precept upon precept, line upon line, line upon line, here a little, there a little," that they might go and fall backward, and be broken and snared and caught.*

He has penned Revelation in such a way that only those who are His can understand it. That means that those who are not His will be exposed by their failure to understand.

---

14 *Therefore hear the word of the LORD, you scornful men, <u>who rule this people</u> who are in Jerusalem,*

He now addresses the carnal leaders who refuse hidden manna. They have lorded over the people for the sake of their own pride and are against anything that threatens that authority...even if it is Christ.

---

15 *Because you have said, "We have made a covenant with death, and with Sheol we are in agreement. When the overflowing scourge passes through, it will not come to us, for we have made lies our refuge, and under falsehood we have hidden ourselves."*

Many will not believe in this revelation of Christ because their whole relationship with Christ is about keeping <u>their</u> life and missing Hell (Sheol). They think that just because they profess Christ,

they need not fear hell. This message is the message of luke-warmness..."we have it all and need of nothing." The Lord told the Laodiceans that if they did not go through the fire, He would spew them out. This revelation of Christ is to remove the lies and prepare a people.**

---

16 *Therefore thus says the Lord GOD: "Behold, I lay in Zion a stone for a foundation, a tried stone, a precious cornerstone, a sure foundation; whoever believes will not act hastily.*

If He is not the chief cornerstone of your life, then...

---

17 *Also I will make justice the measuring line, and righteousness the plummet; the hail will sweep away the refuge of lies, and the waters will overflow the hiding place.*

Christ will judge you and show you the lies that have misguided you. The tribulation will erode the sandy foundation that you have built in Christ.

---

18 *Your covenant with death will be annulled, and your agreement with Sheol will not stand; when the overflowing scourge passes through, then you will be trampled down by it.*

The first lie Christ will wash away from these scoffers is their covenant with hell. He will then show them their need for a relationship with Him, and that the best way to achieve that relationship is to be humbled by the mighty hand of God.

---

19 *As often as it goes out it will take you; for morning by morning it will pass over, and by day and by night; it will be a terror just to understand the report."*

There will be no escaping this revelation. The truth will become self-evident.

---

20 *For the bed is too short to stretch out on, and the covering so narrow that one cannot wrap himself in it.*

No one will be allowed to rest with his or her lies. They will be unable to answer the questions that arise as this "Day of the Lord" comes closer.

---

21 *For the LORD will rise up as at Mount Perazim, he will be angry as in the Valley of Gibeon-- that He may do His work, His awesome work, and bring to pass His act, His unusual act.*

This is His work and He will perform it. It will be an act so unusual that it speaks only of the will of God, not man. That is the nature of the Revelation; it must be done by and through Him.

---

22 *Now therefore, do not be mockers, lest your bonds be made strong; for I have heard from the Lord GOD of hosts, a destruction determined even upon the whole earth.(NKJ)*

The Day of the Lord is at hand! Praise be to the righteous judge...the earth (i.e. carnality) will not stand.

FIGURATIVE AND LITERAL INTERPRETATIONS

The power of any revealed truth is measured by just how consistent that interpretation remains as it occurs repeatedly throughout the Word of God. For example, as a spiritual 'type', *white* represents *purity;* you can expect that everywhere the word *white* is used figuratively, it will mean *purity*. Numbers, too, stay consistent in meaning as a spiritual type.

> **2**=witness **3**=complete **4**=end-time **5**=grace **6**=man **7**=perfection **10**=judgment **12**=Godly authority **42**=His appearing

As you go through the Bible, you will find that these numbers will bring greater meaning to the stories and parables you read. Tares, good soil, seed planting, fishing, pearls, bread, wine, etc., are just a few of the images that have been defined as symbols and will give greater insight into the truth regardless of where they occur.

Communicating through types

Communicating figuratively through types was so normal to Jesus that when He spoke plainly (without types), His disciples were amazed (John 16:29). This is the language of God; and like any language, the words stay consistent. We agree that a 'horse' is a 'horse' and a 'car' is a 'car', so that we can communicate. We may visualize different colors and kinds of horses and cars, but the essence of each is the same for both of us. If I said horse and you thought car, it would make it difficult to share ideas. Jesus' language is much the same. He is consistent with types and truths throughout the entire Bible. If we perceive an inconsistency, it is because our understanding is darkened and not because of a contradiction in the Word.

Today, we require that words be defined explicitly and literally. We want to be sure that all truth is preserved and doctrines properly grounded. Unfortunately, efforts to interpret scripture more narrowly and literally rarely seem to bring men and doctrines into greater agreement; rather, what is created is even more division over the TRUTH. This is why Jesus Christ chose the language of parables and types. Truth must be given that touches the heart and bypasses the carnal mind. When truth is received this way, the Word will sing in harmony. The mind seeks truth which feeds carnal pride and then deprives men of 'spiritual ears' to hear. Notice how many times in the Word Jesus says, "For those who have ears to hear." Jesus was telling us that we need His spiritual language to understand what He is saying. He is looking for hearts that desire and long for truth, because He is the Truth. Therefore, He is trying to find sheep "that will hear His voice" (John 10:27). He once told the Pharisees that they were unable to even hear His words. We know that they understood every word in its literal form, yet they could not hear the language of "life" that He spoke directly to their hearts. They did not open their hearts to truth; they just wanted to be right in their own minds. Today, we have fallen back to reading the scriptures in the same shallow way, missing the full richness of interpretation available to an open heart.

Problems when we reject types

When we fail to rightly understand the language of types, we can fall victim to another of Satan's deceptions; we may be unknowingly tempted to change or add to what is written if it does not support what we believe. We can avoid this snare by requiring that every truth or symbol pass the test of consistency. This will keep symbols from being redefined in Revelation in a manner that is inconsistent with their definitions elsewhere in the Bible. Our desire to conform interpretations of scripture into our own doctrinal beliefs is so intense that sometimes-obvious symbols are interpreted literally. For example, despite the fact that an Angel defined the New Jerusalem for John in Rev. 21:9 as a symbol for the Bride of Christ, most current end-time doctrines interpret the New Jerusalem literally, as a city descending from heaven. Even though the Word itself defines the New Jerusalem as a symbolic description of the Bride, many men choose to ignore the scriptural truth just to support a belief or doctrine. This can be a very dangerous practice. Interpreting the New Jerusalem as a literal city hinders the revealing of deeper symbolic spiritual truths. For example, literal interpretations force us to believe that the gates of pearl or the streets of gold are just ornamentations, not revealed truths. The gates of pearl take on a deep spiritual meaning when seen as a type, freeing us to see the deeper truth; *to become part of the Bride, you must give all that you have and obtain the "pearl of great price"* (Matt. 13:46). Does not this interpretation give a greater revelation of Christ than a literal interpretation? Will I obtain a greater measure of His abundant life by believing that there is a big beautiful city in the Millennium or by believing that I need to increase the measure of Christ in my life to rule with Him?

If images in Revelation could be interpreted both literally and symbolically, then what authority is used to draw distinction between the two? Why 'the Beast' would be interpreted figuratively as a man, but the 'mark of the Beast' is interpreted literally as a tattoo? Why would the New Jerusalem be a literal city, but Babylon a metaphor? Unlike the other books of the New Testament, Revelation is a message given directly by Jesus Christ (Rev. 1:1) using His language. This would mean that all the imagery in Revelation is a parable of sorts; these 'types' are associated with Jesus Christ's appearing. Jesus spoke much of His wisdom using figurative types and parables; this is His preferred method for revealing the kingdom. We will also see that He stayed consistent with His use of types. We will use these spiritual types, which Christ defined, as our keys to unlock the book.

The Bible as the authority

In 2 Tim. 2:15 we are told to "rightly divide" the word of truth. This study is designed to help us rightly divide the book of Revelation. By "rightly divide", we mean that all scriptural interpretation is developed through a process whereby the Bible is used <u>first</u> as its own best source. In other words, to understand a type or term in Revelation, we would follow a three-step process:

- ❖ **First**, see if the term had been defined explicitly *in* the book of Revelation;
- ❖ **Second**, see if the types and terms have been explained by Jesus' own words or by the words of the prophets;
- ❖ **Third**, look to all of the occurrences of that type throughout scripture to discern its common meaning.

In most cases, following these three steps will provide clear definitions of the types or terms encountered in Revelation. However, in some cases, types defined using this three-step process will themselves be used to determine the definition of other types. Here we will use the revealed

Being open to deeper revelation does not mean being unscriptural. Indeed all revelation must be "line upon line". Have you ever studied to be sure that your end-time doctrine is scriptural? Many people just go with the crowd feeling that there is safety in numbers. However, we want you to study the Bible with us, and let it be the source of your beliefs. For example, did you know that all of the scriptures speaking of people being separated and removed refer to evil ones, not believers? In our study of the rapture all of these scriptures will be opened, and you may be very surprised at what they reveal. Many people are surprised to find out that there is no antichrist mentioned in the book of Revelation. Some scholars may want to dispute that point, but the truth is…'antichrist' is not mentioned anywhere in the book of Revelation, nor is there any mention of a world leader. Some choose to interpret the Beast mentioned in Revelation as the antichrist, but how did they decide on this interpretation? Do you know why? Have you ever been

---

"Kings" Literal or Spiritual

The use of the term "king" in Revelation can be interpreted to mean either a natural monarchy or a spiritual type. How do we determine which interpretation is correct? Rev. 1:6 states, "And hath made **us kings and priests** unto God". Therefore, according to this scripture, the "us" are the 'kings'. Jesus gives "us" spiritual authority that makes us *kings* in His kingdom. Based on this scripture, we should adhere to a spiritual definition for the word 'kings' as it occurs in the book of Revelation. If we stick to definitions defined explicitly by scripture, then we will build a sure foundation for God to challenge wrong notions and preconceptions of biblical truths. This will then prevent doctrinal biases from mis-shaping our understanding of scripture.

For example, if our doctrine demands that Christians are absent from most of Revelation, then *that position* predetermines the rejection of 'kings' as Christians. These persons would instead look for a natural or literal definition without regard to contrary scriptural references. Interpreting scripture from a predetermined mindset not only promotes error, but it creates a perspective that severely limits the power of God to divinely inspire new revelation in the heart of a believer. That is why Jesus was rejected by religious leaders of His time. He came as the suffering Christ, instead of a ruling monarch; thus their preconceptions blinded them.

Word of God to build understanding "precept upon precept". For example, in the illustration below where "kings" is defined explicitly by actual scripture in Revelation, we can see how this definition can be used to assist us in understanding other less explicit terms that are used in conjunction with "kings".

What is the source of your doctrines?

Doctrines are just beliefs, and we all have them. However, when they are penned as universal statements of faith by an organization, they tend to become enshrined or "set in stone" and tend to shape our interpretation of what we read and believe in the Word. **What we read in the Word should shape what we believe.** There is absolutely nothing wrong with doctrines or statements of faith, but they should be open to a deeper revelation as God opens "deep unto deep".

presented with the scriptural pros and cons of common beliefs such as the antichrist or the rapture? Instead, you were probably told, as a statement of fact, "we" believe in 'this or that' interpretation; thus you deferred personal revelation. Accepting any doctrine without looking into its scriptural foundation can be dangerous, even if it is a commonly held belief. Today, many Christians are dogmatic about their end-time beliefs, yet they are unable to tell you why. Scripture tells us that it is the obligation of every Christian to study to show himself approved unto God by rightly dividing the word of truth through the revelation of God's Spirit within him. Pray that the Spirit would open your heart and mind to the truths that He would reveal in you as we proceed through our study.

Chapter 2

The Trumpet Sounds for the Elect

Rom. 8:19 — The Chosen Generation

19 The creation waits in eager expectation for the <u>sons of God</u> to be revealed. (NIV)

Joel 2:1-3

1 Blow ye the **trumpet** in Zion, and sound an alarm in my holy mountain: let all the inhabitants of the land tremble: for the day of the LORD cometh, for it is nigh at hand;

2 A day of darkness and of gloominess, a day of **clouds** and of thick darkness, as the morning spread upon the mountains: **a great people** and a strong; **there hath not been ever the like,** neither shall be any more after it, even to the years of many generations.

3 A **fire** devoureth before them; and behind them a flame burneth: the **land is as the garden of Eden** before them, and behind them a desolate wilderness; yea, and nothing shall escape them.

The book of Revelation is partially an end-time manual, designed to give the last generation an understanding of the events that will close down time. As a dynamic part of the corporate appearing of Jesus Christ, that generation will need to know God's plan and what He expects from them. Look at these scriptures from Romans and Joel and let them speak to you. God is raising up a generation, a "great people," the like of which the world has never before seen. They will be so completely in love with the Lord that their very presence will speak of Jesus; thus, they are called the Sons of God. God has chosen them to play a special part in end-time events.

These chosen sons have been preordained to "sound the trumpet" by bringing forth a message that lets everyone know that the Day of the Lord is upon us. They will declare a time of great tribulation for those whose hearts are bound by the deception and blindness of their own desires. Yet, they will also bring a time of unparalleled liberation through a revelation of hope with the power to set the world free. These Elect messengers of God, transformed by the power of Christ, will show us the way back into the garden. Reject the revelation of Christ at the peril of being released into the wilderness of desolation, into a life of hopeless bondage to carnality and death.

Opening the mystery to the Saints of God allows them to be part of the fulfillment to the word of God. Even though there have been individual saints throughout the ages who have received the mystery, there has never been a gathering that would qualify as 'manifest sons'. The chosen generation is so **in-love** with Jesus Christ that they are "a generation" willing to lay down their lives so that His life will be seen in a body of people (true Glory see page vii). They will be able to hear His revelation and live it. They are truly a *chosen* generation and a royal priesthood. These are Saints who have figuratively "lost their heads" for Jesus Christ. This generation can say with Paul, "*And last of all he was seen of me also, as of one born out of due time* (1 Cor. 15:8)." This generation has been chosen for this time to be His appearing!

Deut. 14:2

2 For thou art an holy people unto the LORD thy God, and the **LORD hath chosen thee to be a peculiar people** unto himself, above all the nations that are upon the earth.

We are Israel by faith. We should be set apart, not for our religious works, but by the sold out nature of our love for Christ and each other.

1 Pet. 2:9

9 But ye are a **chosen generation**, a royal priesthood, an holy nation, **a peculiar people**; that ye should shew forth the praises of him who hath called you out of darkness into his marvelous light:

The revelation of the *mystery*, **Christ-in-you,** was given to Paul so that he could give it to us (others out of time). Moreover, by fully receiving it, we become the manifest generation of Saints who take it to the world…just like Paul.

> **Col. 1:26** Even the mystery which hath been **hid from ages** and from <u>generations</u>, but **now is made manifest to his saints:**
> **27** To whom God would make known what is the riches of the glory of this mystery among the Gentiles; which is **Christ-in-you, the hope of glory**:

Galatians tells the story in detail. Paul thought that the *mystery* would be fulfilled in his generation. Yet, as time went on, it became apparent that his generation was not THE generation. Instead, he "finished the course" and "fought the good fight", desiring to cross over and be with Jesus. Listen to the frustration in his writings as he admonished those who should be maturing on the meat of the Word, but instead were babes, able only to digest milk (Heb. 5:12). Others obtained a measure of revelation just to turn back again to the rudiments of this world (2 Pet. 2:21-22).

What Paul had entered into and wanted others to experience was a place of spiritual being where it is possible to say *"...it is no longer I that live but Christ that lives within me"* (Gal. 2:20). He knew that it was possible for them to have their desires and lives so lost in those of Jesus Christ that they no longer lived for self but for Jesus. They could have no other life but His. Yet never has an entire *generation* come to such a profound relationship with Jesus Christ! It has taken almost two thousand years, from that generation of apostles until now, to lay the foundation for a message that would be revealed **IN** a generation or Corporate Body. It is necessary that there be a corporate appearing to fulfill the gospel; otherwise, many of the scriptures that refer to the Elect, the remnant, the manifest sons, the army of God, or the Bride of Christ would be denied. The many references to these people and of the end-time *Harvest* of God indicate that God's people should be eagerly preparing to take their part in the end-time events.

The Timing of the Revealing, Why Today?

There are two reasons why we believe God is opening Revelation to this generation. First, we know that in the end-time, God will raise up a mighty army (Joel Chapter 2) to restore His kingdom on earth. Today there is a mighty move of God that speaks of this army and the promised *'Harvest'* of souls for the kingdom. Unlike other times of religious awakening, the focus of this worldwide move of God is on building a relationship with Jesus rather than just mentally professing faith in Him. That is significant when you realize that the only true Christ-in-us move of God occurs as we begin to love the Lord with all of our mind, body and soul. Intimacy is the strength of Christ appearing in a believer. Second, we are ending the six thousand-year period of man, or the sixth day of the Lord, that sliver of time before the seventh day, when the Lord will have rest upon the earth. What other time could speak through 'types' any stronger than the end of the sixth day?

The end of the sixth day

According to generations of man recorded in the Bible and the Jewish calendar, we are ending six thousand years of the history of God's people. If a thousand years are as a day unto the Lord, it can be said that we are beginning to enter the seventh day of the Lord. We can associate the end of the sixth thousand years as a type of the Sabbath or day of rest, which could be projected to be the millennial reign. Hebrews talks of *the rest* yet to be entered. Nevertheless, before the seventh day, the sixth day must be finished; and it is the end of the sixth day that defines the end-time events in Revelation.

In Matt. 17: 1-5 the transfiguration of Christ takes place on a sixth day[1] (See insert). Each written word of scripture has purpose and significance, so why does God speak of this event as occurring at the end of the sixth day? It is part of the language of types that God uses to describe the kingdom. Having eyes to see types and shadows opens us to the deeper truth that this event describes what is to come at the end of the sixth day of God.

Matt. 17:15   For those who have ears to hear...

1   And **after** [1]**six days** Jesus taketh [2]Peter, James, and John his brother, and bringeth them up into an [3]high mountain apart,

2   And was [4]transfigured before them: and his face did shine as the sun, and his raiment was white as the light.

3   And, behold, there appeared unto them Moses and Elias talking with him.

4   Then answered Peter, and said unto Jesus, Lord, it is good for us to be here: if thou wilt, let us make here three tabernacles; one for thee, and one for Moses, and one for Elias.

5   While he yet spake, behold, a [5]bright cloud overshadowed them: and behold a voice[6] out of the cloud, which said, This is my beloved Son, in whom I am well pleased; hear ye him.

We are at the end of this [1]sixth day (a day is as a thousand years to God), and what occurred in the past can point the way to what is to come. A [2]remnant will be chosen to ascend with Jesus Christ to a [3]mountain top experience (relationship) where they can see Him face to face. Figuratively, this is similar to Moses seeing God and having the Glory of God [4]transfigure him. When this happens, the remnant will begin to see the cloud of witnesses that press in on us (Moses and Elias, Heb. 12:1) and know that it is good to be a part of such a great event. They will then join this great [5]cloud-of-witnesses to speak with a common voice the good news (*this gospel*—Matt. 24:14) and hear the voice[6] of the Lord that goes before them (Joel 2:11).

The beginning of the seventh day since creation is also the beginning of the third day since the Lord's crucifixion. This means those two thousand years from when Christ was crucified is also the beginning of the third thousand years (or third day). Christ arose on the third day, and Revelation indicates that the same pattern will apply to the second appearing of Jesus Christ. Calendars may vary on the exact date, but most agree that Christ's crucifixion occurred between 27 and 34 AD. Therefore, however you count it, all indicators point to this generation as the one that will see the great time of tribulation and *Harvest*.

Come with us as we open the book of Revelation and learn of this Elect Generation. You may find yourself written on the pages of this book that has just NOW been opened. See the truth that countless generations have only seen in shadow, but you can now see in full GLORY.

Rev. 1:1

"The Revelation of Jesus Christ, which God gave unto him, to show unto <u>his servants</u> things which must shortly come to pass; and he sent and signified it by his angel unto his servant John."

The Trumpet Sounds

This Elect, chosen generation is described in the very first verse of the book of Revelation. Notice that **the servants** to whom Christ shows the full 'revelation of Christ' will be the ones who will see the things written in the book of Revelation "shortly come to pass". These bond slaves are a special people because they are the first generation able to fully receive the revelation of Jesus Christ. Had any previous generation been given the Revelation, they would have seen the "things which **must** shortly come to pass." Yet, generations have come and gone and the events spoken of in the book of Revelation have not yet come to pass. Therefore, it is possible to claim with full assurance that the opening or understanding of the book of Revelation is a new experience in human history. It also means that the generation to whom God has chosen to reveal this message is the Manifest Sons spoken of in Rom. 8:19 and the great Army of God spoken of in Joel Chapter 2.

Listen to the Trumpet

God reserved the opening of this book until the end-day generation. This is not only proclaimed in Rev. 1:1, but in Daniel as well. These two verses in Daniel are rich with understanding for the end-time generation of God. Daniel is telling us that those who operate in the Glory will be used to bring many to Christ and the mystery of how they do this is sealed up until the end-time. Daniel is also told that the opening of the book will be in relation to knowledge, which we assume is revelation knowledge. This is truly the day in which revelation is pouring out upon God's children.

Dan 12:3-4
3   And they that be wise shall shine as the **brightness of the firmament; and they that turn many to righteousness** as the stars for ever and ever.
4   But thou, O Daniel, shut up the words, and **seal the book, even to the time of the end**: many shall run to and fro, and knowledge shall be increased.

This is not to say that no other generation has received a blessing from Revelation. Spiritual truth associated with the mystery of godliness has been revealed to godly men since John penned Revelation. However, all the speculation about end-time events in Revelation has done little to increase righteousness in the body of Christ. Instead, many men are stumbled by wild images associated with the events of Revelation. These men are not looking for truth, which leads to righteousness; but instead, they are seeking knowledge, which leads to pride. They are using the ambiguity associated with Revelation to prey on man's natural fears and desires. Movies and books, which appeal to our CARNAL nature, are gaining circulation, thereby threatening to replace sound doctrine. This tactic of Satan is doing its best to use our minds and imaginations to distract us from The Truth. In the absence of divine language or revelation, they set their beliefs on literal interpretations of Revelation that are today being exploited in fictional literature. Are these accounts right? Are these stories based in scripture? Has God inspired them? Are we swallowing unsound doctrine because it is popular or is delivered by well-known teachers? If these interpretations were subject to the stringent criteria of examination applied to any other doctrine, they would be substantiated by cross-references to other solid biblical truths. Interpretations such as, locusts being helicopters should not be accepted at face value. We would not choose to interpret scripture in the light of our preconceived doctrines; but instead, we would look to the Bible to define and illuminate the word "locust". God cannot author confusion. If we approach the Word openly and allow the Bible to give us our answers, we should all come to similar understandings. The book of Revelation has become the only book of the Bible where Christians seem to drop their standards for spiritual truth and replace them with a "Hollywood" presentation. Revelation, like every other word of scripture, should be reviewed and held accountable to the time-honored belief that...

2 Tim. 3:16-17 *All scripture is given by inspiration of God, and is profitable for doctrine, for reproof, for correction, for instruction in righteousness:* <u>*That the man of God may be perfect, thoroughly furnished unto all good works*</u>*.*

The tests that should be applied to any interpretation of the book of Revelation are these: it moves Christians on to perfection and righteous works; it has relevance in their daily life; and it enables them to walk in better relationship with Jesus Christ. These are the conditions that according to Revelation 1:1-3 are inherent in its promise. Any true and scriptural interpretation of Revelation must fulfill all of these things. Christians cannot accept claims that most of the book of Revelation is simply an account of what will happen to the unsaved not relevant for them. The truth is that the book of Revelation is specifically written for today's time and today's Christians. The deep truth is, God has patiently waited two thousand years to open this book to today's sold out, Christ-possessed believers, and they are about to be party to the single greatest revelation of modern time!

Section II   The Mystery Revealed

The *mystery* of the godliness, defined by Paul as *Christ in you*, is not THE revelation, it is the way Revelation is revealed. It is also the way an Elect generation moves into their election. We may think we know all about the mystery of God. But be open to seeing a deeper truth that will lead a chosen generation into the appearing of Christ. For a more detailed study of the mystery, see commentary "The Mystery" on page 128.

Chapter 3

Christ's Appearing

The foundation of most end-time doctrines is the prophecy of the 'Second Coming' of Jesus Christ. Traditionalists believe that Christ will descend from heaven on a cloud and take His church away at one of three points relative to a time of "tribulation". It is the timing of Christ's return that defines these scholars as "pre", "mid", or "post" tribulation. The most popular belief is that Christ will return before any tribulation time. Thus, we have the predominance of the "Pre-tribulation view". We will begin this study by challenging the very nature of all of these understandings of His coming. Jesus did not make His first appearance on earth 2000 years ago as the religious leaders of His time expected. Will His second appearing be just as much of a surprise to the scholars of today? This chapter will discuss the misconceptions surrounding current doctrines of Christ's Second Coming. It will demonstrate how this 'coming' is more of an 'appearing' linked to Christ-in-us (the mystery revealed), than a personal return to remove His Church physically from the earth.

CHRIST'S COMING AGAIN

Many people feel that the central event of the book of Revelation is Christ's *'coming'* again to earth. Therefore, it is important that we understand the full meaning of the word 'coming' as it was originally written. The two most common Greek words that translate 'coming', *parousia* and *erchomai*, have been misinterpreted in many different contexts adding to the problem of understanding what is the end time. A closer examination of these terms will shed light on much of the confusion surrounding this event.

Parousia

The Greek word *parousia* is translated 25 times in the New Testament as 'coming'. This definition is the foundation for some debate, as the original Greek term does not translate well into English. The English emphasis for the word "coming" is on the process of moving from a far place to a near place. The emphasis of the classic Greek is not one of motion, but rather of be-coming or coming into being, as in the "appearing" or "presence" of deity.

This is a very important distinction, especially since this word describes how the Lord will be manifest during end-time events. *Parousia*, translated directly from the original Greek, *allows* us the freedom, not readily apparent in the English translation, to interpret the event of Christ's 'coming' as a figurative 'appearing'. More time will be given to just how and why this "appearing" is manifest later; for now it is sufficient to introduce you to the concept of Jesus spiritually 'appearing'. God has "appeared" to His people in Spirit throughout Bible history (Ex. 16:10, Lev. 16:2). He appeared as the fire on the mountain and a cloud on the tabernacle. He appeared as a pillar of smoke and a burning bush; but in every case, it was God. In the same way, it will be no less Christ should He choose to appear in a "cloud" of witnesses...

Erchomai

The other common Greek word 'erchomai' does speak of moving from a far place to a near place. Today, many Christians are anticipating a literal **erchomai** of Christ, believing He will come bodily from heaven to earth. However, does the use of the word 'erchomai' really provide support for His bodily coming to rapture His Church? How does Jesus use this word in the context of **His** coming again? As you read the following scriptures in which Jesus declares His 'coming' to the high priest, remember that He had already told them in Luke 17:20-21, the kingdom of Heaven is not "here" or "there" nor "cometh with observation". It is *within* you (Luke 17:20-21)!

Matt. 26:63-64

63   But Jesus held his peace. And the high priest answered and said unto him, I adjure thee by the living God, that thou tell us whether thou be the Christ, the Son of God.

64   Jesus saith unto him, Thou hast said: nevertheless I say unto you, **Hereafter* shall ye see the Son of man sitting on the right hand of power, and **coming in the clouds of heaven**.

Another translation error related to the passage above is Jesus' use of the word **hereafter* related to His coming. To our ears, the word "hereafter" sounds as if it is a specific future event that could be experienced by direct observation. Yet the Greek words, '*Apo*' and '*Arti*', which are combined in the original text to translate 'hereafter' actually mean...**FROM THIS MOMENT FORWARD!** Jesus was telling the High Priest that 'from now on', you will see me coming in clouds of heaven. This ongoing event can only be interpreted figuratively. This means that Jesus has been coming out of Heaven for two thousand years. We will see that the clouds of heaven in which Jesus arrives is actually a Glory cloud (**Glory** page vii). This is the 'coming' of Jesus in a person. **As we see the Glory of God's presence on a person, we are really seeing Christ come into this world**. This is consistent with the focus of 'parousia', which means 'appearing'. In other words, every time we see Christ formed in a person, we see the coming of Christ. The book of Revelation will show us that this process will become so profound in the end time that soon a whole generation will allow Christ to 'come'; and then we will see a corporate 'appearing' of Christ.

THE PERSONAL VS. THE CORPORATE 'APPEARING'

Christ wants to be revealed in and through each individual, accomplishing the personal transformation that is the fulfillment of the mystery of God. Paul spoke of the power and the purpose of this personal appearing in Gal. 1:16 when he says, "*To reveal his Son in me, that I might preach him among the heathen ...*" He believed that Christ was being "revealed" in him so that he might reach a large group of unbelievers with the gospel message; that when the Glory of Jesus Christ living in him became visible to the world, people would listen. When people both **see** and **hear** the same message, they can comprehend through faith much more quickly than if they just hear the word alone. In Eph. Chapter 3, Paul prays that by his example of Christ-like suffering, the Ephesians would be strengthened with might in the inner man. It was his prayer that his visible witness of Christ, even through his martyrdom, would touch their hearts and open the gateway of their faith. They could then be partakers with Paul of the same faith that could birth Christ in their hearts (Eph. 3:17)! By both seeing and hearing the mystery of Christ-in-us their faith was increased, enabling the appearing of Christ in them.

Once the mystery of Christ is fulfilled in a person, then they can be used to accomplish another level of the plan revealed in the Book of Revelation – the corporate manifestation of His presence in a Body of Saints, ("**Firstfruits**" of His appearing). The personal revealing of Christ in our body enables us to become members of His Body, "*...Now ye are the body of Christ, and members in particular*" (1 Cor. 12:27). Indeed, it will be impossible to meet the goal of Revelation - to reveal Jesus Christ once again to the world – until the personal revealing of Christ has first taken place in all those who will be a part of the revelation. They will then form a large-scale corporate body manifesting a bodily return of Christ. This Firstfruits Company of Christ-indwelled believers prepares the way for a generation who need to **SEE** Christ revealed before they can experience the revelation. With a visible Body for the world to see, the world will be without excuse for God's last call for redemption.

The pieces come together

In kingdom understanding, when each believer knits together in love, Christ's presence is increased within the Corporate Body (See Eph. 4:16 below). Unlike in the world where the collective is only as strong as its weakest link, in Christ's kingdom, each part adds to the whole and the sum becomes greater than the total of its parts. When enough of His kingdom is in dominion through the lives of His Saints, then His Bride will be distinctly visible to the world. "Thy kingdom come…"

Eph. 4:16
16   From whom the whole **body fitly joined together** and compacted by that which **every joint supplieth**, according to the effectual working in the measure of every part, maketh increase of the body unto the edifying of itself in love.

The additive presence of Christ means that not every member has to be perfect before we can see Christ appear in a corporate body. As the Seals are loosed and Revelation opened, then true believers begin to gather together, each supplying what the other lacks as Christ's love binds them as one. When all the gaps are filled with Christ's love, then the Bride without spot or blemish becomes manifest. Christ is coming to prepare for Himself a Bride; He is just doing it from the inside out!

Whether personally or corporately, the goal of this study is to see Christ appear. The mystery of godliness taught by Paul is primarily about the personal appearing of Christ-in-us, while the Revelation penned by John is about a corporate appearing. The corporate appearing cannot be achieved without the personal; therefore, the personal must be the first priority for every reader. Although it is your personal revelation that is the most important, it must be worked out between you and Christ. Therefore, for the purposes of this study, we will be concentrating on the ultimate Revelation…the forming of the Bride.

Appearing as the Bride

Many believe that what is referred to as the "Bride Church" is the Church that exists in the end-days. Others believe it is the "true" church, and still others believe that those who will be raptured comprise the Bride Church. Rev. 1:1 tells us that *if* we are able to *comprehend* the revelation that Christ gives us, *then* we will shortly or swiftly see the events of the book take place. Whatever we may believe about the events of Revelation, we must agree that no other previous generation has received the full revelation of Christ. If they had, they would have already seen the events of Revelation take place and then the book would be a history book. That means that the book of Revelation must be a book for the end-day servants of God. This end-day generation is the Bride without spot or blemish.

Eph. 5:26-27, 31-32
26   That he might sanctify and cleanse it with the washing of water by the word,
27   **That he might present it to himself a glorious church**, not having spot, or wrinkle, or any such thing; but that it should be holy and without blemish.
31   For this cause shall a man leave his father and mother, and shall be joined unto his wife, and they **two shall be one flesh**.

32 This is a great mystery: but I speak concerning Christ and the church.

These Verses in Ephesians (26 and 27) shows that He wants a spotless Bride, and verses 31 and 32 show how this will happen. He will become one with us. This is the mystery of Godliness…Christ in us, the hope of Glory.

Does the Church today have spots and wrinkles? Let's be honest; for all the great revivals and all the great teachings, the Church today is losing the battle for the hearts and minds of the people. It is going to take more than big churches, good teachings, or even massive revivals to turn the tide of sin. It will take nothing less than Jesus Himself to step in and champion our cause!

In Ez. 34:10-16, the Lord speaks against the pastors (shepherds) who have not fed His sheep on the word of God and declares that He will come to deliver His flock from their neglectful care. He will no longer allow His sheep to wander and feed on false doctrine, but He will gather them together and feed them from His pasture. He is telling us through Ezekiel that He is coming back, not to rapture His church, but to perfect her. He will work through us to perform what the natural man can not do, bring His GLORY to the Church (See Rom. 8:17 and Glory page vii). This marvelous appearing to the world in His Bride will persuade every knee to bow and tongue to confess that Jesus Christ is Lord. Amen.

Traditional doctrines of the rapture and other end-time events can generate apathy. This is not to suggest that everyone who believes in the rapture is apathetic. Nevertheless, without a prophetic vision of His appearing that urges people to prepare their hearts for the indwelling of Christ, most will not. They will get too involved with their religion or the world, thereby taking their eyes off Jesus. People cannot comprehend what they are not seeking. If they are not seeking for Christ's appearing, it will not occur in them. Blessed are those who are seeking, who hunger and thirst after righteousness, for they will be filled (Matt. 5:6). If you are simply waiting to die so that you can receive the riches of heaven, you will not be ready for the Great Day of the Lord to come.

Chapter 4

Christ APPEARING to Harvest the Earth

The true blessed hope for all Christians is for the great Harvest of souls into the kingdom of our Father. The desire of all Christians should be to respond to the Father's heart that "none should perish" by working fervently during these end times to share the gospel of the living Christ with all who would receive. Yet, one of the reasons modern Christians are not eagerly preparing for this great Harvest is because they believe that there is nothing more to anticipate but a rapture of the Church. Thus the rapture can become a distraction that robs Christians of the blessings available to them as they fulfill God's purpose in end-time. We should be like Paul who, though he wanted desperately to be with Jesus, was willing to remain to be available for those who needed him. The true heart of a servant would call out to be left behind as a source of light to a dark world, even if there was but one who could be saved. [For an in-depth study of the scripture used to validate rapture theology, it is recommended that you read the "Rapture", page 117.]

There must be *Harvest*ers if there is to be a *Harvest*. This chapter will show how Christ will appear in a body of believers to harvest the earth. One of the clearest explanations of the harvest in the entire Bible is delivered in the parable of the wheat and the tares. Here Jesus himself takes the time to explain all the parable types so that there can be no misunderstanding about the harvest, and those "that have ears to hear" can recognize their need to be ready.

Matt. 13:24,25,30

24 Another parable put he forth unto them, saying, The kingdom of heaven is likened unto a man which sowed good seed in his field:

25 But while men slept, his enemy came and sowed tares among the wheat, and went his way.

30 **Let both grow together until the harvest: and in the time of harvest I will say to the reapers, Gather ye together <u>first</u> the tares, and bind them in bundles to burn them: but gather the wheat into my barn.**

Matt. 13:39-43
The Parable of the Harvest explained to disciples by Jesus

39 The enemy that sowed them is the devil; **the** *Harvest* **is the end of the world**; and the **reapers are the angels**.

40 As therefore the <u>tares are gathered and burned in the fire; so shall it be in the end of this world</u>.

41 The Son of man shall send forth his angels, and they shall **gather out of his kingdom all things that offend**, and them which do iniquity;

42 And shall cast them into a furnace of fire: there shall be wailing and gnashing of teeth.

43 **Then shall the righteous shine forth as the sun in the kingdom of their Father. Who hath ears to hear, let him hear.**

You will notice several facts that do not correspond to traditional thinking. For example, the wheat and the tares stay together until the harvest, which is defined as the end of the world. The "first" thing done in the harvest is the removal of the wicked. There is no mention of the Church being removed (a rapture), but there is a mention of the wicked being raptured or caught away from the righteous. He says that once the wicked are removed, then the righteous can shine forth…just like the Bride in Revelation shines. According to this scripture, Jesus declares that the next event the world will see is the removal of the wicked from out of the midst of the righteous, leaving behind only His Bride without spot or blemish.

Do not confuse this *harvest* with the harvest spoken of in Matt. 9:37 and Jn. 4:35. Those references are about the harvest to bring in the Church age, while this one is about the harvest that will end the Church age. Verse 13:25 shows the distinction. The end-time *Harvest* occurs after the Church slept and allowed the enemy to sow tares into the kingdom of Heaven. This *Harvest* is to remove those tares and bring forth the glorious Bride of Christ, which will then go forth to harvest the earth. "Thrust in thy sickle, and reap: for the time is come for thee to reap; for the harvest of the **earth** is ripe" (Rev. 14:15).

Nothing should divert the Church's call to wake up and prepare for the harvest. By lulling the Church to sleep and diverting the Church from fulfilling its role in God's *Harvest*, the enemy has accomplished a temporary victory. He has misled God's people into complacency with visions of a quick exit which eliminates their need to prepare for the shaking to come. The *harvest*ers represent the Bride which will give the entire world one last chance to choose the redemption of Jesus Christ. So we should ask the same question the angels asked the disciples in Acts 1:11, "Why <u>stand ye</u> gazing up into heaven…?" Standing around looking for a physical return does nothing to promote the spiritual purposes of God. The bodily return of Jesus to his people is assured; the "how" should not be an issue unless it robs us of our appointed task. We will all meet the resurrected Jesus, and for some of us it may be any day as He steps into the midst of His harvesters and sends them forth into the harvest. In the parable of the vineyard (Matt. 20), Christ asks a similar question, *"Why stand ye idle? It is the eleventh hour and the harvest is under way, why are you not in the fields working?"* The workers said that no man had hired them or put them to a task. Since the Lord has already defined the end time as the harvest (Matt. 13:39), then we know that this parable is about the end-time workers of the Lord. These men stood around because they were not sent; no one directed them to get prepared and be ready.

The laborers are few today because pastors do not teach about the necessity of becoming Harvesters for the great *Harvest* ahead. In the parable of the ten virgins, it says that they all slept until the midnight call. At that call only the wise were accepted at the marriage feast (Great Supper page xviii). The wise were chosen because they prepared themselves and filled their lamps with oil (Christ). That is how the Lord finishes the parable of the vineyard… "Many are called but few are chosen." Many are called to be prepared for the harvest, but few will be chosen as the instruments of His will.

HARVEST VS. PUNISHMENT

Many think of the end-time tribulation period as punishment because they do not understand God's full intent. However, if we keep in mind His purpose for the end-time *Harvest*, 'wrath' and 'tribulation' begin to take on a very different connotation. Scripture shows us that God uses 'wrath' as a perfecting or sorting instrument. He uses wrath to remove wickedness so that righteousness can shine. He forces His people to choose between Himself and the world by demonstrating that choosing the world has very severe consequences. God does not desire to punish people for sin; He allows the natural consequence of disobedience to occur so that they will repent and be redeemed from the penalty of sin. God, through Israel, shows us when His people are wicked, He sends a prophetic word to warn them. If they choose not to heed His word, wrath comes to chasten them. If the chastening causes them to cry out, He will send a deliverer. In this way, wrath is a form of pressure designed to direct our paths toward God. (See Heb. 12 for detail about this process)

Suffering is Good

Sufferings cause us to let go of our carnality and, thereby, make more room for the presence of Christ. Flesh hides the light. Sanctification, or dying-to-self, reveals the light. Verse 19 shows us that God wants a family, and all creation is waiting for them to manifest. He is speaking of the chosen generation who will die-to-self and allow Christ to MANIFEST in them.

Rom. 8:18-19
18   For I reckon that the **sufferings** of this present time are not worthy to be compared with **the glory which shall be revealed in us.**
19   For the earnest expectation of the creature waiteth **for the manifestation of the sons of God.**

Heb. 12:3-8
3   For **consider him** that endured such contradiction of sinners against himself, lest ye be wearied and faint in your minds.
4   **Ye have not yet resisted unto blood, striving against sin.**
5   And ye have forgotten the exhortation which speaketh unto you as unto children, My son, **despise not thou the chastening of the Lord,** nor faint when thou art rebuked of him:
6   For whom the **Lord loveth he chasteneth,** and scourgeth every son whom he receiveth.

7   If ye endure chastening, God dealeth with you as with **sons**; for what son is he whom the father chasteneth not?
8   But if ye be without chastisement, whereof all are partakers, then are ye bastards, and not sons.

Suffering and wrath are the ways that God redeems or perfects His people. If suffering was only a punishment, then why was it necessary for Christ to suffer?

Heb. 2:10
10   For it became him, for whom are all things, and by whom are all things, in **bringing many sons unto glory,** to make the captain of their salvation **perfect through sufferings.**

Christ thought it necessary to bear terrible suffering to be perfect and complete in the will of God, and thereby, to be able to bring more sons unto Glory. Why would less be expected of those of us who want to be joined with Him as manifest sons of God?

Wrath as an act of Love

Many traditional scholars feel that Christians are not *"appointed unto wrath"*; and that God will not allow tribulation to come against Christians. Both wrath and tribulation in this context are considered punishment.

Traditional scholars use the following scriptures to support their belief.

1 Thes. 1:10
10   And to wait for his Son from heaven, whom he raised from the dead, even **Jesus, which delivered us from the wrath to come.**

1 Thes. 5:9
9   For God **hath not appointed us to wrath,** but to obtain salvation by our Lord Jesus Christ,

It is true; God does not **want** us to experience wrath or to be the objects of the wrath to come. Nor does God want any to perish; yet, some will choose it. God will do all that He can (short of forcing them to choose Him) to bring the disobedient to a point of repentance and restoration. This study will demonstrate that both tribulation and wrath should be considered as an act of God's love.

The wrath of God will only be poured out upon the earth (on page v). It is the **earth** or **carnality** that spots our garments and the Church. Anything that is not of Him, including those things in us that are against Him and His will for our lives, will be subject to the wrath of God in the Day of the Lord. This is God's way of motivating us to let go of this world and seek only Him. As the following verse in First Corinthians shows, God wants us to bear the image of the heavenly, not the earthly. What better way to accomplish this than to make holding on to the earth painful and fruitless!

1 Cor. 15:47-48 (also see Rom. 8:5-7)
47   The first man is of the earth, earthy: the second man is the Lord of Heaven.
48   As is the earthy, such are they also that are earthy: and as is the heavenly, such are they also that are heavenly.

There will be a time of great tribulation, but it will be in the form of wrath poured out against carnality, referred to as **earth** (on page v) in Revelation. Those who 'dwell' in or inhabit the **earth** will face tribulation because they choose this world instead of Christ. In addition, the kings of the 'earth' will face wrath. These are the people professing a desire for His Kingdom but who, in reality, desires the things of the world. They will face tribulation because they allow the spirit of this world to reign in their hearts. In both cases, repentance and selling out to the lordship of Christ are necessary to stop the wrath. Christ will be appearing in a body of believers to judge the **earth** and bring wrath or tribulation to all that hold on to this world.

> To clearly see the harvest of Revelation, we must understand the concept of 'death'; because 'death' is the term used to represent those who are harvested unto life. It is also the term used for harvesters-*dead headless Saints*. This section of His Appearing will therefore show us that **death brings life**.

DEATH BRINGS LIFE (READ COMMENTARY, "DEAD IN CHRIST")

In Chapter One we talked about hearing the language of Jesus Christ, but this is an even deeper level of perception. For example, we may define the **dead in Christ** (on page iv) as those in whom Christ appears. Will you be able to abandon your natural understanding of death and understand in the Spirit that being dead is something beneficial? To truly understand something in the Spirit, it needs to be quickened to you. This means that it becomes 'life' to you bringing that "oh, I see what the Lord is saying" understanding. It feels good to the Spirit-man; it is food for the soul. However, if you do not desire to be fed by the Lord, you will never find that life. The Spirit of the Lord can only give you life through your desire to please Him. It is this desire that pierces the veil that covers the heart. If the veil is not taken away, then you will hear only from your carnal mind instead of your heart. You will be subject to pride, judgment, or envy, all of which will taint or tarnish the truth. A steadfast relationship with the Lord is the only thing that can shut down our carnal mind and enable us to listen to His Spirit.

Many people avoid a study of Revelation is because of repeated references to the reaping and killing of millions of people. Interpreting this killing as mass genocide causes you to miss the wonderful promise of the harvest in which many will come into the kingdom. Instead of grieving at the prospect of the death of millions, the Spirit of the Lord will enable you to rejoice because now you can see this "dying" as being transformed into new life. Our God has proven Himself throughout time to be a long-suffering God of love who desires that none should perish but all should receive eternal life.

The Harvesters must be dead before the Harvest can begin

Concerning death, Paul made such statements as "to live is Christ and to die is gain", "I die daily", and "I no longer live, but Christ lives within me." Dying is a blessing! He did not come to this revelation on his own, but was taught this by Jesus. Through the words of the gospels, we, too, can hear Jesus' teaching on death. Once we see that dying is a wondrous miracle of grace, we will rejoice over the Revelation message. Listen intently to what He has to say.

Matt. 10:39

39 He that findeth his life shall [1]lose it: and **he that loseth his life for my sake shall find it.**

John 12:24-25

24 Verily, verily, I say unto you, Except a corn of wheat fall into the ground and die, it abideth [2]alone: **but if it die, it bringeth forth much fruit.**

25 He that [3]loveth his life shall lose it; and he that hateth his life in this world shall keep it unto life eternal.

Jesus' view of death

[1]You have to die to find life, and most Christians have yet to die. [2]Unless you die, Christ is not with you! If you do die, He will be in you; and you will bear forth much fruit. But notice, [3]love of your life or love of this world will keep you from true Life. You must hate this life to gain life eternal!

There you have it! Death is absolutely necessary if you want the life of Christ. There is no room for doubt on this point. Read these scriptures repeatedly until you see that Jesus does not give us an option. If you do not think that Christ-in-us is a revelation, then ask yourself, "Do I hate my life in this world?" How many Christians do you know who hate their lives in this world? Yet, if they do not hate their lives, then they will never be able to let them go and make room for His eternal life.

The Holy Spirit's role in our death

The only way to hate our life in this world is to experience a taste of the wonderful life that a relationship in Christ offers. The Holy Spirit leads us to the place in which we can partake in the life of Christ through the baptism of the Holy Spirit. Christ said it was important for Him to ascend to the Father so that the Holy Spirit might descend upon us. He told us that the Holy Spirit would "take" of Christ and come show 'it' to us so that we would desire Christ (John 16:13-15). The Holy Spirit comes to us not for His own sake, but for Christ's sake. His true role is to be the 'earnest' or 'down payment' of the Christ life, teaching and showing us Christ so that our desire for Him becomes greater than our desire for this world.

Many Christians focus all of their desire on receiving the blessings and gifts of the Spirit. They will not ascend any further in Christ than the taste that the Holy Spirit offers. They get satisfied with the land on the other side of Jordan and fail to go on to obtain the promise. Since the Holy Spirit's sole desire is to birth Christ, then ignoring His direction is to blaspheme Him. He is trying to bring you to that place in which Christ can be formed in you: yet, He cannot do so if you will not surrender. The Holy Spirit is that free gift of Grace to sustain us. Do not frustrate that Grace by settling for less and never allowing the 'abundant Life' of God to form in you.

Paul tried desperately to explain this principle of death to the Galatians. We know now that his frustration was justified because there has never been a generation of men who were transformed in the way described in Gal. 2:20. They failed to see that the same Holy Spirit, who had worked miracles in their midst, was striving to take them on to perfection. (*Knowing* Christ = ascending to perfect man Eph. 4:13).

Gal. 2:20-21
20   **I am crucified with Christ: nevertheless I live**; yet not I, but Christ liveth in me: and the life which I now live in the flesh I live by the faith of the Son of God, who loved me, and gave himself for me.
Paul lived the Revelation for them.
21   I do not frustrate the grace of God: for if righteousness come by the law, then Christ is dead in vain.
Paul shows that we can miss the point and miss Christ-in-us. They seem to have frustrated the Holy Spirit's work. The Galatians stepped off the path of the crucified life of faith and reverted to religious works.

What Revelation says about death

Jesus makes it clear: we are to actively seek after death. It will not happen just because we recognize the truth of the revelation and want it to happen. Each one of us must allow the Holy Spirit to teach us to surrender and be obedient; and as we do, we will experience more and more of that heavenly gift. Death is an act of faith, which shows that we believe that the life which Christ offers, is better than the life we have.

Death speaks of being harvested into life, look at how death is an honor in Revelation, …

> **Rev. 9:6**   And in those days shall **men seek death**, and shall not find it; and shall **desire to die**, and death shall flee from them.
>
> **Rev. 14:13**   And I heard a voice from heaven saying unto me, Write, <u>**Blessed are the dead**</u> which die in the Lord from henceforth: Yea, saith the Spirit, *that they may rest from their labours*; and their works do follow them.
>
> **Rev. 3:1-2**   **1** - And unto the angel of the Church in Sardis write; These things saith he that hath the seven Spirits of God, and the seven stars; I know thy works, **that thou hast a name that thou livest, and art dead**.
>
>   **2** - Be watchful, and strengthen the things which remain, that are **ready to die**: for I have not found thy works perfect before God.
>
> **Rev. 9:20**   And the <u>**rest of the men which were not killed**</u> by these plagues *yet repented not* of the works of their hands, that they should not worship devils, and idols of gold, and silver, and brass, and stone, and of wood: which neither can see, nor hear, nor walk:

As Jesus Christ said, "*If any man come to me, and* ***hate*** *not his father, and mother, and wife, and children, and brethren, and sisters, yea, and* **his own life** *also, he cannot be my disciple (* <u>***disciple means follower***</u> *). Moreover, whosoever doth not* ***bear his cross****, and come after me, cannot be my disciple* (Luke 14:26-27). This truth is profound enough to be called a **revelation**. It describes a life entirely focused on dying to self in order to grow in Glory; nothing but Jesus Christ is important. This is not the message that most churches are preaching. We are called to be a witness to the fruitlessness of this world; yet we seem to be compromising the truth in order that we can have a pleasurable (self-centered) life in this world. When we choose to walk in faith as 'dead men', the world will take notice; and therefore, only <u>**peculiar**</u> people will be allowed to open His book.

Section III Opening the Book
Chapter 5

The Revelation Begins

Are you ready?

In this section, we begin our study of the Revelation. You may have been challenged in some of your doctrines or beliefs yet by making it this far, you have proven yourself ready to open the book and see the mystery held back for generations. Nevertheless, to open the book you must have spiritual ears to hear. You must allow Christ to transform your natural ears into spiritual ears if this Word is to be heard or received into your spirit. This will not happen if you do not have a deep and abiding DESIRE for the revealing of Jesus Christ. Revelation 5:2-7 shows us that Jesus Christ is the only One worthy to open the book. When you allow Him to transform your carnal mind into a spiritual mind, then His Spirit will open the book to your understanding. (See Rom. 8:5-8).

REVELATION CHAPTER 1, THE REVEALING OF CHRIST

Personal appeal

The first nine verses of Chapter One are a personal appeal to YOU to see the special calling on those who are willing to become PART of this message. In nearly every verse the appeal is that we see the chosen, elect nature of the people called to be Firstfruits of His *Harvest*. They are called servants (v. 1), blessed (v.3), loved (v.5), kings and priests (v.6), clouds of His presence 7), brothers in tribulation through patience, and finally, a testimony of Jesus Christ (v. 9). Verse nine can also be translated that we are the evidence or a revelation of Christ. This is why we can be exempt from the tribulation to come on the Church...we are that message of tribulation. The Church will realize that a sold out life can only be accomplished supernaturally through Christ. It will, have no choice but to recognize the truth of the Christ-in-us message. The Christ-like authority of the living message will be recognized by all who encounter it and will create in them a desire to repent.

Since John is a recipient of the message, then he can be viewed as a type of the prophets who carry this message to the Church. We will be able to see ourselves in Him as we determine to be the Firstfruits of the harvest. Listen to these scriptures and see if the Lord is calling you!

CHRIST CALLS TO THE ELECT

Rev. 1:1-9

> *1:1 The Revelation of Jesus Christ, which God gave unto him (Jesus), **to shew unto his servants** things which must shortly come to pass; and he sent and signified it by his angel unto his servant John:*

This is a message to those who have been called to be His bond slaves and who laid down their lives to do so. You may have been chosen, but you must choose to walk as a chosen one.

> *1:2 **Who bare record** of the word of God, and of the testimony of Jesus Christ, and of all things that he saw.*

John possesses the revelation of Christ and all that it means; therefore, he is qualified to speak on Christ's behalf. He is telling us from firsthand experience that what Christ is about to say is true.

> *1:3 Blessed is he that **readeth**, and they that **hear** the words of this prophecy, and **keep** those things which are written therein: for the time is at hand.*
>
> **READ means eyes to see. HEAR means ears to hear. KEEP is to those who take up the offer to be an overcomer.**

He is "blessed" because only Christ can open the book; therefore, the hearer of this revelation must be one of Christ' servants. "Keep" means that this book is to be embraced and cherished. He is looking for those who will rise to the call of this revelation. It will be sweet to the lips but bitter to the inner carnal man. Finally, if there are those who understand this, then the time is at hand. He is reiterating the theme of verse 1, knowing that only the last generation will be blessed in the hearing of this Revelation.

> *1:4 John to the seven Churches which are in Asia: Grace be unto you, and peace, **from him** which is, and which was, and which is to come; and from the seven Spirits which are before his throne;*

John is sending this to the Church but notice that it is Jesus who is speaking. It is from Him "which is to come" (in us).

The **seven Spirits** (on page xvii) which represent the fullness of Christ, are directed at issues of the heart and so is this message to the Church. Only those who operate in the fullness of Christ can speak this message to the Church.

> *1:5 And ¹from Jesus Christ, who is the faithful witness, and the first begotten of the dead, and the **prince of the kings** of the earth.*

²Unto him that ³loved us, and ⁴washed us from our sins in his own blood,

Prince is an heir to kingship. Those of the earth have not recognized Christ as King yet.

This message is ¹from Christ ²to all that are of Christ's (either ³loved or ⁴justified). He is signifying that this message is from the Lord, the faithful <u>witness.</u> All who bring this message will become a witness of Him. These messengers are the **Firstfruits** (page vi) of the harvest; dead to this world.

These 'kings of the earth' (carnality, see **earth**) show that He is sending this message even for those who have "not yet received a kingdom" and are only justified by His blood. Notice that He is not the king of the "kings of the earth"; but He is their Prince desiring to be their King. Disobedient Christians will need to accept this message to become one with the King of Kings.

1:6 And hath made us **kings and priests** *unto God and his Father; to him be glory and dominion for ever and ever. Amen.*

HE *makes us* **kings and priests.** *It is His work not ours.*

Being a king or priest is not something we obtain because we deserve it. In the Old Testament order of David or Aaron, you were given the office because of your birth. We are under a new order by faith (See Melchizedek page x). All authority, in both heaven and earth, is now given to Christ; therefore, we are kings and priests because He makes us such. Verse 6 is telling us that Christ will come in full authority in us.

1:7 Behold, he cometh **with clouds**; *and* **every eye shall see him**, *and they also which pierced him: and all kindreds of the earth shall wail because of him. Even so, Amen.*

Clouds are the saints manifesting His glory (cloud). This is how every eye will see Him.

Christ is coming back in a corporate body. This contradicts the traditional notion of coming "on" a cloud. Clouds are 'those' in whom He is coming, not on that which He is riding (See also **clouds** page iv). This message is a message of His 'appearing' within a cloud of witnesses.

Rev. 10:1

1 And I saw another mighty angel come down from heaven, **clothed with a cloud**: and a rainbow was upon his head, and his face was as it were the sun, and his feet as pillars of fire: (also 1:15-16)

By coming in a cloud of witnesses, everyone on the earth will be able to see Him. He will be seen in every faithful witness who is showing forth the revelation of Christ. Since He is coming to conquer the earth (Rev. 6:2), then those who are 'of the earth' will be upset. This is a hard message for those who are content with the spots in their garments. Nevertheless, Jesus is about to stand before them with the full power of His presence, demanding an account.

1:8 I am Alpha and Omega, the beginning and the ending, saith the Lord, which is, and which was, and which is to come, the Almighty.

He IS the revelation message; its beginning and its ending.. It is Christ in an Elect company that begins the message. It will be Christ in His Bride that brings conclusion to the message. You can help fulfill the word of God for this world by being one of His Saints to manifest Him.

Col. 1:25-26 Christ-in-us fulfills the word

25 Whereof I am made a minister, according to the dispensation of God which is given to me for you, to **FULFIL** the word of God;
26 Even the mystery which hath been hid from ages and from generations, but now is made manifest to his saints:
27 To whom God would make known what is the riches of the glory of **this mystery** among the Gentiles; which is **Christ-in-you**, the hope of glory:

1:9 I John, who also am your brother, and **companion** *in* **tribulation**, *and* **in the kingdom** *and patience of Jesus Christ, was in the isle that is called* **Patmos**, *for the word of God, and for the* **testimony** *of Jesus Christ.*

PATMOS <u>means</u> "my killing" in Greek. Look how sweet God is to bury nuggets of gold at our feet. Hearing the scripture in language of Jesus Christ brings revelation that would otherwise be missed. How else could it read? His word is so perfect. **YOU MUST BE DEAD TO RECEIVE THIS REVELATION.**

Patiently embrace tribulation for the Word's sake and the Word will then manifest in us as a testimony of Christ. The choice is really ours; go through tribulation now to become a testimony, or receive tribulation later because of the testimony.

Having Ears to Hear and Eyes to See
Rev. 1:10-20

1:10 I was in the Spirit on the Lord's day, and **heard** *behind me a great voice, as of a trumpet,*

This is a spiritual book given to those who have ears to hear.

The revelation (trumpet) of this message is to be understood spiritually: a book of types, parables, and spiritual wisdom. This message is only given to those who can hear in the Spirit. Are you in the Spirit? The door is open come up! (see Rev. 4:1-2)

1:11 Saying, I am Alpha and Omega, the first and the last: and, What thou seest, write in a book, and send it unto the seven Churches which are in Asia; unto Ephesus, and unto

> Smyrna, and unto Pergamos, and unto Thyatira, and unto Sardis, and unto Philadelphia, and unto Laodicea.
>
> **Take MY message to the Church and declare their spiritual condition.**
>
> *1:12 And I turned to **see** the voice that spake with me. And being turned, I saw seven golden **candlesticks**;*
>
> **Christ is the voice that John hears. Trumpets (1:10) are the voice of Christ that is heard in the earth.**

This is the Godly witness of the Church (candlesticks on page iv). John sees the Christ in the Church through all seven candlesticks. If you add together all the good from the seven letters (message to the Churches), then you would describe the characteristics of the Bride Church.

> *1:13 And in the midst of the seven **candlesticks** one like unto the Son of man, clothed with a garment down to the foot, and girt about the paps with a golden girdle.*

Christ comes as a judge to judge the earth. These are the garments of a judge. This message tells of Christ's coming as the righteous Judge to judge the Church. He will illuminate the things with which He is displeased. He will reveal the spots in their garments.

In verse 1:5 Jesus is the faithful witness, which is what the Church is lacking. If the Church is fulfilling its witness of Christ, it would not need to be judged; thus we have the symbolism of this verse. He IS in the fullness (seven) of the Church (candlesticks) and its witness to the world. Show nothing but Him and you have a Bride worthy of Christ.

> *1:14 His head and his hairs were white like wool, as white as snow; and his **eyes** [on page v] were as a flame of fire;*

Not only is this the uniform of the judge, it also symbolizes His righteous judgment. 'Wool' tells us that this message is for the sheep of the Church. He has come to clean them by revealing (eyes) the imperfections He wants to burn away. Therefore, He will burn the wood, hay, and stubble of the Church to prepare a spotless Bride.

> *1:15 And his feet like unto fine brass, as if they burned in a furnace; and his voice as the sound of **many waters**.*

Now He reveals that He is coming in a people to fulfill this message (See many water on page xi). This is a company of people perfected like brass from the furnace…through the fire. Also, brass is the foundation of the laver (Ex. 38:8), which is where the priest looked at himself. He was looking for dirt so that he could clean himself before entering into the presence of the Lord.

> *1:16 And he had in his right hand **seven stars**: and out of his mouth went a sharp two-edged ¹sword: and his countenance was as the sun ²shineth in his strength.*

These holy messengers (**seven stars** on page xvii) bring a message (mouth) that kills the flesh through judgment. The ¹revelation and its strength will be seen through the ²Glory of Christ, which shines through these messengers. He is warning the Church to be ready for the message and messengers to come.

> *1:17 And when I saw him, I fell at his feet as dead. And he laid his right hand upon me, saying unto me, Fear not; I am the first and the last:*

They come to kill the flesh, not the believer. They are a manifestation of love, which should be embraced, not feared.

> *1:18 I am he that liveth, and was dead; and, behold, I am alive for evermore, Amen; and have the keys of hell and of death.*

Christ is the one who should be seen in the message and the messengers. This is His work even though it seems like a fearful message. For later reference, notice that He has the keys of hell and death. Rev. 9:1 & 20:1…Jesus has all the keys!

> *1:19 Write the things which thou hast seen, and the things which are, and the things which shall be hereafter;*

Some of the things are present already (like the condition of the Church and the spirit of antichrist), and some are yet to come.

> *1:20 The mystery of the seven stars which thou sawest in my right hand, and the seven golden candlesticks. The seven stars are the angels of the seven Churches: and the seven candlesticks which thou sawest are the seven Churches.²*

UNLOCKING OF THE BOOK – BREAKING THE SEALS

Chapter One tells us that those who have eyes to see will see Christ in a deeper way. They will be allowed to see His plan for His people and will become kings and priests who will be prepared to reign and rule with Him. Chapter One is meant to inspire those who want more of Christ like John did. This book will take us into the Spirit and allow us to "see". If that inspires you, then push on and let us see how we unlock this promise for our life.

Christ must be your *focus* to *see* His 'parousia' (appearing). The more you grow in your relationship with Christ, the more the things of this world begin to dim. Personal entertainment and pleasure, sports, travel, and making money, once so important will have little value to you if they are not part of the Lord's kingdom. By allowing His will to operate in us, instead of operating in our own will, we build a personal relationship with the Lord. As we die to our self and He increases within us, He imparts to us an ability to minister to others. Do not however; be fooled with a counterfeit works program. Sacrificing your personal life for a life of ministry does not in itself merit God's favor. God's favor cannot be earned. It comes by choosing to be in the place where Christ is manifest. It is the difference between working to earn a blessing and living in the Blessed One. We choose, like Paul, to know nothing but Christ and to be obedient to His will. Obedience is better than sacrifice.

Once you begin to move into this realm of relationship, you will [1]marvel at how people distract themselves with details of doctrine and nuances of theology, - everything else but the experience of Christ-in-us. If you are not about "knowing" Him, then you are more likely to look for natural understanding in the scriptures while overlooking the fact that they all point to "relationship" with our Lord. Scripture is an outline of the plan of God to bring us to Sonship. All of the New Testament, including the Book of Revelation, is about our relationship with God through Jesus Christ WHEN YOU HAVE EARS TO HEAR! To get spiritual ears we will look to the fifth chapter of Revelation where instructions are given for opening and understanding the Little Book…Revelation.

What makes the study of the book of Revelation such a blessing is that we must have Christ birthed within us to even open the book. This puts the emphasis on our relationship with Him and not on our knowledge of Him. This book demands a relationship before you can receive the essence of its message. Chapter Five of Revelation tells us that only Christ can open this book and unlock the seals that have kept it hidden for generations.

This corresponds to Revelation 1:1, where we see Christ 'giving' the revelation of Himself to His servants which allows us to see that He must be *in us* to give it *to us*.

We believe that the Holy Spirit is our guide through the scriptures opening our mind to the truths that lie therein. Yet there is a promise which says "when that which is perfect is come" the imperfect is done away with (1 Cor. 13:9-10). This refers to Christ feeding us the Living Word of His presence; giving us the fullness of His Spirit which is the Spirit of Prophecy. He is transforming us not teaching us. We are not about learning or doing, but we are about receiving and becoming through the transforming process whereby we see Him face to face. That is why this is called the Revelation of Jesus Christ. He wants to reveal Himself to us and then to the world.

Our study of Revelation Chapter 5 will help us strive to 'become' instead of know. He offers a greater revelation of His person to those willing to 'become' His witnesses.

STUDY TEXT – REVELATION CHAPTER 5

Only Christ in us can open the Little Book (it's for the dead to self)

Rev. 5:1-14

> *1   And I saw in the right hand of him that sat on the throne a **book** written within and on the backside, **sealed** with.*

This is the revelation of Jesus Christ. The book has to be unsealed. The King of Kings has it and wants to give it to someone. But who can open it. Daniel 12:4 told us that the book would be opened at the end of time. We will now see how the book is going to be opened.

But notice that the book has 7 seals. In Thunder 7 we find out that **all these seals must be broken in us** before there can begin the corporate unveiling of Christ.

> *2   And I saw a strong angel proclaiming with a loud voice, Who is worthy to **open the book**, and to loose the seals thereof?*
>
> *3   And **no man** in heaven, nor in earth, neither under the earth, was able to open the book, neither to look thereon.*
>
> **No man…or carnal mind can open the book or even understand it. Only Christ will be able to open it.**

Only those who have eyes to see will be able to look into the Revelation of Christ. Who then can be worthy of

such a calling. Jesus said to Nicodemus that you must be born of Spirit to even SEE the kingdom.

> *4   And I wept much, because no man was found worthy to open and to read the book, neither to look thereon.*
>
> *5   And one of the elders saith unto me, Weep not: behold, the Lion of the tribe of Juda, the Root of David, hath prevailed to open the book, and to loose the seven Seals thereof.*

You must be a servant to have a king. In our study of Rev. Chapter 4, the Lion represents Christ sitting on the throne of our heart. He will need to have dominion in our lives to loose the seals. The revelation of Christ comes as we come to 'know' Him as Jesus Christ our LORD.

> *6   And I beheld, and, lo, in **the midst of the throne** and of the four beasts, and in the midst of the elders, **stood a Lamb** as it had been slain, having seven horns and **seven eyes**, which are the **seven Spirits of God** sent forth into all the earth.*

To be a servant you must die to yourself. Also in Rev.4, we learn that we must die to self to receive Christ in us. Here the Lamb slain represents the Spirit of Christ in those who have died to self. The seven horns and **seven**

eyes will help us see the carnality (sin) within us that needs to die. This happens as we look into the sea of glass in Chapter 4, which is the 'brazen laver'. (All of this will be reviewed in detail in our study of the 'throne room'.)

> **7** And he came and took the book out of the right hand of him that sat upon the throne.

Only the Lamb in us can take the book. The lamb speaks a deep truth about those who can receive the book. The Lamb represents Christ in a sacrificially slain vessel. The one that the lamb takes the book from is the "lion", which again is Christ. Therefore we must be the lamb. Remember the 'servant' of Rev. 1:1.

> **8** And when he had taken the book, the four beasts and **four and twenty elders** fell down before the Lamb, having every one of them harps, and golden vials full of odours, which are the prayers of saints.

Through praise (harps) and prayerful intercession (vials), the Elect will manifest as the 'sons of God' (Saints). God will use the Saints as He used Moses, as intercessors for the carnal church. This is the beginning of the generation who will usher in the appearing of Christ. By manifesting the revelation of Christ, they establish themselves as living testaments to His appearing for all to see.

> **9** And they sung a [1]**new song**, saying, Thou art [2]worthy to take the book, and to open the seals thereof: for thou wast slain, and hast [3]redeemed us to God by thy blood out of every **kindred, and tongue, and people, and nation;**

The [1]**new song** (page xiii) rises from the Elect as they give Christ the Glory for the opening of the book and the seal. They recognize that [2]Christ gives the Revelation to those slain and this will deliver (redeem) them from the carnal church. The **kindred, and tongue, and people, and nation** collectively is a type used for the carnal church (page xiii). **"Come out from among her"** will be spoken loudly and clearly throughout this study.

In the definition of 'new song' on page xiii), tribulation is an expression of love from God. Christ sings this song through the Elect. In addition, the Elect are thanking Christ because He has delivered them from the wrath that will come to the Church. Being purchased away from that wrath means that they [3]owe everything to Him. In this way, Christ sets them apart for God to use.

> **10** And hast made us unto our God kings and priests: and we shall reign on the earth.

Christ makes us kings and priests. Any use of the term 'king' in Revelation is a reference to the redeemed. However, kings must have Christ _IN_ them to reign, which is the only way to have a kingdom. Rev. 17:12 speaks of the kings associated with the Harlot who do not have a kingdom: these are the Christians who have not gone on to make Jesus Christ Lord of their life.

> **11** And I beheld, and I heard the voice of many angels round about the throne and the beasts and the elders: and the number of them was ten thousand times ten thousand, and thousands of thousands;

This is the "cloud of witnesses", who are 'pressing in' on our behalf. These are the Elect of generations past who are waiting for the appearing so that they can obtain also. In the same way that Moses and Elijah appeared on the Mount of Transfiguration, we will see these Saints at the end of our 6th day (Matt. 17:1). They are praying for us to "run the race" and establish the New Jerusalem.

Heb. 11:39-12:1
11:39 And these all, having obtained a good report through faith, <u>received not the promise</u>:
11:40 God having provided some better thing for us, that they <u>without us should not be made perfect</u>.
12:1 Wherefore seeing we also are compassed about with so great a <u>CLOUD OF WITNESSES</u>, let us lay aside every weight, and the sin which doth so easily beset us, and let us <u>run</u> with <u>patience</u> the <u>race</u> that is set before us,

> **12** Saying with a loud voice, Worthy is the Lamb that was slain to receive power, and riches, and wisdom, and strength, and honour, and glory, and blessing.

Worthiness comes from being slain…dying to self and living for Christ. It is our dying that qualifies us for His power, riches, wisdom, strength, honor, Glory and blessing.

> **13** And every creature which is in heaven, and on the earth, and under the earth, and such as are in the sea, and all that are in them, heard I saying, Blessing, and honour, and glory, and power, be unto him that sitteth upon the throne, and unto the Lamb for ever and ever.

> **14** And the four beasts said, Amen. And the four and twenty elders fell down and worshipped him that liveth for ever and ever.

The great truth of this chapter is that "no man…is able to open the book." The only way to receive the revelation is to let Christ open it for you. He is the only one worthy to open the book and give you eyes to see. He will only do it for the **DEAD** (verses 6, 7) in Christ, those who have become a willing sacrifice (lamb). We will only be able to see clearly the plan of God when we are separated from our carnal desires and the fellowship in the carnal church (verses 8, 9). Being thus enlightened, we will be used of God for the great end-time _Harvest_ (verses 10, 11) and be partakers with the heavenly host in the worship of God (verses 12-14).

However, there is still more for us to do than just allow Christ to open the book. The next chapter will introduce us to the fullness of Christ that we are to show the world. God has ordained that those operating in this fullness of Christ will not only open the book, but also prophesy it to the world. They will be a living Revelation.

Chapter 6

Growing in Christ...Kingdom

It is necessary, before we can go any further, to see what part the mystery of godliness, Christ-in you, plays in understanding the kingdom. It is also necessary to understand the process of growing in Christ until He can be fully manifested in a person. The 144,000 will all operate in the **fullness** of Christ. If you feel that God is calling you to be part of this "Firstfruits" company of people, then you will want to know all you can about continuing to grow in godliness.

God is preparing a people described in Joel Chapter Two as...a people "the like has never been seen before." This will be the body of believers in whom He will first appear. Because they love not their lives unto death (Rev. 12:11), they will corporately embody the "good news" gospel of the Christ-in-us revelation. They will become living testimonies to the entire world (Commentary "the Mystery" on page 128). However, before this corporate appearing can occur, there must be a personal appearing in each of the lives of these Holy Messengers.

We have talked about Christ being birthed or formed in us through the work of the Holy Spirit, but that is only the beginning. We can go beyond that initial experience into all the fullness of Christ. In other words, we will grow in Christ as He grows in us. Understand this very important truth is critical to the appearing of Christ in the end times.

Step 1 ... Christ sends the Holy Spirit to show us Christ John 16:14-15

14 He shall glorify me: for he shall receive of mine, and shall shew it unto you.

This is where the Holy Spirit, sent by Christ, brings a taste of Christ so that you may desire Him and allow Him to be "formed" in your life.

15 All things that the Father hath are mine: therefore said I, that he shall take of mine, and shall shew it unto you.

(see also: Rom. 8:8-9)

Step 2 ... Death and...On to the fullness

A good place to begin to look at the process established for coming into God's 'fullness' is Eph. 3:16-19. Paul's prayer begins by asking the Holy Spirit to strengthen our inner faith by allowing us to sample the Glory of Christ. As the Spirit guides us to experience more of Christ, our faith increases until finally, we are able to claim to have Christ birthed in us. This is really the death-to-self process that has been covered in previous chapters. It is only when we are weak that the Holy Spirit can strengthen us. Therefore, the tribulations of life are necessary so that the Holy Spirit can "birth" Christ into our life. This is un-

derstood by many as a "Lordship" issue. For there to be a 'kingdom' there must be a King.

Once we have surrendered and been "strengthened", then Christ can sit on the throne of our heart.

Study Help   The Fullness Doctrine

Eph. 3:16-19

16   That he would grant you, according to the riches of his glory, to be strengthened with might by his Spirit in the inner man;

First, the Holy Spirit strengthens the inner man, normally by tests and trials, letting us taste of Christ. Only a hungry man will seek food.

17   (so) That Christ may dwell in your hearts by faith; that ye, being rooted and grounded in love,

Christ-in-us is a work of faith empowered by the work of the Holy Spirit. If it were not for the Holy Spirit bringing us that taste of Christ's love, then we would never surrender and let Christ be birthed in us.

18   May be able to comprehend with all Saints what is the breadth, and length, and depth, and height;

With a Christ Revelation, we can come to understand (with the other Saints) the greater measure of Christ.

Now on to the fullness of God

19   And to know the love of Christ, which passeth knowledge, that ye might be **filled with all the fullness of God.**

This verse shows us that we are able to "know" Christ beyond the limitations of our mind which will open the path to the fullness of God. Since we see that there is a fullness to be had, we should never be satisfied with "partness"! It is the totally sold out saints that will be the army of God.

Growing in Glory ('Glory' on page vii)

Growing in Glory is really growing in Christ. Below, Rom. 8:18 makes it very clear; suffer with Him to be glorified with Him.

Rom. 8:18-19

18   For I reckon that the sufferings of this present time are not worthy to be compared with **the glory which shall be revealed in us.**

19   For the earnest expectation of the creature waiteth for the **manifestation of the sons** of God.

His Glory will only increase as we maintain a face to face relationship with the Lord. Chapter Four of Revelation reveals that by looking into the glorious face of Christ, our blemishes and spots are illuminated so that we can surrender them to the Lord. We can only grow as the carnality of this world is washed away, letting the treasure within us shine forth.

2 Cor. 4:6-7	
6	For God, who commanded the light to shine out of darkness, hath shined in our hearts, to **give the light** of the knowledge of **the glory** of God **in the face of Jesus Christ.**
7	**But we have this treasure in earthen vessels, that the excellency of the power may be of God, and not of us**.
	Based on verse 6, 'Glory' is the treasure. We are told to lay up treasure in heaven (in us); yet, here it says the treasure is in earthen vessels. This is to remind us that the kingdom of Heaven resides in our heart, and that He places His treasure (Christ) in our earthen vessels. Therefore, to lay up treasure in heaven is to add to the Glory within us. In this way, we can show the Glory of God to the world.

Those who truly have a heart after God will want all of Christ (the **fullness**…Eph. 3:19 and 4:13). The question is, are we willing to do what it takes to obtain such a great *treasure* and to receive the *pearl of great price* (Matt. 13:45)? In the parable of the pearl, the man had to sell all that he had to obtain the special pearl. The same was true for the hidden treasure (Matt. 13:44); no price was too great to obtain the prize. Are you willing to sell-out to get the fullness of Christ?

If Christ is the *treasure* that we are to lay up in heaven, then how can we get our inheritance while we yet live? The fullness of Christ is something we are instructed (Eph. 3:19) to obtain now. So there must be a way to gain our inheritance without going to the grave. The Word tells us that Christ 'tasted of death' (Heb. 2:9) for us and that we need not see death (John 8:51). Our abundant **eternal life** is for today (John 10:10 & I John 5:11). Yet, how can the "mortal put on immortal"? It can be done simply…by changing our minds, by allowing Him to transform us from a carnally minded being to a spiritually-minded being (Rom. 8:6). Rom. 8:1 says that this will happen as we walk after (follow) the Spirit.

Rom. 8:6	
6	For to be carnally minded is death; but to be **spiritually minded is life** and peace.

Once we understand the purpose of tribulation, we suffer to experience a greater measure of Christ and make choices that give us a greater inheritance now. The riches of Christ and His kingdom are available NOW to those who will allow their spots revealed, and then surrender them to Christ. Tribulation may come, but you will rejoice in it, counting all earthly things lost and as dung to win Christ (Phil. 3:8).

Heb. 11:35	
35	Women received their dead raised to life again: and others were tortured, <u>not accepting deliverance</u>; **that** they **might obtain a better resurrection**:

Remember Christ said <u>He is the resurrection</u>. It is our choice as to how much of Him we want, but notice that "no pain…no gain." The trials and tribulations we face are to reveal the carnality in us so that we can release it. As tribulation comes we can choose to be delivered from it and not grow in the life of Christ, or we can welcome it and be glorified. This is the choice of the overcomer.

30, 60 or 100, the choice is yours

Dying to reveal Christ creates an opportunity to receive the wealth of benefits inherent in Him; the less of me, the more of Christ's life there is in me. Once a decision to sell-out or die-to-self is made, we begin to offer ourselves as a willing sacrifice. Piece by piece we are transformed into His image, receiving an ever-greater "measure" of His Glory. In His Word God, measures his gifts in parts of three: 30, 60, 100; or 1, 3, 5; or stars, moon, sun. *Three* is the number of Godly completeness (page xviii) and represents God's triune nature. God is complete in three, and we can move toward godliness through three stages. In the parables of the Talents (Matt. 25:14-30) and the Pounds (Luke 19:12-27), greater Glory is seen through the fruit of faithfulness. **This means that faithfulness is a form of intimacy**. "For how can two walk together lest they be agreed?" (Amos 3:3) **The greater the intimacy, the greater the Glory**.

The following scripture from Corinthians begs the question, "How bright is your light?" The Glory of the 'manifest sons' will be as bright as the sun (son), but this is not a competition. God loves us all the same; He offers us all the privilege of participating in the appearing. Nevertheless, those who hunger and thirst for righteousness will be filled equal to their desire.

1 Cor. 15:41-42	
41	There is one **glory** (page vii) of the *sun,* and another glory of the *moon*, and another glory of the *stars*: for one star **differeth** from another star in glory.
	There are levels to our manifesting Glory. Our relationship (face to face) with Jesus Christ qualifies us in this resurrection. "Fruit…some 30, some 60 and some 100" (Mark 4:8). Are you satisfied with less than the fullness?
42	So also is the resurrection of the dead. It is sown in corruption; it is raised in incorruption:
	The Glory is also a determining factor in the resurrection. The Glory we obtain here is the Glory that defines us in the world to come! Remember, those who choose can seek their resurrection now.

Now let us see what awaits us as His Glory is revealed in a vision of the Throne of God.

The Glory Throne Room of Revelation…

Revelation Chapter Four (see below) gives us a vision of the throne room of our heart. This is where the images portray spiritual types, which guide our understanding as we ascend into the greater truth of Christ's revealing. We see in these figures the stages of spiritual growth, which help to motivate the believer towards the fullness of God. Some may be tempted to see this as a way to promote elitism or pride, but that misses the point. Jesus always had His chosen, even among the disciples. He did not take all twelve up on the mountain ('great mountain on page xiii). He took only Peter, James, and John. The real truth is, "Blessed are those who hunger and thirst after righteousness, for they shall be filled."

Understanding the progressive stages of growing in Glory is an important part of Revelation. It will change our focus and reshape our priorities. As the last days approach, growing in our relationship with Christ will no longer be an option. God will orchestrate circumstances so that each of us will be forced to move on to His Glory or move out of His will; no fence sitting will be acceptable and no gray areas will be allowed. This is in stark contrast to the attitudes of Christians today who fail to see the need for a relationship with Christ and are content to be exempt from Hell. They feel free to enter into an idolatrous relationship with this world, losing sight of God's plan. They neglect God's command to love Him with all their heart, mind, body, and soul, and are satisfied simply to be the <u>object</u> of God's love. They believe they are covered by the blood and that their lack of relationship has no real consequence in their eternal position with God.

Understanding the purpose of life in Christ will reshape the focus of our life. It will allow us to see that everything outside of our relationship with Christ is a snare that robs God and us of Glory. When the Bridegroom shuts the door, all opportunities are lost. God has waited two thousand years to find a generation who can finally hear this truth and become the generation who hastens His appearing.

Revelation Throne Room (Chapter 4)

1 After this I looked, and, behold, a door was opened in heaven: and the first voice which I heard was as it were of a **trumpet** talking with me; which said, Come up hither, and I will shew thee things which must be hereafter.

2 And immediately I was in the spirit: and, behold, a throne was set in heaven, and one sat on the throne.

3 And he that sat was to look upon like a jasper and a sardine stone: and there was a rainbow round about the throne, in sight like unto an emerald.

4 And round about the throne were four and twenty seats: and upon the seats I saw **four and twenty elders** sitting, clothed in white raiment; and they had on their heads crowns of gold.

5 And out of the throne proceeded lightnings and thunderings and voices: and there were **seven lamps** of fire burning before the throne, which are the seven Spirits of God.

6 And before the throne there was a sea of glass like unto crystal: and in the midst of the throne, and round about the throne, were four beasts full of eyes before and behind.

7 And the first beast was like a **lion**, and the second beast like a **calf**, and the third beast had a face as a **man**, and the fourth beast was like a **flying eagle**.

8 And the four beasts had each of them six wings about him; and they were full of eyes within: and they rest not day and night, saying, Holy, holy, holy, Lord God Almighty, which was, and is, and is to come.

A walk in the Throne Room

Chapter Four of Revelation begins with John hearing the voice of the trumpet (a type that represents an understanding of the revelation). He immediately ascends in the Spirit and sees Christ on the throne. This represents that Christ has been birthed in our hearts and has established His lordship as the King/Priest of our life (Eph. 3:16, 17). John stands outside the throne room and cannot see the full nature of who is on the throne. He is allowed to see just enough to motivate him (us) to go on and draw closer to the Most Holy Place, where he will see the Lion on the Throne.

Let us walk with John and see what he sees. Our first vision of Christ is that of a beautiful King, much to be desired (*verse 3*). **We want a closer look so we move forward.** We see God's power and the flashes of His Glory (lightning and thunder *verse 5*) and get a taste of what it means to be in His presence. **We begin to hunger** for more

of His presence and desire to do whatever it takes to "know" Him. **We decide to come closer**. Before we can enter the throne room, we encounter seven lamps representing perfection (the fullness), some of which are burning very dimly. **We need a closer look.** We look and see that the Lamps reflect the degree that Christ's presence is operating in specific areas of our lives. We need to get more of His transforming presence so our lamps can burn brightly; yet, we must cross the "sea of glass" to get to Him. **We go forward.** The sea (brazen laver) reflects our face, and we see the dirt (carnality). We offer our carnality as a sacrifice to the Lion on the throne. He accepts and **WE ENTER THE THRONE ROOM.**

Christ now starts the transforming process. As long as we continue to bring sacrifices, we can stay in the throne room and be counted as one of the ministering beasts. This is where the Calf, Man, and Flying Eagle represent the measure of Glory in our lives. These Beasts reveal the High Priest nature of this perfecting work within our hearts.

Heb. 8:3 says that Christ, as our High Priest, requires an offering and we are the sacrifice. The eyes of the Beast represent the all-knowing aspect of Christ in us, revealing the issues that hinder us. As the issues are revealed, Christ will burn them from our lives so we can grow in His Glory. This is the sacrifice of our wills, so that His will can fill our life... less of us, more of Him.

As our sacrifices are made, we can enter into direct fellowship with God where he dwells. Thus these Beasts also represent the Cherubim which stand over the mercy seat in the most Holy Place, the place where **Moses saw God and learned of Him**. (What could be a better representation of "face to face" transforming?)

Exod. 25:22

22 And there **I will meet with thee**, and I will commune with thee from above the mercy seat, from **between the two cherubim** which are upon the ark of the testimony, of all things which I will give thee in commandment unto the children of Israel.

Section IV
Ending the Church Age

The heart of Revelation will be seen in the message of the **seven Thunders** (starting on page 40), in which the story of Christ's return to reclaim His kingdom, hidden for generations, is revealed through an amazing, three-dimensional pattern. However, before these events of Revelation begin, Jesus sends a warning message to the Churches explaining why the Church must be subject to tribulation. This is in fact the closing of the 'Church Age' which will end with a call to the Church to "buy gold tried in the fire." This will then open us to Revelation 4:1 where a door to the throne awaits all that are willing to ascend through the fires of affliction. The whole purpose of these seven letters is found in the promises to the overcomers. Throughout these letters a promise is given to those who are willing to be tried in the fire. "To him that overcometh will I grant to **sit with me in my throne**, even as I also overcame, and am set down with my Father in his throne. He that hath an ear, let him hear what the Spirit saith unto the churches (Rev. 3:21-22)."

Chapter 7

The Message to the Church – Rev. Chapters 2-3

MESSAGE TO CHURCHES - END OF THE CHURCH AGE

Satan does not want the Church to receive this revelation and has been subtly working for generations to prevent it. His strategy has been to divide the Church so that the unity of the brethren, spoken of in Chapter Four of Ephesians, is unattainable. He has already succeeded in separating the Church to such a degree by denominationalism that a common 'appearing' of Christ in a unified Bride Church would seem impossible. Satan has succeeded in turning the hearts of many to believe that unity in the body of Christ is just setting the stage for the antichrist so that they are unable to receive this message. He has so blinded the eyes of many in the Church that he no longer has to fight it; the Church fights itself! Content with the Church's condition, he is free to set his sights on the messengers who will try to change things. *What better way of stopping the message than to kill the messenger?*

Satan's attack is portrayed in Chapter Twelve of Revelation where we see Satan standing over the woman (which is the Church) seeking to devour the 'man-child'. The woman is no threat to him; he is only interested in the mature company of believers who will be birthed. These messengers will, later in Chapter Twelve, take the Church into the wilderness to protect her from Satan's lies. However, there are those in her that would rather 'swallow' the lies of the enemy than be transformed into 'manifest sons of God'. Chapter 8 of Romans tells us why. Although tribulation is the path to Glory and to the "manifestation of the *sons of God*", it is not a comfortable path.

Rom. 8:18-19
18   For I reckon that the **sufferings** of this present time are not worthy to be compared with the **glory** which **shall be revealed in us**.
19   For the earnest expectation of the creature waiteth for the **manifestation of the sons of God**.

Many in the Church will not want to hear this message. They are comfortable with "their life" and "their doctrines" which allow them to be lukewarm in Christ. This is why the first three chapters of Revelation are dedicated to declaring the state of the Church through the eyes of Christ. He wants the Church to know what He has "against" them so that they can repent and receive His revelation. Until they see that they need this Revelation, there will be no hope of getting them to become a part of the end-time manifestation of the Bride.

Guidebook to the end-time

The book of Revelation is a guidebook, given by Jesus to His servants, so that they will see and understand the conditions that they will face as this message is taken to the Church. When Jesus said that Revelation was given "to show us the things that must shortly come to pass," He was not merely providing a preview of end-time events; He was creating an instruction manual for the Elect to use during the end-time *Harvest* of God. The **seven Thunders** of God will be revealed to enlighten the Elect as to their appointed place in the harvest.

These letters declare contemporary truths that will allow the prophets of God who take this message to the Church to see and know the plan of the enemy and to anticipate his responses. They will understand that it is not their responsibility to convince or persuade, but to declare. Christ must be the essence of the harvester. Knowing our part in His plan fulfills Jesus' desire. John was told to 'eat the book' (Rev. 10:9). We, too, should let every page of this guidebook quicken our spirit. Since Revelation is THE revelation of Christ, then to eat the book is to eat the flesh of the Lord: a true communion.

These letters show both where Christ is present in the Church and where Satan has successfully infiltrated the Church over the last two thousand years. We can discern from these letters the failures of the Church in its call to show forth Christ' power and presence to the world. It is a way for Christ to show why we must move into the kingdom phase of our relationship. If He is not allowed to reign, both in us and in the Church, then we will never see the Bride "without spot and blemish" take her position in the earth.

Letters to Church (Rev. 2:1-3:22)

Church 1 Ephesus
Ephesus = 'permitted' ok, but no relationship.

> **2:1** Unto the angel of the Church of Ephesus write; These things saith he that holdeth the [1]**seven stars** in his right hand, who walketh in the midst of the seven golden [2]**candlesticks**;

He is the one sending the holy [1]messengers (7 stars), and this message is about His presence in the [2]churches. This church has much that He likes and can use. This is a church in which He can harvest some good fruit. Some churches just need to know the truth, and they will embrace it. They want to become great instruments in the hand of God.

> **2:2** I know thy works, and thy labour, and thy patience, and how thou canst not bear them which are evil: and thou hast tried them which say they are apostles, and are not, and hast found them liars:

Let's keep track of the good characteristics because they describe what He wants for all the Church. Those characteristics are 1) patience, 2) exclusion from the world, 3) hatred of hypocritical leaders…

> **2:3** And hast borne, and hast patience, and for my name's sake hast laboured, and hast not fainted.
> **…4) patience with the Saints, and 5) works long and hard.**
> **2:4** Nevertheless I have somewhat against thee, because thou hast left thy first love.

Nevertheless, with all of these good things, the one thing that keeps this church from being the Bride is not having a relationship with Jesus Christ thus losing His presence. They forgot to keep Jesus "in their midst." This shows the importance of the Christ-in-us message for today's Church. They need to redirect their focus towards loving Jesus, not changing the world or building buildings.

> **2:5** Remember therefore from whence thou art fallen, and repent, and do the first works; or else I will come unto thee quickly, and will remove thy candlestick out of his place, except thou repent.

Any Church that misses this truth about an intimate relationship through Christ-in-us, will not be His Church

for long! There is a time line in place, now that the book is open and the message is out; therefore, there is not much more time to repent. If your church is not repenting, hear the call to "come out from her, my people (Rev. 18:4)."

> **2:6** But this thou hast, that thou hatest the deeds of the **Nicolaitans**, which I also hate.

The good news is that since they hate the deeds of the "**Nicolaitans**"(on page xiv), they are on the right track; indeed, hating the works of carnal Christians sets your face toward a righteous judge.

> **2:7** He that hath an ear, let him hear what the Spirit saith unto the Churches; To him that overcometh will I give to eat of the tree of life, which is in the midst of the paradise of God.

The Spirit tells us that the 'overcomers' are headed back to the **Garden** (paradise). Praise God! He also reveals that only those who are overcomers can eat of the tree of Life!

Church 2 Smyrna
Smyrna = 'Myrrh' an ingredient of the anointing.

> **2:8** And unto the angel of the Church in Smyrna write; These things saith the first and the last, which was dead, and is alive;

This church has much that makes them alive. They may be in error but their heart is right; indeed, life is offered as the promise for this church. But there is a distinction between Smyrna and the last church. Ephesus is headed for the harvest as a harvester, meaning that there is a lot there that He can use for reaping the harvest. This gives us insight into the state of the Church today. Some are harvested for 'harvesters'; others will just be harvested.

> **2:9** I know thy works, and tribulation, and poverty, but thou art rich and I know the [1]blasphemy of them which say they are Jews, and are not, but are the **synagogue of Satan** [on page xviii],

This church is obviously showing Life because they are coming under attack for it. He tells them that He likes their…1) work, 2) tribulation, 3) poverty for Him, and 4) persecution by carnal Christians (synagogue of Satan).

Notice: those who bring this message will suffer much at the hands of [1]self-righteous persons. He tells this church not to be concerned about them because they are really acting from an antichrist spirit. As you can see, this spirit has been worshiping alongside the Church for two thousand years. It is not a person, but a spirit that will try to act religiously; but it is against the manifestation of Christ. It seeks to establish itself in your throne room and declare itself as God. This means that the persons acting from this spirit will be full of SELF 'will' and show little care for the brethren.

> *2:10 Fear none of those things which thou shalt suffer: behold, the devil shall cast some of you into prison, that ye may be tried; and ye shall have* **tribulation ten** *[on page xiv]* **days:** *be thou faithful unto death, and I will give thee a crown of life.*

Again, we see Jesus warning the Church about the tribulation that is coming. He wants them to stay faithful until the end and receive His Life into them; therefore, tribulation is an act of love, a path to life. However, you must let it kill you or die-to-self (**death**) to receive life. Overcoming is the price for a crown of life.

> *2:11 He that hath an ear, let him hear what the Spirit saith unto the Churches;* He that overcometh *shall not be hurt of the* **second death***.*

See '**second death**' page xvi. Notice that it takes spiritual ears to hear this message. No one likes to hear that they must overcome their own flesh to be exempt from the Lake of Fire. This does not demean the Blood of Jesus. For if it was not for His sacrifice, you would not even be qualified to overcome.

Church 3 Pergamos
Pergamos = 'Height / Elevated' a place for all to see.

> *2:12 And to the angel of the Church in Pergamos write; These things saith he which hath the sharp* **sword** *with* **two** *edges;*

This church will face the truth that kills (two edged sword). The first two churches were 'harvestable', but this one stands in jeopardy and could go either way. The Revelation message to this church is a warning; whereas, to the other two, it was a promise.

> *2:13 I know thy works, and where thou dwellest,* **even where Satan's seat is***: and thou holdest fast my name, and hast not denied my faith, even in those days wherein Antipas was my faithful martyr, who was slain among you,* **where Satan dwelleth.**

Not denying His name is about the only thing good this church has done. We do not see much of the Lord in this church; indeed, twice He makes the point that Satan has a seat of authority here. It seems that whenever there is an absence of the Lord, there is a presence of Satan. Today people think that if they just keep from denying Christ, that He will be pleased. In reality, if there is not a witness of Christ's presence in them, then is He really there? The end time will put an end to this hypocrisy…you must show Him to know HIM.

> *2:14 But I have a few things against thee, because thou hast there them that hold the doctrine of Balaam, who taught Balac to cast a stumbling block before the children of Israel, to eat things sacrificed unto idols, and to commit fornication.*

See definition of **Nicolaitans** on page xiv. This is a doctrine of self, wealth, and pride. It emanates from the seat of Satan. It is what will cause the Church to commit fornication with the world.

The focus of this verse is on the religious confusion this doctrine creates. People do not expect to see the world or its habits when they are worshiping God. Moreover, if a leadership allows or even promotes this, then they are "casting a stumbling block before the children of God." It is bad enough when we sin; but to bring others into our sin just to justify ourselves is an attack on the body of Christ.

> *2:15 So hast thou also them that hold the doctrine of the* **Nicolaitans***, which thing I hate.*

Similar to the verse above, self-righteous doctrine is the focus instead of worldliness. This can be even worse because people feel that they are worshiping God when they are really worshiping a religious spirit.

> *2:16 Repent; or else I will come unto thee quickly, and will fight against them with the* **sword** *[page xviii] of my mouth.*

He threatens with a sword from His mouth. The Revelation will cut them to pieces and remove the **candlestick** of His authority from its place. He will cut out the good for His Bride and leave the rest for the dogs.

> *2:17 He that hath an ear, let him hear what the Spirit saith unto the Churches; To him that overcometh will I give to eat of the hidden manna, and will give him a white stone, and in the stone a new name written, which no man knoweth saving he that receiveth it.*

If you overcome yourself, then this hidden Revelation will be your sword. It will then create in you a new nature. This is a heavenly nature, not for the 'fleshy-man' to see or understand, but only for the Spirit-man.

Church 4 Thyatira
Thyatira = 'Odor of affliction' a place of tribulation which becomes a sweet smelling savor to the Lord.

> *2:18 And unto the angel of the Church in Thyatira write; These things saith the Son of God, who hath his* **eyes** *[on page v] like unto a flame of fire, and his* **feet** *[on page vi] are like fine brass;*

This church, like the church at Pergamos, stands in jeopardy. Yet, this church is told how to have victory if they want it. They must submit themselves to the **eyes** and **feet** of Jesus Christ. In this way they will overcome the evil spirit that has risen up in their carnality…Jezebel. Surrender and obedience will be the path for this church.

> *2:19 I know thy works, and charity, and service, and faith, and thy patience, and thy works; and the last to be more than the first.*

He approves of many of their Christ-like attributes and offers them the option of having the 'last' to be more than the 'first'. "Stick it out and all of this tribulation will be worth it." As Paul says, "I reckon that the tribulation of this time is not worthy to be compared to the Glory that shall be revealed."

> **2:20** *Notwithstanding I have a few things against thee, because thou sufferest that woman **Jezebel**, which calleth herself a prophetess, to teach and to seduce my servants to commit fornication, and to eat things sacrificed unto idols.*

This is the spirit that tries to kill the men of God and separate them from Christ (kingship). It will try to take the attention away from God and direct it towards itself. It first manifested in Eve because her husband was not the "high priest" he needed to be. Then it came after Adam to separate him from the kingdom. The same is true in the story of Jezebel, who took the powers of the kingdom, because the husband was not the king he was supposed to be. He was just selfish and self-centered, which allowed this spirit to come into Jezebel. She, therefore, has received the 'honor' of naming this spirit.

Once in authority, this spirit will try to lead the kingdom into adultery (world worship) and will try to destroy the man of God. In this verse, Jezebel takes for herself a 'position' in the kingdom (prophetess), not to help the body, but to seduce the servants. This particular spirit always tries to shift attention onto the natural things, away from Christ.

Personal Note: For the men of God to reenter the kingdom, they will likely face this spirit. Please do not take this as a sexist issue, both the man and the woman are to blame when this spirit manifests. This is because it comes to test the King and Priest of God.

> **2:21** *And I gave her space to repent of her fornication; and she repented not.*
>
> **2:22** *Behold, I will cast her into a bed, and them that commit adultery with her into great tribulation, except they repent of their deeds.*

These two verses are a warning: you can dismiss this only at your own peril. If the men of God buy into the lies of these spirits and become separated from the body, then tribulation will come. As Jezebel separated the nation of Israel from God, she is again trying to separate the Church from God. The Church has become so worldly that they have ceased doing spiritual warfare. We know that Jesus Christ has won the victory, but will we give Him the authority to win in us?

If we fail to see where spirits use our carnality, then we will never be able to give Jesus the authority to conquer 'our earth'.

> **2:23** *And I will **kill her children with death**; and all the Churches shall know that I am he which [1]searcheth the reins and hearts: and I will give unto every one of you according to your works.*

Kill with death? This is actually a positive statement; the people who have been brought under her dominion can be delivered. But it will take the death spoken of in this Revelation…death to self. This spirit's tribulation will expose any carnality it meets. (Once you recognize these spirits, you will see the truth of this statement.) This will help the Saints die-to-self as they overcome these areas in the heart. These evil spirits have no power over our spirit man. They live in our flesh; therefore, whatever they can touch in us needs to die. In revealing this to the Church, He wants to see [1]if we will recognize our heart issues or defer the problems to others.

The true mark of a saint is seen in the way they look inwardly to resolve conflict. They will overcome their own issues and not try to fix everyone else. That is how these spirits operate. They lie to us, telling us that it is everyone else who has the problem. To understand the revelation of Christ is to understand that we do not battle against flesh and blood, but against spirits that sit in heavenly places. (Eph. 6:12, 2 Cor. 10:3-5)

> **2:24** *But unto you I say, and unto the rest in Thyatira, as many as have not this doctrine, and which have not known the depths of Satan, as they speak; I will put upon you none other burden.*
>
> **Do not buy into the lies and you will be alright; otherwise, be prepared for tribulation.**
>
> **2:25** *But that which ye have already hold fast till I come.*
>
> **2:26** *And he that overcometh, and keepeth my works unto the end, to him will I give power over the nations:*

Hold fast to Christ's life and do not let these spirits rob you of your inheritance. If you will surrender to the perfecting power of God, then He will be able to use you as one of the Elect during the upcoming Harvest.

> **2:27** *And he shall rule them with a **rod of iron**; **as** the **vessels** of a potter shall they be broken to shivers: even as I received of my Father.*

See the 'rod of iron'(page 101). Notice that we must be broken to be the rod. This means that in the same way Jesus had to suffer to be made complete, we too must suffer to learn obedience. Then we can be used of God. We are to rule with a rod of iron. Keep this in mind when we look at Rev. 12:5.

> **2:28** *And I will give him the **morning star**.*
>
> **See 'bright morning star' on page xviii. Christ is the morning star; and if we overcome (die to self) and rise to the calling, then we can have Him and His Glory.**
>
> **2:29** *He that hath an ear, let him hear what the Spirit saith unto the Churches.*

Unlike the previous three churches, there is no promise at the end of this letter. Instead, a command is given to hear in the Spirit. That is the only way for deliverance from the evil spirits that plague our lives. We must be willing to hear the truth. The truth in this letter promises to make you anew after crushing you (verse 27). When we give rise to evil spirits, a simple makeover is not good enough; we need to be rebuilt in the image of Christ. (Look at the parable of the unclean spirit Matt. 12:43-45.)

Church 5 Sardis

Sardis = 'Red ones' those with some life in them.

> *3:1* *And unto the angel of the Church in Sardis write; These things saith he that hath the seven Spirits of God, and the* **seven stars***; I know thy works, that thou hast a name that thou livest, and* **art dead.**

This church, like Ephesus, is harvestable. He wants to use them as harvesters. They are dead to this world and alive unto Christ.

> *3:2* *Be watchful, and strengthen the things which remain,* **that are ready to die***: for I have not found thy works perfect [complete] before God.*

Being dead does not mean that you are complete. Refer to the commentary, 'complete vs. perfection' on page 124, if you do not yet understand being 'complete'. Complete is more than being dead; it is walking out God's plan. He wants this church to redeem the time and focus on the harvest ahead.

Too many Christians without this Revelation get involved with things that have no importance in the kingdom of Heaven. If you believe that you have all that God wants you to have, you will stop hungering for more. God wants us to see our lives as a grand plan that can only be lived as we follow closely after Jesus.

> *3:3* *Remember therefore how thou hast received and heard, and hold fast, and repent. If therefore thou shalt not watch, I will come on thee as a [1]* **thief***, and thou shalt not know what hour I will come upon thee.*

The first thing that Christ demands is repentance for our selfish nature. We are wrapped up in our world, forgetting that we are redeemed for a reason. He wants us to be looking ahead to the work prepared for us. He also wants us to prepare for that work.

Completion comes through obedience; and if we fail to use what time He gives, then God promises to get our attention through tribulation. Just when we get comfortable with OUR life, Christ will [1]surprise us with reality. He will then begin to take away what we do have, and blessings will dissolve into cursing.

> *3:4* *Thou hast a few names even in Sardis which have not defiled their garments; and they shall walk with me in white: for they are worthy.*

Some are already complete and spotless, ready for the 'robe of righteousness'. Notice that completion (signified by the robe) is an act of continually walking with Jesus.

> *3:5* *He that overcometh, the same shall be clothed in white raiment; and* **I will not blot out his name** *out of the book of life, but I will confess his name before my Father, and before his angels.*

Once saved, always saved … is not what the Word says. Eternal life is only for those who "overcometh" and make it to the end. God does have an eraser!

> *3:6* *He that hath an ear, let him hear what the Spirit saith unto the Churches.*

Church 6 Philadelphia

Philadelphia = 'Brotherly Love' His loved ones

This is the Church He has crowned with His Love. This is a description of those who will soon be His Bride. He has nothing against this group and everything for them. He declares this Church as His and gives them His power (verse 9). He promises them that they will be at His side during the end-time tribulation. Finally, in verse 12, He promises them a new nature (HIS) and an everlasting citizenship in the New Jerusalem…the Wife of the Lamb.

There is no commentary on these verses so that the uninterrupted anointing of God might have an opportunity to pour over you as you read these words slowly. Try listening with your heart to the promise for those who overcome.

> *3:7* *And to the angel of the Church in* **Philadelphia** *write; These things saith he that is holy, he that is true, he that hath the key of David, he that openeth, and no man shutteth; and shutteth, and no man openeth;*
>
> *3:8* *I know thy works: behold,* **I have set before thee an open door***, and no man can shut it: for thou hast a little strength, and hast kept my word, and hast not denied my name.*
>
> *3:9* *Behold, I will make them of the synagogue of Satan, which say they are Jews, and are not, but do lie; behold,* **I will make them to come and worship before thy feet***, and to know that I have loved thee.*
>
> *3:10* *Because thou hast kept the word of my patience,* **I also will keep thee from the hour of temptation***, which shall come upon all the world, to try them that dwell upon the earth.*
>
> *3:11* *Behold, I come quickly: hold that fast which thou hast, that no man take thy crown.*
>
> *3:12* *Him that* **overcometh will I make a pillar [see jacinth page x] in the temple** *of my God, and he shall go no more out: and I will write upon him the name of my God, and the name of the city of my God, which is new Jerusalem, which cometh down out of heaven from my God: and I will write upon him my new name.*
>
> **The New Jerusalem is for overcomers.**
>
> *3:13* *He that hath an ear, let him hear what the Spirit saith unto the Churches.*

God is telling us, the potential Firstfruits, to get ready. There will be much to be done during this time. If we seek to be part of the Appearing, then our lives will not be our own. His coming is not to take us away but to bring the Bride to earth (**New Jerusalem**). To help us get ready, the Lord has given us a sign that hearkens us to His soon appearing. When we see His appearing begin to 'bud' in a generation, then we know that He is at the door.

The GENERATION OF THE LORD
Matt. 24:31-35
31	And he **shall send his angels with a great sound of a trumpet**, and they shall gather together his Elect from the [1]four winds, from one end of heaven to the other.
	The Firstfruits Angels gather the Elect from the [1]last-time tribulation
32	Now learn a parable of the fig tree; When his branch is yet tender, and putteth forth leaves, ye know that summer is nigh:
	<u>*He is beginning to bud in the lives of a generation (verse 34); therefore, we know that the time is at hand.*</u>
33	So likewise ye, when ye shall see all these things, know that it is near, even at the doors.
	See Rev. 3:8 above, this is decision time.
34	Verily I say unto you, This **generation** shall not pass, till all these things be fulfilled.
	THE GENERATION in which he buds is the one that will not pass away. This fits with verse Rev. 1:1 "that they (chosen generation) would see the things shortly come to pass."
35	Heaven and earth shall pass away, but my words shall not pass away.
	We are His words, the living revelation of Christ. There will be a new heaven and a new earth, but His 'words' will still be here.

Church 7 Laodiceans
Laodiceans = 'Justice of the people' 'self'-righteous, self-guided individuals.

This is the final word to the Church. If the Philadelphian church represents those who are destined to overcome through love then the Laodiceans represent those who are destined to be rejected because of their 'self' assurance. They represent the final word to the carnal church. Rev. 3:18 is the only hope of those who are blind to God's desire. "They have need to buy OF Christ, Christ' anointed presence." It is a mater of standing in the fire and allowing 'self' to be burnt up!

3:14 And unto the angel of the Church of the Laodiceans write; These things saith the Amen, the faithful and true witness, the beginning of the creation of God;

3:15 I know thy works, that thou art neither cold nor hot: I would thou wert cold or hot.

No more middle ground for the Church. You are either with Him or against Him. All else is sinking ground.

*3:16 So then because thou **art lukewarm**, and neither cold nor hot, **I will spue thee out of my mouth**.*

Lukewarm Christians make Him sick. The plow shear is about to divide the land between hot and cold. The plan of the Revelation is to force every person to make a decision. No more fence sitting, or He will spew you out.

3:17 Because thou sayest, I am rich, and increased with goods, and have need of nothing; and knowest not that thou art wretched, and miserable, and poor, and blind, and naked:

The problem, as He has said so many times already, is the world in the Church. We judge based on outward appearances. God looks into the heart. Brokenness and poverty can be very godly.

*3:18 I counsel thee to **buy of me [1]gold tried in the fire**, that thou mayest be rich; and white raiment, that thou mayest be clothed, and that the shame of thy nakedness do not appear; and anoint thine eyes with **eyesalve, that thou mayest see**.*

He wants [1]perfection (gold in fire), completion, and a spiritual nature to be in His children. None of these have to do with prosperity, accomplishments, or abilities. Until you get your eyes on Christ and His kingdom, you will never see or hear the truth. Tribulation will be the only path to bring sight to the blind.

*3:19 As many as I love, I rebuke and chasten: be zealous therefore, and **repent**.*
Word to the Carnal...REPENT!!!

Open Door to the Kingdom

*3:20 Behold, I stand at the door, and knock: if any man hear my voice, **and open the door**, I will come in to him, and will sup with him, and he with me.*

Are you ready to let Him in and strengthen you?

*3:21 To him that overcometh will I grant to sit with me in my throne, even as I also overcame, and am **set down with my Father in his throne**.*

THE KINGDOM PROMISE!!!

The kingdom is for overcomers. This is the fulfillment of Christ' prayer in John 17 to be with Him NOW.

3:22 He that hath an ear, let him hear what the Spirit saith unto the Churches.

If you have **ears to hear** what Christ is saying to the Churches, then you understand that there is a revelation of Christ that the Church needs desperately to hear. The threat has been given, "Behold I will come quickly and take my candlestick out of its place." If the Church will not hear His message, then God will choose another witness to the world, just as He did two thousand years ago. The following chapter provides the framework for how this message which was "hidden for generations" has now been made manifest. It will also demonstrate clearly that Christ will have His Bride without spot or wrinkles.

THRONE ROOM STUDY TEXT - REVELATION CHAPTER 4

At the end of the Church Age we see the door to Christ closed (3:20). Yet there is a promise that if we will overcome, He will allow us into the throne room and to sit with Him in heavenly places. This means the door is opened to those who overcome and allow Christ to strengthen them with His presence. This is where we begin the kingdom. John as us, reveals that if we hear His first call (knock, knock) and let Him in, then that same voice will invite us up even higher. His voice will sound as a trumpet calling us up into the Spirit to receive the revelation. Rev. 1:1 told us that the Revelation was to show us the things that will swiftly come to pass and here we see that event in greater detail.

Do not be fooled into thinking that what we are about to see is natural. Revelation Chapter Four is about issues of the heart. Christ invites us up into the Spirit and His throne room then shows us the path of His unveiling. This is the most important part of Revelation. It is where the unveiling takes place. If we do not desire to ascend into His presence and be transformed into His likeness the rest of Revelation is of no effect.

Christ's kingdom appearing in a people must first begin in the hearts of individual believers. We begin the study in Chapter Four, in which we see Him beginning to call forth an **Eagle** company of believers to soar above the rest showing the way. This is the 144,000 (page i) who will take this message of Christ to the Church. This chapter describes the path taken by those who hunger for the fullness of Christ and are willing to do whatever it takes to receive more of Him. We just took a visual tour of the throne room to get comfortable with the imagery used to describe the types represented there; now, let's visualize this place as it is described by the language of Jesus Christ.

Rev. 4:1-11

> **4:1** After this I looked, and, behold, a **door** was opened in heaven: and the first voice which I heard was as it were of a [1]**trumpet talking** with me; which said, Come up hither, **and I will shew thee things which must be hereafter.**

Now that the door of Rev. 3:20 is open we can hear the Revelation[1] because Christ is now in a place to feed us the truth. If we tie this to Rev. 1:1, where Jesus is giving the revelation, so that His servants would see the things shortly come to pass, then we see that it is here that He will show us our destiny. What Christ shows us is the throne room where the fullness of Christ is offered (seven lamps). The trumpet (**trumpet** page xix) is inviting us into the Spirit to see the throne room and its function within the kingdom of our heart.

> **4:2** And immediately **I was in the** [1]**spirit:** and, behold, a throne was set in heaven, and one sat on the throne.

[1]This book is to be perceived spiritually. He did not go anywhere in the physical; he just entered the spiritual kingdom of Heaven. Eph. 2:6, **"And hath [already] raised us up together, and made us sit together in heavenly places in Christ Jesus:"** This is the place that 'rapture' proponents place the rapture. First, it is obvious that there is no reference to a snatching away of the Church; second, the place in which John arrives "immediately" is not a place but a condition…"in the Spirit."

John's journey and ours into the fullness of Christ begins with seeing Christ as Lord. This is where our relationship must begin: Christ living in us on the throne.

> **4:3** And he that sat was to look upon like a **jasper** and a **sardine** stone: and there was a **rainbow round** about the throne, in sight like unto an **emerald.**

We will need to desire Him as if He were as precious as these. These descriptions reveal precious spiritual truths for believers looking to make Christ Lord and King of their lives.

> **4:4** And round about the throne were **four and twenty seats**: and upon the seats I saw **four and twenty elders sitting,** clothed in white raiment; and they had on their heads crowns of gold.

With Christ on the throne of our hearts we can now be partakers of the righteousness of God (white raiment) and the authority of God (crowns of gold); partakers if we allow Christ to rule. Later, we will see the elders fall down at the feet of Jesus and this is the surrender necessary to have more of Christ in our life. (**four and twenty fell** page vii).

> **4:5** And out of the throne proceeded **lightnings** and **thunderings** and **voices**: and there were **seven lamps** of fire burning before the throne, which are the seven Spirits of God.

These "out of the throne" manifestations entice the viewer (those who have not yet had Christ formed in them) to surrender and move on into a true relationship with Christ.

If you do surrender before the throne, you, too, will be part of this Glory (lightning), authority (thundering), and corporate appearing (voices) of Jesus Christ. These things issuing out of your throne room will then entice others.

Matt. 24:27 speaks of His appearing, "as the lightning comes from the east (where the door to the temple is) and shines to the west…" Those who have Christ formed in them become God's voice to the world. This is what motivates us to go on and die to self, represented by the **seven lamps**. We are qualified to obtain more of Christ' Glory because we are willing to surrender and hear from God. We see in Exodus, the Hebrew children were not willing to hear from God; and when He came close to them (see the parallel to Rev.), they retreated. Therefore, only Moses obtained the Glory of God.

Exod. 20:18-19

18 And all the people saw the **thunderings, and the lightnings, and the noise of the trumpet**, and the mountain smoking: and when the people saw it, they removed, and stood afar off.

19 And they said unto Moses, Speak thou with us, and we will hear: **but let not God speak** with us, lest we die.

> **4:6** And before the throne there was a **sea of glass** like unto crystal: and in the midst of the throne, and round about the throne, were four beasts full of eyes before and behind.

Now that we are qualified by our desire to hear from God, we can see the spots that veil us. Here is the sea of glass, a form of the TABERNACLE LAVER, a place in which a person is to wash prior to entering the Holy Place. The mirror action of the Laver represents the way that Christ, through His face to face relationship with us, shows our imperfections. The lack of light from one of the lamps (seven spirits) shows us an area of need. For example, we may see that 'Might' is lacking (dim lamp) in our life, then the Sea of Glass will point out what we need to surrender to have might restored in our lives.

2 Cor. 4:6

6 For God, who commanded the light to shine out of darkness, hath shined in our hearts, to give the light of the **knowledge of the glory of God** in the **face of Jesus Christ**.

The face to face relationship with Christ brings perfection and transforms us from glory to Glory. Once these spots are surrendered, Christ is poured into our lives. The four beasts will be described in verse 7. Yet, we see here that we are qualified for one of the stages they represent, because we have let Christ look us over and cleanse us. Remember, that the beasts are the stages of Christ-in-us. The eyes are His and they are focused inwardly (within verse 8).

> **4:7** And the first beast was like a lion, and the second beast like a calf, and the third beast had a face as a man, and the fourth beast was like a flying eagle.

Our growth in Christ in the Throne Room

Lion - Christ on our throne, – Represents our surrender to the Lion...Christ in us transforming us.

Transforms us into...

Calf - Immature in Christ (Greek Moschos-"tender shoot, sprout or fresh delicate child").

Man - Mature in Christ (Greek Anthropos-defined as "mature man yet subject to weakness").

Flying Eagle - Overcomer in Christ (Greek aetos-flesh eating bird). They are soaring. *NOTE: in Rev. 8:13 this same word is used for an Angel giving warning...these are the Angels of Revelation.*

Kingly

The Lion in the midst of the throne represents our completeness in Christ through obedience. It is being complete in Christ that brings the 'robe of righteousness' (page xvi and 'completeness vs. perfection' page 124).

The three other beasts represent our growth in Christ or victory over carnality as we engage in the process of dying to self. This process has just been described in verse six. Perfection can continue until we are flying Eagles. This can only be done as we follow Him.

> **4:8** And the four beasts had each of them six wings about him; and they were full of eyes within: and they rest not day and night, **saying, Holy, holy, holy**, Lord God Almighty, which was, and is, and is to come.

The wings, eyes and cries of these beasts link them with the Cherubim over the mercy seat. In Psalms 80 and 99 we learn that the Lord dwells in the midst of the Cherubim. Today, these beasts (stages of Christ-in-us) represent the way in which God appears to this world. He is no longer speaking to just one man from the mercy seat, but to all of us through His Temples, "whose temple we are."

2 Cor. 6:16

16 And what agreement hath the temple of God with idols? **for ye are the temple** of the living God; as God hath said, I will dwell in them, and walk in them; and I will be their God, and they shall be my people.

Christ is showing Himself to the world through Christ-in-us, as represented by these beasts. This is a singular form of the appearing, which lays the foundation for the corporate appearing through the Bride. It also shows that our willingness to go on to the fullness is a way of ministering to our Lord God. Our sold out nature declares His holiness for all to see.

> **4:9** And when those beasts give [1]glory and honour and thanks to him that sat on the throne, who liveth for ever and ever,

> **4:10** The four and twenty **elders fall down** before him that sat on the throne, and worship him that liveth for ever and ever, and cast their crowns before the throne, saying,

Verses 9 and 10 show that the process of surrendering (elders falling down) brings **Glory**. Since this process shows more of His **Glory** to the world, then we are in effect [1]'giving' Him Glory. Our perfecting sold out relationship with God shows Christ's Glory to a dark and carnal world. Surrendering is defined as giving up our will (casting our crowns to Jesus), which is necessary to be one of the Glory-giving beasts.

4:11 Thou art worthy, O Lord, to receive glory and honour and power: for thou hast created all things, and for thy pleasure they are and were created.

The Garden was created for His pleasure and so was man. This verse is showing that we are headed back to that original plan, where God can commune with His creation in the Garden.

In Conclusion

Chapter Four teaches us that we have a choice about the level of our relationship with Christ. For those who choose to press in to the fullness, a 'glorious' event occurs. Revelation clearly demonstrates that not everyone will participate in all aspects of God's plan for the end-time. Some events are reserved for those who 'overcome to the end' (of themselves). Eagles will be called upon to achieve things that those who have settled for less will not. God loves us all, but only the headless Saints will be able to overcome the Beast.

Not only is there a choice to have victory over carnality through surrender, there is also a choice to be completed through obedience within the body of Christ. Even though it is tough to die to self, it is more difficult to love others more than yourself. Eph. 4 shows clearly that the body of Christ is a critical part of all that will take place in this last generation. We must learn to cherish His body and fully supply our part, which is essential for its edification. There will have to be fullness seen in a body of believers…the Bride… before the lost world can be brought into the fullness of Christ

The true Church, as the body of Christ, plays a critical part in our sanctification. Yet, as the next chapter will show us, the Church in its current condition is not ready to play that part. The seven letters that Jesus sent to the Church brings an end to the Church Age. Christ will show the mixture of good and evil within the Church thus revealing the need for cleansing. This cleansing will take the form of the washing Church with the water of the word (Revelation) transforming the Church through tribulation so it can become the Bride that Christ desires.

Chapter 8

The Revelation of the "Seven Thunders"

This is the last chapter before we proceed to the Seven Thunders of Revelation. We have seen to whom Christ wants to carry His revelation message and for whom it is intended. Now we will uncover the hidden 'Seven Thunders' upon which His revelation is built. We must understand this three-dimensional framework to see the depth of Christ's message of the things "which will shortly come to pass." Fortunately for us, the pattern is already in place. We can look to what has been to see what will be.

The Timeline of the End Time

Eccl. 1:9

9   The thing that hath been, it is that which shall be; and that which is done, is that which shall be done: and there is no new thing under the sun.

The pattern that Jesus Christ established two thousand years ago is the same one that reveals Him to us today. **First**, He sent forth His messengers (spirit of Elijah/John the Baptist) to sound the trumpet preparing the way for His coming. In the days of Christ, John the Baptist sounded the trumpet from the wilderness to announce the coming of the Messiah, which began the gathering of the first apostles. Today, the 'Seven Thunders' is sounding the Trumpet from the wilderness, gathering this same apostolic group from among the churches. The Spirit of Elijah is the chosen messengers of the last days calling forth the apostolic Firstfruits company.

Second, He will call forth these Firstfruits to visit His own people (the Church), to declare the acceptable Day of the Lord. Two thousand years ago, men of God were called to come out of a Judaic system that had become corrupted, and those that responded formed the first Church. Today, in the first dispensation of Revelation, the message of Christ will be directed exclusively at the established church. The call will go forth to "come out from the carnality in the Church" and become spotless…the Bride. Those who have ears to hear will separate themselves from their carnal ways and become a Bride for Christ to appear in; those who will not, will become the Harlot.

Finally, in the same way that the message of the first Church was spread to the Gentiles, the message of His appearing in His Bride (**Parousia**) will go forth into the entire world. "Then this message of the <u>kingdom</u> will be preached in all the world, then the end will come." (Matt. 24:14) The similarities between the first and second appearing of Christ end here because **this time Jesus' <u>seven-year ministry is fulfilled</u>**. It is time for the great *Harvest* of God, and His mercy and love for the disobedient will bring life-changing wrath and tribulation such as the world has never before seen.

The seven years ministry of Christ

In most traditional views of Revelation, it is believed that end-time events will take place over a period of seven years. We will review some of the evidence that supports this position.

Revelation is separated into two halves; forty-two months and three-and-one-half years. Add these together and you get seven years. But it is the second half, the three-and-one-half years, which gives greatest strength to a literal seven-year interpretation of Revelation.

Forty-two is the number of 'His appearing' (refer to page xiv) and tells us that the first half of the seven years (42 months) will bring forth His appearing. The second half (three-and-one-half years) is also the number of years Christ ministered on earth two thousand years ago. When we add the three-and-one-half year ministry of Christ 2000 years ago, with the three-and-one-half year ministry of Christ in the second half of Revelation, we get a seven year ministry of Christ on the earth. But why does Christ need to add to His first three-and-one-half years of ministry? We know God's perfect number is seven; therefore, it is reasonable to assume that Jesus will have a seven-year ministry to fulfill a perfect earthly ministry. This will be accomplished by Christ's second appearing in a body of believers who become the habitations of Christ appearing.

Seeing revelation in this way allows us to understand the two edge sword coming forth out of His mouth as He appears during the end-time (Rev. 1:16). It is a message that will first cut a bride out of His Church and then use that same Bride to cut away the sin of the earth. A study of **'third day'** (page xviii) types will reveal that the first forty-two months is given for Christ to prepare a people for His 'appearing', and the second three-and-one-half years is Christ indwelling people so HE can finish His ministry.

The last week of Daniel's 70 weeks (Dan. 9:27)

Christ coming back to complete the last half of a seven-year ministry is found in Dan. 9:27 where the reference to a one-week or seven-year Messiah ministry is split in half. The first half was completed 2000 years ago, and the second half is yet to be fulfilled. A study of the seventy weeks of Daniel is beyond the scope of this chapter, but it is commonly understood to be a vision of the end of man or the end of carnality and sin. (See Dan. 9:24).

Dan. 9:27 represents two three-and-one-half year time periods in which God will confirm His [1]covenant 'to many', producing a 'perfect' seven year ministry of confirmation. He confirmed the first half of the week personally 2000 years ago. In Dan. 9:27 this would correspond to the time up to the middle* of the week, where Christ' sacrifice at the cross brought an end to Old Testament sacrifices. Therefore, the "confirmation" was established through His direct intervention and presence. This then must be the pattern for the second half of the week because the confirmation is for a whole week (seven years). It reveals to us that confirmation of God's covenant is established through the direct intervention of Christ Himself. Ezekiel 34:10-16 tells us this same thing when He declares that He will set aside man's efforts and come personally to finish their work. This is why He must be the one who establishes the covenant because our efforts are too 'self'-centered. Only He can finish the work of 'His' desire.

The second line in verse 27 is concerned with the latter half of that week and helps to explain why Christ would split up His ministry into two, three and one-half year periods. [2]The statement in Dan. 9:27 underlined reads, "and on the wing of abominations shall be one who makes desolate…" A thorough study of the original Hebrew reveals a better translation which is supported by both the KJV and NIV. The verse might be better interpreted: after the end of sacrifice (natural law), Christ will show (wing) that the evil in a person's life is caused from within by an evil one who is making them desolate (without life).

Christ must come again to finish the work that the Church has been unable to finish. His glorious presence will reveal the hidden evil and allow the sources of the heart to be revealed. If these sources are from the antichrist, actions and lives will be made "desolate" and thus marking the person for wrath and judgment.

This verse prepares us for the glorious [3]end-time ministry of Christ where He will pour out His [4]wrath upon all the desolate. 'Consummation' means 'end or finish,' and therefore this wrath will bring mankind to the end of themselves: a wonderful place to meet Jesus.

He is coming to appear in a people to pour out that "which is determined" (wrath) upon the desolate. Nothing will be hidden from the eyes of the Elect; all things of a spiritual nature will be revealed so that they can focus their ministry on those who need it most. This will be of great help in ministering to hypocrites and people who may seem outwardly religious, but inwardly are desolate and in need of godly chastening. This will make all carnality visible and will allow Him to conquer the **earth** and take us back to the **Garden** (on page vii).

The Seven Thunders of Revelation

Seven years is a literal period with spiritual meaning. The first forty-two months is about Christ coming to prepare for Himself a Bride, and the last three-and-one-half years is Christ appearing to the world in a body. The problem comes when you try to put the events from Revelation Chapter 5 to 22 into chronological order. Traditional doctrines, which try to explain these events on a linear time line, must shift the prospective of the reader from Heaven to earth and back again in order to logically account for differences. Many parenthetical (side-bar) discussions also present problems for these linear doctrinal positions because they do not fit into a natural flow of events. However, the biggest problem with linear interpretations is that they force arbitrary decisions as to the literal or figurative interpretation of events. This has been the subject of much

debate even within the ranks of those who accept the traditional doctrines. Without a divine rule or pattern to follow, they are forced to base their theology on man-made doctrines or predefined personal opinions. What we want to do is to allow God to teach us a pattern that can be applied objectively.

This pattern is revealed through the **Seven Thunders** which were sealed by John until this day. These Seven Thunders provide a framework by which the rest of Revelation can be attached. We have seen there are seven years in Revelation, but what we must also see is there is more to the seven years than just a period of time. Each year represents a **Thunder** (xix) in which God's purposes are fulfilled in the earth. A year then is not just 365 days, but a time of destiny for mankind. Understanding just what God wants to accomplish in each of these Thunder-years is the purpose of Revelation.

Again, there are Seven Thunders corresponding to seven years, with each Thunder/revelation being poured out in a one-year period. But this is not about natural events, the book of revelation is a spiritual book that gives us a three dimensional look at the purposes of God. Like the parables of the kingdom in Matt. Chapter 13, this revelation is better seen in 'types' and 'shadows'. To do this the Lord takes each Thunder and breaks it into pieces that help reveal the whole. These pieces we call segments and are the foundation to understanding the "height depth and breadth" of each Thunder. These segments reveal a different aspect of each Thunder and, like a puzzle, they come together to form a picture of God's heart hidden until now.

These five segments come from the: seven Seals, seven Trumpets, seven Angels, seven Vials, and seven Vial Angels of Revelation. However, the front to back reading of Revelation does not give us a Thunder because a Thunder is only a piece of these assembled together in a predefined manner. This is where past studies have erred.

Personal Note: This is where God had to step in…

During the early part of this study, we came to a standstill. God was being faithful to give us insight into the meaning of most of the 'types' that had long been misunderstood. However, it was still not enough to fully understand the story of Revelation. So we stopped the study and spent the rest of the time in prayer, waiting on God. Then one night, God gave me a vision in which I was told to see the 'three- dimensional geometric expression of God'. That may sound like a mouthful, but God speaks in ways that we can hear. We knew that this meant something about a story behind a story, but we were not told what it was. None of us were able to interpret God's words. A few weeks after we paused our study, a large drawing (similar to a blueprint) arrived in the mail. The paper was a visual depiction of biblical references to the five groups of sevens from the book of Revelation (as well as references to other prophetic passages in Daniel, Joel, etc.) They were displayed in such

---

Dan 9:27

27   Then he **shall confirm** a [1]covenant with many **for one week**; but in the ****middle of** the week he shall bring an end to sacrifice and offering. [2]And on the wing of abominations shall be one who makes desolate, even until the [3]consummation, which is determined[4], is poured out on the desolate."(NKJ)

a way that all the Ones, Twos, etc., appeared laid one upon another (Chart below). There was no commentary, just a note from a friend who stated that someone had sent this to him long ago and God told him to send it to us. I immediately knew this was the 'three-dimensional' geometric expression of God' foretold. It was possible to see how each of the seven segments and numbered events corresponded nicely to seven years. God had given us a pattern in which to place our events!

THE ANATOMY OF THUNDERS

Each of the groups of *Sevens*: Seals, Trumpets, Vials, Angels, and the Vial Angels present one facet of an interconnected story. Each Thunder/year is divided into five segments that represent one aspect of the revelation and must be viewed in relation to all others. In other words, all the *Ones, Twos, etc.* must be viewed together, each with a defined purpose in mind. When we apply these definitions and patterns to Revelation scripture, the story unfolds. Look at the definitions for each group of Sevens below. You will need to refer to these definitions often throughout our study, so mark this page for future reference. In each category we can see that the 'natural meaning' provides an indication of the spiritual meaning.

Seals — The **Natural meaning**- A locked item, must be opened by proper key or authority.
Revelation type- The authority or key by which each of the seven revelations is executed.

Trumpets — The **Natural meaning**- An item heralding an event, often associated with Jubilee.
Revelation type- A Revelation voice (Rev. 4:1) of God that reveals the truth.

Angels — The **Natural meaning**- Holy messengers of God.
Revelation type- The proclaimed message of each of the seven revelations.

Vials — The **Natural meaning**- An item used to dispense or pour out from.
Revelation type- Method used to pour out the seven revelations.

Vial Angels — The **Natural meaning**- Dispensers of the Holy Truth.
Revelation type- Message to the dispensers (Holy Messengers)…the purpose of each revelation.

For example, in the *ones*, **Seal 1** will be the *authority* in which the first Thunder operates. This means that Christ makes spiritual authority available for His Holy Messenger to use. Once they understand this power is available for them to dispense, then they can become the 'dispensers' (vials) for that particular Thunder. Nevertheless, we will not know the *'revelation' or insight of* the **First Thunder**, until He reveals it through **Trumpet 1**. The Trumpet in any Thunder explains the problem that God is going to conquer. The **Vials** explain how He is going to do it, while the **Angel** proclaims the Thunder in the form of a message that all can understand. Finally, Christ speaks to His Holy Messengers through the **Vial Angel** to explain background or needed information they must have before they are sent forth. All of these events comprise the story of the first Thunder (seen in the *Thunder 1*), a story that will play out in year *one* of tribulation.

Each one of the seven years brings a revelation of Christ called a Thunder. These Thunders are also designed to produce a specific and unique outcome. These outcomes fall under the goal of each dispensation, which means that

THREE DIMENSIONAL VIEW OF REVELATION

		Dispensation 1 Prepare the Bride			Dispensation 2 Harvest the World			
Year		*THUN-DER 1*	*THUN-DER 2*	*THUNDER 3*	*THUNDER 4*	*THUNDER 5*	*THUNDER 6*	*THUNDER 7*
Judgment Themes		The Earth	The Sea	Rivers and Fountains	The Sun	Seat of the Beast	Euphrates (Sources of Babylon)	Air (Spiritual Realm)
7 Seals		Seal 1	Seal 2	Seal 3	Seal 4	Seal 5	Seal 6	Seal 7
7 Trumpets		Trumpet 1	Trumpet 2	Trumpet 3	Trumpet 4	Trumpet 5	Trumpet 6	Trumpet 7
7 Angels		Angel 1	Angel 2	Angel 3	Angel 4	Angel 5	Angel 6	Angel 7
7 Vials		Vial 1	Vial 2	Vial 3	Vial 4	Vial 5	Vial 6	Vial 7
7 Vial Angels		Vial Angel 1	Vial Angel 2	Vial Angel 3	Vial Angel 4	Vial Angel 5	Vial Angel 6	Vial Angel 7

(left margin: Five segments within each Thunder)

the events occurring during the first three-and-one-half years of the seven years are to sanctify the Church. This sanctification is to birth the Bride without spot or blemish. Christ will indwell this Bride for the appearing. This first three-and-one-half year period is called the **first dispensation**. The events occurring during the second three-and-one-half years are aimed at harvesting the world. This we call the **second dispensation**.

Whether in the first or second dispensation, each Thunder, with its five parts, is a critical piece in the process. We must study each Thunder individually to understand the full meaning of God's plan. Each type not only gives insight into the corporate appearing of Christ, but it can also assist us in our personal walk with Christ. Revelation can be interpreted from the perspective of Christ appearing in the Corporate Body or our personal body. Using language descriptive of a corporate appearing does not take away from the awesome depth of personal revelation available in this book.

THE HIDDEN THUNDERS OF REVELATION

This method of studying Revelation differs from almost all other previous studies. Generally, the book is studied front to back, beginning in Chapter 1 and moving through to Chapter 22. Although this is not wrong, it will not "open the book" and reveal the **Hidden Truth of Revelation.** We must see the truths represented in each Thunder as well as each dispensation. Truth that could never be seen in any other way is revealed through the story that evolves from this three-dimensional view. This non-linear reading of scripture, coupled with God's imperativeness to let the Word of Revelation define itself, makes this a truly unique study.

It will quickly become apparent that God intended this book to be revealed in this manner, especially when you see His recurring theme in the associated year. For example, **Trumpet 1** (Rev. 8:7) of Thunder 1 speaks of casting things upon the **earth**. In **Angel 1,** the message is to those dwelling on the **earth** (Rev. 14:6). Still further away in Rev. 16:1, the **Vial 1** is poured out on the **earth**. The **earth** is the consistent theme in the Thunder 1 and in no other Thunder. Trumpet 2 and Vial 2 of the second Thunder share the same correlation with the 'sea', and it does not stop there. You will see truths in every Thunder that could never be seen in a front to back reading of Revelation.

The five segments of each Thunder
-Review-

Each of the 'seven Thunders/years' is a story in and of themselves. They are all connected, and each plays a part in the whole. The seven Thunders are divided into two dispensations. The first three-and-a-half-years is a time of 'preparing' the Bride for habitation. The next three-and-one-half years are the time that Jesus harvests the world. These two halves of the seven years will be called: first and second dispensation respectively.

Each Thunder is broken down into five segments that give us the complete revelation of that Thunder. As we have learned, it is through these five segments that we can understand the story associated with that number.

Segment 1– The **Seal** is the **authority** by which each Thunder operates in Christ.

Segment 2 – The **Trumpet** is the **revelation** of each Thunder. The Trumpet provides insight into what is taking place in a Thunder.

Segment 3 – The **Angel** is the **message** associated with each Thunder, and it describes how God wants the revelation presented. The message may also tell us for whom the message is intended.

Segment 4 – The **Vial** is the **dispensation** of the Spirit associated with each Thunder. Here God is showing us what is taking place behind the scenes. The Vial shows us the process from God's perspective. Remember, that in the Seal (authority), He reserved for Himself the right to deal with mankind in this way. God is always just; He has allowed the cup of wrath to fill so that it can be dispensed at this time, in this way, to accomplish His will for man.

Segment 5 – The **Vial Angel** is the **message to those who are the dispensers** of each Thunder. It shows them the purpose or completion of their task. Like the Vial, this is a spiritual peek behind the scenes so that the 'holy messengers' know what God will accomplish in the Spirit through them.

Christ will work through a 'Firstfruits' company of people to separate the wheat from the tares. He will have His Church without spot or blemish...the Bride. When He has finished sanctifying the Church into His Bride, He will appear in and through her to the world. That is where the next three-and-one-half year dispensation comes into the picture. This is the time of the great *Harvest* in which Christ will use His Bride to *Harvest* the world. The world will be without excuse as they see Christ again in a cloud of witnesses. He will minister great signs and wonders (the greater works referred to in John 14:12), doing all He can to turn up the pressure and force unbelievers to choose.

Section V Preparing the Bride
The Seven Thunders Begin
THE FIRST DISPENSATION

Section five begins the study of the Seven Thunders which you may remember is both a slice of time, and a step in God's restoration process. It is like stepping up 7 steps; each step designed to elevate and prepare you for the next step. In the book, Secret of the Stair by Wade Taylor, he describes this journey as steps in which we walk out what we have until we come to a new revelation. That revelation is the "riser" of the step designed to take us higher, but if we do not rise and walk it out, that revelation (riser) did us no good. These Thunders are both a revelation of things to come and our preparation for what is being revealed.

IMPORTANT: Do not get confused as we switch back and forth between the corporate events that lead up to the "parousia" of Christ and the issues that affect our heart. Every Thunder will approach the revelation from both sides. There are two bodies Christ must be revealed in…ours and the Corporate man. Each of the seven Thunders must sound in your life to make you a part of the corporate end-time ministry of Christ. I, like Paul, pray that you be counted worthy of this call… "When he shall come to be glorified in his saints, and to be admired in all them that believe (because our testimony among you was believed) in that day. Wherefore also we pray always for you, that **our God would count you worthy** of this calling [to be a vessel of His appearing] (2 Thes. 1:10-11)."

This first dispensation, which consists of the first half of the seven Thunders, is also designed to prepare us for the second dispensation. God is recruiting an army of sold out saints in the first dispensation, who will become the habitations for His appearing. Yet a habitation alone does not fully describe His purposes for us in the second dispensation. The second dispensation (the second half of the seven Thunders) is where these 'habitations' become vehicles through which the Lord will harvest the earth. Having no will of our own and being possessed by the mind of Christ, the world will see the coming Army of God as a single person…Jesus Christ. What a glorious day that will be, to be part of the "parousia" or appearing of Christ. He will, through us, say, *"The Spirit of the Lord is upon me, because he hath anointed me to preach the gospel to the poor; he hath sent me to heal the brokenhearted, to preach deliverance to the captives, and recovering of sight to the blind, to set at liberty them that are bruised. To preach the acceptable year of the Lord… This day is this scripture fulfilled in your ears" (Luke 4:18-22).*

As we open each Thunder, know that the things described therein are more than just revelations for the sake of knowledge. The Lord will allow this revelation to judge your heart and prepare you so you can be part of the revelation of Jesus Christ and not just a reader. Each segment of

each Thunder will resonate within you, providing you with a mirror that reveals the essence of your own heart. This will bring forth the passion and compassion necessary to make you a vessel of honor; meat for the masters table.

CAUTION:

Each of the Thunders (1-7) represents a slice of time. However, as you read the five segments within each Thunder (Vial, Angel, etc), you will have a tendency to think of them chronologically as separate events that occur one after another. You may think Seal 1 is broken *before* Trumpet 1 sounds. Or that the message of Angel 1 precedes the pouring out of Vial 1, etc, etc. NO, NO, NO, this is not the way it works. It is important to understand each of the five segments within each Thunder represents a different aspect of the same Thunder. Each of the individual Thunders should therefore be studied as a whole, with each of the five segments complementing and clarifying one another to convey a single experience in depth.

These next seven chapters will demand some patience and study. All of the Revelation scriptures pertaining to the Seven Thunders will be discussed one verse at a time, and each type and symbol will be reviewed in detail. A thorough study of these scriptures will require repeated reference to the comprehensive dictionary of terms provided at the back of the book. Use the dictionary to become familiar with each type as you encounter it before moving forward in your reading of the commentary. You are being introduced to many new terms and types that will be used repeatedly throughout the Seven Thunders, each of which has been defined, thoroughly studied, and tested using the method described in Chapter One. All words included in the dictionary appear in a special **dictionary font**. In most cases, the dictionary page number of the word is included with the reference. Each chapter also begins with a summary description of the story associated with that number which is followed by a study of the verses that provide the foundation for the story.

May God bless the reading of this book and the study of His Holy Bible.

Chapter 9

The First Thunder - The Judgment of the 'EARTH' (Carnality/Worldliness)

Thunder 1 begins the process continued throughout the first dispensation in which Christ comes to claim the victory that He earned at the cross, conquering the **earth** (carnality) which has spotted His Church. The challenge of Revelation is to show the Church that the true enemy God and His church is not Satan but the carnality in us that feeds him. on. In Genesis we see that Satan was not cast out of the Garden but sentenced to an existence where he is forced to eat the earth. This is to show us that our carnality is keeping Satan alive and that the only power Satan has in our life is through our "stinking thinking".

Therefore, Christ has to destroy the source of all sin which is the 'carnal mind' and replace it with the mind of Christ. Romans 8:7 says our carnal mind is at enmity against God. This means it hates God and it the opposite of all that is God. It goes on to say that the carnal mind can not obey or be guided by God! That is God's enemy.

Therefore God is sending Judgment Day, a time when all *carnality that hinders Christ's appearing will be revealed and cast out of His kingdom.* This is a judgment of the heart; the choice given to every individual to choose Christ or the world. Jesus, through His messengers, will demand that everyone acknowledge the truth He spoke in Matt. 6:21, "where our treasure is there will our heart be." They will be forced to answer clearly and definitively the difficult question, "Is your treasure (your time, your ambitions, your desires) in Christ or is it in this world?" They will no longer be able to excuse or justify Christian carnality, or be deceived into thinking they can live in both worlds. They will be judged by those who have clung to the promise of a better 'Way' and have walked in the authority of Christ-in-them, who will not fear what men will say but will speak the truth that judges all carnality.

Seal 1 unlocks the authority of Christ as He comes through His Elect as a conqueror to destroy the **earth** (carnality) revealed by **Trumpet 1**. **Angel 1** brings the message to "fear God" for the Day of Judgment has come first to the Church (1 Pet. 4:17). The Elect are instructed to preach the everlasting gospel of Christ-in-us to those who claim His name, declaring that redemption is available only to those who bear witness of relationship to Christ through sacrificial, sold out commitment to His purposes. *Perfecting fire* will begin to pour out from **Vial 1** to mark carnality for all to see and to guide those who receive this fire toward perfection. Those who understand that He chastens the sons whom He loves (Heb. 12:6-7) will choose to accept God's judgment so their spots may be removed, and they can enter into the fellowship of the Bride. Those who reject God's judgment will receive even greater tribulation to come.

It will be painful and grievous to see how much of the spirit of antichrist inhabits Christian lives today. This judgment will cause the **Beast** to rise up out of some of their hearts, and many will gnash their teeth at Christ in the messengers who bring this judgment. This is how, in **Vial Angel 1**, Christ begins to separate the Bride from the Harlot, the wheat from the tares. Those who have a spirit of antichrist, refusing to hear the Thunder of God and to be chastened, will be marked as the Harlot (*on page ix*). They seek strength in common worldly doctrines and lifestyles, but their doctrines of devils and demons make them spiritually desolate and easy to recognize. They may appear to be religious to the natural man, but God judges the heart and will not let this Harlotry go unpunished!

THUNDER 1

Seal 1 - Christ coming to conquer
Rev. 6:1-2

> *6:1 And I saw when the* **Lamb** *[on page x] opened one of the Seals, and I heard, as it were the noise of* **thunder** *[page xix], one of the four beasts [first beast is Lion look back on page 34] Saying, Come and see.*
>
> **Only the Lamb gives has the authority to break the seals. This represents dead-to-self Christians who have become a living sacrifice. They have ears to hear the thunder which is the revelation voice which gives us eyes to see.**

> *6:2 And I saw, and behold a* **white horse** *[on page x]: and he that sat on him had a* **bow** *[on page xv]; and a* **crown** *was given unto him: and* **he went forth conquering, and to conquer.**
>
> **We are the vehicles (white Horse) through which Christ comes to conquer. His promise (bow) is about to be fulfilled as the authority of Christ (crown) is manifest against the earth.**

"Come and see" it says; Christ wants us to have 'eyes to see and ears to hear'. Our first glimpse into Thunder 1 shows us Christ is coming back "conquering, and to conquer", and we are the vehicles He will use to go to and fro throughout the earth. This is not a strange concept because the Word calls us His *temples, a Christ house* and even *a holy habitation.* We must allow Christ to posses us with His presence so that He can ride us into His end-time purposes.

The bow represents the 'promise' that we will find the city Abraham looked for; a city whose builder and maker is God (Heb. 11:10). This is our offer to be part of the New Jerusalem, a city of Glory. The 'crown' He wears represents the authority by which the Elect conquer. They are the 'crowns' tossed at the feet of Jesus! They have authority because their will (crowns) has bowed to Jesus; similar to the **Lamb** designation. (Be sure to read all definitions for the full revelation.)

It is the Lamb, working in the hearts of His people, which has the authority to unlock the revelation of **Seal 1**. The Lamb will open every seal for us if we let Him. But only those who will lay down their own lives can claim the authority of the blood of the One who has laid down His life for us. As we die to self we receive more of the revelation that is Christ. The degree to which we receive the revelation is dependent upon the degree to which we are willing to submit our own lives unto death.

The white horse upon which He rides represents the Elect 144,000 sold out vessels of His will, clothed in their white garments of righteousness. They are obedient to His calling; the gentle hand of His Spirit bridling each step of their path. They will validate this Revelation by providing irrefutable evidence of God's supernatural transformation of their lives. His appearing in this apostolic group brings forth the tribulation of Christ's judgment, which in turn brings repentance, increasing the body until the Bride is formed.

Trumpet 1

Rev. 8:7

> 7   The first angel sounded, and there followed **hail** *[on page ix]* and **fire** *[on page vi]* mingled with **blood** *[on page iii]*, and they were cast upon the **earth** *[on page v]*: and **the third part** *[on page xviii]* of **trees** *[on page xix]* was burnt up, and all green **grass** *[on page viii]* was burnt up.
>
> *The revelation of Thunder 1 is unveiled, and we see the object of His wrath...the **earth**. The earth is the object of destruction. This is the carnality in His people (**third part**). We also see the means by which He plans on conquering our carnality; intense personal judgment (**hail**) which brings the perfecting **fire** and thus, the resurrection life (**blood**) of Christ. All of our works (**green grass**) is burnt up to make room for the righteousness of God.*

Trumpet 1 brings God's opportunity for redemption to those who are willing to face personal judgment (**hail**) and perfecting **fire** for the sake of partaking in the Christ Life (**blood**). They are the ones who have the desire spoken of in Ps. 139:23-24 ..."*Search me, O God, and know my heart: try me, and know my thoughts: And see if there is any wicked way in me, and lead me in the way everlasting.*"

42

God's people (**third part** of **trees**) and their works (**grass**) are tried in the fire to expose and destroy all that does not reflect the nature of godliness. Heb. 12:27 says, "*And this word, Yet once more, signifieth the removing of those things that are shaken, as of things **that are made**, that those things which cannot be shaken may remain.*" Notice that life (blood) is a part of the judging and perfecting process. It is those who have allowed the visible life of Christ to be manifest in them who become the **hail** and **fire** of the judgment.

The **third part** represents God's part, the part that is redeemable. It is the **green** part of the **grass** that has *life*; therefore, it is God's part (the Church) and can be tried in the fire. By seeking the **third part**, those who possess a measure of life, the messengers of God, are guided to those who are ready to hear their message and embrace the fullness of Christ's life. **This "third part" will be a recurring theme in almost all of the seven Trumpets because it refers to the redemption of that which is redeemable.** Contrary to what the world may believe, the revelation of Jesus Christ was not given to bring terrible punishment to the disobedient. It was given to reveal the path which God, in His incomprehensible love, has made for them to come back into fellowship with Him. The Church will be sanctified into a Bride worthy of the Bridegroom.

Angel 1

Rev. 14:6-7

> **14:6** *And I saw another angel fly in the midst of heaven, having the everlasting gospel to preach unto them that* dwell [sit] on the earth, **and** *to every* **nation**, *and* **kindred**, *and* **tongue**, *and* **people**, *[see these definitions on page xiii]*
>
> *This revelation is going to those who sit or take their strength from the earth (worldliness). It is also a message for the Church (nation, kindred, tongue and people). Where ever carnality prospers, this message will be heard.*
>
> **14:7** *Saying with a loud voice,* **Fear God**, *and* **give glory** *to him; for the* **hour** *of his judgment is come: and worship him that made heaven, and earth, and the sea, and the fountains of waters.*
>
> *Rev. 3:1 says that the time is at hand and here we see it is a time of judgment.*

Message 1st Angel

"Fear God" means Holy reverence that has been lost in many of today's Christians.
"Give Him Glory" means that this is about praising Him in deed as well as word. Christians are to pursue death-to-self so that His presence will increase in them and therefore, more of His Glory will be seen by the world.

Angel 1 is the first message of the Thunders, a message to fear Him and give Him Glory. It is a message that smacks in the face of carnal Christians. Those without 'eyes to see and ears to hear' will **blaspheme** (on page 44) God by robbing this message of the dynamic truth it represents. Nevertheless, since the "hour" of judgment is here, all Christians had better be certain that they have a right relationship with Christ or face the wrath that is to come.

The "Angels" (Holy Messengers on page i) are really **Eagles** who operate from within the "midst of Heaven", where Jesus resides (John 17:24). These sold out Eagles (page v) dwell in the fullness of Christ and are bringing His everlasting gospel back to the Church.

The message of Revelation **Angel 1** is brief and plain, but do not be fooled by its simplicity. "Fear God" is more than just respecting the power of God. It is the deep, consuming belief that honoring Him is the only worthwhile purpose in life (Matt. 10:28). It is a message that the Church has lost. Worldliness and pride veil most Christians from understanding their need for a deep and abiding relationship with God. The Angel declares that we are to "give Glory to Him", but we can only give Him Glory if we have it. Christ in us is our *only* hope of Glory; therefore, if we are to give 'Glory' to Him, we must have Christ who is the source of Glory. As we die to self, His life increases in us infusing our life with an ever more visible witness of His GLORY. Nothing else should occupy or concern us because **'the hour of judgment has come", and Christ will be manifest in His fullness!**

Them that Dwell on earth

Do not confuse the group in verse 6 ["them that dwell on earth"] with the **inhabitants of the earth**. The translation for 'dwell-in' (Greek- Kathemai) is misapplied. It means to 'sit' or to 'be seated **on**'…not to 'dwell **in**'. These are people, including Christians, who are undisturbed by their sin, resting comfortably with their earthly carnality. Inhabitants of the earth, on the other hand, are a group of people who have never been redeemed, they just live here. The distinction is important because the everlasting gospel is aimed first at the Church and then at the unredeemed world. Here the message is to those who **dwell on the earth,** who are content with "their lives" of self-direction and self-fulfillment. These kinds of Christians are the lukewarm Christians spoken of in the letter to the Laodiceans.

Vial 1
Rev. 16:1-2

> *1* And I heard a great voice out of the temple saying to the seven angels, Go your ways, and pour out the vials of the wrath of God **upon the earth.**
>
> **'Wrath' is poured out against the earth (carnality), which is any thought, word, or deed of self-will that is counter to the will of God.**
>
> *2* And the first went, and poured out his vial upon the earth; and there fell a noisome and **grievous sore** upon the men which had the **mark of the beast** [on page xi], and upon them which worshipped his image.
>
> **The sore is a visible, spiritual mark upon Christians to make all carnality obvious and reveal those who love this world. See the definition of 'mark of the beast'.**

What a wonderful way for God to help Christians deal with the carnality in their life. He will pour out of His Spirit and make carnality painful so Christians will have a powerful incentive to let go and let God. Since carnality is freely accepted within Christianity today, there must be this kind of spiritual awakening to sin. The sold out message of Christ-in-us, spoken and lived by His holy messengers, brings forth Spirit and Truth (later referred to as the 'two witnesses', page xix) to mark with "grievous sores" all carnality wherever it dwells.

It will be apparent to carnal Christians that they have been **worshiping the image of the Beast** (the world) and that you can only worship one God. They will no longer be able to deceive themselves about their level of commitment. Many will be grieved to know it is the end time and that all of their worldly plans have brought them nothing. They now have no recourse except to choose whom they will serve; and **'sold out'** is the only acceptable worship (Jn. 4:23). It must be all, or it will be nothing.

Vial Angel 1

Vial Angel 1 references the two Parentheticals: **The Harlot** (page 90) and **The Beast** (page 94). It is important that you take time to read and understand these Parentheticals before proceeding with this study text.

IT IS IMPORTANT TO NOTE that the events described in the two parentheticals are not taking place during Thunder 1, but are used to show the reason for the judgment of the carnal church by Vial Angel 1. The actual defeat of the Harlot will not take place until Thunder 4…the end of the first dispensation!

Rev. 17:1-18

> *17:1* And there came one of the seven angels which had the seven vials, and talked with me, saying unto me, Come hither; I will shew unto thee the judgment of the **great whore** [on page ix] that [1]sitteth **upon many waters** [on page xi]:
>
> **Judgment has come to the Harlot church (great whore) who takes her power from the number (many waters) of people and organizations who [1]**support** carnal worldly worship. Any who are part of this harlotry will be the object of this judgment.**

Since carnality is being revealed in the lives of Christians, then the Church is not exempt. Judgment must and will begin at the house of the Lord. The Church has, in many cases, taken on the image of the world instead of the image of Christ. Inspired faith seems to have been replaced by worldly wisdom. We are to convict the world not mimic it. Harlotry will tell us to make the Church more appealing and less confrontational.

The Harlot will have a hard time changing because it takes its strength from its numbers (**many waters**). There are more against this sold out message than are for it. "There is strength in numbers."

> *17:2* With whom the **kings of the earth** [on page x] have committed fornication, and **the**

inhabitants of the earth *[on page x] have been made* **drunk** *with the* **wine** *of her fornication.*

Those with a desire for worldliness are the ones quick to fornicate with the Harlotry in the Church. They are in agreement with this hypocrisy and are confused (drunk) by the type of life (wine) they are drinking. This is carnal religion.

This majority (**Kings of the earth**) have bought into the carnal lies because it brought them pleasure. They believed they could have the best of both worlds. And why shouldn't they be confused, they have been taught that this carnal wine is the same as the new wine even though it does not satisfy.

The real losers are the unredeemed (**inhabitants of the earth**). These are the unbelievers who needed to taste of the new wine of Christ' presence, but instead they got a dose of the wine of hypocrisy, which tasted just like the junk that they have had to drink in the world. They are very confused (**drunk**) by this hypocrisy (fornication); therefore, they are reluctant to believe the message of the Church. This is why Christ will purify the Church before He finishes evangelizing the world.

> **17:3** *So he carried me away in the spirit into the wilderness: and I saw a woman sit upon* **a scarlet coloured beast,** *full of names of blasphemy, having* **seven heads** *[on page xvii] and* **ten horns** *[page xviii].*
>
> ***This shows the same picture but with deeper understanding. The only reason the Harlotry is allowed to exist in the Church is because there is a beast which resides in it to support her. Seven heads is the Godly plan for this beast and ten is the judgment this beast will cause. Horns are the mercy God is extending to those confused by her.***

This Harlot sits upon people (**many waters**) with a carnal heart issue (**Beast**), who support worldliness. However, this Beast has been divinely (7 heads) appointed to judge (**ten horns**) the Harlot. These **10 horns** are the Kings of the Earth who God will later use to judge the Harlot (Rev. 17:12). **Horns** are used to show the clemency that is extended to those who are part of this judgment. These Kings think they do God service by attacking the Elect and do not know that they are part of the Harlot. When they battle the Lamb, God will correct them (Matt. 24:9-10, Jn. 16:2). Then they will turn against the Harlot and be instruments of her destruction by the hand of the Lord.

Blasphemy – Greek=blasphemia 1) slander, detraction, speech injurious to another's good name 2) impious and reproachful speech injurious to divine majesty.

The message of the Harlot sounds religious which is represented by the scarlet/royal color of life. But it is full of names injurious to God; speech laced with more of the world than the Spirit.

> **17:4** *And the woman was arrayed in* **purple** *and scarlet colour, and* <u>decked with</u> *gold and*

precious stones and pearls, having a **golden cup** *[on page iv] in her hand full of abominations and filthiness of her fornication:*

This Harlot looks like a queen but look out! She is ready to poison you with her worldliness.

She may seem spiritual with all of the religious ornamentation, but what she is drinking shows her true appetite. She is drunk with worldliness and it makes God sick, but will she listen? Rev. 18:7 says "How much she hath glorified herself, and lived deliciously, so much torment and sorrow give her: for she saith in her heart, I sit a queen, and am no widow, and shall see no sorrow." Boy, is she wrong.

She appears to be the Church of Rev. 12:1 and even wears the royal color. Yet, instead of dispensing salt, light and love, this group dispensed abominations. God is beginning to make a distinction between the Bride and the Harlot. Since their fruit is abomination instead of peace and joy, they will now be marked for all to see.

> **17:5** *And upon her forehead was a name written, MYSTERY, BABYLON THE GREAT, THE MOTHER OF HARLOTS AND ABOMINATIONS OF THE EARTH.*

The Harlotry in the Church is responsible for all the abominations of the earth. If the Church had cleansed itself, then the world would not be in its current condition. The Church would have certainly been the salt of the earth, reproving sin instead of deciding not to be offensive.

All 'socially acceptable' sin is a result of the Church failing to honor its covenant with God. Many think that the Church should not see any wrath to come; instead, here we see that it is THE HARLOTRY IN THE CHURCH THAT IS RESPONSIBLE FOR THE WRATH.

> **17:6** *And I saw the woman* **drunken with the blood of the Saints,** *and with the blood of the martyrs of Jesus: and when I saw her, I wondered with great admiration.*

The Harlot herself is confused (drunken) because she sees the life in the Saints and believes that she has that same life; after all, they are part of the same Church. These are the Christians who think that because they are a member or a contributor to a Church, they are equal participants in the righteousness of the Church. They may even feel that through their participation or contribution they are an author of that life.

The Harlot takes credit for the Saints' works, believing that they could not be where they are if it were not for her. Religious spirits tend to take credit for the good and shed off all criticism or correction. But as time goes on, we will see that the 'true Bride' separates from the Harlot and takes the **candlestick** of authority with them. These are those who "come out from among her" (Rev. 18:4).

> **17:7** *And the angel said unto me, Wherefore didst thou marvel? I will tell thee the mystery of the woman, and of the beast that carrieth her, which hath the seven heads and ten horns.*

> **17:8** *The beast that thou **sawest** [1]**was**, and [2]**is not**; and [3]**shall ascend** out of the **bottomless pit**, and go into perdition: and they that **dwell on** [on page 43] **the earth** shall wonder, whose names were **not written in the book of life** from the foundation of the world, when they behold the beast that was, and is not, and **yet is**.*

The Beast… [1]**WAS** – *This was the Beast in the form of a religious Pharisee spirit (Matt. Ch. 23) which was bringing the kingdom into captivity. (Mat. 23:15) This same spirit led Israel astray 2000 years ago.*

[2]**IS NOT** – *Then after Christ's coming, the Beast was removed from the kingdom; because the kingdom was removed from the hands of the Jewish leadership and given to the disciples. The kingdom of Heaven is now within the hearts of believers.*

Luke 22:29-30
> *29 And I appoint unto you a kingdom, as my Father hath appointed unto me;*
> *30 That ye may eat and drink at my table in my kingdom, and sit on thrones judging the twelve tribes of Israel.*

[3]**SHALL ASCEND** – *Finally, the Beast finds its way back into the kingdom through the carnal hearts of Christians.*

The Beast has not yet fully ascended and formed; it is still waiting for the day when the Holy Spirit, now restraining His ascent, is moved aside. Then it will ascend out of the collective heart of the carnal believers (**Sea**).

Earlier we saw that the Beast was supporting the Harlot, and that is by design. Satan is supporting the harlotry in the Church until there is enough worldliness to come forward (ASCEND) and attack the Elect who are the true threat to Satan. It was in Genesis that there was a promise in which the seed of Eve (church type) would bruise Satan's head (Gen. 3:15). This is a picture of the Man Child of Rev. 12:5.

Notice, once it enters the kingdom, it goes into perdition (destruction). This is because the Glory of the Lord will begin to destroy it. Those 'who dwell on the earth' are in "wonder" to see their worldliness given credibility by the Harlot/Beast church. NOTICE THAT THESE CARNAL CHRISTIANS HAVE NO ETERNAL LIFE, which puts the demand on this message, get them out of the world and into Life before it is too late. Any believer should be moved to action with such a warning.

> **17:9** *And here is the mind which hath wisdom. The seven heads **are seven mountains** [on page xvii], on which the woman sitteth.*

This is the third thing that the Harlot sits on. These mountains are the visible authorities and programs that support her carnal life. It could be a denomination or a separate program that seems to justify the Harlots authority. But remember it says that during this time the mountains will be brought low (Rev. 16:20)

In Rev. 18:7 the Harlot says, "I am not a widow, I sit as a queen" in response to the accusations that she is not the Bride. The Harlot Christian would say, "I am saved and a church member. I do not need to fear or change anything." The Harlot believes she is OK because she is part of the religious system; however Israel thought the same thing. The Harlot Christians lose their husband when they go whoring after the world. Relying on the title of Christian or Church membership will not be enough to keep the veil in place. The Beast will keep telling her, "Look at the money and time you give. You even read your Bible and sometimes witness. You must be the true Bride." The Elect will ultimately expose her nakedness.

> **17:10** *And there are seven **kings**: five are fallen, and one is, and the other is not yet come; and when he cometh, he must continue a short space.*

The Laodicean Church is the seventh (see below) and is now coming into being. This represents the foundation for the Harlot church to come.

> **17:11** *And the beast that was, and is not, even he is the eighth, and is of the seven, and goeth into perdition.*

Perdition=Gk. a perishing, destruction, Remember 'kings' are the making of the Lord…us and His church. These are the authorities that represent THE King in this earth. That is why the Beast has 7 horns, mountains, etc. This is still His church even with the spots. But the Harlot Church, which is not His, will soon appear.

Now, we backup and see the birthplace of the Harlot Church. It comes as Christians and the organizations that support them choose the wrong path in serving God.

Rev. 17:10-11 is the story of the Church age (chapters 2 & 3). Look again at the letters to the churches. The first five showed the general condition of the Church through the age of grace (five is the number of grace); yet, the last two are distinctly different. The Philadelphia church and the Laodicean church represent the culmination of the Church Age of Grace. The Philadelphia (brotherly love) Church shows the path the Elect will take. The Laodicean Church (carnal church) shows the path that leads to the Harlot Church.

The road to perdition is found in the Laodicean doctrine: "We are rich and have need of nothing." The Laodicean church gives life to the Harlot, which is really not the Church but what is left in the old dead meeting houses when the Elect begin to shine. The Harlot church is really those who refuse to "buy of Him gold tried in the fire", or the tares that the angels remove (parable of wheat and tares). The Harlot will go into perdition (destruction) because its authority in the true Church will be removed. Notice the eighth (Harlot) is NOT a king. This is the true spirit of antichrist that will show itself as the revelation continues.

> **17:12** *And the **ten horns** [on page xviii] which thou sawest are ten kings, which have received no kingdom as yet; but receive power as kings one hour with the beast.*

Ten is the number of judgment so these have something to do with judgment. They are of God (kings) yet have no kingdom and have given their authority to the Beast for a short time.

Here we are introduced to a key player in the end-time book of Revelation. These are the ones whom God is ultimately going to use to judge the Harlot, even though they originally were a part of the Harlot. They are really a byproduct of the Harlot. They are kings (**kings of the earth**, page x), but they have not entered the kingdom of Heaven. They are innocent (see **horns**) of this because they have not rejected Christ; in contrast, they have been deceived into believing they serve Him. They have a form of godliness that the Harlot gives to them, but they do not yet have Christ in them which is the kingdom.

*17:13 These have **one mind** [carnal], and shall give their power and strength unto the beast.*

It is carnality that feeds the Beast. Remember that Satan is still in the Garden eating dirt.

These kings have bought into the carnal message of serving God and mammon. Do not be fooled, they do not look worldly. The problem for many is a misplaced loyalty; some love their church more than they love Christ, and they will follow their doctrines almost to the death. Others are satisfied to do as little as possible as long as they can continue to pursue (or be loyal to) their lives.

*17:14 These shall **make war with the Lamb**, and the **Lamb shall overcome them**: for he is Lord of lords, and King of kings: and they that are with him are called, and chosen, and faithful.*

The Harlot/beast convinces them that the Elect are fanatical and cultish and that they must attack them. Yet, since they are Christians, the Lord (lamb) is still their Lord and will straighten them out.

The kings of the earth will make war with any who would dare to speak evil of their denomination or doctrine, even if it is Christ in a body of believers. Thank God that our Lord is faithful to those who choose Him. The kings of the earth desire God, but they have not died to self yet. This scripture describes how many of the **Kings of the Earth** get victory over their earthiness and have their veils removed so that they can see themselves as they truly are.

What finally overcomes them... the 'parousia' (on page 12), Christ appearing in a body. This 'parousia' in a body of believers pierces their veils and allows them to realize that they do not fight against evil people with false teachings; but rather, they fight against Christ revealed in the sold out lives of His surrendered vessels.

*17:15 And he saith unto me, The waters which thou sawest, where the whore sitteth, are **peoples, and multitudes, and nations, and tongues** [on page xiii].*

The water is the sea (See definition sea, xvi) and the peoples, multitudes, etc. is harlot church.

Even though the kings of the earth are misguided, they still have to bear the responsibility for their carnality.

It is still what has allowed the Harlot to come into being. That realization is what causes them to become such zealots for the faith once the veil has been removed. "They who have been forgiven much, love much."

*17:16 And the **ten horns** which thou sawest upon the beast, these **shall hate the whore**, and shall make her desolate and naked, and shall eat her flesh [carnality], and burn her with **fire**.*

Judgment now comes to the Harlot through the very ones who supported her.

This is how the **ten horns** become instruments of God's judgment against the Harlot. Now that the veil is lifted, they hate the harlotry within the Church and become a vocal critic. Since many of these kings may be important people within their organizations, they will have a tremendous authority to make the Harlot naked before the other kings of the earth. They will eat (fire) her carnality (flesh) through their righteous judgment. They do not want her to deceive any others.

*17:17 For **God hath put in their hearts** to fulfill his will, and to agree, and give their kingdom unto the beast, until the words of God shall be fulfilled.*

God allowed this to happen to fulfill His 'will'; the revelation of His prophecy in them.

God is in control and this verse is where the godly 'seven' of the **seven headed Beast** originated. It was God's plan all along to entrap Satan in his own plans. This is why Paul was such a strong witness before the Jewish leadership; he had been one of them, and yet he saw the light.

17:18 And the woman which thou sawest is that great city [Babylon], which reigneth over the kings of the earth.

Babylon is the unity or gathering together of the carnally minded. There is strength in numbers and a greater manifestation of their common carnality...the Harlot.

There is now more of the Glory of Christ to be seen. Those who refuse the light being shown by these converted kings of the earth are now spiritually sentenced to Babylon. Babylon is the next manifestation of the Harlot/Beast. God continues to be patient, yet if after such a witness men will still not bow before the Glory of God, then more heat will be applied.

Vial Angel 1 introduces us to the Harlot. The differences between the Beast and the Harlot are almost indiscernible. The Beast that has made the Church give rise to a Harlot by rising up and defiling her, but the carnality in the Church has created a place for the Beast (spirit of antichrist) to enter. The Beast is Satan's tool to influence the Church and do battle with the Lamb's Elect. He entices believers with lies and lust for the world in an effort to make the sold out message of Christ look fanatical.

As Chapter 17 of Revelation reveals, many Christians have become carnal and a tool of the enemy; therefore, as spots in our love-feast; they must be judged. It is important to understand why this judgment must come to separate His Bride from the Harlot. Using "the body" as a metaphor, we can see that Paul makes clear the dangers of uniting with a harlot (as a person or a church). Christ cannot be unequally yoked with a part of His body that is fornicating with the world. Instead, He told us to cut off our arm or pluck out our eye if it offends us. He can only be joined in Spirit with a body without spot or blemish…the Bride.

1 Cor. 6:15-17

15   Know ye not that your bodies are the members of Christ? shall I then take the members of Christ, and make them the members of an Harlot? God forbid.

16   What? know ye not **that he which is joined to an Harlot is one body**? for two, saith he, shall be one flesh.

17   But he that is joined unto the Lord is one spirit.

Vial Angel 1 shows both the depth of love and the severity of judgment of our God. Although the Harlot is judged, there is a way provided for those who choose to repent and are willing to accept and learn from their chastening. God's plan is not only to redeem the repentant kings, but to ultimately bless them by making them a part of the Bride that returns to carnal Christians with the good news of His deliverance. In this way, the flesh of the Harlot will be eaten from the inside out. However, the Elect can expect that the unrepentant kings of the earth will cause them much pain. Some will seek to kill the Saints, thinking they do God service. *"They shall put you out of the synagogues [churches]: yea, the time cometh, that whosoever killeth you will think that he doeth God service."* (John 16:2)

Jesus, speaking of this day, said, "*And the brother shall deliver up the brother to death and the father the child: and the children shall rise up against their parents, and cause them to be put to death*" (Matt. 10:21). The good news is that the death we face is of the flesh, so even the enemies of Christ will be instruments of perfection for the Elect's sake.

Chapter 10

The Second Thunder - Judgment of the 'SEA' (heart of carnality in the Church)

In Thunder 1, the true ememy of God was revealed. Carnality and the carnal mind is the enemy of God and actually hates God. It must be defeated for Christ to have the fullness of the victory promised in His word. This is a major revelation to the Church and Christians, who have long evaluated sin from the outside in. Now, we will see Christ reveal the inner heart and judge it at the very source of sin.

However, knowing who the enemy is does not defeat the enemy. It is one thing to see carnality as our problem, it is quite another to have it removed from our life. In Thunder 2, the carnality that plagues us will be made visible so that the Lord can destroy it. The carnality which plagues our life will be made visable so the Lord can ultimately destroy it. The Lord will acomplish this first in His Elect and use them as the lamps to shine forth and reveal the carnality in the Church.

The story of Thunder 2 begins with the Spirit (**Seal 2**) of Christ coming to take "peace from the earth" and to destroy complacency and compromise with sin in all who claim His name. The "great sword of truth" in the lives of the Elect is drawn against the false righteousness perpetuated by religious spirits in the ungodly, preventing believers from standing before the Spirit of Christ with the mark of carnality in their lives. They will either surrender to Christ so He can burn away their spots, or they will reject His message and run from His presence.

In **Trumpet 2,** Christ unveils a great promise: He will perfect the heart (**sea**) of the Church and make it His by bringing the revelation of Christ (**mountain burning** page xiii) to everyone who has the 'life of Christ' birthed in them. The humbled Christ life poured out through the Elect in **Vial 2** brings an unconditional love and giving of self which touches and purifies any heart who desires Christ. This will bring perfection to the Church, enabling them to turn from their vain and prideful activities, which will in turn make it possible to be about the true work of the Lord…showing and declaring Christ.

Life floods the Church, eliminating the confusion held by many who wrongly believe that a relationship with their church is a substitute for a relationship with Christ. As the carnality in the heart of the Church is clearly revealed, **Angel 2** tells us that Babylon is fallen. The Bride Church is being clearly separated from the Harlot. As in the parables of the 'wheat and tares' (Matt. 13:24) and the 'net' (Matt. 13:24), the wicked are being removed from the righteous as the Bride is formed through the spiritual cleansing of the Church. The Harlot is around and continues to confuse with religious spirits, which the world still mistakenly believes is God. But **Vial Angel 2** declares that those with the eyes of Christ, (e.g. having eyes to see), will recognize that Babylon is fallen (religion is no substitue for Christ). What was seen as religious just years before is now revealed for what it truly is: the dwelling place of carnality and unclean spirits, where hypocrites and mammon worshipers fellowship. Soon, however, the wickedness of the Harlot will be judged, and the **lampstand** (authority and witness of Christ, page xi) will be moved to the Bride. The Harlot will be removed; yet, rejecting Christians will continue in their form of religion despite being separated from the true worshipers of God. These rejectors will become **Babylon** (on page ii).

THUNDER 2

Seal 2 - Peace taken from earth

'Taking peace from the earth' sounds in the natural like a promise of world-wide war which is why natural interpretations of revelation are full of such images. Why would Christ fight a war He has already won at Calvary? Instead we know through the Spirit, that war will rage in the hearts of men. According to Paul, this is exactly what is taking place right now in the heart of every believer. The old carnal nature, trying to make you captive to sin (Rom. 7:23), is warring against the Spirit of the Lord.

Jesus Christ is only the hope for those who want to be set free from this battle. Therefore, the war has to be won inside of us before we can hope to see victory in either the Church or the world. We must "walk after the Spirit" by pursuing Christ so that our mind will be transformed into a Spiritual mind. Complacency toward carnality will keep you from pursuing the "Hope of Glory" and the victory that comes with it.

Rev. 6:3-4

> 3 And when he had opened the second seal, I heard the second beast say, Come and see.
>
> 4 And there went out another ¹**horse** that was ²**red**: and power was given to him that sat thereon to **take** ³**peace from the earth**, and that they **should kill one another**: and there was given unto him a ⁴**great sword**.
>
> *We are the vehicles (horses) of life (red) that bring the Lord's Glory to remove complacency (peace) with carnality (earth). Red represents*

> *the visible life within the blood of Christ. The revelation of Christ (sword) will be the "iron that sharpens iron" (kill), which perfects the Body of Christ.*

The [1]Elect, by exhibiting a [2]Christ' life, will show His victory over the sin nature and will have the power to remove [3]carnal complacency within the Church. The glorious victory they manifest is the great [4]sword of truth which will have the power to kill the 'self' life. During this time, worldly or uncommitted Christians will have no peace with their carnality in the light of Christ, manifesting Glory. All their efforts to fill the void in themselves will come to naught. This void was created when, as Christians, they failed to come to KNOW Christ. Therefore, only laying down their lives to gain Him will fill it. This will give the revelation of Christ (great Sword of Truth) a sharp enough edge to kill their carnality.

Jer. 12:12

12   The **spoilers** are come <u>upon all high places</u> through the wilderness: for the sword of the LORD **shall <u>devour</u>** from the one end of the land even to the other end of the land: **no flesh shall have peace** .

The Elect will wield the great sword of truth, which will remove the spots of carnality in other believers.

Trumpet 2

Rev. 8:8-9

> 8   And the second angel sounded, and as it were a **great mountain burning** [page xiii] with fire was **cast into the sea**: and the **third part** of the **sea** became **blood**;
>
> **This great mountain is the revelation of Christ being revealed in the lives of His Elect, which causes Babylon to burn. It is the beginning of the end for man-made religion. God's people (third part) in the Church (sea) will be perfected and come into the full life (blood) of Christ.**
>
> 9   And the **third part** of the creatures which were in the **sea** ~~and~~ ['and' added word] had [1]life, died; and the third part of the **ships** were destroyed.
>
> **Those [1]<u>with life already</u> (Christ's) will die (to-self) and bring more life into the heart of the Church (sea). The next sentence speaks of a shift in emphasis from programs to personal evangelism, much like the Church of the first century. Ships (man-made programs, idols of pride - page xvii) will no longer be the tools of carnality. They will be redeemed for use in God's end-time harvest.**

Seal 1 showed us that the Glory of God will remove the complacency with carnal sin and in **Trumpet 2** we see how God will do it. He will make carnality too hot to stand. Conviction will force a response. This is a two part process. First, the Beast will rise up in response to the Glory that is being revealed in the elect. This is seen in the Parenthetical of the Beast (page 94) as John sees the Beast come up out of the sea. But what made him come out of his hiding

place? It was this influx of Glory through the Elect (mountain burning).

Secondly, those with eyes to see will begin to realize they have been in fellowship with the Beast and will be convicted. Many will repent of their self-life and pursue the revelation of Christ.

The **great mountain** is an image of high communion with God. Perhaps the best example is Moses' encounter with God on Mount Sinai where he demonstrated that man could have face to face intimacy with God on the mountain of God. Intimacy brings Glory as witnessed by the countenance of Moses when he descended from the mountains. The power of God shone forth from his face with such magnificence and authority that it brought judgment and condemnation to all that beheld him, and he had to cover Himself with a veil. This happens as the **Great Mountain** enters into the **Sea**. The very presence of the Elect, spiritually showing forth the Glory of an intimate relationship with Christ, brings condemnation to the Church. Their perfecting fire or Glory will bring [1]life to those who have tasted of the life of Christ (note: it can only 'kill' those who have life) and who have ears to hear.

2 Thes 1:7-8, 10-11

7   And to you who are troubled rest with us, when the **Lord Jesus shall be revealed from heaven** with his mighty angels,

8   **<u>In flaming fire</u> taking vengeance on them that know not God, and that obey not** the gospel of our Lord Jesus Christ:

10   When he shall come to be **glorified in his saints**, and to be admired in all them that believe (because our testimony among you was believed) in that day.

11   Wherefore also we pray always for you, **that our God would count you worthy of this calling**, and fulfil all the good pleasure of his goodness, and the work of faith with power:

The life presence of Christ afresh in the Church (fire) will destroy man-made idols and create new patterns and pathways of life focused on building relationships with Christ. Programs and plans once designed to attract the carnal side of man will be transformed into heart-changing tools of righteousness. However, notice that you have to be worthy to be a vessel of fire who reveals Christ. Do you want to be worthy of this calling?

Angel 2

Rev. 14:8

> 8   And there followed another **angel**, [on page i] saying, **Babylon** [page ii] **is fallen**, is fallen, that great city, because she made all [1]nations drink of the **wine** of the wrath of her fornication.
>
> **The Bride now being made visible also shows that the end of Babylon is near.**

The lies of the Harlot are now revealed, making it impossible for the carnality of the Harlot to deceive those who seek truth. Angel 2 tells us carnal religion is now defeated by the truth of Christ' Glory. True worshipers who worship Him in Spirit and Truth will carry the candlestick and BE seen as THE witnesses of Christ to the world. The world will not be confused any longer (drunk) by hypocrisy.

Babylon is a dead-end for those who continue to reject the revelation of Christ. The **message** of **Angel 2** is simple: choose to follow after the way of truth, not the way of men and religion. Many of those who have [1]worshiped carnally have done so in ignorance, deceived by religious doctrines of apathy and worldly compromise. Now the Bride Church will provide another example and another choice, demonstrating the nature of true worship as they show forth Christ. Judgment has now come against carnality; the Saints have shown the way of life. The great city…man's carnal religious system…has fallen.

Vial 2

Rev. 16:3

> 3   And the second angel poured out his vial upon **the sea**; and it became as the **blood of a dead man** [on page iii]: and _every living **soul** died_ in the sea.
>
> **Only the living can die it says. This means that only those who have partaken of Christ will be able to die to self and obtain the full revelation of Christ. The Christ life (blood) in the Elect (dead men) dispenses this death.**

What a great promise for those with spiritual ears to hear! Angel 2 declared the beginning of death for carnal religion and Vial 2 declares the life that comes through that defeat. The dispensing (vial) of death through the life of the Saints will bring soul life to the sea (the heart of the Church). The Church will be purified through the poured-out life of the Saints who share the revelation of Christ to all who have ears to hear. Since the soul is the seat of the "will and desires', this means that those who _desire_ God and hear His message will receive His Glory.

Vial Angel 2

Rev. 18:1-3

> 1   And after these things I saw another **angel** come down from heaven, having great power; **and the earth was lightened with his glory**.
>
> **These are the Elect wearing their glorious robes of righteousness.**
>
> 2   And he cried mightily with a strong voice, saying, Babylon the great is fallen, is fallen, and is become the **habitation** of devils, and the hold of every foul spirit, and a cage of every unclean and hateful bird.
>
> **Babylon is now revealed as the spiritual place of gathering for those who reject the life of Christ. These people are now the habitation for all kinds of spiritual evil. Satan will do all he can to mislead and distract those gathered under his influence.**
>
> 3   For all nations have drunk of the wine of the wrath of her fornication, and the **kings of the earth** have committed fornication with her, and the **merchants** [on page xii] of the **earth** are waxed rich through the abundance of her delicacies
>
> **Notice 'her' indicates that Babylon and the Harlot are the same. She will put on a good show for the world, but ultimately those with spiritual eyes will see through her disguise. They will see that the Harlot has become a gathering place for carnal, lifeless, rejecting Christians.**
> **Merchants: organizational leaders who loved their positions more than the Lord …also 18:11 where souls are a commodity to them.**

As all of this life comes into the Church, where is all of the darkness going to go? In **Vial Angel 2** we begin to understand the separation taking place in the heart of the Church. Christians are separating themselves into habitations of the heart. Those who desire more of Christ will join with the Elect as the New Jerusalem. Those who love their life will separate into Babylon and become subject to a spirit of strong delusion.

The mixture in the heart of the Church is falling away as each dwelling place becomes purer in the essence of its source. Soon the visible witness of just how evil carnality is to God will bring forth the message of "come out from among her." Obedience and disobedience will be judged and the "**horns**" of clemency will no longer apply.

Through the Glory of the Christ-in-you messengers, the Harlot is seen for what she really is…the "habitation of devils, and the hold of every foul spirit." In Thunder 2, the Angels of the Lord who are His holy messengers of truth in word and deed, are to show forth the power of His resurrection as a living epistle. This is the judgment that separates. Their message will be strong (verse 2); they will not be afraid to reveal the Harlot for who she is. All who choose her worldliness ("the abundance of her delicacies") will be declared the inhabitants of Babylon. CHOOSE THIS DAY WHOM YOU WILL SERVE!

Chapter 11

The Third Thunder – Judgment of the 'Rivers and Fountains' (Sources)

In Thunder 3, the judgment of God will work its way even deeper into the spiritual source of the Church (the hearts of its people) until every individual heart has been weighed in the balances. The standard for judgment is simple: does the desire of the heart reflect a willingness to submit to God's way or does it seek to follow the way of the world? Now that carnality is unmistakably revealed, **Seal 3** provides the authority to judge each person based upon his personal choice to follow after or reject the will of God. In **Trumpet 3** He helps us make the right decision by transforming anything that is not after Christ into bitter waters, making it difficult to be involved with vain and worldly preoccupations when the Day of the Lord is at hand. The message in **Angel 3** is stern: if you worship carnality, be prepared to face a Day of Judgment and Wrath, a time when the revelation of Christ will torment you with the Glory of God. **Vial 3** shows the Elect pouring out the words of Life, which is found in the revelation of Christ unto the entire Church. No matter where the ungodly turn, Jesus is there judging their hearts. In **Vial Angel 3** the message is made crystal clear as Jesus Christ speaks directly to disobedient Christians…COME OUT OF HER, MY PEOPLE! **For the Old Testament type, read Hab. Chapter 3.**

THUNDER

Seal 3

Rev. 6:5-6

> *5* And when he had opened the third seal, I heard the third beast say, Come and see. And I beheld, and lo a **black horse**; and he that sat on him had **a pair of balances** [on page ii] **in his hand.**
>
> *This seal represents the authority of Christ to the judge (balances).*

He is ready to weigh us in the balances and to see if our actions match our profession: do we "walk the walk?" The revelation of Christ in the Elect is visible evidence of God's power and purpose; their lives are the plumb line by which the entire Harlot will be measured.

> *6* And I heard a voice in the midst of the four beasts say, A measure of **wheat** [on page xix] for a penny, and **three measures** [on page xviii] of **barley** [on page ii] for a penny; and see thou hurt not the oil and the wine.
>
> *The authority is now given to judge all by a two-fold judgment: first, to discern who are truly His (wheat); and second, to increase their walk toward the fullness of Christ (barley).*

The third Thunder will make visible the hidden things of the heart through a move of the Spirit. Both the carnal and the Elect will see where they stand. This is a message to all the Church; press in while there is still time.

The oil and wine represent those anointed in His joy and peace. These are the Elect who have come into their Glory are now seen as God's representatives on earth. To come against them is to come against God. This judgment is also a warning that if you do not measure up, time is short.

Dan 5:22-28

Parallel scripture to this segment –

Judgment of Babylon

	Judging the heart of the prideful is as clear as… "Handwriting on the wall"
22	And thou his son, O Belshazzar [king of Babylon], **hast not humbled thine heart**, though thou knewest all this;
	Pride came in.
23	But hast lifted up thyself against the Lord of heaven; and they have **brought the vessels of his house** before thee, and thou, and thy lords, thy wives, and thy concubines, have drunk wine in them; and thou hast praised the gods of silver, and gold, of brass, iron, wood, and stone, which see not, nor hear, nor know: and the God in whose hand thy breath is, and whose are all thy ways, hast thou not glorified:
	Worldliness came in and they acted like a church, but they did not give God Glory.
24	Then was the part of the hand sent from him; and this writing was written.
GOD SENDS A CLEAR MESSAGE…	
25	And this is the writing that was written, MENE, MENE, TEKEL, UPHARSIN.
26	This is the interpretation of the thing: MENE; God hath numbered thy kingdom, and finished it.
	Harlot/Babylon is judged; your time of deception is over.
27	TEKEL; Thou art **weighed in the balances**, and art found wanting.
	She is lacking; you do not measure up to my standard.
28	PERES; Thy kingdom is divided, and given to the Medes and Persians.
	I will divide your people, some of whom are declared Persians (means pure and splendid)

Seal 3 unlocks the authority that places all hearts in the balance and requires them to measure up sufficiently. If we endure judgment and are willing to be weighed according to God's scale, then our value will be established. The price is the same whether you are being measured for salvation (redeemed/wheat) or for completion (sons/barley). It is a Penny (Greek denarion), which means **containing ten** (on page xiv); for our purposes, **containing judgment (10)** signifies that all must face the judgment of God. The oil and the wine speak of Christ in the heart of the believer, which is the test applied to those who declare His name. This judgment is not to hurt our anointing or our spiritual life, but to increase them. For those who will not allow Christ to reveal the contents of their hearts, doom and destruction wait. This will be a time of true judgment of the heart which will declare definitively who of those that profess Christ are truly His - and who are not.

Trumpet 3
Rev. 8:10-11

> **10** And the third angel sounded, and there fell **a great star** [on page xviii] **from heaven,** burning as it were a **lamp,** and it fell upon the **third part** of the **rivers,** and upon the **fountains of waters**;
>
> *Christ is beginning to descend (**great star**) into His organizations (**rivers**) and into the hearts of His people (**fountains**) through the ministry of His Elect (See **horses**).*

The Life of Christ is beginning to revive His Church. True revival has come to His Church. Thunder 2 was about purification of the corporate heart, but to keep the heart pure the judgment must move upstream to the sources of the heart. The fountains and rivers, which are the very sources of the corporate heart (**sea**), are beginning to flow clearly and cleanly. In this way, Life will bring life. If those who are partaking of the death realm taste this new wine, they will taste more death.

> **11** And the name of the **star** is **called Wormwood** [on page xx]: and the third part of the waters became wormwood; and many men died of the waters, because they were made bitter.
>
> *This is the "Daystar" bringing glory and it is coming through His Elect. The Revelation (waters) becomes bitter (**wormwood**) to the carnal Christian.*

"To the one we are the savor of death unto death; and to the other the savor of life unto life. And who is sufficient for these things?" (2 Cor. 2:16)

There will be only bitterness for those who drink of the true gospel and continue in sin. But to those who taste of the sweetness of Christ, they will find that the bitterness in their belly brings strength to lay down their lives and "diligently hearken to the voice of the Lord" (15:26 below). They will be freed from the wrath to come.

Take a look at the Old Testament type of Thunder 3 where God used the bitter waters of Marah to test His children.

The bitter waters are to prove their hearts
Exodus 15:23-26

23 And when they came to **Marah**, they could not drink of the waters of Marah, for they <u>were bitter</u>: therefore the name of it was called Marah.

24 And the people murmured against Moses, saying, "What shall we drink?"

25 And he cried unto the LORD; and the LORD shewed him a **tree**, which when he had cast into the waters, the waters were made sweet: there he made for them a statute and an ordinance, and THERE HE PROVED THEM,

26 And said, If thou wilt diligently hearken to the voice of the LORD thy God, and wilt do that which is right in his sight, and wilt give ear to his commandments, and keep all his statutes, I will put none of these diseases upon thee, which I have brought upon the Egyptians: for I am the LORD that healeth thee.

Such an in pouring of Christ in us (Great Star coming to earth) will cause anything that is not of Christ to become bitter to those who are Christ's. The 'lamp', which is the revelation of Christ, will illuminate the carnality and judge the heart of every professed believer. Many will die to self and receive life as they drink of the bitter truth.

"I Jesus have sent mine **Angel** to testify unto you these things in the Churches. I am the root and the offspring of David, and the bright and morning star. The Spirit and the Bride say, Come. And let him that heareth say, Come. And let him that is <u>athirst</u> come. And whosoever will, let him *take the water of life freely* (Rev. 22:16-17)."

Two thousand years ago Christ commanded that those who are of the light should walk in the light. Now, it will no longer be an option. Hypocrites, who profess a relationship with our Lord but will not walk in the light of that profession, will now drink bitter waters.

The revelation of Christ that '*it is no longer I that live but Christ that lives in me*' makes the Elect a walking condemnation to carnality and a perceived enemy of the world. "*If ye were of the world, the world would love his own: but because ye are not of the world, but I have chosen you out of the world, therefore the world hateth you*" (John 15:19). They will either change the direction of their hearts or separate themselves from the bitterness of the truth, bringing the final separation of God's people from the Harlot.

Angel 3
Rev. 14:9-12

> **9** And the third Angel followed them, saying with a loud voice, If any man worship the beast and his image, and **receive his mark** in his forehead, or in his hand,
>
> *Carnality is a decision (forehead) that is made visible in action (hand). Therefore, this is a judgment against those who show forth the worldliness of their heart.*

> **10** *The same shall drink of the* **wine** *of the wrath of God, which is poured out* [2] *without mixture into the cup of his indignation; and he shall be* **tormented with fire and brimstone** *[on page iii] in the* [1] *presence of the holy Angels, and in the presence of the Lamb:*
>
> **As you sow so shall you reap. This is pure wrath with out grace. Repent or everlasting destruction is to be your end.**

The message (angel) of Thunder 3 is: worldliness is no longer tolerated and when present, will bring the wrath of God. This is the first place where **brimstone** is used in the Thunders because this is where God is telling Christians who are sold out to carnality will be tormented with a 'last-chance' judgment (See definition of **brimstone**).

If they do not repent, these believers will face the reality of a final separation. Later we are told that these marked with carnality cannot rule with Christ in the Millennium. This mark seems to never completely wear off…this is serious!

As they partake of the spiritual (wine) of Christ-in-us [1] presence and life in the Elect become wrath to them. Plus, the wrath is no longer [2] seasoned with grace. God knows the time is short and they are facing a final decision. *Notice:* the lamb is here with us and is at the source of everything.

> **11** *And the* **smoke** *[on page xviii] of their torment ascendeth up for ever and ever: and they have no rest day nor night, who worship the* **beast** *and his image, and whosoever receiveth the* **mark** *[on page xi] of his name.*
>
> **Smoke is Glory showing that the "tribulation of this time is not worthy to be compared to the [everlasting] Glory that will be revealed in them." Peace (no rest) with the earth (from Thunder 2) has increased to torment for worldly Christians.**

We can not loose focus on what God is doing. This is all an act of His love and patience with disobedient Christians. God's love is seen in their chastening because their torment will brings Glory if they finally "make straight paths for their feet" (Heb.12:13). The Glory that is a result of this torment is eternal. It will be a testimony of the enduring patience of God to do so much to bring Life to these rejecters. Now that the waters are bitter, carnal Christianity will have no peace.

> **12** *Here is the* **patience of the saints:** *here are they that keep the commandments of God, and the faith of Jesus.*
>
> **We are God's vehicles for the judgment and will continue to endure with those carnal Christians as long as necessary. This is God's love for them seen through us.**

We are nearing the end of the first dispensation, and God is making an impassioned plea to Christians bound up in Babylon to turn from their carnal path. The price of refusal is a dispensation of terrible wrath like the world has never seen.

Those who have been marked because they are worshiping carnality will be clearly visible. The fire (judgment) and brimstone (perfecting power) of His wrath will destroy or make unfruitful all earthly things in order that those who repent might receive Glory (14:11). God does not torment to hurt or punish, but rather to correct or perfect. His patience to do so will be seen in His Saints (14:12) who endure to pour out the full cup of wrath upon those who choose to serve mammon.

Angel 3 also speaks to those who think they can postpone dying. The longer you wait, the more difficult it becomes when the wrath of God is poured out on your disobedience. At some point there is no more time, and the door will be shut! The world (or worldliness) will be judged, and it will perish along with all that cling too tightly to it.

Vial 3
Rev. 16:4-7

> **16:4** *And the third angel poured out his vial upon the* **rivers** *and* **fountains of waters;** *and they became* **blood.**
>
> **The lives of the Elect are poured out (vial), bringing life (blood) to the hearts of carnal Christians (fountains of water), making abundant life visible and obtainable. The local ministries (rivers) will also feel the effect of this judgment.**

Being sold out is the standard demonstrated by the Elect, but it is their abundant life which brings Revival to the Church, laying the foundation for the Bride to come forth.

> **16:5** *And I heard the angel of the waters say, Thou art righteous, O Lord, which art, and wast, and shalt be, because thou hast judged thus.*
>
> **Angel of the waters = messengers to the Church.**

What a way to judge man! Show an example that provides living <u>proof</u> of God's righteousness! The Bible was not sufficient to burden these carnal Christians to seek the fullness, although the fault was not entirely theirs. Leaders did not preach the fullness of Christ, leaving many ignorant about its existence or attainability. However, when this fullness walks before them as a living testimony, they will be without excuse.

> **16:6** *For they have* **shed** *the* **blood** *of saints and prophets, and thou hast given them blood to drink; for they are worthy.*
>
> **'Shedding blood' means that they have helped 'bestow' (Gr. 'ekecheo' metaphorically to shed forth) the Life of the Saints.**

In the Church, carnal Christians have been a part of (shed) the lives and ministries of the saints (prophets). They have prayed for and given time and money to the work of the saints. They have witnessed and been a part of all that Christ has done in the lives of these Saints. Therefore, they are without excuse and worthy of tribulation because they are still objects of God's love.

We, as the blood (Life) they drink now, want them to partake of the same life we have. We shed our lives in God's purposes for His people because love for the brethren is crucial to the work of the Saints.

> **16:7** And I heard another out of the altar say, Even so, Lord God Almighty, true and righteous are thy judgments.

The pouring out of **Vial 3** is a 'righteous' judgment because no one is to be judged unless they are in full knowledge of the truth and choose to reject it. There is nothing new in what God requires to please Him. He has given ample witness through the ages to the truth of Christ in you, the hope of Glory. The whole Bible speaks of His requirement for relationship (... *love the Lord with all your heart, soul, mind, and strength*). He has always required ALL of us.

Even in the last hours, God's patience and love still endure to bring forth yet a final living example in the form of His Saints who pour out truth at the very source – upon individual hearts. This is the Gospel of the Love of Christ, *Eph.3:19 "... to **know** the **love** of Christ that goes beyond understanding that you might be filled to all the fullness of God" Eph.3:19.* Saints show this Love one on one by investing themselves into the lives of others. The unteachable Love of Christ is then made "knowable", and rejecting His love then becomes a matter of choice. Ignorance is forever removed as an excuse.

Vial Angel 3
Rev. 18:4-20

Vial Angel 3 is where the messengers to the churches (vials) must do all they can to separate carnal Christians from their carnality and all of its sources. The greatest source is Babylon or the carnal religious system whereby they are being deceived.

> **18:4** And I heard another voice from heaven, saying, Come **out of her** [the Harlot], **my people**, that ye be not partakers of her sins, and that ye receive not of her plagues.
>
> **My people are carnal Christians. The plagues are the physical judgment that will fall on all those who hold on to their worldliness. Come out is to separate.**

Wrath is going to come on those who are disobedient and unwilling to separate from their pride and worldliness (Babylon). Reject any further and God's righteousness will bring wrath on you just like Egypt.

All of the Hebrews that lived in Egypt were subject to the same plagues that fell on the Egyptians. Only those who were in Goshen were protected from the judgments of Egypt.

> **18:5** For her sins have reached unto heaven, and God hath remembered her iniquities.
>
> **The cup of wrath is filling up.**

> **18:6** Reward her even as she rewarded you, and double unto her double [1]**according to her works**: in the cup which she hath filled fill to her double.
>
> **Reward translates: "to give of your own to another."**

As the Harlot gives of her carnality to the **kings of the earth**, the Saints will give a double portion of Life. Satan in both the carnal system and in carnal saints is desperate to maintain his place. In response to this desperation and the lateness of the hour, the Elect will double their efforts. This will heap "coals of fire" upon her head 'ship'. The more they fight, the faster they lose.

A believer's heart condition is [1]revealed by their works. The angrier they are, the harder they fight; consequently, the more it reveals who is in them. Anger and strife will stand in contrast to the peace and joy of the Saints. Christ is peace and joy; Satan is strife and bitterness.

> **18:7** How much she hath [2]**glorified herself**, and [2]lived deliciously, so much torment and sorrow give her: for she saith in her heart, I sit a queen, and **am no** [1]**widow**, and shall see no [3]sorrow.
>
> **Back to shedding the blood of the Saints of 16:6, the Harlot in the Church tries to justify herself by taking credit for all that is good in the Church. 'No widow' reveals she has lost her husband, Jesus and will not repent because, like the Laodicean church, she does not think she is lacking anything.**

The Harlot thinks she is part of God's Bride. But she is not [1]married to the Lord for [2]she does not do the things that please Him (John 14:21-23). Although all the evidence shows a selfish, carnal, worldly life, many will still think they are part of the Bride. There is a veil distorting their vision.

Spirit of antichrist brings veils
II Thes. 2:9-12
9   Even him, whose coming is after the working of Satan with all power and signs and **lying wonders**,
10   And with all deceivableness of unrighteousness **in them** that perish; *because **they** received not the love of the truth*, that they might be saved.
The "him" is a spirit of antichrist because the "him" is revealed "in them" that perish. It is not a person, but a spirit that brings delusion. It sits on the throne of God in our hearts, if we let it.
11   And for this cause <u>God shall send them strong delusion</u>, that *they* should believe a lie:
12   That *they* all might be damned who believed not the truth, but had pleasure in unrighteousness.
This is about the spirit of antichrist IN a people. Because they gave themselves over to the carnal message (pleasure in unrighteousness). He sends them a veil to cover the truth. The veil can only be removed by turning to the

> Lord and receiving a revelation of Christ. 2
> Cor. 3:16 tells us, "Nevertheless when one
> turns to the Lord, the veil is taken away."

> **18:8** Therefore shall her plagues come in [1]one
> **day**, [2]death, and [3]mourning, and [4]famine, and
> she shall be utterly burned with [5]**fire**: for
> strong is **the Lord God who judgeth her.**
>
> **Day refers to a specific time when things hidden
> are brought into the light. [1]'One' shows the
> quickness of this work (as seen in verse six). In
> the light of the Glory of the Saints comes
> [2]death, [3]remorse for the old life, [4]fruitlessness
> of spiritual things, accomplished by [5]perfecting
> fire.**

Verse 8 shows why the Elect are so diligent and desperate in their ministry to the carnal. These things will be accomplished suddenly and only those ready will receive their reward.

They may get angry with the messengers, but it is the Lord who is judging them not the Elect. It is His Glory in the Saints that burdens them with conviction.

> **18:9** And the **kings of the earth**, who have
> committed fornication and lived deliciously
> with her, shall bewail her, and lament for
> her, when they shall see the **smoke** of her
> burning,
>
> **Smoke is Glory coming from the fire of 18:8**

Those who still qualify as **kings of the earth** will be recognized as such because they mourn instead of rejoice at the cleansing of the Church. They will long for the old days. The 'smoke of her burning' is the Bride Church's Glory and the removal of the spots. This recognition is what makes the kings of the earth bewail her.

> **18:10** Standing afar off for the fear of her
> torment, saying, Alas, alas, that great city
> Babylon, that mighty city! for in one hour is
> thy judgment come.

These remaining kings of the earth will run from the judgment that is meant to perfect them. Fellowships and friends who begin to exhibit the Glory will repel them. They want to remain the way they are. Yet standing back and refusing to partake of the Glory will separate you even more. Only those who want to be judged will be judged.

> **18:11** And the **merchants** of the earth shall weep
> and mourn over her; for no man buyeth their
> merchandise any more:
>
> **The merchants are those who profit through the
> harlotry in the Church. This is not just about
> commerce, but about keeping YOUR life because the Church let you.**

The spiritual impact of this judgment makes those who trade in carnal Christianity unable to continue their religious career.

But the natural impact of this judgment is that there will be no more market for the things of this world that bring false security. The economy in general will be af-

fected as Christians start walking in faith seeing the 100-fold realm of God become a reality.

> **18:12** The merchandise of gold, and silver, and
> precious stones, and of pearls, and fine linen,
> and purple, and silk, and scarlet, and all
> thyine wood, and all manner **vessels of**
> ivory, and all manner vessels of most
> precious wood, and of brass, and iron, and
> marble,
>
> **These vessels are Christians.**

Look and see what God tells you about the content and makeup of these vessels that the kings of the earth are merchandizing.

> **18:13** And cinnamon, and odours, and ointments, and frankincense, and wine, and oil,
> and fine flour, and wheat, and beasts, and
> sheep, and horses, and chariots, and slaves,
> and [1]**souls of men**.

God is declaring the death of carnal religion. God is not interested in the embellishments we place on worship. Nor is He interested in the "positions" many organizations offer as a prize or mark of accomplishment. "Vessels of" also represent the embellishments men tend to place on people and things in their church organizations. Church membership or salvation for the sake of such will be seen as [1]merchandizing for the souls of men. It is the growth in the hearts of Christians that will establish the real value.

> **18:14** And the fruits that thy soul **lusted** after
> are departed from thee, and all things which
> were dainty and goodly are departed from
> thee, and thou shalt find them no more at
> all.
>
> **The 'fruits' of the Spirit are what they wanted.
> The 'dainty' stuff is Godly approvals associated
> with being in ministry.**

The Glory of Christ in the Elect will dim the light of all the religious stuff carnal ministers and ministries have lusted after as a mark of their 'right'eousness. The true intent of the heart will be seen.

> **18:15** The **merchants** of these things, which were
> made rich by her, shall stand afar off for the
> fear of her torment, weeping and wailing,
>
> **See note in verse 18:10.**

These carnal ministers and ministries will be some of the last (if at all) to enter in. It will be embarrassing to admit they were wrong and they will justify themselves as long as they can declare everyone else is wrong but them.

> **18:16** And saying, Alas, alas, that great city, that
> was clothed in fine linen, and purple, and
> scarlet, and decked with gold, and precious
> stones, and pearls!
>
> **The death of carnality is mourned by the carnal.**

These are those whose hearts have not yet seen the love in what God is doing. They will long for the days before the Day of the Lord.

> *18:17 For in one hour so great riches is come to nought. And every **shipmaster**, and all the company in **ships**, and **sailors**, and as many as trade by **sea**, stood afar off,*

Carnal programs (ships). Shipmasters are the carnal ministers of these programs. Sailors are those who make up these carnal programs. "Trading by the sea", are the rest who use the carnality of the Church as their source of income.

Carnal ministers are revealed as more involved with pride than relationship. They become "turf" to be possessed and protected by those who seek individual glory more than obedience and surrender to the will of God. Many who make their 'living' at providing 'programs' will see them "come to naught." This will cause their hearts to be judged and their real motivations exposed. "Many" will refuse such judgment and choose instead to be separated.

> *18:18 And cried when they saw the smoke of her burning, saying, What city is like unto this great city!*

They, like many Christians today, step back when the perfecting fire of God falls on people and ministries. They think that only natural blessings can represent Godly approval. They are confused by the lack of worldly blessing on the true ministries and ministers of God. They can only see with natural eyes.

> *18:19 And they cast dust on their heads, and cried, weeping and wailing, saying, Alas, alas, that great city, wherein were made rich*
> *all that had ships in the sea by reason of her costliness! for in one hour is she made desolate.*

Dust is worldliness or carnality.

To keep from repenting, they will cover themselves in carnality (dust), busying themselves with the things of this world so that they do not have to face the judgment offered. As they move away from the fire, they become immersed in things. The loss of mammon and not the loss of a relationship with Christ is what they mourn. They are hard-hearted Christians.

> *18:20 Rejoice over her, thou heaven, and ye holy apostles and prophets; for God hath avenged you on her.*

Vial Angel 3 shows that the fire of judgment is going to get more intense. It is unclear in what form the judgment will manifest: through natural destruction or spiritual hardship. Perhaps it will be both, for God is willing to use whatever means are necessary to get the attention of people. It is certain that all of the carnal trappings of religion will be made desolate, and only those who love their harlotry more than Jesus Christ will mourn as she is sent to perdition. It is getting close to the last call for the redeemed (those who ultimately will desire perfection and want to be overcomers); for those who still lust after the world will find that their hearts are hardening and it will be increasingly difficult to die to this world.

Chapter 12

The Fourth Thunder – The Bride is Made Ready …Time of Transition

The fourth Thunder is a time of transition between the first dispensation and the second and final dispensation in which Jesus completes His earthly ministry to the world through His Bride. It is the time when the Bride Church becomes the perfected Wife of the Lamb because all Harlotry is utterly removed from her. It is a time when the last vestiges of Christ's authority (candlestick) is removed from the carnal worshipers and given exclusively to the purified Bride Church.

In Thunder 3, God increased the pressure on carnal Christians through tribulation to convince them to turn from their worship of the Beast before the coming wrath. In Thunder 4, God's matchless patience has come to an end; the balances have been read, and the time of reckoning is at hand. The Church receives judgment which will cause a final separation between believers, preparing them for Thunder 5. Here they will be offered **robes of righteousness** or the wrath to come.

FINAL JUDGMENT IN THE HOUSE OF GOD
Rom. 1:18-23

18   For the *wrath of God is revealed* from heaven against all ungodliness and unrighteousness of men, <u>who hold the truth in unrighteousness</u>;

19   Because **that which may be known of God is manifest <u>in</u> them**; for God hath shewed it unto them.

20   For the **invisible things** of him from the creation of the world are **clearly seen**, being understood by the things that are made, even his eternal power and Godhead; so that <u>they are without excuse</u>:

21   Because that, *when they knew God, they glorified him not as God*, neither were thankful; but became vain in their imaginations, and their foolish **HEART WAS DARKENED.**

22   Professing themselves to be wise, they became fools,

23   And changed the glory of the incorruptible God into an image made like to corruptible man, and to birds, and four-footed beasts, and creeping things.

This judgment then is directed upon those who "knew God" because He was clearly IN them (verse 19). God does not excuse those who profess to be part of the Bride and then seek the things of the world (verse 22 & 23). This same process will be seen when the 'woes' are manifested to the inhabitants of the earth. They will see Christ in us and be "without excuse"; this is the way God uses the Truth as a "plowshare" (Is. 2:3-4).

In **Seal 4** Jesus comes riding the pale horse of Death (…that's us! We are the ones dead to this world) bringing the world into judgment. In other words, His appearing is so profound that to reject Him as He is (seen in His Bride) is to face judgment…HELL. They will be without excuse (Rom. 1:20 above); they will choose Christ or they will choose Hell.

GOD'S PEOPLE BRING WRATH OR PARADISE
Joel 2:3

3   A fire devoureth before them; and behind them a flame burneth: the land is as the **garden of Eden before** them, and **behind them a desolate wilderness**; yea, and nothing shall escape them.

This verse in Joel shows that you can join with the Wife of the Lamb (head towards the Garden), or you can reject her and face a desolate place. This is the last dispensation (**fourth part**) of God's work. Reject Jesus Christ now and there will be no mercy.

The overriding purpose of Thunder 4 is that **POWER has come to the end-time messengers of Christ.** This Power will be manifest in the form of Christ appearing in His Bride who has made herself ready for Him. **Trumpet 4** reveals 'part one' of the Bride's preparation, as she is hidden from the world in her bridal closet for the final perfecting and cleansing prior to being presented to the world in her wedding splendor (also seen in Joel 2:16). Before Christ's power can be released through His appearing, more carnality must be removed from the Saints; and all carnal Christians must be removed from Christ's body. This period of time is signaled by a warning from the Eagles not to delay repentance, for the world is about to face terrible tribulation (woes).

Angel 4 sends a message to all Christians who have not made a final decision that mercy is coming to an end, and there is little time remaining before the wrath to come. The "dead rest from their labors" even during tribulation, but the suffering will get so intense that only 'those in Goshen' will stand (Goshen on page viii).

The Elect Angels bring the message that Christ is coming to harvest the world. The **woes** of tribulation **4,** in conjunction with the power of His witnesses, make His purposes visible to the world. Men know that it is God who brings the hardship; still, many will not repent, even though the Bride stands ready to show them the path to freedom if they will surrender. Finally, in **Vial Angel 4,** the Harlot's influence in the Church is destroyed so men no longer have the option of placing their trust in a carnal faith when the saints move forward to pursue the world. The voice of the Bride/Bridegroom, or works of righteousness, will be clearly removed from all association with harlotry, worldliness or pride. Satan is a deceiver, not a redeemer; and the Harlot will cease to exist as the plowshare separates her from the flock – all are either part of the Bride or cast forth to experience the woes that are to come to the carnal world!

THUNDER 4

The ministry to the Church is ending and the preparation for His "parousia" becomes the focus. **Mal. 3:2 says, "But who may abide the day of his coming? And who shall stand when he appeareth?** For he is like a refiner's fire, and like fullers' soap:"

This is the question the Lord is about to answer. No flesh can enter the kingdom.

Seal 4

Rev. 6:7-8

---

7 And when he had opened the fourth seal, I heard the voice of the fourth beast say, Come and see.

8 And I looked, and behold a pale **horse**: and his name that sat on him was Death, and Hell followed with him. And power was given unto them over the **fourth part** [page vii] of the earth, to kill with sword, and with hunger, and with death, and with the beast(s̶) of the earth.

The pale horse is the manifest glory of God's elect, who have dimmed in the natural and begin now to shine forth in His appearing. Fourth part is the end-time.

This is last call for Christians: die to this world or face Hell. These last chance (**fourth part**) messengers have all the power needed to bring to completion any who have ears to hear. All the power of Christ is upon them as a witness to the inhabitants of the earth. The Elect will then be able to kill the inhabitants of the earth with: SWORD = truth, HUNGER = desire, DEATH = visible life, and the BEAST. Even the Beast (not plural in Greek) of the earth will help our cause because he will reveal the evil in the hearts of the people.

These instruments of death represent the different ways that the Elect bring the realization of Christ's Revelation to those blinded by carnality. They realize, as the Lawyer did of Jesus, that "we know that no man can do these works but he is from God."

Seal 4 announces the authority that ends the first dispensation for all those who profess Christ: the demand to submit to Christ or Hell. The second dispensation opens with *power* coming to the Bride as she is made ready for the 'appearing'. Now, all will recognize that this is THE DAY OF THE LORD! This power enables the Saints to minister death to a world who has never known Jesus Christ, killing them with the truth, soul famine, visible Glory (death), and spiritual affliction.

The visible presence of Christ, with its blessing and power, will create in the world a desire that moves them into a relationship with Christ. His person will be so visible through this body of Saints, and the power will be so profound, that every knee will bow and every tongue will confess that Jesus Christ is Lord (whether they accept Him as

such or not). Even the carnal spirits (beasts of the earth) will work to bring pain to people and to push them toward Christ. During Thunder 4, the Beast loses his power as the Lord of Glory appears!

Trumpet 4

Rev. 8:12-13

---

12 And the fourth angel sounded, and the third part of the sun ~~was smitten~~ [struck], and the third part of the moon, and the third part of the **stars**; so as **the third part** of them was **darkened**,[on page iv] [1]and the day shone not for a third part of it, and the night likewise. [1][Translation: "and for a period of time (day), God's part was not seen by those without revelation (night)."]

The sun is those eagles.

Rev. 19:7

7 Let us be glad and rejoice, and give honour to him: for the marriage of the Lamb is come, and **his wife hath made herself ready.**

The Bride is prepared for the 'appearing' out of the sight of the world. These references to sun, moon, and stars are about God's part (third part) becoming complete through the "striking" of the Eagles. In the second dispensation, these references to sun, moon, and stars will change to define man's glory ('Glory' on page vii). Nevertheless, here the Sun struck the Church to find any last tares and bring a final perfecting call to the Church. Search your hearts and remove any natural light in you or among you for it is the time of His Appearing.

The Bride makes herself ready

See Trumpet 5 on page 65 for part 2.

Part 1
The Darkening

*Strong's Greek Dictionary shows some confusion in the use of the Greek word 'plesso' (was smitten). This word is used only once in the Bible giving translators little evidence to discern. Nevertheless, Homer and others who used this word used it to mean "to strike", not "was smitten". We understand the problem the translators must have had in trying to understand how the sun, could strike something, especially when it becomes "darkened" because of the striking. Be sure to look up **darken** on page iv to understand this process. Verse 12 reveals that God's qualified ones (**third part**), whether they are a sun, moon, or stars will be perfected one last time. This is also a last removing of the tares so that there is no natural light in the Glory of the Bride.*

By this time the Bride has been separated from the Harlot. Yet not everyone gathered is qualified. The betrothed Bride has to consum-

---

mate the relationship with Christ and become His Wife, signified by her wedding garment (the robe of righteousness). Matt. 22:8-14 tells us we must be worthy of a garment to be a part of the wedding supper. For the Bride to make herself ready for the appearing of the Bridegroom, those who are disobedient must be removed (see parable of tares). The first of two processes that will weed out the disobedient (second on page 65) brings a profound truth, which will smite those who claim to be God's (third part). This revelation (trumpet) sounded by every one 'qualified' (sun, moon, stars) will "strike" or cause tribulation for those who profess to be a part but are not. The overall message of Trumpet 4 is about the coming WOES. It is here many will realize that life, as they have known it, is over. They followed Jesus for personal carnal reasons, but now they will realize they must truly "love not their lives until death." This happened 2000 years ago to many of the followers of Jesus who were asked to sacrifice the world for His sake, and it will happen to them again. This will be too much for some to take. "And they walked no longer with Him" (John 6:66). (Witness God's sovereignty – the carnal disciples who rejected Christ are mentioned in 6:66...the number of carnality! What an awesome God!)

The second half of Rev. 8:12 tells us that God's work on the Bride will be beyond the critical eyes of the world for a period of time. The inhabitants of the earth will pay no attention to the Church until the appearing.

> *13 And I beheld, and heard an ~~angel~~ [eagle] flying through the midst of heaven, saying with a loud voice, **Woe, woe, woe,** [page xx] to the inhabiters of the earth by reason of the other voices of the trumpet of the three angels, which are yet to sound!*
>
> *Verse 13 translated Angel incorrectly; it should read 'Eagle' (Greek – aetos). This is the warning to the inhabitants of the earth. Be prepared for the disaster spoken of by the next three (5,6,7) Trumpets (Woe on page xx).*

The Bride has made herself ready and the harvest is about to take place. It is the Eagles who come forth to declare the woes to the world. Eagles are the only ones dead enough to stand before the world and make such a strong statement. We will see others join in during Thunder 5, but the Eagles/Angels are powerful enough in Jesus (Phil. 4:13) to endure the initial reaction the world will give. These are the apostolic ones chosen by God to endure the ridicule also ascribed to the first disciples. They, too, had to go to their brethren first before they could go to the gentile world.

Matt. 24:14

14 And this **gospel of the kingdom** shall be preached in all the world for a witness unto all nations; and **then shall the end come**.

Three Harvesters will come out after them. Their message will be disaster and horror for those who will not accept Jesus Christ. Woe 1 is in Thunder 5 and is dispensed by the locusts/scorpions. Woe 2 is dispensed by Joel's

army and occurs in Thunder 6. Finally, Woe 3 in Thunder 6 is the last Harvester, the Righteous Judge who gathers the remainders (those who have not accepted Christ).

The Revelation **Trumpet 4** of 8:12 tells of the completion of the Bride during the first half of Thunder 4. The reference to the sun, moon, and stars are the Elect. This is their last opportunity to die to self before their eternal weight is established with the **robes of righteousness** (page xvi). The level they attain when the robes of righteousness are given will be their measure of resurrection life in the Garden. Unfortunately, this is also the time when those who give only lip service to being part of the Bride are removed. The tribulation of giving up their lives and the loss of all personal freedom (just like the disciples of old) is too much for them. Their hearts are hardened, and they return to their carnal lives.

Woe, Woe, Woe (page xx)

Finally, in verse 13 the Eagles declare the coming woes. But they are calling out from heaven, which means that most of the earth will not have ears to hear. They will find it hard to hear that our God is the one true God, and His Son is the only path to Life. The world is put on short notice: there is little time remaining before the woes are dispensed. Most, however, must experience the woes in their flesh before they will repent. Thank God, the redeemed will be in Goshen (Goshen page viii)!

Angel 4
Rev. 14:13-14

> *13 And I heard a **voice from heaven** saying unto me, Write, Blessed are the dead which die in the Lord from henceforth: Yea, saith the Spirit, that they may rest from their **labours** [on page x]; and their works do follow them.*
>
> *The voice of the Lord goes before His army (Joel 2). The Bride will speak out of Heaven operating from such a spiritual place they may even see Christ face to face as Moses did.*
>
> *14 And I looked, and behold a **white cloud**, and upon the cloud one sat like unto the **Son of man**, having on his head a golden crown, and in his hand a sharp sickle.*
>
> *Here we are in the middle of the tribulation, and now Christ appears upon a cloud...His Glorious Bride.*

It is a blessing if you are able to die to self during the days of His wrath; and it is the only way to rest from your labors. We will read of those who seek death and are not able to obtain it. Only the dead obtain relief from pain. Therefore, the **message for everyone...sell out to God through surrender to Christ in you.** Lay down your life (hopes, ambitions, desires, etc.) if you hope to find peace from the woes to come.

II Thes. 1:7-11

7 And to you who are troubled **REST WITH US**, when the Lord Jesus shall be **revealed from heaven** with his mighty angels,

8   In **flaming fire taking vengeance** on them that know not God, and that obey not the gospel of our Lord Jesus Christ:

9   Who shall be punished with everlasting destruction from the presence of the Lord, and from the glory of his power;

10   When **he shall come to be glorified IN his saints**, and to **be admired IN all them** that believe (because our testimony among you was believed) in that day.

11   That the name of our Lord Jesus Christ may be glorified **IN YOU**, and ye in him, according to the grace of our God and the Lord Jesus Christ.

The Fours are a time of transition. As the final perfecting of the Bride is occurring, the second dispensation message of **Angel 4** is announced by His Eagles to the world. The world is put on notice that the harvest is at hand, and the pain they are beginning to experience will worsen until they surrender to Jesus. Lip service, shallow commitment, and "faith without works" or evidence (James 2) are not sufficient for salvation. The world will know the whole truth as Jesus Christ becomes very real through the **cloud** of witnesses. Notice that the appearing of Jesus Christ, which will take place in Thunder 5, is associated with a crown on the head and a sickle in the hand. The crown on the head is the authority by which these Eagles speak, and the sickle is the truth they wield to harvest souls. These Eagles are not their own, but belong wholly to Christ…they no longer live, but Christ lives through them.

Vial 4

As we have seen, the vial is the way Christ brings to pass the revelation of each Thunder. In Vial 4, we see that the final perfecting work of God, before the harvest of souls, is accomplished by His appearing. This is the "parousia" or corporate appearing of Christ, which the Church has longed for. Christ will begin to finish His ministry on earth.

Rev. 16:8-9

> **8**   And the fourth angel poured out his vial upon the **sun** [on page xviii]; and power was given unto him to scorch men with fire.
>
> **POWER IS GIVEN to HIM (the Bride Church represented as the sun), so the Glory that appears through them will scorch men.**

This corporate appearing will bring burning perfection. Trumpet 4 told us that this scorching will happen in the Bride first, then the world. Individual perfecting accomplishes the corporate appearing. Matt. 13:43 tells us what happens after the tares are removed!

> Matt. 13:43 Then shall the righteous shine forth <u>as the sun</u> in the kingdom of their Father. Who hath ears to hear, let him hear.

> **9**   And men were scorched with great heat, and **blasphemed** [on page 44] the name of God, which hath power over these plagues: and they repented not to give him glory
>
> **Blasphemed is to distract from God…normally through carnality. Not giving glory shows that they would not die to self, which brings Glory.**

God will keep turning up the heat on mankind so that He can redeem as many as possible. Men are aware that God is bringing these woes against them. They will not be able to discard the events of the day as happenstance; nevertheless, some prefer to curse Him instead of repent.

The 'Power' reveals His Glory in the Bride; Jesus Christ will be before them, and they will have no place to hide. The spirit of Elijah will come again to put all scoffers to the test that faced the priests of Baal on Mt. Carmel. The one true God through Jesus Christ will challenge their false religions, and His power will scorch them with the truth. They will blaspheme God by denying the bodily presence of Jesus Christ; because to see Him in a body of believers (antichrist page xviii) is to acknowledge their own rebellion.

Vial Angel 4
Rev. 18:21-24

> **18:21** And a mighty angel took up a stone like a great **millstone**, and cast it into the sea, saying, Thus with violence shall that great city **Babylon be thrown down, and shall be found no more at all.**
>
> **Millstone is where the wheat is ground out. The function of saving souls (wheat) is completely removed from Babylon.**

The days of religion without relationship are gone forever. The millstone tells us that the last of the wheat is ground out of the Babylon. Babylon is thrown down, not fallen, meaning it is not an option for wheat (believers) any more. It may exist, but not for true Christians.

> **18:22** And the voice of harpers, and [1]musicians, and of pipers, and [2]trumpeters, shall be heard no more at all in thee; and no [3]craftsman, of whatsoever craft he be, shall be found any more in thee; and the sound of a [4]millstone shall be heard no more at all in thee;
>
> **There is now no true [1]praise, [2]revelation knowledge, [3]ministry, or [4]salvation among carnal worshipers (Harlot).**

By this time Satan's plans are revealed to all believers; if they continue with the Harlot, it is with acceptance of her unmistakable barrenness. The gathering of harlotry which calls itself church will no longer show any form of true ministry. It will be more of a social club than a church.

> **18:23** And the light of a candle shall shine no more at all in thee; **and the voice of the bridegroom and of the bride shall be heard no more at all in thee:** for thy **merchants** were the great men of the earth; for by thy sorceries were all nations deceived.
>
> **Candlestick is the witness of Christ. Pride has truly caused this fall (great men).**

The candlestick (page xi) is completely removed…Christ is no longer associated with carnal religion. Carnal Christians were warned in Rev. 2:5, "Remember therefore from whence thou art fallen, and repent, and do the first works; or else I will come unto thee quickly, and will remove thy candlestick out of his place, except thou repent."

The guiding voice of Christ will not be heard in Babylon, and anyone who chooses to be part of her is NOT part of the Bride.

> **18:24** [1]*And in her was found the blood of prophets, and of saints, and of all that were slain upon the earth.*
>
> **Verse 24 is the reason for verses 21-23. The word translated [1]'And' (Gr. Kai) would better translate 'For'. In other words, because she had part in the Life of the Saints, she should have known better. Verses 21-23 use a future tense, 'this will happen'. Verse 24 uses a past tense, 'because this happened'.**

Babylon is thrown down (verse 21) because all of the wheat (Elect) is gone. She has been abandoned by Christ (verse 23), and nothing godly remains. Those who are left are rebellious, refusing to see the truth, no matter how profound. Their only hope is to come out of her, but it will take wrath (woes) to change their hearts. Verse 24 closes this segment by showing that God is a righteous God, and any harlotry deserves the wrath it receives at God's hand.

To hear God's judgment to the leadership, who did not shepherd the Church, read Chapter 34 of Ezekiel.

There will be no refuge for the redeemed that refuse to sell-out. Babylon's unrighteousness in the face of the truth (given by the Saints and prophets) will seal her fate with that of the world. The time of men gathering themselves together to form man-made religions (denominations) is over. You are either a member of the Bride Church, or you will face the same wrath as the inhabitants of the earth. **See Jer. 51:47-58, 6:8-9, 51:33**

Look Back at Thunder 4

Thunder 4 should accomplish several things. **First,** the Bride begins to perfect herself and make way for Christ's appearing, which will be finished in Thunder 5.

Second, we get a glimpse of the wrath of God to be poured out on the **inhabitants of the earth**. This will begin in the "house of God" and pour out into the whole earth. Once Christ appears in His Bride, the intensity of the tribulation, both spiritual and natural, will become so great that it is no wonder this is called the Great Harvest and the "awful Day of the Lord.."

Third, Christ is coming in **power** through the Bride as a witness again to the world. *"Verily, verily, I say unto you, He that believeth on me, the works that I do shall he do also; and greater works than these shall he do; because I go unto my Father (Jn. 14:12).* Joel declares that there have never been a people like these before. Prior to the coming of power, dying to self was the witness of the Elect. This is because they became separated from the passions of this world, and Christians were convicted by such Holy lives. But the ***world*** will need more than holy lifestyles to get their attention...signs and wonders must accompany the Elect's message. *"God also bearing them witness, both with signs and wonders, and with divers miracles, and gifts of the Holy Ghost, according to his own will"* (Heb. 2:4). This is a body of believers who are sold out to Christ so that He is seen in every aspect of their lives and ministry. The dead will be raised, the lame made to walk, the blind made to see, because they will 'love not their lives unto death'. This will be the Church without spot or blemish.

Finally, the most significant aspect of Thunder 4 is the dogma that overwhelms Christians. They will possess a single-minded desire for salvation of the entire world. *"And this gospel of the kingdom will be preached in all the world...then the end will come"* (Matt. 24:14). Anything that distracts them from this cause will be set aside. Much the same as the apostles of old, they live the rest of their lives as **nomads in the service of Christ**.

Section VI
Restoring the Kingdom
The Seven Thunders Continue

THE SECOND DISPENSATION

Section 5 covered four Thunders or years, which puts us solidly into the second half of the Seven Thunders (i.e. the second dispensation). Ideally, Section 5 would represent the first dispensation only and Section 6 would represent only the second dispensation. However, since Thunder 4 represents the transition between the first and second dispensation, and the events that occur in Thunder 4 occur partially in the first dispensation and partially in the second dispensation, following that model would require splitting Thunder 4 into two sections, making it difficult to understand. Therefore, we begin Section 5 with Thunder 5, realizing that we are already well into the second dispensation.

Section 6 consists of the three chapters that cover the years of Christ's appearing in His Bride Church as they come to reap the harvest of the world and reclaim His kingdom before the millennial reign. In Thunder 5, the betrothed Bride consummates her relationship with Christ and becomes the Wife of the Lamb (Rev. 21:9). She receives her wedding garment (the robe of righteousness), a glorified spiritual body, as a mark of the change in her status. Saints qualify for these glorified bodies because they no longer walk in carnality; rather they choose, like Enoch, to walk with God in every moment of every day, pleasing Him in all they do. In Thunder 6, Christ appears through the Corporate Body of the Bride to bring Final Judgment to the world. In Thunder 6, those who have rejected Christ will gather in Babylon, while all who will accept Him will gather to create the New Jerusalem, the place from which the Lord will rule the nations. *This is the city promised to Abraham... "a spiritual city whose founder and builder is God."* To understand the second dispensation, it is important to understand the difference between Babylon and the New Jerusalem.

BABYLON VS NEW JERUSALEM

Read first the following Parentheticals: Bride/New Jerusalem page 97, The Beast page 94.

To understand the second dispensation, you need to see the difference between Babylon and the New Jerusalem. Here in Thunder 5, we will see the 'marriage of the Lamb' to His true Bride. As the Bride consummates the relationship with Christ, her distinction moves from betrothed Bride to Wife of the Lamb (Rev. 21:9). Marking this change in status, the Saints receive their wedding garments (the robes of righteousness). Everyone who is a part of the New Jerusalem will wear a Robe of Righteousness, which is our glorified spiritual bodies. Saints qualify for these glorified bodies, because they no longer walk in carnality. Like Enoch, they choose to walk with Him in every moment of every day, pleasing Him in all they do. To see them is to see Christ; thus, the Bride is now seen as the New Jerusalem: the place from which the Lord will rule the nations (*the Bride will be explained in greater depth later in this chapter*). *This is the city promised to Abraham... "a spiritual city whose founder and builder is God."* Everyone recognizes this as the gathering of the Saints for the "appearing of Christ". They willingly sacrifice their individualism for the sake of providing a corporate body for Christ.

In the first dispensation, the Harlot was the alternative to the Bride. By Thunder 5, the Harlot is totally removed from the picture and is no longer an option for Christians. Carnal worship will no longer be part of God's witness to the world. Relationship replaces religion. God's true Bride is now visible; everyone will recognize her as God's representative. Those who refuse to repent of their carnality will have only one option…Babylon. Therefore, Babylon is a different type of designation; it is a place for those with a

heart so hardened to the Spirit of the Lord that it is unable to be "pricked" by any move of the Spirit. Therefore it is a place of habitation for devils and all types of evil spirits. Nevertheless, just as it occurred with the "demoniac", a personal encounter with Jesus could change their status.

Up until Thunder 5, Babylon and the Harlot were described as the same. In reality, we were seeing the future Babylon as the Church was purified from the Harlot. Satan was trying to fool Christians into believing that they were pleasing God when they were really of the 'synagogue of Satan' (page xviii). This is because Satan's lies entered into the Church through man-made religion, thus creating the Harlot (page ii). By now, God has judged the Harlot (See Vial Angel 4), allowing us to clearly see the influence Babylon has on the Church.

Babylon is not <u>just</u> worldly thinking in the Church; those in Babylon have made a deliberate choice to pursue self-interest and reject a relationship with Christ. However, **NOT EVERYONE WITHOUT GOD IS IN BABYLON**; they must be forced into a choice. That is the function of the Bride…bringing the world into accountability. Our burning presence and message give people two options: accept the revelation of Christ (New Jerusalem) or Satan's message of 'self determination' (Babylon). By choosing Satan's message, they choose to dwell in Babylon and thus, reject Christ. This will bring them the wrath of God destined for Babylon and reveal that they are enemies of God. The good news is that once they feel God's fury, the inhabitants of Babylon will know they need to repent. This means that the woes are an instrument of God's salvation, a way to get the world to repent. However, some will feel the pinch of the 'woes', but not associate it with God's end-time plan. That is when the role of the Lamb's Wife (the Bride) becomes evident. They will be the plowshare that goes through the world giving the Revelation that will divide the people into two camps...New Jerusalem or Babylon!

The 'Corporate Bride' creates the New Jerusalem

To become part of the New Jerusalem, Christians will need to consummate their relationship with the Lord in intimacy and become the Wife of the Lamb. As we surrender to the Corporate Body of Christ, our brothers and sisters in Christ help constrain our walk. This is iron sharpening iron in corporate accountability until completion is achieved (See **complete vs. perfect** on page 124). His appearing can only be manifested in a body in which individuals are no longer recognized apart from their corporate unity in Christ. That body cannot be complete unless each member supplies its part to the whole (Eph. 4:16). In turn, this complete body will bring its members into completeness (Eph. 4:11-13). Being a Christian does not in and of itself make you part of the Body of Christ. Eph. 4 points out that if you are not willing to yoke with a body (of people) and receive headship from that same body, then the "full measure" of union with Christ will elude you.

Chapter 13

The Fifth Thunder - Christ Appearing…Parousia

This is the day for which all of creation has waited, and the great cloud of witnesses has pressed in to see (Heb. 12:1). In Thunder 5, the Bride has made herself ready, and the harvest is under way. **Seal 5** shows the authority under which Thunder 5 operate. The "poured out" blood of the Saints makes a path for Christ to appear. Because these Saints are no longer their own, they can thrust in the sickle to glean the harvest. They pour out their spiritual life for the world, and the world owes them. This may be figurative, but there is an element of natural truth as well. The righteous bloodshed of Saints of God who have literally died to the world, for a testimony of Christ, created an authority through which God harvests the world. This is a type of the Lamb whereby we are partakers of Christ's sufferings.

Col. 1:24

24　　I now rejoice in <u>my sufferings for you</u>, and fill up in my flesh what is lacking in the afflictions of Christ, **for the sake of His body, which is the Church,**

The Bride asks, "How long?" in **Seal 5** before she can start the harvest of the world. By sharing Christ's life, she also shares His fervent desire to pursue God's plan to reap the harvest. The corporate Bride is of one accord; they are ready to give their lives for the revelation of Christ. They are worthy to be called the Wife of the Lamb and to receive their robes of righteousness (which are the righteous acts of the Saints). God asks them to be patient while He brings some of their fellow brethren into completion through **corporate accountability**.

Woe 1

Trumpet 5 reveals the first 'woe'. Christ, as the Morning Star, descends from heaven into prepared earthen vessels (the completed Bride). His **appearing** or **parousia** brings **locusts** out of the **heart** of the Bride. Unlike the Beast, which comes out of the carnal Christian's heart (**sea**) with the intention of killing the spiritual life of men, the **locusts** will bring spiritual life by devouring the earth (carnality) that has bound and separated mankind from Christ. In the same way that the **kings of the earth** had to die to self, the inhabitants of the earth must die to this world. Yet they will not be able to sacrifice their lives until they come to know and desire Christ. So, for five months (verse 5) during this period, the Saints will preach the Glory of the kingdom, pouring judgment out on all flesh (Joel 2:28-32). The **Five** speaks of grace. The cup of wrath brings redemption through tribulation in lieu of punishment, which is God's grace. Joel 1 describes these **locusts** [on page xi] in detail. They represent the New Jerusalem or those who have received their robes of righteousness. They are of

different levels of Glory (calf, man, or eagle), which Joel describes metaphorically as the growth stages of the locust (Joel 1:4). However, the mature stage of the locust represents the entire Bride as a cloud of witnesses, which shows forth the power of a corporate appearing. Naturally speaking, there is not much power or fear associated with a single locust; but when they mature into a cloud, they bring nations to their knees. New Jerusalem represents this corporate appearing. The world will not be able to ignore so great a cloud of witnesses.

The Saints were an offense to the **kings of the earth** by their total commitment to Christ. Likewise, New Jerusalem offends the **inhabitants of the earth** with their lack of interest in worldly things. What the world fights for and struggles after comes freely to the Elect. The inhabitants of the earth will try to ignore the Saints and their message of Christ; but their revealed power and corporate Glory make this impossible. Natural disasters will bring added strength to the Bride's message, and then the Glory of Christ-in-them will begin sifting them into either New Jerusalem or Babylon.

The message of **Angel 5** clearly declares that the great *Harvest* of the Lord has begun. The call to harvest comes from the Angels who operate from the throne room. These are the *Eagles* leading the way for the rest of the Bride. It is a time to reap and sift; the carnal killing will come later.

Vial 5 is similar to Vial 1; the pouring-out reveals carnality. In Vial 1, however, the focus was on revealing the truth of carnality to those in the Church deceived by worldliness. By contrast, Vial 5 is poured out on the inhabitants of the earth who have never known Christ. They are ignorant, blind, and dumb, with no spiritual eyes to see, or ears to hear. It will take natural disasters as well as a powerful spiritual witness to free them from worldly patterns of thinking and convince them of how much God hates carnality. That is why the locusts come forth and torment men. They represent the manifestation of Christ necessary to reveal the carnality in people who have been, until recently, all carnal. The Bride will become a gazing-stock for the world who will marvel at the Bride's willingness to surrender this world for the sake of Christ. To the *inhabitants of the world,* the sold out message is excessive and undesirable; however, this is a day of shaking (Heb. 12).

The greatest event of all of Revelation comes forth in **Vial Angel 5**. With the Harlot out of the way and the Bride made ready (robe of righteousness), **THE MARRIAGE SUPPER OF THE LAMB BEGINS** as the Bride goes forth with her husband to harvest the earth. **Are you ready, do you want to be a harvester**?

THUNDER 5

Seal 5 Prepare for Harvest

Rev. 6:9-11

> ***6:9*** *And when he had opened the fifth seal, I saw under the altar the **souls** of them that **were slain** for the word of God, and **for the** [1]**testimony** which they held:*
>
> **The slain souls (minds) are the 'dead in Christ'. They chose to be dead so that they could be a testimony or living revelation of Christ.**

These completely surrendered dead-to-self Saints are a testimony for the entire world to see. 'Soul' represents a saved and transformed mind. "Under the altar" shows their sacrifice is now complete. Together, the reference to 'slain' and 'altar' reveals a [1]Revelation Christ that brings a sold out relationship. These members of the Bride are qualified for the appearing.

> ***6:10*** *And they cried with a loud voice, saying, How long, O Lord, holy and true, dost thou not judge and avenge our **blood** [on page iii] on them that **dwell on the earth** [on page 43]?*
>
> **The phrase, "avenge our blood", means to vindicate our sacrifice and show everyone it was worth it.**

Because they have fellowshipped in the Lord's sufferings, His life will be available to the world. They know that their sold out lives will bring discontentment to the inhabitants of the earth. It will also bring Christ's life (blood) to those who repent.

They also realize that the time of the great Harvest of God is at hand, and they are anxious to be a part of the greatest conversion of souls in the history of man!

> ***6:11*** *And **white robes** [on page xvi] were given unto every one of them; and it was said unto them, that they should rest yet for a little season, until their **fellow servants** also and their brethren, that should be **killed as they were**, should be fulfilled*
>
> **The white robes are glorified bodies.**

THE ROBES ARE READY FOR THEM NOW...

The Lord gives them their white robes (**robes of righteousness**) as a wedding coat for the supper about to take place. These are the members of the Bride, recognizable by the Glory upon them. However, the Lord asks them to wait just a little longer. Waiting does not mean that they do nothing; they will be about the Fathers business. The reason they have to wait is because some fellow servants have not yet been corporately slain, which means that they have not been made 'complete' by the constraining action of Christ's body. (See commentary ' Complete vs. Perfect' on page 124.)

The Saints who have received their robes were completed by each other. Look back at Seal 2, page 48 to see when this process started. The iron sharpening iron process will complete those who are to be part of the appearing. God is waiting for a 'critical mass' so that the appearing is so profound that it will shake up the inhabitants of the world. It will take quite a phenomenon to get the attention of all those who are committed to false religions and atheism.

The authority of **Seal 5** rests in the power of 'lives given' (spiritually and physically) for this day. All who have shed blood, both literally and spiritually, have paved the way for the great end-day *Harvest*. Their reward is a robe of righteousness given to them as proven, manifest sons of God. The **robe of righteousness** is the glorious **APPEARING** of Christ. The 'Firstfruits Company' of 144,000 received their robes in the Thunder 1 of the first dispensation before tribulation began. This did not represent the 'Parousia', the visible completion of Christ's seven-year ministry to the world. The 'candlestick' of His authority had yet to be transferred to them after the tares were removed.

Their power was in 'dying to self', providing in the first dispensation a model for other believers to gain more of the life of Christ. The Firstfruits were persecuted as was Jesus and they only returned love. In the second dispensation, power comes on this Corporate Body. It brings a witness of His appearing to unbelievers through the signs and wonders; this is what the inhabitants of the world require to be able to hear the message of truth.

Verse 11 gives great insight into the nature of this corporate appearing. Complete dying-to-self that produces an 'appearing' of Christ can only be accomplished through corporate accountability. John 13:35 says, *"By this shall all men know that ye are my disciples, if ye have love one to another."* The 'parousia' will only occur among a body of believers in a love relationship whereby iron sharpens iron, and even immature Christians are covered sufficiently by the body to be able to demonstrate the Christ life. This is the death of individualism in the body of Christ, a concept that flies in the face of American tradition, whereby the individual is worshiped. Losing ourselves in a group for the sake of God's greater plan is a bitter pill for many to swallow. Yet, without the constraining path of a larger body, our effort to walk after Christ will fail; because we will "do what seems right in our own eyes." See Prov. 12:15 and 21:2.

Trumpet 5

Trumpet 5 is complex. Take the time to get familiar with terms and concepts that may be interpreted differently than that with which you are accustomed. Satan has had two thousand years to use our language to defeat the Word of God. Even a simple term such as 'Glory' loses its power over time until many today feel that to give God 'Glory' means nothing more than giving Him credit for the good things that happen. "Christ in you, the hope of GLORY" means so much more. Another phrase, the 'bottomless pit', has been given a frightful meaning by popular literature; yet, the original Greek words do not have a negative connotation. The bottomless pit [see reference on page iii] should be read as a 'deep well', an appropriate symbol for the 'heart', which is the deep gateway to the spiritual realm. This term is covered with traditional dark veils, but it is really the place we connect with God or Satan. To understand these truths, you will, like Nicodemus when Christ tried to explain "born again", have to set aside customary patterns of imagery designed to defeat you.

Rev. 9:1-11

WOE 1

> **9:1** And the fifth angel sounded, and I saw a [1]**star** [see **morning star** [page xviii] _fall from heaven unto the_ [2]_earth:_ and to him was given the **key** of the [3] **bottomless pit.** [on page iii]
>
> **Jesus is the star (Christ appearance in a people…parousia. The bottomless pit is the heart and the key is the gateway to either heaven or hell from within our heart.**

[1]Before the great appearing of Christ occurs, one more separation must take place. Christ will judge hearts of those professing Him. He is looking for [2]earth and will declare that carnality represents rebellion within the believer. "Why do you hold on to this carnality in the face of My presence (great appearing)?"

It is one thing to have a heart made pure by the blood of Christ and quite another to keep it pure. The attack of circumstances can cause us to stumble and allow wrong thoughts and intentions to begin to rise up out of our heart. The '**key**' to the '**pit**' speaks of Jesus and His ability to heal any heart issue and keep the source of the heart pure. Anyone who knows Jesus and holds on to any carnality is being self-willed and disobedient. He will be the author and the finisher of our faith. For those who submit, He will use this key to forever lock their access door to Hell. For those who reject, all Hell will break loose on them.

The Angel receives the key to the [3]heart, so the qualified Saints can receive their robes of righteousness. Once a person puts on (metaphorically) a robe of righteousness, they will never stumble again. Stumbling begins when carnal desires draw us away by virtue of our own lust. Those who have robes will have their desires brought into line with Christ's desires as the Body of Christ enables them to fill their mind with the Spirit. What little desire still exists is not strong enough to draw us away; therefore, our lust cannot conceive. Finally, Christ locks the gate in our hearts that opens to hell; therefore, death cannot rise up into our members and defile us.

James 1:14-15
14 But every man is tempted, when he is drawn away of his own lust, and enticed.
15 Then when lust hath conceived, it bringeth forth sin: and sin, when it is finished, bringeth forth death.

It is understood that this process automatically takes place for all of the Saints who entered the kingdom by way of the grave. However, the scriptures plainly teach that some will step over the grave. Do we want to be that people? Jesus said, "If you will do what I say you will NEVER see death" (Jn. 8:51).

> **9:2** And he opened the bottomless pit; and there arose a **smoke** [page xviii] out of the pit, as the smoke of a great furnace; and the **sun** [on page xviii] and the **air** were **darkened** [on page iv] by reason of the **smoke** of the pit.

The Bride makes herself ready
See Trumpet 4 on page 58 for part one

Part 2
The Great Furnace

This describes the last separation of Christ's body before the 'appearing'. God searches hearts, separating from the Bride those who still refuse to relent from their carnality (sin). In the next verse, we see the appearing of Christ as locusts on the earth. The heart-felt, single desire of the Bride must be conformed to the will of Christ. In other words, all Christians who are to be part of the appearing must be **completed** [on page iv]. (If you are unfamiliar with 'completion vs. perfection', go back and read the Commentary on this issue on page 124.) If you are out of step with Jesus (which happens when you let carnality reign), then you will be separated. Christ will have a Wife without "spot or blemish." The Glory, which rises up from the hearts of the Elect Saints, acts as a great perfecting instrument.

Air (Greek 'aer' not 'ouranos') is a symbol of the lower spiritual realm, which has been under the control of the power of Satan. It is about to be redeemed by the Glory of the Bride.

Eph. 6:12, 2:2
12   For we **wrestle not against flesh and blood, but against principalities, against powers**, against the rulers of the darkness of this world, against spiritual wickedness in high places.

2   Wherein in time past ye walked according to the course of this world, according to the prince of the power of the air, the spirit that now worketh in the children of disobedience:

In this case, it refers to the spiritual presence of the Bride bringing Glory into that realm and diminishing Satan's light. This is God's way of driving out the snake from the Garden, preparing it for our return.

> **9:3** And there came out of the **smoke locusts** [on page xi] upon the **earth**: and unto them was given power, as the scorpions of the earth have power.

The locust are His great army (Joel 2:25) being sent by God. The Glory of Christ shining forth from them will hurt (sting).

In the natural scorpions sting people who are not watching their walk. In the Spirit His Bride will be scorpions who sting those who are walking in the earth. These

66

locusts will give revelation that stings the inhabitants of the earth and makes them "sick" of this world. Their only hope will be to come into the "kingdom", where Christ can pull out the stinger of self will and pride.

> **9:4** *And it was commanded them that they should not hurt the grass of the earth, neither any* **green thing***, neither any* **tree***; but only those men which have not the seal of God in their [1]foreheads.*
>
> **Green grass is good works. This is a heart issue not works issue. This is not for those saved (green and tree) but those disobedient (foreheads) unsaved.**

In Trumpet 1 of the first dispensation [on page 42], Christ directed our efforts toward those who had a measure of life (green). However, here in Trumpet 5 of the second dispensation, He directs the efforts of the Elect at those totally without life. The way is being prepared for those who have not yet made a sincere [1]decision regarding Christ, testifying of the wonderful grace of God and the power of His Christ. We are the plowshare.

> **9:5** *And to them it was given that they should not kill them, but that they should be tormented five months: and their* <u>torment was as the torment of a scorpion</u>*, when he striketh a man.*
>
> **Five is the number of Grace. This torment is what happens when the venom causes pain long after the sting.**

But since time is short there is no point in trying to disciple people (kill them). Instead, the Elect will show the love of God through His manifest Glory so that they will want the life He offers.

Here in 9:5, God's grace is holding back judgment on the inhabitants of the earth until they have felt the full impact of the Revelation of Christ. As the Elect impact them with Christ' Glory, this world will dim and *their* world will be shaken. Hearing that this world is ending, and seeing the love and patience of the Saints causes their carnal hearts to melt. Many will desire and seek Christ as they see the love and liberty in His revelation. Again, we are leading them, not killing them. This will be living evangelism, not demanding evangelism. God wants to gather His family through love. See the sidebar "scorpions" in Locust definition on page xi.

> **9:6** *And in those days shall men* **seek death***, and shall not find it; and shall desire to die, and death shall flee from them.*
>
> **Death is sold out by being dead to self.**

At first the inhabitants of the earth will do what comes naturally, they will try to negotiate God's life on their terms. They will desire to remove the pain of the woes and even desire the life they see in us, but look for a fast and easy solution. They seek the death the Elect speak of, but are not ready to receive it. The benefit of a life in Christ will drive them to say things and do things before it can be manifested as a heart issue, but lip service to God will not bring Life. There will be no more quick and superficial conversions. Laying down your life is a heart issue, and you must first count the cost. You will not be able to have Christ *and* this world.

If they can endure and keep from rejecting God, He will finish the work and death will come. The horsemen of the sixth Thunder will finalize the dying process...Praise God!

> **9:7** *And the shapes of the locusts were like unto* **horses** *prepared unto battle; and on their heads were as it were [1]crowns like gold, and their* **faces** <u>were as the faces of men</u>*.*
>
> **Look at Joel 2:4, 'Faces' represent both the essential essence of a person (I Thes. 2:17) and personal contact or relationship. Crowns are the power that has now come, and gold is its source...divinity.**
> **Joel 2:4 "The appearance of them is as the appearance of horses; and as horsemen, so shall they run."**

This is described in Joel Chapter 2. This army of Glory will not be able to be stopped. They will be in the face of every person in this world. This is what is meant by the Glory of the Lord filling the earth and every eye beholding Him.

The Bride comes in her [1]power through Christ appearing; she may even appear angelic to some (Phil. 4:13). The locusts are men who will do battle one to one, through the personal sharing of Christ throughout the world.

> **9:8** *And they had hair as the* **hair** *[on page ix] of women, and their teeth were as the* **teeth** *[on page xviii] of lions.*
>
> **Hair represents their covering...Christ. These teeth are for eating flesh.**

These locusts will operate under the covering and direction of Christ's glorious body from whence they draw their strength. This scripture was always meant to be interpreted spiritually. The power is in the covering of Christ. This is what makes us the Holy Messengers; Christ is over us through a body of believers. In Joel 2 it says that the voice of the Lord will go before His army. The Locusts are operating in the power of God, because He covers us by His Body. <u>The love that unites us is the blood by which Christ's body lives.</u>

Study Help
Hair...The Power of Covering

This is **'appearing power'**. We all know that two thousand years ago Christ showed forth a very powerful witness, and we have longed for that manifestation of Christ ever since. The Church has made excuses about why we do not see miracles and manifestations today like those in the days of Christ. The simple truth is that Christ has not been present enough within a body to minister healing, blessing, and victory over death. When He **appears** through His Bride, He will again be able to minister fully to the world. The whole becomes greater than the sum of the parts.

This does not mean that a group of gathered Christians would manifest this kind of powerful witness. Instead, it is the knitting together, through corporate accountability and love, which brings a greater measure of Christ. This happens because His presence in our brothers and sisters enables Him to speak into our lives. No one person can manifest Christ's appearing because our selfish carnality will prevent us from hearing the voice of God, and we will choose to walk "in a way that seems right in our own eyes." Our brothers and sisters in Christ show us the spots that the Holy Spirit has been trying to remove. The body will produce a greater manifestation of Christ in us as we submit to this chastening. Pride, which goes before a fall, has denied us access to this benefit of the Lord's body. Soon His powerful witness will walk this world again!

As individuals within the body obtain more of Christ's Glory, a greater measure of Christ will appear in the Corporate Body and will transform us even more. This will continue until there is a true **appearing** of Christ through His body and in His Saints.

Eph. 4:13 "till we all come to the unity of the faith and of the knowledge of the Son of God, to a perfect man, to the measure of the **fullness of Christ."**

> **9:9** And they had breastplates, as it were **breastplates** [on page iii] **of iron**; and the sound of their wings was as the sound of **chariots** of many horses running to battle.
>
> **The 'breastplates' are robes of righteousness and iron is its perfecting power.**

We see that the iron, which sharpens other iron, is what prepares us. This accountability enables us to go into the battle (See definition of **breastplates**). Joel 2:5 speaks of God's army coming with the sound of chariots, the sound of Christ's Bride going forth into the world. This is a Bride work, not an individual work. We will lose ourselves in the purposes of Christ.

> **9:10** And they had tails like unto scorpions, and there were **stings in their tails**: and their power was to hurt men **five** months.
>
> **The stings in the tail represent the point of their message...Christ...and the result of not joining them. In Joel it says that behind them "a flame burneth." Five may be literal but it also represents the grace of God to endure with these rejecters.**

This powerful appearing will bring us into battle with the world, destroying everything they think is important. We know that worldly things distract from Christ therefore, it is really grace (5) which we bring.

> **9:11** And they had a **king** over them, which is the angel of the bottomless pit, whose name in the Hebrew tongue is **Abaddon**, but in the Greek tongue hath his name **Apollyon**.
>
> **Abaddon, the destroyer—see Abaddon [on page i]—brings God's wrath. Yes, this is the Lord's doing even if it is Satan that He may use. Look up the definition; it was the Lord (using the Destroyer on His enemies) who passed over on the "Passover".**

God always said that He will fight our battles; this is no exception. Christ is coming to the world (in us) to destroy all carnality and set His people free. Satan may be the direct agent or it could be the Glory, but the outcome will be destruction of the flesh.

The King will rise out of our hearts and appear to conquer the earth. The unsaved (Greek) will see only destruction if they shun this call of God.

Trumpet 5 reveals the power of the corporate appearing of Jesus Christ as the army of God comes forth to reap the harvest. This army is under the leadership of Jesus Christ, who will be intimately guiding all that takes place from here forward. In Verse 1 and 2 we see that His appearing opens a way for the kingdom of Heaven to pour into this world, so that all of the world will know the King of Kings ("Thy kingdom come, thy will be done, here on earth as it is in heaven."). The 'appearing' is so glorious that all natural light will dim, and many men will turn to God when Christ becomes so evident. History has told us even when God reveals Himself to man, there is no guarantee that all men will repent. Some will try to disregard what God is doing and will allow a spirit of strong delusion to veil them.

II Thes. 2:11-12
11   And for this cause **God shall send them strong delusion**, that they should believe a lie:
12   That they all might be **damned who believed not the truth, but had pleasure in unrighteousness**.

The locusts (Christ appearing) will go forth tormenting the flesh and devouring worldliness (9:2 & 3). All of mankind will hear the radical message of the kingdom with which Christ will confront the inhabitants of the world. "To be friends with this world is to be an enemy of God." His presence, as seen in a sold out peculiar people, will challenge people to regard the status of their personal relationship with Jesus Christ as an issue of conflict and concern (verse 4 & 5).

This torment will turn to fear in some; and because of that fear, they will seek "death". Others will desire to be part of the Bride for the sake of its 'rewards'; however, they will still be unwilling to commit their lives and surrender. Desire in itself is not sufficient to be worthy of Christ's appearing; they must die-to-themselves to enter into a relationship with Jesus Christ (Matt. 10:37-38).

The Wife of the Lamb

Verses 7-9 give insight into the method of His appearing. Many men and women of God believe that they can mature in Christ by working through their own power, adhering to a strict doctrine or certain lifestyle, or perhaps dedicating themselves to a ministry. However, it is brother **accountable** to brother in love that brings completion to our walk with Christ.

Joel 2:7-8
7   They shall run like mighty men; they shall climb the wall like men of war; and they shall **march every one on his ways**, and **they shall not break their ranks**:
      Accountability brings everyone to task, focusing on their walk...never moving to the left or the right.

8   **Neither shall one thrust another**; they shall **walk every one in his path**: and when they fall upon the sword, they shall <u>not be wounded</u>.

Thrusting means hitting, pushing, or harming. Walking in peace and obligation to the body keeps us under the protection of Jesus. Then we are protected when we go into the battle.

Learning to be <u>part</u> of the whole makes us a <u>whole</u> part. This is so important to understand. Surrender to our brothers and sisters in Christ is the greatest evidence we have of dying to self. Today, if Christians do not like what the preacher says, they go to another church. Pastors can also fail to become accountable to the flock; instead they see only "their" ministry. This lack of love for the body, which is Christ, disqualifies them from having a robe of righteousness before the grave. Those who submit for the sake of Christ will be completed in Christ. This Glory will motivate some of the loners to enter and give over their personal ministry to the whole. That is why He has asked the Saints to be patient (See Seal 5) until the self-centered ones come around.

Religion has made us so self-righteous that 'fixing others' is our focus, and we refuse to be judged ourselves. True AGAPE LOVE is what will make the world take note. It is the only possible way to become an Eagle in Christ's kingdom. Those who want to be a Bride of Christ look in-side themselves when things offend them and seek to die to that thing IN them which becomes offended. Remember, Christ has become a rock of offense, a stone of stumbling, so that we can clean out the selfish carnality cluttering our lives and make way for His appearing.

Finally, Trumpet 5 tells us that Christ does all the de-stroying. His locusts torment (sift and separate) through their testimony and bring the good news that surrendering to Him destroys the carnality that separates them. The Bride speaks the truth and points the way; and God will then "bear witness" through the powerful Glory that shines forth from His Beloved.

Angel 5
Rev. 14:15-16

> **15** *And another angel* **came out of the temple**, *crying with a loud voice* **to him that sat on the cloud**, *Thrust in thy sickle, and reap: for the time is come for thee to reap; Thrust in thy sickle, and reap: for the time is come for thee to reap; for* **the harvest of the earth is ripe.**
>
> *Cloud is the Parousia of Christ. Sickle is the final work of the "two edged sword".*
>
> **16** *And he that sat on the* **cloud thrust in his sickle on the earth**; *and the earth was reaped*

"Harvest is beginning" is the message of **Angel 5** to the inhabitants of the earth. The Eagles (those in the tem-ple) start the harvest by sending the Wife of the Lamb (**clouds** on page iv) into the earth amid a great cloud of wit-nesses. In this way, Jesus can be seen by the entire world at one time. Some will believe His message, others will scoff; but all will hear the truth. The sickle is the truth designed to

separate - either from this world or from Christ. Being forced off the fence brings accountability. They must either accept Him or reject Him.

Remember that during the parable of the tares (Matt. Chapter 13), as the harvest ripened, it was easy to discern the wheat from the tares. God is making this a time of black and white issues; there are no more gray areas.

Vial 5
Rev. 16:10-11

> **10** *And the fifth angel poured out his vial upon the* **seat of the beast;** *and his kingdom was full of darkness; and they gnawed their tongues for pain,*
>
> **The seat of the Beast is worldliness/carnality. The Beast's kingdom is Babylon, and to dwell there is to dwell in the pain of darkness. All worldliness will be evil (darkness) and painful, even to the inhabitants of the earth.**
>
> **11** *And blasphemed the God of heaven because of their pains and their sores, and repented not of their deeds.*

In **Vial 5** God will pour out such destruction that this world's riches and pleasures will seem unimportant by comparison. God will show those who are carnal how un-stable their world really is. No one knows what kind of devastation will take place, but it will be more severe than anything in previous human history. God will get the world's attention, and they will know that the wrath is of God. If they still refuse to repent, the pressures and pain will intensify. Their deeds (fruit) will bear witness against them that they belong to a spirit of antichrist.

The reference to blasphemy is not about cursing God, but about diminishing God. It occurs when the natural dis-asters and tribulation are attributed to natural causes, deny-ing that they are produced by the wrath of God.

Vial Angel 5
Rev. 19:1-16 Elect Praise Him

This is a time of great joy for the Elect. All of the tribulation is having an effect. Countless numbers of souls are being saved through the manifest Glory. This is PRES-ENCE EVANGELISM. The joy, love, patience and Glory of the Elect are all that is needed to accomplish the greatest harvest the world has ever known. PRAISE GOD!

Look at the boundless joy in the hearts of God's Elect. Will you be in this number?

> **19:1** *And after these things I heard a great voice of much people in heaven, saying, Alleluia; Salvation, and Glory, and honour, and power, unto the Lord our God:*
>
> **19:2** *For true and righteous are his judgments: for he hath judged [past tense] the* **great whore**, *which did corrupt the earth with her fornication, and hath avenged the blood of his servants at her* [1]*hand.*

The Harlot corrupted the earth by portraying a carnal testimony of Christ to the World, hindering the ministry of being the salt of Christ to the world. Now the Church will redeem the name of Jesus through the Wife of the Lamb. Her [1]actions means the Church, now spotless, will share a much more glorious revelation of Christ.

> **19:3** And again they said, Alleluia. And her **smoke** rose up for ever and ever.

The Wife of the Lamb is the Glory of the Harlot's burning; her burning (the purification of the Church) has revealed the Bride. Her judgment is now Christ' Glory to the world, because it means salvation is coming to the world.

> **19:4** And the four and twenty elders and the four beasts fell down and worshipped God that sat on the throne, saying, Amen; Alleluia.
>
> **Elders** *(our will)* **falling down** represents a time of great surrender and ascension (See four and twenty on page vii). Any time we see the elders fall (will surrendered); it is a reference to completion through ascension.
>
> **19:5** And a **voice came out of the throne**, saying, Praise our God, all ye his servants, and ye that fear him, both small and great.
>
> *Small and great, there will be distinctions…Calf, Man, and Eagle even among the robe wearers.*

God is speaking to His Elect in such an intimate way that it can only be expressed by stepping in and out of the very *throne* of God. The types tell us that His voice will be speaking loudly out of the 'heart' of the Elect.

> **19:6** And I heard as it were the voice of a great multitude, and as the voice of **many waters** [on page xi], and as the voice of mighty **thunderings** [on page xix], saying, Alleluia: for the Lord God omnipotent reigneth.
>
> *The army of God will speak in one voice, and it will be a tremendous sounding revelation of Christ.*

The corporate "Man-Child" is speaking (many waters) and it is revealing the seven thunders to the world. The world will receive ears to hear due to the corporate nature of the manifestation of the parousia.

> **19:7** Let us be glad and rejoice, and give honour to him: for the marriage of the Lamb is come, and his wife **hath made herself ready**.
>
> *The great marriage has come and the Lord has entered the vineyard with His beloved. Song of Solomon says, "Come, my beloved, let us go forth into the field; let us lodge in the villages. Let us get up early to the vineyards; let us see if the vine flourish, whether the tender grape appear, and the pomegranates bud forth: there will I give thee my loves (Song 7:11-12).*

Many believe that for the Church to become a Bride without spot or blemish, Christ must transform it at the rapture. However, based on this scripture, any notion of an instantaneous work is false. The Bride <u>has made herself ready</u> through the perfecting power of the revelation of Christ. He comes to prepare for himself a Bride, and now He has accomplished His will (See Trumpet 5…Wife of lamb). The Bride is ready to become the Wife of the Lamb and to consummate the relationship.

> **19:8** And to her was granted that she should be arrayed in fine linen, clean and white: for the **fine linen is the righteousness of Saints**.
>
> *These are the glorified bodies that qualify you to be a part of the great and final harvest…the marriage supper of the Lamb.*

He is revealing one more time that the Bride is ready because of the Robes of Righteousness. Again, the 'covering' of the body came from the "right acts" of the Saints. The right-acts came by iron sharpening iron in the Body of Christ.

> **19:9** And he saith unto me, Write, Blessed are they which are called unto the **marriage supper of the Lamb**. And he saith unto me, These are the true sayings of God.
>
> *Rev. 1:3 says that we are able to be one of these blessed ones if we will keep the words of Revelation.*

If you endured the perfecting work of Christ in His body, you are truly blessed as is signified by being part of the New Jerusalem and of the harvest (See 'great supper' page xviii). The harvest is the marriage supper of the Lamb.

> **19:10** And I fell at his feet to worship him. And he said unto me, See thou do it not: I am thy fellowservant, and of thy brethren that have the testimony of Jesus: worship God: for the **testimony of Jesus is the spirit of prophecy**.
>
> *Since Jesus is the Spirit of prophecy, only He can make you a "Revelator" like John.*

The Eagles/Angels are so Christ like even John mistakes them for angelic beings. Thank God for the manifest Sons of God (Rom. 8:19). They are not Jesus, but they are so transparent His Glory is all there is to see.

The Spirit of Christ is what opens your understanding to all these things. He is the Spirit of this prophecy. You are able to understand this prophecy so you can be a part of this prophecy… see 1:1.

Heaven revealed - the appearing

> **19:11** And I saw **heaven opened**, and behold a white horse; and he that sat upon him was called Faithful and True, and in righteousness he **doth judge and make war**.
>
> *WHO His Bride is…What she reveals*
> *THE BRIDE IS HIS WHITE HORSE.*

The Elect are His vehicles in this world through righteousness (robe or appearing). We saw this in Seal 1 as an appearing to the carnal Church. This time it is to engage in a war with the world.

12 *His **eyes were as a flame of fire**, and on his head were many **crowns**; and he had a name written, that no man knew, but he himself.*

THE BRIDE IS HIS CROWNS. The Bride is His appointed authority in this world, His anointed. The name that NO MAN (natural carnality) can know is for those who are intimate with Him.

Through the Elect, carnality is revealed and then burned (eyes-flame-fire).

13 *And he was clothed with a **vesture** dipped in blood: and his name is called The Word of God.*

THE BRIDE IS HIS VESTURE, baptized into His death and raised into His life, the robe of righteousness.

Referring back to verse 12, He is His revelation (Word) and we represent it. Only those with Him *in them* can know the Revelation …and live it!

14 *And the **armies** which were in heaven **followed** him upon white horses, clothed in fine linen, white and clean.*

We must be His follower to be a part of this. THE BRIDE IS HIS ARMY. See Joel 2 and locust.

We must be where He is (i.e. follow Him) to see the Glory and to be the glorious vehicle of the Lord. Notice that only those with the robes can go out with Him.

John 17:24
24   Father, I will that they also, whom thou hast given me, **be with me where I am; that they may behold my Glory**, which thou hast given me: for thou lovedst me before the foundation of the world.

John 12:26
26   If any man serve me, let him follow me; **and where I am, there shall also my servant be**: if any man serve me, him will my Father honour.

15 *And out of his mouth goeth a sharp sword, that with it he should smite the nations: and he shall rule them with a rod of iron: and he treadeth the winepress of the fierceness and wrath of Almighty God.*

THE BRIDE IS HIS SWORD. THE BRIDE IS THE ROD OF IRON. See Rev. 5:10, also see page 101.

He wields (sword) the Elect as a manifest truth to the world of the Word of God. They will rule through the righteous acts (rod of iron) of Christ. This is the same way that Christians are formed into the Bride.

The Bride will go forth (tread) with the Word to declare the full Revelation. It will be a terrible thing for many. Their life in this world will be coming to an end.

16 *And he hath on his vesture and on his thigh a name written, KING OF KINGS, AND LORD OF LORDS.*

THE BRIDE IS HIS "KINGS" AND HIS "LORDS".

He is our King and our Lord because our name is written on His thigh, which shows they know Him in the most intimate sense.

Vial Angel 5 began with a message that declares Judgment Day to the world. For His Bride, it is a great day. To others, it will be a day of destruction because they will not let go of this world and repent. The cup of wrath is full and pours out (verse 1 & 2). The whore is the reason (judged - past tense), but the world is the recipient. Nevertheless, the ones who benefit are those who partake in the Glory revealed through her destruction (verse 3).

Since this is the Judgment day, then it is the Lord's Day (2 Pet. 2:7-10). Paul himself longed to be part of this day. He says in 2 Tim. 4:8, "Henceforth there is laid up for me a **crown of righteousness**, which the Lord, the **righteous judge**, shall give me **at that day**: and not to me only, but unto **all them also that love his APPEARING**." Paul predicts that he will be here along with all the Saints of the past who sold out and looked for this day. In verse 6, it refers to a great multitude and many waters (voices). These are two different groups: the cloud of Saints pressing in (Heb. 12:1) and the sold out Bride. This is the seventh day, the Lord's day.

The Wife shows that she is ready (verse 7) because she is wearing the wedding garment (verse 8). Now is the time when Christ will harvest the earth through His Elect (verses 12-16). Praise God to be part of such a great event!

Being completely surrendered, the Bride becomes His: White Horse, Crowns, Vesture, Armies, Sword of Truth, Rod of Iron, Kings, and Lords. The only way we can be all of these things is to be clothed in a robe of righteousness. Therefore, Christ wants us to seek Him in each other so that He can transform us into His image. We will only be useful to Him as we lose ourselves in the body of Christ. If you want to receive that blessed invitation to the marriage supper of the Lamb, you must begin now by becoming accountable to your brothers and sisters in Christ.

Phil. 2:3
3   Let nothing be done through strife or vainglory; but in lowliness of mind let **each esteem other better than themselves.**
4   Look not every man on his own things, but **every man also on the things of others.**

Rom. 12:5
5   so in Christ we who are many form one body, and each member belongs to all the others.

Chapter 14

The Sixth Thunder - Final Judgment

The harvest begun in Thunder 5 will swell in Thunder 6 to encompass the entire world. Although many will flee from the face of God as it is revealed in the Wife of the Lamb, confrontation is inevitable. Christ's presence will demand a final decision by all. There is a great sense of urgency brought on by the message that is heard as the horsemen go forth, "final judgment has come on the children of disobedience." At any moment during this time, the Lord "as a thief" will snatch them away to the lake of fire and brimstone. This happens only because they have been given every opportunity to choose Christ and still will not.

In **Seal 6,** we see that God begins the task of making the whole world accountable. This accountability will come as Truth removes the deception through which Satan has blinded them to their worldliness. The Glory of Christ's appearing will shake the world, bringing it to its knees, showing them how much they love the glories of this world. They will understand that while Satan has deceived them, it was their sins in the form of love of the world and rejection of God that allowed them to be deceived. It is this love that continues to make them an enemy of God. As they desire to hold on to this world, wrath and judgment will pour into their lives. Many will realize the futility of their worldly desires and accomplishments and repent from their sins as the message of the Bride touches their hearts.

In **Trumpet 6,** the message from the four **horns** (**horns** page xviii), which represent clemency, send forth the end-time Angels (Eagles) prepared to slay men (bring them life). Grace and clemency is over and the ignorance brought about by the deceit of Satan is no longer an excuse for unbelief. **Woe 2** brings the horsemen of the harvest to pour out the final warning to the world and demand a decision. For those who repent, these horsemen will be able to prophesy the life of Christ into their hearts. Rejecters will face the lake of fire and brimstone.

(**Angel 6**). The Elect operate out of the temple, meaning that they have been 'completely' prepared for this day and equipped to swing the sharp sickle that will enable a harvest on a level never before seen. As these horsemen pour out **Vial 6**, they pierce the veils of many who have been deceived; no one can escape their last opportunity for redemption. God will encompass the world at Armageddon and will pour out His presence for judgment on every remaining undecided soul. No one will escape, although some will still reject.

Acts 2:17-21

17   And it shall come to pass in the last days, saith God, I will <u>pour out of my Spirit upon all flesh</u>: and your sons and your daughters <u>shall prophesy</u>

[*the little book*], and your young men shall see visions, and your old men shall dream dreams:

18   And on my servants and on my handmaidens I will pour out in those days of my Spirit [*"my" Spirit of Christ*]; and they <u>shall prophesy</u>:[*speak the revelation of Christ*]

19   And I will shew wonders in heaven above, and signs in the earth beneath; blood, and fire, and vapour of smoke:[*Life, perfection, and Glory*]

20   The **SUN** shall be turned into darkness [*natural glory will pale*], and the moon into blood [*our evil desire turned to life*], before that great and notable day of the Lord come:

21   And it shall come to pass, that whosoever shall call on the name of the Lord shall be saved.

Vial Angel 6 reveals that the heavenly banquet takes place here on earth. "The Marriage Supper of the Lamb" is actually a great time of *Harvest*, a time when all will become accountable and many in the world will choose Christ.

Study Help
The Nature of Man

God shares a profound truth in Vial Angel 6; a truth that is applicable to our lives today. We like to believe that Satan is our enemy and the cause of our stumblings, but God shows us that **we** are to blame for our woes. In Vial Angel 6, we see that the agents of Satan's lies are cast into the lake of fire and brimstone. This means that their lies are removed and can no longer deceive those remaining (the remnant). Nevertheless, even without the influence of Satan's agents, men still reject God. Why? Because they want to be as a god, and Satan takes advantage of that evil nature within them. It was for this reason that Eve ate the apple. Satan did not trick her. She knew the truth. However, the temptation to be as a god was just too much for her. Today, this takes place every time we choose to live our lives our way.

Therefore, bringing a man to truth or bringing about a change in his behavior is not a sure indication that his heart has changed. It takes a surrendered, obedient relationship with Christ to change the heart. If we refuse to surrender and become obedient, we reveal an evil heart. No amount of 'rebuking' Satan can change that.

In Thunder 6, God will force everyone to see and admit to the evil nature of their heart (Matt. 15:18-19). They will also see clearly that only Christ living in the heart can purify a man. With nothing to hide their nakedness, will they see their shame and put on Christ? Those who still reject God at this point have no one to blame but themselves for the eternal separation from God, which is their just reward. Because of the plan of salvation and Harvest patiently wrought by God through the witness of Christ's appearing, millions will accept. Praise God, praise God, and praise God for His incomprehensible mercies! **Blessed are all that are called to the great supper of God.**

THUNDER 6
Seal 6
Rev. 6:12-17

This is the time of the great harvest. Everything that can be shaken will be shaken until all that is left is of the kingdom of Christ. Woe to the inhabitants of this world; another Woe is on the way.

> **6:12** And I beheld when he had opened the sixth seal, and, lo, there was a **great earthquake** [on page v]; and the **sun** [on page xviii] became black as **sackcloth** of **hair** [on page ix], and the **moon** became as **blood**;
>
> *The reference to 'sackcloth' means mourning, while the reference to* **hair** *means covering. The* black *represents the hopelessness. The* **moon** *represents the lusts which guide mankind's dark desires and perversions.*

This is the great Harvest…"Taking the gospel of the kingdom to the world and then the end shall come" (Matt. 24:14). Christ's Glory will remove all of this world's glory (sun). For those who draw their strength from this world (i.e. covered by this world…hair) this will be a time of such intense tribulation, that the life (blood) in Christ will shine as the only hope. The black represents the hopelessness they feel as they realize their life has become pointless (lost its glory). The carnality and riches of this world no longer deceive men in the face of the Glory of Christ Jesus.

The **moon** represents the lusts that guide mankind's dark desires and perversions. These will be revealed by the life (blood) of Christ. Remember, we are dealing with a world that has become lovers of pleasure more than lovers of God. Their "PLEASURE" becomes despair; it is unsatisfying in the light of what God is doing. All will be revealed as vanity, and many will cry out in despair for Christ's Life (**blood**).

> **6:13** And the **stars** of heaven fell unto the earth, even as a fig tree casteth her [1]untimely figs, when she is shaken of a mighty wind.
>
> *Time is up for those professing Christ, yet not having Life.*

Now we hear about the Kings of the earth who still have not repented. The [1]untimely figs are figs that refuse to mature. The Old Testament called them bad or evil figs. They looked good to the natural eye, but they would stay on the vine all winter without ripening. When the winds came, these untimely figs would fall to the ground. As it is in the natural, so it is in the spiritual Harvest. When tribulation shakes the vine, it should mature these figs. They should start to soften and repent and be available for the harvest of God. Instead, these figs do not mature and are now shaken off the vine because they bore no "good" fruit.

In John 15:1-8, we see that if the branch does not bear good fruit, it will be cut off; this is what happens to these

stars. The falling of these stars reveals that their foundation is not in Christ. Unlike natural figs, however, once these stars are no longer deceived, they have the opportunity to repent.

> **6:14** And the heaven [1]**departed as a scroll** when it is rolled together; and every **mountain** [on page xii] and **island** were moved out of **their** places.
>
> *The veil between the first and second heaven is rolling away. The mountains and islands stand for the independence that has been the fruit of carnality.*

[1]It is all but over. Even heaven (all of the spiritual realm) itself has been sifted, which declares that the kingdom is the Bride of Christ (New Jerusalem). There is no "place" for independent mountains (page xii), or other organizations that could compete with the Bride.

There will be no selfish separations (islands) of people or ministries in the body of Christ; all of Christ's body will come together (Joel 2). Only one body can hold the **candlestick**. Islands represent the self-centered nature of ministries that have never come into the full flow of the unifying river of God. They try to stand alone promoting themselves above their brethren and sometimes even before Christ. They are the kings of the earth yet to be enlightened.

> **6:15** And the **kings of the earth** [**stars** cast to earth], and the great men, and the rich men, and the chief captains, and the mighty men [**sun**], and every **bondman** [**moon**], and every free man, hid themselves in the dens and in the rocks of the mountains;
>
> *This speaks of the pride of man and all those who have operated in it.*

Men will do whatever they can to keep from facing the judgment of God. People must submit voluntarily to the judgment of God. If they are too busy or distracted, then they will never be able to repent. These men use the 'Glory' of this world to distract them, and keep them, from the face of Jesus Christ.

This verse refers back to Rev. 6:12-13 (sun, moon, and stars) where the natural glory of this world blinds carnal persons to the true Glory of Christ. All three of these natural strengths have one thing in common…they use a desire for this world to hide the Glory of Christ. However, Christ's presence in conjunction with the wrath poured out, will demand a response. Their religion, their natural life, or their sensual desires will not be able to distract them any longer. Time is up.

> **6:16** And said to the mountains and rocks, Fall on us, and hide us **from** the **face** of him that sitteth on the throne, and from the **wrath** of the Lamb:

They refuse that face to face relationship which brings Jesus Christ. (READ Isa. 2:10-22.) The Bride will radiate that relationship, so they are without excuse...no place to hide. All the world religions start falling in the face of the Truth of Jesus Christ. They now recognize that it is HE who sits on the throne. Every knee will bow and every tongue will confess that Jesus Christ is Lord...whether they accept Him or not.

> **6:17** For the great day of his wrath is come; and who shall be able to stand?

This is the day of final judgment. Only those who are His can stand final judgment. For them, this is a day of Harvest and joy. For the children of disobedience, it is doom and destruction.

Seal 6 unlocks the long awaited final phase of Revelation, the full Harvest...THE REAPING OF THE EARTH. All recognize that God is on the throne, and that their earthly religions and desires cannot protect them from judgment. Many will try to hide from the face of Christ to no avail. His appearing in the Wife of the Lamb gives them every possible chance to choose God. Ultimately, they will be forced to stand face to face before God and make a final decision. The Saints in Thunder 5 asked, "how long"? God said to wait until all thy brothers are ready...now they are ready.

Trumpet 6
Rev. 9:12-21
Final Judgment is here
WOE 2

> **9:12** One woe is past; and, behold, there come two woes more hereafter.
>
> **Woe is an expression of a disaster to come. These are tough times. Who will stand?**
>
> **9:13** And the sixth angel sounded, and I heard a voice from the four **horns** [on page xviii] of the golden altar which is before God,
>
> **This is the voice of clemency (horns), signifying no more grace for those who were innocent...everyone is accountable. All must choose, because there is no more time left.**
>
> **9:14** Saying to the sixth angel which had the **trumpet**, Loose the **four** angels which are bound in the great river Euphrates.
>
> **Euphrates means to "break forth". Euphrates is also the natural source of water for Babylon.**

Later on in Vial 6, we will detail this event. The emphasis here is on being able to "break forth" from what has hindered them. These end-time (**four**) "holy messengers" were unable to get their revelation of Christ-in-us heard, because of the lies that support Babylon (Euphrates). These lies that distract men's hearts from the word of God keep them in captivity to Babylon. During the time of Thunder 6, the end-time messengers (**Four** on page vii) will pierce through these lies and set mankind free while also making the entire world accountable to their message

> **9:15** And the four angels were loosed, which were prepared for an hour, and a day, and a month, and a year, for to slay the **third part** of men.
>
> **This is the harvest of men. Men represent the unsaved. Third part is the redeemable of God.**

The purpose of all tribulation and perfection was to allow His messengers this designated point in time to reap the earth. This is the time for which the cloud of witnesses has long awaited. The focus is now on those who are redeemable and not to chase after those who reject God's offer of Life.

Mankind has been under the bondage of Satan and his lies for too long. This is the time for God to redeem all who can be His (**third part**). Therefore, God has put together this marvelous plan (Revelation) to enlighten man, and thereby, help many come into the kingdom.

> **9:16** And the number of the **army of the horsemen** were two hundred thousand thousand: and I heard the number of them.

This is the first number we receive about the fruit of the Firstfruits (144,000). The number is two hundred million. This number should give us hope to endure pain and tribulation for the sake of bringing more "sons" into the kingdom. Just imagine two hundred million sold out manifest sons of God giving last call!!!

> **9:17** And thus I saw the horses in the vision, and them that sat on them, having breastplates of **fire**, and of **jacinth** [on page x], and **brimstone** [on page iii]: and the heads of the horses were as the [1]heads of lions; and out of their [2]mouths issued **fire** and **smoke** and **brimstone**.
>
> **Jacinth represents smoke in the next verse; therefore, 'Glory' is what it means here as well. Brimstone speaks of 'last call'. They speak it and they live it (breastplates).**

The horsemen (Army of God/New Jerusalem) have a right to issue forth judgment, because they have already been through the perfecting fire of Christ. They have died to self and received His Glory (jacinth - Christ-in-us). They are made **complete** by being of one mind with Christ's body ([1]lions head); therefore, they have faced His final judgment (**brimstone**) and received their **robes** of righteousness (**breastplate**). With the robe of righteousness, the world sees one body...Christ.

Speaking in [2]unity will empower these horsemen to kill (verse 18). The horses represent the tribulation of the earth, which we use to ride into the lives of the inhabitants of the earth. The horsemen issue perfection and Glory by declaring final judgment.

> **9:18** By these three was the **third part** of men killed, by the [1]**fire**, and by the [2]**smoke**, and by the [3]**brimstone**, which issued out of their mouths.
>
> **God's portion (third part) is redeemed and thereby comes into life by the power of the**

Bride to issue: [1]perfection, [2]Glory, and [3]final judgment.

This means that the Bride is able to cause someone to desire Christ in these three ways. This has been the truth all along, but now we are told that final judgment is upon the world. This means that if the appearing does not persuade them, then the fear of final judgment might. Remember, the appearing is over two hundred million strong. It is hard to ignore this body.

> *9:19 For their **power is in their mouth**, and in their [1]**tails**: for their tails were like unto serpents, and had **heads**, and with them they do hurt.*
>
> **Power comes from the revelation of Christ and declares last chance. Choose or loose. Heads is the authority or power that has come to them.**

Everyone that encounters this final judgment will hurt. [1]Behind them waits desolation. The tail speaks of the pain that will come to those who reject this message of Woe. To reject Christ and let His Revelation pass is desolation. At any moment during this time, the Lord will take the wicked from among the righteous (See commentary Rapture on page 117).

Joel 2:3
3 __A fire devoureth before them__; and __behind them a flame burneth__: the land is as the garden of Eden before them, and *behind them a desolate wilderness*; yea, and nothing shall escape them.

> *9:20 And the rest of the **men which were not killed** by these plagues yet repented not of the works of their hands, that they should not worship devils, and idols of gold, and silver, and brass, and stone, and of wood: **which neither can see, nor hear, nor walk**:*
>
> **Death was achieved by those who repented. Death is only available to those who repent therefore, these could not get what the Elect have...visible resurrection Life.**

Regardless of all that has been witnessed, the sinfulness of man will still prevent some from repenting and coming under God's protection. These children of disobedience are a very stubborn, prideful group of people, prone at any moment to be cast "alive" into the Lake of fire.

Also note that repenting brings death (to self). These people that are not killed are refusing to repent.

> *9:21 **Neither repented** they of their murders, nor of their sorceries, nor of their fornication, nor of their thefts.*

This is the obvious failure of man, continuing in their lawlessness and sin, even in the face of Jesus Christ. REPENT AND AGAIN I SAY REPENT!

Trumpet 6 sets loose the army of God on the world with a shout that final judgment is at hand, and their God demands an accounting. The power and determination with which this body shows forth Christ in **Woe 2** will be the single greatest event of all time. The million Hebrew children moving through the desert pales in comparison to Jesus walking the earth in a body of believers 200 million strong! The robes of righteousness that they wear will astound the world. These robes are the same Glory that Moses wore after returning from the mountain that struck fear into the hearts of the people. Christ's appearing promises to be even more awe inspiring and terrible to behold. The most profound part of this revelation is that some still refuse to repent; therefore, they face a dragon's hell!

Angel 6
Rev. 14:17

> *17 And another angel came out of the temple which is in heaven, he also having a **sharp sickle**.*
>
> **The Bride now operates from the temple, face to face with Jesus.**

The message of the **Angel 6** calls forth the Harvesters from out of the temple to reap, kill, and perfect the Great Harvest of God. The plowman will overtake the reaper, and the reaper will overtake the sower (Amos 9:13).

Vial 6
Rev. 16:12-16

> *16:12 And the sixth angel poured out his vial upon the **great river [1]Euphrates**; and the water thereof was dried up, that the way of the kings of the **east** [on page v] might be prepared.*
>
> **Euphrates is the source of water for ancient Babylon. Truth will dry up the lies of the Beast and make a way for the kings of the East (the Elect who have entered into the sanctuary through the eastern gate) to reach the __last strongholds of sin__.**

God will bring tribulation and wrath (probably on a global level) that will destroy the sources through which Satan's lies originated. As God shakes this world, He will remove Satan's ability to deceive, exposing the deception that has covered the emptiness of worldliness. "Drying up" the [1]"river of lies" will make a new pathway into the hearts of the lost and make them accountable. They will learn that this world is an enemy of God, and they have been distracted from the truth of Christ by barren illusion.

> *16:13 And I saw three unclean spirits like **frogs** [on page vii] come out of the mouth of the **dragon**, and out of the mouth of the **beast**, and out of the mouth of the false **prophet**.*
>
> **The snake of Genesis has grown up, fed by earthly carnality, for two thousand years. __Dragon, Beast, and prophets__ represent the levels of deception of these people.**

This verse is a continuation of verse 12. When Satan cannot deceive people with the 'glitz and glamour' (sun of seal 6) of this world, then His lies are exposed. The **frogs** tell us that the things that come out of his carnal servants' mouths are lying spirits. The inhabitants of the earth will realize that they have been the ones telling these lies. All that they have proclaimed regarding this world was a lie straight out of Hell. This means that they, too, have been the 'sources' of Satan's lies, and they are subject to wrath and judgment because they are partakers with Satan. Now that these antichrist spirits are exposed, people are fully accountable; they either repent now, or they may never be able to repent.

Dragon, Beast, and false prophets represent the levels of deception of these people. In the same manner that Christ transforms people, Satan can transform them as well. If people continue with a spirit long enough, then they will begin to resemble that spirit. For Christians, the calf, man, and Eagle, (where Eagle represents the fullness of Christ) symbolize their level of spiritual growth in Christ. For the deceived victims of Satan, the false prophet, beast, and dragon, (where the dragon is the fullness of antichrist spirits) symbolize their level of sin. Unlike times past, God makes men accountable to these spirits. If they do not repent, these spirits will have greater hold on their lives than ever before. They will become active enemies of God.

> **16:14** *For they are the spirits of devils, working* **miracles***, which go forth unto the* **kings of the earth** *and* **of the whole world***, to gather them to the* **battle** *of that great day of God Almighty.*

Satan responds to this exposure with even more deception. He will offer some "sign" (Gr. *semeion*) in an effort to bring doubt on God's judgment. The same thing happened when the Egyptian priest duplicated the judgment of the frogs sent by Moses. (Yet, only Moses could eradicate the frogs.) With that, they succeeded in creating just enough doubt in Pharaoh's mind to harden his heart against God. Satan may accompany his 'sign' with some kind of lie about God sending wrath just to hurt people. In this way Satan tries to distract and harden the hearts of the people, so that they speak against God and become His enemy.

Satan calls out his army – Satan is trying to mimic what God has accomplished. He is trying to use the hardened hearts of those who reject God as a prime breeding ground for these "spirits of devils".

> **16:15** *Behold, I* **come as a thief***. Blessed is he that watcheth, and keepeth his garments, lest he walk naked, and they see his shame.*
>
> **THE LAST WARNING FOR THOSE NOT WATCHING!!!**

Christ is not a thief, but He comes as one to remove the wicked. The people in Noah's day were surprised by the judgment of God and lost everything: this is the same type all over again. While people are distracted, Christ will appear and demand an account. They will make the same excuses made by the poor steward of his one talent, and their end will be the same as well. Jesus will take all that they have and give it to another (Matt. 25:24).

> **16:16** *And he gathered them together into a place called in the Hebrew tongue* **Armageddon.**
>
> **This Hebrew word has two root words: one means "to pour upon"; and the other means "to surround, take, or seize."**

God will totally surround the enemy of Babylon at Armageddon and pour out His wrath on them. In the natural, this means that God has eliminated all excuses and distractions; people will deserve what they get. These people are gathered together to do battle (16:13); they are hopeless and THERE IS NO PLACE TO HIDE.

Satan is a liar and his vessels are liars; his miracles are deception and his purpose is distraction. As **Vial 6** is poured out, his tactics are revealed; the evil of carnality is clearly visible in all of its vileness and corruption. The inhabitants of the world and the kings of the earth can no longer be deceived as Truth lays a path of accountability before them. They have full knowledge of Satan's enmity with God and the tools of deceit he has used to distract them. Still, Satan perseveres and continues to try to gather people to his purposes by creating signs and miracles that imitate the miracles of Christ but are void of life. Christ's signs are reserved as a witness for God's messengers (Heb. 2:4). Satan's signs must be "lying signs", whose direction is to distract from God's Love.

John 8:44	
44	Ye [they] are of your father the devil, and the lusts of your father ye will do. He was a murderer from the beginning, and abode not in the truth, because there is no truth in him. **When he speaketh a lie, he speaketh of his own**: for he is a liar, and the father of it.
I Jn. 2:22	
22	Who is a **liar** but he that denieth that Jesus is the Christ? He is **antichrist**, that denieth the Father and the Son.

The actions of Man reveal that by nature he likes to think of himself as a god. He has been stumbled by this desire since the garden. In Gen. 3:5, we read, "For God doth know that in the day ye eat thereof, then your eyes shall be opened, **and ye shall be as gods**, knowing good and evil." Eve wanted the apple for just this reason. Therefore, even though the lies are exposed, the sinful heart of man may still cause him to choose himself over God. Even in knowledge many willfully harden their hearts and determine to reject their God, making the final choice that ranks them as part of Satan's army and a declared enemy of God. We see in Second Thessalonians that all of Satan's work will be revealed at this time. This is not a scripture about a person called the antichrist.

II Thes. 2:8-12	
8	And then shall that ['ho' the] ~~Wicked~~ wicked (not a proper noun) be revealed, whom the Lord shall consume with the spirit of his mouth, and shall destroy with the brightness of his coming:
	The translators added the capitalization and translated 'ho' as 'that' when it is normally translated

	'the'. Therefore, a more proper translation is "And then shall the wicked be revealed with the Spirit…"
9	~~Even him~~ (added), whose coming is after the working of Satan with all power and signs and lying wonders,
	To back up the first error, they added "Even him", which was not in the original. This was a reference to the wicked ones who would be revealed because of the deceptive works by which Satan deceived them. The next verse makes it clear that he was speaking of a people… "in them."
10	And with all deceivableness of unrighteousness <u>in them</u> that perish; because they received not the love of the truth, that they might be saved.
11	And for this cause **God shall send them strong delusion, that they should believe a lie:**
12	That they all might be damned who believed not the truth, but had pleasure in unrighteousness.
	The spirit of antichrist is revealed in those who break the law of God and refuse to believe Him. The warning is that if they continue in deception or unrighteousness and do not receive the Truth (Christ-in-us), then they will be damned!! Therefore, Satan only has to distract them with "lying wonders" long enough to keep them from repenting in time.

Remember…**SATAN IS DEFEATED. <u>OUR</u> CARNALITY IS THE TRUE ENEMY!**

Vial Angel 6

Rev. 19:17-21

> *19:17 And I saw an angel standing in the* **sun**; *and he cried with a loud voice, saying to all the* **fowls that fly** *[eagles] in the midst of heaven, Come and* <u>**gather yourselves together**</u> *unto the* **supper** *[on page xviii] of the great God;*
>
> **The Bride comes forth and declares that it is time for the feast. The angel standing in the sun represents the Bride in her robes of righteousness declaring the fullness of the harvest. The demand to 'gather' emphasizes that New Jerusalem is a corporate body, in which Eagles will feast in the power of Christ.**

The Eagles are the ones in charge. They are so sold out, they speak in the power of Christ. Only those in the fullness will be able to bring forth the fullness of the harvest. They will have no will of their own so they will stand in the Son (sun).

> *19:18 That ye may eat the* **flesh** *of kings, and the* **flesh** *of captains, and the* **flesh** *of mighty men, and the* **flesh** *of horses, and of them that sit on them, and the* **flesh** *of all men, both free and bond, both small and great.*
>
> **Look at what is on the menu…FLESH (CARNALITY).**

The Eagles love to devour carnal lives with living Truth. With the world subject to wrath, carnality is easy prey. The Eagles have no problem overcoming those who

do battle and indeed will harvest many who repent of their carnality.

> *19:19 And I saw the beast, and the* **kings of the earth**, *and their armies, gathered together to make war against him that sat on the horse, and against his army.*

Vial 6 began the last spiritual battle between the Eagles and Satan to claim final victory over the hearts and minds of the nations of the earth. Satan can capture the mind if the heart longs for this world. "For where your treasure is there your heart will be." (Luke 12:34). Those who have not repented by this point and have made themselves enemies of God are about to lose BIG. They will never live to see Thunder 6 or the white Throne…they will be annihilated!

> *19:20 And the* **beast** *was taken, and with him the* **false prophet** *that wrought miracles before him, with which he deceived them that had received the mark of the beast, and them that worshipped his image. These both were* **cast alive** *into a* **lake of fire** *[on page x] burning with brimstone.*
>
> **All manifestations of carnality are destroyed.**

All who have sold out to carnality and not repented have made themselves enemies of God. They will now be judged and taken away, so that those who have repented can be given a solid last chance. This is different than the White Throne Judgment which occurs at the end of the Millennium. At the White Throne, all who have never seen the appearing will be judged. But those who have witnessed the appearing and still rejected Jesus deserve no other chance. They are instantly cast into eternal separation from God. The dragon (Satan) is excluded because Satan himself will be shut up in the hearts of those ruled during the Millennium.

Notice that this is another confirmation, echoed throughout this study (rapture commentary, reference to the days of Noah, parable of wheat and tares, etc.) that it is the wicked ones who are removed from the presence of the righteous. See also Ps. 104:35 and Prov. 2:21-22.

Prov. 10:30
30 The righteous shall never be removed: but the wicked shall not inhabit the earth.

This is the end of the line for those who have been transformed into the image of their master. There is no time or hope left for them. God judges these now.

> *19:21 And the* **remnant were slain** *with the* **sword** *of him that sat upon the horse, which sword proceeded out of his mouth: and all the* **fowls** *[eagles] were filled with their flesh.*
>
> **The remnant are those who are still redeemable.**

The Eagles swarm down to kill any that are left and ready (remnant or third part). Their testimony and power are too much for those who have made lies their refuge. This does not mean that all were saved; but those who are now slain are slain because of the word of truth…the end is here.

Vial Angel 6 testifies to the end of carnality in all of its forms as the Eagles eat the remaining flesh from all who would be saved before the final destruction. Those who will not repent and die to themselves declare themselves forever the enemy of God, leaving Him no recourse except to cast them and their self-life into eternal separation. The last remnant has been slain as we begin to enter the Lord's seventh day of rest. Time and hope are at an end.

Chapter 15

The Seventh Thunder – The End is the Beginning

Thunder 7 begins with the awesome revelation that those who read this book and "hear' and "keep" the revelation of Jesus Christ **are the Seals** that must be broken before the revelation can begin. What a thrill to understand the mystery that has been hidden for generations and to be the very instruments of the Revelation which unlock authorities and events that will begin the final phase of history. We are a living part of the book and of the end times.

In the children's fantasy, the Never-Ending Story, a young boy receives a special book. As he begins to read it, he discovers that the passages he reads are connected in a mysterious way to the events in his life. His thoughts and actions are woven into the fabric of the story, and he begins to realize that he is a principle character in the unfolding story. It is his life and his drama that he is reading, and he is critical as to its outcome. **Seal 7** tells us that our relationship to the book of Revelation is much the same. Christ has written each of us into His Never-Ending story of eternity. The seven trumpeting angels of Seal 7 cannot bring the truth ("show the things that will swiftly come to pass") until we ("His servants") are unlocked. The generation which is broken enough to receive a revelation of Christ, is the generation which will be a part of His revealing (appearing). Revelation must be eaten (10:9) and digested through brokenness (10:10) before it can be prophesied again (10:11). The Elect must have the entire book of Revelation play out in their lives before they will be able to prophesy to others. Revelation is not just a book of end-time events; it is also a Revelation to revive the Elect into an apostolic office.

Woe 3

Trumpet 7 continues Revelation by declaring the victory of Jesus Christ over all the kingdoms of the world; in us and in the natural world. As the final Seals of Revelation are released, the Lord through His Bride will take all authority. He declares that those who overcome to the end will reign with Him! In reality, we will reign _as_ Him, for it will be Christ living in us who will rule the nations. What fellowship with the Lord this represents! This does not mean that the Elect will not see the Lord bodily. We will be His rod to rule the nations.

There is only a small sliver of time from when the Lord's presence takes dominion over the world until the judgment. This is **Woe 3**. The remnant will know that the end is upon them. They will reveal to these inhabitants of Babylon that wrath has come; therefore, their only hope is to call upon the name of the Lord. This message (**Angel 7**) of final destruction will bring anger, fear, and terror to the hearts of man, but it will also bring the great Harvest of man. This is the time of the great **winepress** of God in which He will squeeze the earth and harvest to capture every last drop of Life that is His. Any that are broken (figuratively) by the pressure of the woes _and_ call upon the name of the Lord will be saved from destruction and will qualify to enter the Millennium. This is the final act of Grace.

In **Vial 7,** Christ will take dominion of the kingdoms of this world by removing the veil that separates this world from the second heaven (garden). His presence will then be so evident that His will (which is the Father's) will be done here on earth as it is in heaven. His voice will be heard saying, "it is done." Once the world hears this and sees the rewards (more robes given out) of the Saints, the final separation (great hail) will take place. This is not the judgment itself; it is the separation because of the judgment. Men, for fear of what is in store for them, will quickly fall into Christ's or Satan's camp.

Finally, in **Vial Angel 7,** we see the dawn of the Millennium. We also learn that only those who have been faithful to the end, or those who have yet to be tested, will enter into the Millennium. The rest will not rise again until the end of the Millennium at the White Throne judgment.

THUNDER 7

Seal 7

You are the last seal to be broken.

Christ has now taken us through six seals, but the last seal is more important than all the rest. Here we find that before any of the first six can be broken in the corporate man, they must first be broken in each of us. Since the revelation must be seen as well as heard, our part is simple…eat the book.

> **1** And when he had opened the seventh seal, there was **silence in heaven** about the space of half an hour.

There is a very specific time for the authority of this Revelation. Nothing is going to happen until the seventh seal (us) is broken. The cloud of witnesses is waiting on us!!

> **2** And I saw the **seven angels** which stood before God; and **to them were given seven trumpets**. [could that be you?]
>
> *Since the voice of the trumpet in the first chapter of Revelation is Christ, then this must be His sold out messengers who speak for Him.*

The End is NOW the beginning

In the beginning of this study, we stated that the "revelation of Jesus Christ" could be received both corporately and personally. We have focused on the corporate "parousia", which will close the Church age; but there cannot be a corporate appearing without a personal appearing. For example, many of you feel a strong sense of purpose. You have not only read, but also received. You have seen yourself in the pages of Revelation and are prepared to sound the trumpet as a Holy Messenger of Christ. In this way, you are the beginning and the ending of this book.

Christ is the Alpha and Omega, the beginning and the ending. The final authority of the book of Revelation is… you… being broken. YOU ARE THE FINAL SEAL. You had to be broken (from this world) to manifest enough of Christ's authority to become a Holy Messenger. You, as a broken Seal, open the authority that is used to reveal the revelation of Christ-in-us to the world. This means that if you have come this far in your submission and understanding, you are evidently His. Only Christ can break the Seals. Since you have been broken, Christ, through you, can trumpet the revelation to the world. Therefore, you are the Seal, Angel, and Trumpet; and in verse 3, you are the Vial and Vial Angel. Christ-in-you is the authority for all of Revelation.

> **3** And another angel came and stood at the altar, having a **golden censer** [Divine containers…you]; and there was given unto him much **incense**, that he should offer it with the prayers of all saints upon the golden altar which was before the throne.
>
> *All the saints, (even the cloud of witnesses?) Christ can now appear in a pure dispenser (golden censer)…you. Notice that this all takes place at the altar or place of sacrifice.*

Your sacrifice is what qualifies you (this is seen as being broken in verse Rev. 2:27). You have been given the awesome responsibility of finishing the course paved with the prayers of the Saints. For countless generations Saints have prayed for just this day, and you have been chosen to be one of the 'Vial' Angels.

> **4** And the [1]smoke of the [2]incense, which came with the prayers of the saints, ascended up before God out of the angel's [3]hand.

Smoke is the Glory.

We are a sweet smelling savor (incense) to the Lord. The [1]Glory of [2]Christ-in-us is empowered by the prayers of the Saints, but it is manifest in the [3]righteous acts of the Elect.

> **5** And the angel took the censer, and filled it with fire of the [1]altar, and cast it into the earth: and there were [2]voices, and thunderings, and lightnings, and an [3]earthquake.

Will you be a dispenser? If so, count the cost. To be a 'dispenser' (Vial), you must keep (live by) the words of this book.

The Angel speaks

Rev. 22:9   Then saith he unto me, See thou do it not: **for I am thy fellow servant**, and of thy brethren the prophets, and of them **which <u>keep</u> the sayings** of this book: worship God.

You must let the fire burn away the carnality of your life through [1]sacrifice and obedience to Christ. Then you must lose yourself in the [2]body, so that the corporate appearing can dispense the [3]tribulations of Revelation.

> **6** And the seven angels which had the seven trumpets prepared themselves to sound.

Revelation bumper sticker… IF YOU CAN UNDERSTAND THIS, THE END IS NEAR.

Your invitation…

You are the authority of Revelation in Seal 7. Christ must manifest in an Elect company (the 144,000) to finish His ministry to the world. The things that you have read regarding tribulation, vials, trumpets, plagues, Glory, angels, clouds, etc. have all been about you. Indeed, it is Christ in you, but it is still you. If you do not rise to meet this high calling, the body of Christ will be diminished. You must be the living revelation of Jesus Christ. You must be the fullness of the two witnesses (Spirit and Truth) that comes alive for the entire world to see. The golden oil of Christ's anointing must flow through you. Do not be as the foolish virgins who had no oil for their lamps and were not prepared for the great marriage supper. Your light (Christ' Glory) must shine into the darkness of this world at midnight to show the way to Christ.

Trumpet 7 (last Trumpet)

This completion of the Trumpets is told in Chapter 10 and carried forward into Chapter 11.

Rev. 11:14-19   WOE 3

> **14** The second woe is past; and, behold, the third woe cometh quickly.

The third Woe follows immediately after the second. This is the last terrible event for man. There is just a sliver of time remaining. Once we enter the time of the seventh Thunder, the final Woe (**great hail** on page ix) eradicates the remaining carnality. What the lake of fire and brimstone did not get, the great hail will get now.

> **15** *And the seventh angel sounded; and there were great voices in heaven, saying,* The <u>kingdoms of this world are become the kingdoms of our Lord</u>, *and of his Christ; and he shall reign for ever and ever.*
>
> **Kingdoms in us first.**

Personally: As an Angel-to-be, this Trumpet is important. This Trumpet must happen in us. The kingdoms inside you must become the kingdoms of our Lord. You must be SOLD OUT completely for "the mystery of God to be finished" in you. You will then be ready to start. (See Rev. 10:7 Parenthetical Time to Start page 103.)

Corporately: During the time of the seventh Trumpet, Christ will take world dominion through His chosen people. This is not a worldly "kingdom now" doctrine, which sees political and social dominion by Christ as all-important. Instead, this is to be understood spiritually as another part to the redemption of man. Notice the 'are become' shows that the events follow a defined path. First, Christ will become Lord of all His kingdoms, and then the final Woe will be administered. During the short time between, many will rush to Christ to ward off the third Woe.

> **16** *And the four and twenty elders, which sat before God on their seats, fell upon their faces, and worshipped God,*

All of heaven rejoices as the Lord takes dominion both in us and in the world. Truly, thou art worthy to be praised, mighty God. For your ways are perfect and your judgment righteous. Amen.

> **17** *Saying, We give thee thanks, O Lord God Almighty, which art, and wast, and art to come; because* **thou hast taken to thee thy great power, and hast reigned.**
>
> **18** *And the nations were angry, and thy wrath is come, and the time of the dead, that they should be judged, and that thou shouldest* **give reward unto thy servants** *the prophets, and to the saints, and them that fear thy name, small and great; and shouldest* **destroy them which destroy the earth** *[creation].*

The revelation of Christ's dominion makes those without life angry. The party is over; this is God's day. These people were not part of those in Thunder 6 who were sold out to carnality. They are given one last chance because there is still hope for them. Now that Christ is in control, every last one will have to decide. New Jerusalem, the Wife of the Lamb, is now the authority of the entire world; there is nothing to distract or hide them. This is where their hearts will quickly be revealed. The good news...

Acts 2:20-21
20 The sun shall be turned into darkness, and the moon into blood, before that <u>great</u> and notable day of the Lord come:

21 And it shall come to pass, that **whosoever shall call on the name of the Lord shall be saved.**

...is that any who call upon Him in this last sliver of time will be saved and given another chance to manifest Christ in the Millennium.

> **19** *And the* <u>**temple of God was opened in heaven**</u>, *and there was* **seen in his temple the ark of his testament**: *and there were lightnings, and voices, and thunderings, and an earthquake, and* **great hail** *[on page ix]*

The appearing brought Christ's presence (ark) in a body (lightnings, voices, and thunderings) to the world. His presence will separate (earthquake), through great judgment (great hail), those who are His and those who are not. 'Great hail' means that this is the last great judgment that man will endure. If this does not turn them, nothing will.

We will see into the spiritual realm of God because of Christ in us. Since the world is now His, "His will is done here on earth as it is in heaven." Men's disobedience will quickly be made visible and used to reveal the intents of their hearts.

Review...

The revelation of **Trumpet 7** through **Woe 3** is Judgment Day, the day of **Great Hail**. This is a day when the following happens:

- The final judgment will come for inhabitants of earth and kings of earth. (verse 14)
- The world becomes the Lord's.(verse 15)
- Rewards are given to the Saints, who have not received their robes and have endured to the end. (verse 18)
- The inhabitants of the earth see the end and are angry about it. (verse 18)
- The restoration of all things begins; a new heaven and a new earth are created because Christ has removed the veil that separated these two realms. (verse 19)
- **The last trump...**

This is the last trump spoken of in 1 Cor. 15:52, in which the dead are raised. Indeed, in the parenthetical "end-time" (on page 87), we see the "dead in Christ", who are asleep, rising up and ruling with us during the Millennium. The world is His, and Christ is removing the veil that separated us from the spiritual realm. This is the gathering in the air (garden realm of heaven) of the cloud of witnesses, spoken of in Heb. 12:1. We do not leave, rather the wicked leave.

1 Thes. 4:17
17 Then we which are alive and remain shall be caught up together with them **in the clouds**, to meet the Lord in the air: and so shall we ever be with the Lord.

We will not be literally 'in the air' forever with the Lord; this is a spiritual reference. "Air" is translated from a Greek word that means an area that is only about 20 feet high relative to the surface of the earth. It is also used to describe the spirit world where Satan is prince. A better understanding would be that everyone who is faithful to the end will pierce the veil separating us from the spiritual world.

1 Cor. 15:51-53

51 Behold, I shew you a mystery; We shall not all sleep, but we shall all be changed,

52 In a moment, **in the twinkling of an eye**, <u>at the last trump</u>: for the trumpet shall sound, and the dead shall be raised incorruptible, and we shall be changed.

53 For this corruptible must put on incorruption, and this mortal must put on immortality.

Many use these verses to support the rapture doctrine. However; not only does this event take place at the last trump, but Paul's use of "we" indicates that he expected to participate in this event. This leaves no room for a rapture before or during the tribulation. This is really about the robes that everyone who endures to the end will receive. Even those who are asleep in Jesus will arise to be part of the Millennium.

Angel 7

Rev. 14:18-20

> *18 And another angel came out from the altar, which had **power over fire**; and cried with a loud cry to him that had the sharp sickle, saying, Thrust in thy sharp sickle, and gather the clusters of the vine of the earth; for her **grapes are fully ripe**.*
>
> **Only those who are tried in the fire can be used in the harvest.**

The message of Thunder 7 is that the harvest is all but over. The grapes (fruit of the vine…Saints) are fully ripe, full of life as shown forth in the fruit. That is how these people are different from those in the next verse. These have manifest eternal life by dying to self, which brings the fruit of righteousness. Look back to "the true vine", and see what makes them different.

> *19 And the angel thrust in his sickle into the earth, and gathered **the vine of the earth**, and cast it into the great winepress of the wrath of God.*
>
> **The tribulation of this time will "squeeze" the life out of any left that will respond.**

Now, He gathers up the vine. In the same "true vine" description of Jn. 15:1-5, there is another group associated with the vine…those who have not borne fruit. Normally, they are cut off; but in this case, Christ will give them a last chance because they chose to be part of the vine and did not reject Him. Furthermore, they have not received their promised "natural lifespan", and thus greater grace is given. Since God shuts down time, He will make allowances. This group will have to be tested again at the end of the Millennium.

Ps. 90:10

10 The <u>days of our lives are seventy years</u>; and if by reason of [1]strength they are eighty years, yet their boast is only labor and sorrow; for it is soon cut off, and we fly away. (NKJ)

Of course, sin shortens life, through either generational curses or personal sin; therefore, many die before the appointed seventy years. In the same way, their obedience ([1]strength) may increase their life span.

You usually only gather the grapes, letting the vines stay to make more grapes for next season; but there are no more seasons. The winepress is the final test of how much life is in you ("life" on page 128).

> *20 And the winepress was trodden **without the city**, and **blood** came out of the winepress, even unto the **horse bridles**, by the space of a thousand and six hundred furlongs.*
>
> **This is a work for those who are not of the New Jerusalem. "Horse bridles" is about the obedience needed to get through this phase.**

The purpose of the wine press is to apply enough pressure to squeeze out the last of the redeemable in the earth. The reason that this gathering is not part of the New Jerusalem is because they have received the **mark of the Beast** or worshiped his image. This is why this part of the harvest is taking place "without the city" of the New Jerusalem. The only thing that can keep fruit-bearers from becoming part of the New Jerusalem is the 'mark of the Beast', which prevents them from getting their garments "spotless" and becoming part of the New Jerusalem. There was just too much carnality in them to submit to the body of Christ and become 'complete' in Christ. They will not rule in the Millennium and will be in jeopardy of separation until either the grave or the White Throne. They are like Esau who traded part of the kingdom for this world (bowl of pottage). They were never a part of the "parousia" and thus, New Jerusalem.

The troddening of the press is only for those who have not received robes of righteousness (the New Jerusalem). The horses' bridles tell us what kind of test it is. It is a test of obedience unto life…holding on until the end. If the press can squeeze out any form of Christ life, then you qualify for the Millennium. Grace is not diminished here; Christ's grace is the only way men qualify to have their hearts revealed.

The '1600' is interesting. The significance of the number is unclear, but furlong comes from the Greek 'stadion' or place of contest (where we get the word stadium). It is also a distance associated with a race/course, which is six hundred Greek feet long. The translation "by the space of" is incorrectly applied to the Greek word 'apo' which properly translated should be 'from' or 'of'; it never denotes duration of time or space. Translators probably had a difficult time understanding "blood came out of the winepress to the depth of a horse's bridle <u>from</u> sixteen hundred furlongs", but that is what it actually says. In other words, LIFE COMES FROM RUNNING THE RACE UNTIL THE END. For those who finish the course (and do not reject Him), there is a prize of Christ's grace, which gains them access to the Millennium.

The focus of verse 20 is not the blood, but the bridle. The horses' bridles speak of the obedience. In James 3:3 we read, "Behold, we put bits in the horses' mouths, that they may obey us; and we turn about their whole body."

This verse is the only other place in the NT where "bit" is used. The disobedient will stay in the press; the obedient will be broken and gain access to the Millennium.

The overall message of the Revelation **Angel 7** is that God is going to reap the earth. The only way you can be excluded from this great tribulation is to be a part of the Bride without spot or blemish. The final wrath of God is to show God's patience and love. His plan ensures that even those who have worn the mark of the Beast but who have repented at that last moment and received even the smallest amount of Christ's life will have the opportunity to grow in Him.

Vial 7
Rev. 16:17-21

> **17** And the seventh angel poured out his vial into the **air**; and there came a **great voice out of the temple** of heaven, from the throne, saying, **It is done**.

The story of the Vials concludes with the pouring out into the air or spiritual heaven. (This is also a reference to the 'air' of 1 Thes. 4:17.) All things both in heaven and in earth have been purified. Christ's second, three and one half year ministry is finished, and He ends this segment of His ministry with the same statement as He ended the first: "IT IS DONE" (John 19:30).

Study Help
The Restoration

The Vials are poured out progressively on the: 1>earth, 2>sea, 3>rivers & fountains, 4>sun, 5>seat of Beast, 6>Euphrates, 7>air. This is also the path that restoration must take: from inside out. God starts with the intent of our heart and finishes by removing Satan from the spiritual garden.

This is the fall in reverse, a path back to the garden. Look at the vials in reverse to see how sin caused the fall of this world and the Church. Now, you can see why Christ began and finished His work as He did.

Vial / Type / Satan's *plan*

7   **Air** – *Spiritual Realm* – Sin begins with the snake in the Garden...

6   **Euphrates** –*Sources for worldliness* – then, *sin enters the world. The sin of the fallen earth is nourished by lies...*

5   **Seat of Beast** –*Worldliness* – then, *sin encompasses the world. Worldliness makes a throne for Satan. He can rule the world because he is the father of lies. Therefore, all that partake of this world partake of him.*

4   **Sun** – *Church* – then, *sin enters the kingdom because the world enters the Church.*

3   **Rivers and Fountains** –*Sources of the heart of the Church* – then, *the Church bodies and individuals begin to feed from the world instead of the Lord. Worldly leaders begin to rise and soften the Church to sin.*

2   **Sea** – *Heart of the Church* – then, *the heart of the Church becomes filled with the Beast because Christian's hearts are filled with the world.*

1   **Earth** – *Carnality* – then, *sin is acceptable and no longer even noticed.*
These are the seven steps by which sin/Satan came to reside in Christians (remember Peter's rebuke). Now Christ will start in us and bring forth the Seven Thunders which will ultimately restore us and the Garden!

The seventh Vial shows Satan's vessels removed from the earth while the final test is being completed through the perfecting wrath of God. God pours out His wrath to accomplish His perfect plan for man's redemption. He has also cleared the Garden of snakes (so to speak), and He will meet us there.

Personally speaking, if we can operate from the throne room, then our perfection is finished; therefore, we are Angels of God. If you refer to the Parenthetical of Angels (page 101), the last verse states that no man can enter into the temple until these last plagues are finished. Earlier in that Parenthetical, we saw that one of the things that qualifies a person as an Angel is his ability to operate from the temple. Therefore, you need to see all the Vials poured out in your life if you want to be a Holy Messenger of the revelation of Jesus Christ.

> **18** And there were **voices, and thunders, and lightnings**; and there was a great earthquake, such as was not since men were upon the earth, so mighty an earthquake, and so great.

The final separation is brought about by obedience to Christ-in-us (voices, thunders, lightnings) and a great shaking (earthquake) of all remaining carnality. The Elect will give instruction on how to "call upon the name of the Lord and be saved for any who have ears to hear."

> **19** And the great **city was divided into three parts**, and the cities of the nations fell: and great Babylon came in remembrance before God, to give unto her the cup of the wine of the fierceness of his wrath.

Payday... either reward or fierce wrath. The "parts" are the citizens of New Jerusalem who have not yet received their reward (robe of righteousness). If you are not part of the New Jerusalem, which will rule during the Millennium, then it is too late. The best you can hope for is a robe of righteousness at the White Throne. All of this takes place just before the great wine press, which is "the fierceness of His wrath." Now that the disobedient are all part of Babylon, the great squeeze of the winepress begins and the last separation of sheep and goats can take place. Whatever the manifestation of this pressure, it must be great.

> **20** And every island fled away, and the mountains were not found.
> **'Islands'** are any form of individualism, and **'mountains'** are the false religions. Both of these will be completely gone by the end of the Thunder.

Christ will be all in all. This also speaks of the individualism in us that must be removed before the Angels can come forward.

> **21** And there fell upon men a great **hail** out of heaven, every stone about the weight of a talent: and men blasphemed God [1]because of the plague of the hail; for the plague thereof was exceeding great.
>
> [1]**Man is aware of the source of wrath associated with Woe 3.**

He uses a 'talent' to describe the weight of the hail that brings perfection. A talent is ninety-three pounds! That should take care of anyone who needs wrath. Talent is a play on words to show that the spiritual pouring out will mostly be through mammon (not ninety-three pound ice cubes). Expect a world collapse.

See Great hail page ix. This is the judgment of man; some call it the judgment seat of Christ. If you are not chosen as part of His kingdom of Heaven here, then ultimate separation awaits you at the White Throne.

Vial 7 is poured out in the spiritual realm. In some ways, we can say that all Revelation vials are about pouring out in the spiritual. However, Vial 7 has special spiritual focus because it is here that the spiritual begins to manifest in the natural. The veil of carnality that separated man from the Garden of Eden is about to be removed. In Thunder 6, we saw that the Beast and false prophets were removed. This means the lies have stopped; and **Truth** begins to reign. Without the lies to dim our spiritual vision, we begin to see in Spirit and Truth (two witnesses). Christ has been waiting for just this moment, for the realm of His Spirit to be visible in the realm of the natural; thus He says, "it is done."

His presence (verse 18), now even more profound, really forces a separation. It also causes those who have never received their robes to go on to completion; then they will be given their robes of righteousness.

Vial Angel 7

'Epilogue for the Angels'

Rev. 20:1-5

> **1** And I saw an angel come down from heaven, **having the key of the bottomless pit** and a great chain in his hand.
>
> **See 'key' page x and 'pit' page iii. Christ-in-us has the key to the hearts of men. Christ through the Eagles will lock Satan away in the hearts of the ones ruled during the Millennium.**
>
> **2** And he laid hold on the dragon, that old serpent, which is the Devil, and Satan, and bound him a thousand years,

This is not literal, but represents Satan being bound in the hearts of those who will be tested at the end of the Millennium. Christ is not yet manifested as their Lord; Satan is still in their hearts but unable to lie to them, not having a manifest vessel to work through. What a righteous plan of second chance grace!

> **3** And cast him into the **bottomless pit**, and shut him up, and set a **seal** upon him, that he should deceive the nations no more, **till the thousand years should be fulfilled**: and after that he must be loosed a little season.

He is locked away in the hearts of those who will be ruled. Ultimately, their seals must be broken. This will show that Satan is not the one that made the carnal… carnal. There will still be those who disobey even in the millennium.

> **4** And I saw thrones, and they sat upon them, and judgment was given unto them: and I saw the **souls** [commentary on page 127] of them that were **beheaded** for the witness of Jesus, and for the word of God, and which had not worshipped the Beast, neither his image, **neither had received his mark upon their foreheads, or in their hands; and they lived and reigned with Christ a thousand years.**

These persons died to self (beheaded) and are counted worthy to rule with Christ. However, this also means that those who were sold out to carnality and pride are not proper role models for the Millennium, even though they have eternal life. Christ wants His best examples for teachers; therefore, He will use only the ones never soiled by the Harlot or marred by carnal, man-made worship. The implication is clear: those who are marred by the Harlot will never fully mature in the love of Christ even though they endure to the end. This is a warning to all that pursue religion instead of Love.

> **5** But the **rest of the dead lived not again** until the thousand years were finished. This is the first resurrection.

This is called the 'first resurrection'; so somebody must come through the veil. The ones who come through the veil must fit the qualifications of verse four and are deserving of this honor. Like Paul, they ran the race and deserve to rule (crown of righteousness). Unfortunately, some will not be brought back for the same reason that some did not get to stay; they were marred by the Beast. They also obtained life through the 'horns of clemency'. They were the ones who had spotted garments or battled with the Lamb. Sorry, no Millennium. They will join the rest of us later at the White Throne, but not until the final temptation is complete and all have had opportunity to test their faithfulness.

The message in **Vial Angel 7** is to be understood by those mature enough to hear it. Be careful with this message of grace; it could deny some their portion if promoted as the gospel. It could be used as an excuse to hold off dying to self, and thereby jeopardize their chances. Man is to know that final judgment is serious. Last minute calling upon His name is a dangerous game. The final door will be shut without warning (See parable of 10 virgins). Even if you could time your redemption, you would lose the opportunity to be rewarded with the greater measure of Christ's presence, which is the treasure of all treasures that will last an eternity.

Conclusion to Thunder Seven

Here we see that the purpose of all of Revelation is to complete God's plan for man to return to fellowship with Him in the Garden, reuniting the Father with His family who will never again rebel and leave Him.

It takes time to surrender and die to self, allowing Christ to take dominion over your life. We are promised 70 years, but the last generation is cut short, like the fig tree dropping its untimely figs. Therefore, God will give those who come in at the end of time a last chance to die to themselves during the Millennium. Those who have been redeemed under grace but have not yet manifested Christ will be ruled and taught by the Kings and Priests of New Jerusalem for the remainder of the thousand years. At the end, Satan will be allowed to come up out of their hearts and tempt them. It will be their chance to overcome and obtain their weight of Glory or be deceived, as were their forefathers.

The end of Revelation brings the final judgment, but it also brings ultimate victory. Christ will be Lord of all, and we will reign with Him. God has always been a God of grace, and He finishes with grace. Even those who came to Christ out of fear will be allowed another chance. One thousand years may seem unfair, compared to the generations that preceded the last generation, but this is not true. Without a tempter like Satan, these redeemed will not be fully tested until the final test. It is tribulation that brings strength of relationship with Christ. These will not have tribulation, because there will be no more tears or suffering. It may sound good, but these redeemed will have a more difficult time than those who preceded them. Obedience will be their teacher.

Behold the Bridegroom, Come out to meet Him

Section VII The Epilogue

This last chapter of the book of Revelation, which is also the last chapter of the Word of God, reiterates the promise of blessing given in the first verse of the book to those that will keep this prophecy. It also promises His quick return.

Revelation 22:7-21

22:7 Behold, I come quickly: blessed is he that __keepeth__ the sayings of the prophecy of this book.

You are without excuse. You now know the truth. The question is what will you do with it? Are you going to get ready or will you reject it?

For the second time in Revelation, He makes the promise that if you will keep the sayings of this book, you will be blessed. That means that Revelation is more than just a book of events; it is designed to be an operator's manual for the last generation. It should provide a pathway to a greater "Revelation" of Christ in your life. It is important for you to see this book at work in your heart. We have said it many times: Christ must be revealed in a body (personal and corporate). Use it to see the hindrances in your life which prevent the manifestation of the fullness of Christ. Then allow Christ to destroy them with the brightness of His appearing.

22:8 And I John saw these things, and heard them. And when I had heard and seen, I fell down to worship before the feet of the angel which shewed me these things.

Those Angels must be really sold out. Christ in them must make them look supernatural. John shows that he is overwhelmed by the message, and he mistakes the holy messenger for an angelic creature. As Christ is revealed in power through us, we must be careful to "do all for the Glory of God."

22:9 Then saith he unto me, See thou do it not: for I am thy fellowservant, and of thy brethren the prophets, and of them which keep the sayings of this book: worship God.

He is just one of us! Wouldn't you like to be one of these Angels? You can be if you keep the sayings of this book. You might even be the one who has to step out of time to deliver this to John. There may be more truth to that than you realize. The Angel states that he is keeping the sayings of this book, and John has not even written it yet. It sounds like this Angel could well be one of the readers of this book.

22:10 __And__ he saith unto me, Seal not the sayings of the prophecy of this book: for the time is at hand.

If, by now, you have not felt the stir in your spirit to be part of this, we cannot imagine why. What are you waiting for? The time is at hand, no one has ever before understood as you do now. "To whom much is given, much is required."

The phrase, "time is at hand", was revealed as meaning that you show what you believe by what you set yourself to do. Look at the verse below to support what that means. If you truly believe the revelation as it has been described, then you will focus on letting God prepare you.

22:11 He that is unjust, let him be unjust still: and he which is filthy, let him be filthy still: and he that is righteous, let him be righteous still: and he that is holy, let him be holy still.

Another translation from the original Greek is, "he that is unjust will hereafter unjustly act." Your heart cannot be veiled by your actions. Instead, we should examine ourselves in light of the revelation of Jesus Christ and let our actions tell us just what is in our hearts. No more excuses, "Lord search my heart and my ways and reveal to me who I really am."

22:12 And, behold, I come quickly; and __my reward is with me__, to give every man according as his work shall be.

Your works determine how He will interact with you. Glory or judgment - you choose! He is our reward and being open to more of Him makes us open to more blessing.

22:13 I am Alpha and Omega, the beginning and the end, the first and the last.

He started it in Genesis and finished it in Revelation. He starts it in our lives as our Savior and ends it as our Eternal Life.

22:14 Blessed are they that do his commandments, that they may have right to the tree of life, and may __enter in through the gates__ into the city.

Do His commandments, and you, too, can eat of the tree of eternal Life and enter the 'pearl of great price' gate into the Wife of the Lamb. However, selling out is the price you must pay to enter these gates.

If you have eyes to see, then you will see that we cannot ignore the demand on us to be obedient if we expect to obtain eternal life. The Blood of Christ qualifies us as spiritual Jews to come into the temple and give sacrifice; but if, like the "Rich Man" of the Bible, if we fail to be obedient to the sacrifice, then hell awaits us as well. Jesus must be Lord as well as Savior.

22:15 For without are dogs, and sorcerers, and whoremongers, and murderers, and idolaters, and whosoever loveth and maketh a lie.

Now you know that there is no gray area. You are either in or out. Your willingness to do His commandments allows you to enter. Do not believe that you can come in with unrighteousness.

> **22:16** *I Jesus have sent mine angel to testify unto you these things in the Churches. I am the root and the offspring of David, and the bright and **morning star**. [on page xviii]*

Revelation 2:28 says that He will give us the 'morning star' if we overcome and keep His works. Then He is telling us that if we overcome (ourselves) and 'tend to' (Greek definition) His works, we will receive Him. Is this not a Christ-in-us scripture? This surely does not fit a 'sinner's prayer' approach. Look at the conditions He places before us so that we can have Him. This is the message that He wants spoken to the Churches. "I will give you more of me that you might overcome the earth."

> **22:17** *And the Spirit and the bride say, Come. And let him that heareth say, Come. And let him that is athirst come. And whosoever will, let him take the water of life freely.*

The invitation is made…will you be a part or will you be the target? The Spirit of Christ beckons His friends to come and receive Revelation (water of life) that becomes life to all that come. The question implied, "Are you thirsty?" The blessed are those who hunger and thirst after righteousness for they shall be filled.

> **22:18** *For I testify unto every man that heareth the words of the prophecy of this book, If any man shall add unto these things, God shall add unto him the plagues that are written in this book:*

So where was the anti-Christ, the helicopters, Russia, the fancy dinner in heaven, or the rapture? The revelation you have just read is Bible explaining Bible. This is not 'doctrines of men' trying to manipulate scripture to prove personal doctrines. Remember, this book is designed to be the revelation of Jesus Christ. Do other interpretations seek to reveal Him? Adding worldly interpretations or personal doctrines will keep people from the blessing offered in Revelation. This is the spiritual word of God, not a Science Fiction novel.

> **22:19** *And if any man shall take away from the words of the book of this prophecy, God shall take away his part out of the book of life, and out of the holy city, and from the things which are written in this book.*

Recently, a famous Revelation teacher said on his broadcast that we must take the book of Revelation literally because the "Bible means what it says and says what it means." Sounds good, right? He went on to tell how the four horses of Revelation represented different countries. Why could he not see that his own explanations were symbolic and not literal? The reason is simple; he offered a worldlier, natural view of Revelation, which he believes means it is more literal. This is not so. He had to add to the types from a "natural mind" perspective. There is no foundation to his teaching. Someone else could come along and declare these horses are *other* countries. Who would be right? Instead, we use the "line upon line" interpretation of looking to the Word for our definitions. Indeed, some readers of this book may disagree with interpretations of certain types. Praise God, as long as they use the scriptures to validate their claim, then they are open to greater revelation still to come. We applaud all line upon line interpretations.

This verse makes it clear that to take away from this book is a curse. How do you take away from the things that are spiritual - by natural interpretations?

> **22:20** *He which testifieth these things saith, Surely I come quickly. Amen. Even so, come, Lord Jesus.*
>
> **22:21** *The grace of our Lord Jesus Christ be with you all. Amen.*

The Epilogue

Now that you know the truth, listen to the words of Jesus…I COME QUICKLY, to bless those (verses 7, 12) who keep the saying of this book. If you want to be part of the truth spoken of in this book, then you must be prepared to prophesy this book to the world (verse 10). He declares that you must be obedient to have life or to become part of His Bride/Wife.

The last of the book is an invitation to go to the churches to show Jesus to them. It is also an invitation to follow the words of this prophecy so that you will not be as those left on the outside of the marvelous city of the Bride. He does not want you to be taken by surprise when you see the door shut. If you choose to ignore what you have heard and try to remove the pull He has placed upon your heart, He will take it away from you. If you try to add tickling doctrines to diminish the demand He has placed on your life, He will add the plagues. This means, if you will not heed the message NOW, then do not be surprised if the wrath falls *on* you instead of *through* you.

If at this point you still do not believe what has been revealed in this book, but love Jesus Christ and desire Him, then know that we still embrace you as brothers and sisters in Christ. If you have been offended by some of the definitions or interpretations of scripture, then try at least to believe that the heart's desire behind this message is that you come to have Christ revealed in your life and that you will choose Him. May the Love of Jesus Christ shine richly in your life.

Supplement I: Parentheticals

A Parenthetical is an amplifying or explanatory word taken from the remaining chapters and verses of the book of Revelation. Some of the Parentheticals make references to the events that lead up to the tribulation, while some continue the story into the Millennium.

After Thunder 6

Are you looking forward to a future time with Christ? Most doctrines teach us that our heavenly home is a wonderful place of eternal bliss, and it is. However, our conceptions may hold more death than life.

To illustrate, let us review an experience that occurred recently with a group of youth. They were involved in a discussion about the end time. When asked if they were looking forward to heaven, most raised their hands. However, when asked to be really honest about the things they looked forward to, most stumbled and stammered. Their 'pat' religious answers evaporated under examination. When asked what about the end-time they found unattractive, some said they did not want the end to come before they had a chance to live (not sinfully, just naturally). They want to grow to adulthood and experience life with a wife or husband and children. They felt the end-time would rob them of the fulfillment of life. The adults in the group were more timid about their responses, but they admitted to a melancholy about their 'heavenly' home. What is wrong with this picture? What about the image of our heavenly home makes people reluctant to face eternity? If the end-time is only appealing to preachers and people worn out by this world, could it really be paradise? Paradise with Jesus should be glorious, something everyone desperately desires.

In the following Parentheticals, God will reveal truths which will cause you to yearn for paradise. After the young people heard this message, many rededicated their lives and focus to Christ, not wanting to miss any of the events that will take place after the tribulation has past. God is about to open the doors of paradise and let you peek in and see what He has in store for you. If you are not interested in reading all the supporting scriptures, read the summary at the end and hear the story of the Parenthetical. Since many of the Parentheticals are about the same thing but with a different 'type' for illumination, then some of the summaries will sound similar. It is up to you to go back into the study text to see the details. What God is doing is giving us the same story, but He is turning it three-dimensionally. Now we are able to experience it from all angles and not miss a thing.

Parenthetical 1

The End of Time/Millennium overview

Immediately after the seven seals have been unlocked, the seven trumpets sounded, and the seven vials poured out upon the earth; then the Elect will rule with Jesus as the heavenly city for the remainder of the one thousand years. This group will be discussed in Parenthetical 4, the New Jerusalem. Yet, there is another group of people in the Millennium: those who are ruled by Jesus through the Elect. This Parenthetical is about the events that occur during this time to those who enter the Millennium by the grace of God. They cried out to the Lord at the last moment and out of unfathomable love and faithfulness to His word, He gives them another chance to receive Him during the Millennium. They were grafted into the vine but had no time to bear fruit. "Calling upon the name of the Lord" qualifies them for life in the Millennium, but not for the New Jerusalem. They must wait until the end of the one thousand years before they can be tested to determine if they qualify to receive robes of righteousness.

Satan is locked in the hearts of these ruled for the balance of the one thousand years, to be loosed at the end for a time of testing. References to Gog and Magog tell us that the test Satan provides at the end of the Millennium will follow the pattern of ages past, urging men to offer up a new 'golden calf' to worship. Just as they did at the base of Mount Horeb, men will turn their backs on God again in spite of the great deliverance He brought to them. In the end, God will prevail and destroy all who fail the test. During the White Throne Judgment, those who have never received Christ will enter into everlasting punishment; those who have received Christ but never received their robe will get their glorified bodies.

Life during the Millennium may be different than what you may have thought. It is very similar to what we see today; however, it will be without the influence of Satan.

Revelation Chapter 20:6-15

> **20:6** Blessed and holy is he that hath part in the **first resurrection:** on such the second death hath no power, but they shall be priests of God and of Christ, and **shall reign with him a thousand years.**

Since this is called a <u>resurrection,</u> then there will be those who are raised from the grave. They are the dead-in-Christ who sleep or the Saints who pass through the grave (i.e. Paul, etc.) They suffered and stayed obedient to Christ until <u>their</u> end (verse 6 below), so that He was <u>in</u> them. The only Saints not coming to life now are those marred by the Harlot / Beast. They are not worthy to reign, but are worthy of a measure of Glory. This verse speaks of the ones who, outside of the 'parousia' (See page 12), manifested Christ's presence and did not receive the mark of the Beast or worship his image.

Worthy to Rule?

2 Tim. 2:11-12

11 It is a faithful saying: For if we be **dead with him,** we shall also **live with him**:

12 **If we suffer, we shall also reign with him**: if we deny him, he also will deny us:

Heb. 3:6

6 But Christ as a son over his own house; whose house are we, **if** we hold fast the confidence and the rejoicing of the hope firm **unto the end**.

The second death is at the end of the one thousand years (See page xvi). It is called the second death because those who died without the life of Christ in them are awakened to consciousness again just to die the death of separation (lake of fire).

> *20:7 And when the thousand years are expired, Satan shall be loosed out of his prison,*

This is the place where Satan will be loosed from the hearts of men to tempt them. It will prove whether they "called upon the Lord" from fear or from a true desire to know Him.

> *20:8 And shall go out to deceive the nations which are in the four quarters of the earth, Gog and Magog, to gather them together to battle: the number of whom is as the sand of the **sea**.*

Greek: Gog = mountain (page xii) / Magog = covering. At the end of the one thousand years, many will be manifested as an enemy of God. They are those who reject God's will for their own.

The Golden Calf

Gog and Magog represent a place of worship (as a covering), like a religion. Even the reference to the 'sea' speaks of the corporate carnal heart again. When Moses was on the mountain for a long time, the people became restless, and they created their own religion (Golden Calf). By the end of the one thousand years, with Christ's physical appearance not yet a reality to them, men will get restless. It is easy to see how they may follow the same pattern and choose disobedience instead of surrender. Satan will again be loosed, through their disobedience, to do his best to convince mankind that they can live their lives their way. The lies will flow again, and it looks like many (sand of the sea) will be deceived.

> *20:9 And they went up on the breadth of the earth, and **compassed the camp of the saints** about, and the beloved city: and **fire** came down from God out of heaven, and devoured them.*

These deceived ones are everywhere. They accost the Saints with questions, criticism, and cynicism in a manner very similar to the way in which the Hebrew children harassed Moses about his commandments from God. They challenge Christ's authority (New Jerusalem) and probably ask, "Why must these people rule over us?" God quickly answers with fire from heaven. As before, this is the truth, revealed by their carnality, used by God as a perfecting fire. Just the fact that they will not submit shows that they are unworthy of the kingdom of Heaven.

> *20:10 And the devil that deceived them was cast into the **lake of fire** and brimstone, where the beast and the false prophet are, and shall be tormented day and night for **ever and ever**.*

This is Satan being cast into the lake of fire. Whatever you believe this to be, it isn't where anyone would want to be. It is separation from our Lord, and it is eternal.

> *20:11 And I saw a great **white throne**, and him that sat on it, from whose face the earth and the heaven fled away; and there was found no place for them.*

The kingdom of Heaven is fully in place. The intimacy with Christ removed the distinction of heaven and earth. The garden is back in place. We will all be gathered together in the garden with the Glorified Resurrected Jesus Christ in person, the Son of God with His friends. Yet one more judgment must take place.

> *20:12 And I saw the dead, small and great, stand before God; and the books were opened: and **another book** was opened, which is the book of life: and the **dead** were judged out of those things which were written in the books, according to their works.*

Books - plural. There is the book of life; however, there are the books of works that judge the dead, who already have the life of Christ in them. These books establish the weight of Glory for the righteous for all eternity. This group differs from the group in verse 13 because that group has "given up", meaning they have been into the grave but under Christ's covering. This group came out of the Millennium with Life; they passed the test and will be judged according to their works.

> *20:13 And the **sea** gave up the dead which were in it; and **death and hell** delivered up the dead which were in them: and they were judged every man according to their works.*

This verse is about those who have not been through the Millennium but deserve a glorified body. Some of the dead came out of the heart of the Church but were "marred by the Harlot" and unable to receive their robes or rule in the Millennium. Now, they receive their reward. Some came from the Old Testament hell, which was a holding place for those who slept in the bosom of Abraham. Some scholars believe that this 'Sheol' was replaced by paradise until the new heaven and earth is established.

> *20:14 And death and hell were cast into the lake of fire. This is the second death.*

There is no more need for death or hell. This is the second death (second death page xvi).

> **20:15** And whosoever was not found written in the book of life was cast into the lake of fire.

This is the judgment of the damned: short and simple. He who has Christ has life… (he who does not, does not!). Notice that the lake is no longer referred to as fire and brimstone, now it just burns.

Matt. 3:10 And now also the axe is laid unto the root of the **trees**: therefore every tree which bringeth not forth good fruit is hewn down, and **cast into the fire**.

END TIME PROPHECY OF ISAIAH

Isaiah contains much of the information pertaining to the millennium and no study of this time would be complete without a study of these scriptures

Isaiah 65:17-25

> **17** "Behold, **I will create new heavens and a new earth**. The former things will not be remembered, nor will they come to mind.

> ***We are the new heavens and earth (See Parenthetical 'Bride', page 97 and 'new heavens", page 98).***

Notice that the word 'heavens' is plural, which is a direct reference to the Bride; yet, the word 'earth' is singular. As the kingdom of Heaven pours through us onto this earth during the Millennium, it restores the earth to the Garden again. In Gen. 3:17 God said, "cursed is the ground for thy sake." Adam's sin cursed the earth; therefore, the righteousness of Jesus Christ will restore it through His Saints.

> **18** But be glad and rejoice forever in what I will create, for I will create Jerusalem to be a delight and its **people a joy**.

As the New Jerusalem, we are at total peace and joy, a visible embodiment of the two witnesses (Spirit and Truth)…in His presence is fullness of joy.

> **19** I will rejoice over Jerusalem and **take delight in my people**; the sound of weeping and of crying will be heard in it no more.

"New Jerusalem are 'my people', and they will weep or cry 'no more'." Those who are part of New Jerusalem will no longer be subject to 'natural' emotions, but will take on the character of Christ. This is because we will understand as He understands, "knowing even as we are known."

> **20** "Never again will there be in it an **infant** who lives but a few days, or an old man who does not live out his years; he who dies at a hundred will be thought a mere youth; he who fails **to reach a hundred will be considered accursed.**

There will be deaths and births during the Millennium. Remember, there are two groups: the rulers and the ruled. Those without glorified bodies will be subject to death, but only through disobedience. Otherwise, the perfected, restored creation and the glorious, healing presence of Christ will protect them. However, as in the case of Ananias or Sapphira, if you deceive or rebel against the "rod of iron" with which New Jerusalem rules, you will be subject to physical death. There is no excuse for anyone who dies during this time. There will be no disease or acts of violence. It is only the evil nature of the heart that will kill someone during this time. If any of the ruled do not reach one hundred years of age, it will be because of a major 'heart' condition. This is a time of joy and peace, a day of plenty. It is a wonder that anyone would want to disobey God to follow a selfish path that would cause death. Yet, that is exactly what Adam and Eve did.

> **21** They will build houses and dwell in them; they will plant vineyards and eat their fruit.

We will be engaged in normal activities. This is very difficult for some to hear who have a natural vision of heavenly types still filling their mind. They heard that 'mansions' were being prepared for the Elect and believed them to be houses. But the dwelling places are those with Christ-in-us. Heb. 3:6 says, "But Christ as a son over <u>his own house; whose house are we</u>, if we hold fast the confidence and the rejoicing of the hope firm unto the end."

What will happen after the Millennium? Perhaps there may be another place prepared. But ask yourself this question: if God's plan is perfect, and He built the Garden for man to live in and to commune with Him in, why would He move the place of eternal dwelling to a different place? Would it not be more likely that as soon as the final judgment is over and His family of man is perfected through Jesus Christ that Jesus will return the kingdom of Heaven back to the Father, fulfilling the original plan of the Master Designer? This would be perfect restoration, where we meet Him and "so shall we ever be with Him." (1 Thes. 4:17)

There is less scriptural support for a cloudy, mystical place of final dwelling than there is for the view that what God created initially, He will want to see fulfilled. He has planned for a family that will never leave Him again. Praise God!

Joel 2:3
3   A fire devoureth before them; and behind them a flame burneth: <u>the land is as the garden of Eden before them</u>…

The "is as" is added in the translation. Land can be translated as 'the whole earth'. The translators must have had a hard time with the statement, "the earth is the Garden of Eden before them." The Cherubim and flaming sword that the Lord put to keep watch over the Garden direct the way back to the Garden. We must have a face to face relationship (Cherubim) with Christ in the most Holy Place. Letting the truth of Christ-in-us kill us does this. In addition, Joel called the people of this time those of 'the years of many generations', thus showing that they will go right on living.

> **22** No longer will they build houses and others live in them, or plant and others eat. For as the days of a tree, so will be the days of my people; my chosen ones will long enjoy the works of their hands.

The tree referred to here is the tree of Jer. 17:8, which was planted by the river of life and will always bear fruit. What a wonderful picture of the Millennium: a place that is always bearing fruit. This is because the one who robs and destroys will not be there to hinder.

> **23** They will not toil in vain or bear children doomed to misfortune; for they will be a people blessed by the LORD, they and their descendants with them.

Even the Elect will bear children during the millennium. The children will be without the sin nature, because the curse is gone out of the Elect. However, only those who have not been through the grave can come into the Millennium as married and have children. The marriage covenant is still in place for them and God will honor it. Only death frees us of the covenant of marriage. Jesus says that in the resurrection (passing through the veil of death), "they neither marry nor are given in marriage." Those who have been through the veil of death will not marry in the Millennium nor have a desire to.

Based on the Word Paul got from the Lord on marriage, we should keep true to the marriage covenant and not marry even after being widowed. If we stay true to one mate throughout life and death, we will have some form of the 'made one' relationship even in the resurrection. Paul balances this issue with practical advice saying, "it is better to marry than burn." Christ is the most important issue forever; so if you are in danger of losing a relationship with your spouse or Christ, you better choose losing that eternal position with your spouse. For those of you who are divorced do not worry; Christ will be all you ever need.

> **24** Before they call I will answer; while they are still speaking I will hear.

You do not get any closer than this. This shows the intimacy of our relationship with the Father during the Millennium.

> **25** The wolf and the lamb will feed together, and the lion will eat straw like the ox, but dust will be the serpent's food. They will neither harm nor destroy on all my holy mountain," says the LORD. (NIV)

This refers back to the first verse on the new heavens and earth, where creation is restored back to the Garden state. At the end of the one thousand years, Satan will again be allowed to feed on the carnality of the ruled; but he will not be able to harm the resurrected rulers.

Parenthetical 2

The Harlot

In the Revelation letters to the seven churches, we see the reference several times to the "synagogue of Satan" among you (page xviii). This Parenthetical will allow us to review the reasons and methods Satan uses to infiltrate the Church. Satan's desire has always been to stop God's plan to restore His family to the Garden through the lives of the Elect. Therefore, Satan's target has never been the general Church, but rather the Elect who are birthed from the Church (See **Man-Child on page 92**).

Satan, as the great liar, is always trying to counterfeit the works of God. The end-time is no exception. Satan attempts to duplicate every step that God takes. For example, the progression of events laid out by God in the tribulation is: 1) the Spirit of Christ being birthed in His Elect so that He can prepare for Himself a Bride Church; 2) the Bride Church "appearing," as she consummates the relationship with Christ; and finally, 3) Christ appearing (parousia) and harvesting the earth as the New Jerusalem. The pattern Satan uses to counterfeit God and stumble man, is similar: 1) he impregnates the Church with a spirit of antichrist through worldliness that is accepted by the Church. For almost two thousand years, the earth (carnality) has infiltrated the Church through the disobedience of the children of God. 2) When tribulation begins, the spirit of antichrist will be revealed through Christian hypocrisy. Their love of this world will visibly exceed their love of God. Now that Satan is entrenched in the Church, the Harlot is born. She has a beast nature and is fully recognized by her carnality (**mark of beast** on page xi). Look at the Sadducees and Pharisees to see this same manifestation. These are a people with spirits of religion and pride dominating their lives and veiling their heart. She (the harlot nature) is made visible to the Saints as the Beast that rises up from her (their) heart. 3) The Beast/Harlot Christians will then provide a rallying point for those like-minded rejecters of the Bride. This will come in the form of carnal doctrines, apathy, false teachings, and even religious anger. The Harlot veils men's minds to the revelatory word of God, thus revelation will be the *sword that becomes a plowshare* and separates out the wheat and tares...

Spirit of Christ > Bride > New Jerusalem "OR"
Spirit of Antichrist > Harlot/Beast > Babylon

Satan has a plan to destroy the Bride before she can threaten him. To do this he will bring forth his Elect from the Harlot. These are false prophets who believe that they do service to God. They are blind to the fact that they serve the Beast/Harlot, and they believe that the true Elect are the enemies of God. They will judge the outward appearance and not the heart and they are deceived by the edifices and religious traditions that support the Harlot. This will be a new day with new ways. The Beast will take advantage of the breaking down of traditions and the call for a conse-crated life through religious spirits, who will bring con-demnation and disdain on the people of God. This may be nothing new, but in this case Satan knows his time is short, and he will accuse and attack with a desperate nature. Men under the influence of the Beast will exhibit more of a Beast nature than ever before. Consequently, they regard with disdain the zeal of the Elect. The false prophets will do battle with the Lamb in hopes of destroying them. The Elect meet the attack of these kings of the earth and false prophets with love. They answer their lies with truth, and darkness with light. Even though these kings of the earth are given power over God's Elect in the first dispensation, it only helps the Elect die more to self and provide more of the Glory that will ultimately bring victory over the ene-mies of Christ.

Watch the following transformation as Rev. Chapter 12 shows how the Elect is born, and the Church (without the Elect) gives access to the Beast/Harlot.

Revelation Chapter 12

12:1 And there appeared a great wonder in heaven; a **woman** *[on page xx] clothed with the* **sun***, and the* **moon** *under her feet, and upon her head a crown of* **twelve stars***:*

This is the Church from a spiritual perspective (in all her Glory); this is the way Christ created her. The sun, moon, and stars show the path of Glory obtained within her (Eagle, man, calf, see page 34). The twelve stars are the apostolic authority (crown) given to her by Jesus Christ. Jesus gave the kingdom to his apostles (Luke 22:29).

12:2 And she being with child cried, travailing in birth, and pained to be delivered.

Verses 1 and 2 represent the first of three marvelous signs (Greek 'semeion') of Revelation (marvelous signs page xii) given for the Elect to see. It occurs even before the gathering of the 144,000. Today, we are already seeing the Elect come into awareness that there is more to their relationship with Jesus Christ than what they have received in traditional, denominational church services. They begin to hunger for more of Jesus. They begin to question the traditional notions of what it means to "know" Jesus.

At first, their churches will embrace the new Spirit of Christ now evident among them. Then the Word of truth begins to challenge traditional doctrines or leadership stan-dards; the Elect try to raise everything to the standard of Jesus Christ. They begin to be a 'sword of truth', which pierces the heart of Religion. In their quest to be 'manifest sons', the Elect begin to gather out of the traditional lifeless churches. This is the beginning of the birthing process for the 'manifest sons' (144,000 page i).

12:3 And there appeared another wonder in heaven; and behold a great red dragon,

having [1]*seven heads and* **ten horns***, and seven crowns upon his* [3]*heads.*

This is Satan from a spiritual perspective. Satan has a [1]God given [3]authority seen by the use of seven heads. He got that position by being the tester/tempter of man for the sake of [2]judgment and perfection. Satan hates man and is really an unwilling instrument for the perfecting of the Church. Satan unwillingly purifies the Church by helping birth the Bride, and then this mature Man-Child (Christ-in-us) will crush his head. Gen 3:15, "And I will put enmity between thee and the woman, and between thy seed and her seed; he **[Christ-in-us]** shall bruise thy head **[remove his authority]**, and thou shalt bruise his heel **[the perfecting of our walk]**."

12:4 And his tail drew the **third part** *of the* **stars** *of heaven, and did cast them to the* **earth***: and the dragon stood before the woman which was ready to be delivered,* **for** *to devour* **her child** *as soon as it was born.*

Satan's plan against God (part one)

Satan's plan against God is not targeted against to-day's church (woman); it is against His Elect (her child) who will lay the foundation for the Bride. Instead of attack-ing the Church, Satan will use some of them (stars) to try to destroy the Elect. This is not new; Satan tried the same tactic when he used Judas and the Pharisees to kill Jesus. He knows that the Manchild will crush his head; therefore, he wants to devour them before they can gather to become the Bride. To do this Satan goes all out to recruit Christians (**third part**) by enticing them into carnality ("cast to earth"). They then become an enemy of God, hindering any spiri-tual move of revival. Remember that "the carnal mind is an enemy of God." With many carnal Christians in the Church, He has access to devour the Manchild. The word says…

Matt. 24:10-12
10 And then shall **many be offended**, and shall be-tray one another, and shall hate one another.
11 And many false prophets shall rise, and shall de-ceive many.
12 And because **iniquity shall abound**, the love of many shall wax cold.

This scripture is also referred to in Mark 13:12-13 as the events which will reveal the abomination of desolation in the Holy Place. This is a place in which the spirit of anti-christ is on the throne of the hearts of many of God's peo-ple.

How Satan entices the Church
The tail that cast down the stars
Isa. 9:15-16
15 The ancient and honourable, he is the head; and **the prophet that teacheth lies, he is the tail**.
16 For the **leaders of this people cause them to err**; and they that are led of them are destroyed.

The **tail** (false prophets) signifies that Satan deceives the Church with false doctrines packed with lots of feel-good preaching. These false prophets will feed them with so much milk that they will not endure sound doctrine. We know that since the **earth** is involved, the doctrine must play to the carnal desires of man. Any doctrine that justifies carnality or worldliness or diminishes our need to know more of Jesus is a false doctrine. If a doctrine does not demand a Christian to lay down his life or suffer eternal separation from Christ, then it is suspect. The teachings of Jesus are straight forward on this issue, and today's preaching falls far short of His words.

Praise God, Satan will be foiled. He may succeed in getting many Christians to swallow a bunch of carnal lies, disguised as grace, but God will ultimately turn the ill-intended efforts of Satan to bring good to His people. Carnality leads to worldliness, and worldliness will actually cause the Man-Child to be born. Those who desire more in their relationship with Christ will hear the call "come out from her" (Rev. 18:4)...thus the birth.

> **12:5** And she brought forth a **man child**, who was to rule all nations with a **rod of iron**: [on page 101] and her child was caught up unto God, and to his throne.

Man Child (verse 12:5 below) = John always uses this form of male (Greek-huios) to refer to Christ, unless quoting a conversation. Yet, these are the overcomers (Rev. 2:26-27), who will rule with a rod of iron (verse 5). Therefore, to stay consistent, we must declare that these are the Christ-in-us, manifest sons, who come out of the Church.

His efforts have backfired; as a result, the very thing he used to devour the Elect actually helps to bring forth the Elect. The carnality that Satan brings into the Church is the catalyst that births the Manchild. This happens when the Elect, who have a heart after God, leave fellowship with those who partake of this world. As they begin to appear, Satan will go all out to devour them. He will consume their lives with everything he can to keep them from manifesting against him. It is these overcomers, who are never marred by the Harlot, who rule in the Millennium. This gives us a strong indication that this Man-Child is the 144,000 (page i) who initiate the Bride Church.

'Caught up to God and His throne' is a description of the spiritual place of the Elect; they do not actually leave the planet. In verse 17, Satan is doing battle with them (here on earth).

> **12:6** And the woman fled into the wilderness, where she hath a place prepared of God, that they **should feed her** there a [1]thousand two hundred and threescore days.

'They' are the manifested sons who feed her. Their ministering is the wilderness experience that keeps the Church alive; for without tribulation, the Church would become a Harlot. God wants to feed the truth to the Church during the first [1]dispensation. "Should feed her" shows the Elect's love for the Church and desire to see the spots removed. Suffering is what will bring us to His Glory (Rom. 8:17).

> **12:7** And there was war in heaven: **Michael** and his angels fought against the dragon; and the dragon fought and his angels,

Michael means "who is as or like God." Michael is the Angel who said, "the Lord rebuke you, Satan." This is an Elect response to Satan. Michael may be a real angelic being who leads the fight in the heavens but here he represents the Lord who, through His Elect **Angels,** does battle with the carnality that provides Satan access to the Church.

> **12:8** And prevailed not; neither was their place found any more in heaven.

Satan is cast from his high and lofty position the day that carnality is exposed as his only weapon on earth. Carnality is the seat of authority in Satan's kingdom. Men will come to know that Satan can only work within us. This means we are able to choose victory by denying him authority. We can do that by giving that authority to Jesus Christ. True worshipers will worship Him in Spirit and Truth, and all that have a heart after God will operate in the kingdom of Heaven.

> **12:9** And the great dragon was cast out, that old serpent, called the Devil, and Satan, which deceiveth the whole world: he was **cast out into the earth**, and his angels were cast out with him.

Satan wanted to devour the Elect before they could gather so he could prevent them from revealing that he only has power through carnality (earth). This means that it is through our carnality that Satan affects our life. He uses our desires to destroy our lives. That is why Jesus was not worried about Satan. He said about Satan, "...for the ruler of this world is coming, and he has nothing in Me." (NKJ John 14:30) Remove the carnality, and Satan's authority is removed.

This ruins the image of Satan as some enormous spiritual giant waiting to destroy our lives. Instead, he is seeking whom he "may" devour...we have to give him permission! Satan is unveiled, his lies are revealed. It is not the satanic evil demons that we need battle, but rather our own natural fleshly desires. His evil spirits live on our pride, lust, envy, etc. The world now will see that Satan lives in carnality.

> **12:10** And I heard a loud voice saying in heaven, **Now is come salvation**, and strength, and the kingdom of our God, and the power of his Christ: for the accuser of our brethren is cast down, which accused them before our God day and night.

"Greater is He that is in us than he that is <u>in the world</u>." Now that Satan is unveiled, he can be brought down. We can now discern the sin from the sinner; consequently, we can help people release the very things that allow evil spirits to destroy their lives. We do not battle against flesh and blood, but against the spirits that we feed.

> **12:11** And they overcame him by the **blood of the Lamb**, and by the word of their testimony; and **_they loved not their lives unto the death_**.

The power of the surrendered, Christ-in-us life is our greatest weapon against Satan. It is the living Word that has power over carnality. This is the ultimate victory over carnality: loving not OUR life unto death.

> *12:12 Therefore rejoice, ye heavens, and ye that dwell in them. **Woe** to the **inhabiters of the earth** and of the sea! for the devil is come down unto you, having great wrath, because he knoweth that he hath but a short time.*

The true Gospel (good news) is that we can have our victory over Satan.

Just because he cannot touch the overcomers does not mean that he has no authority. He brings his influence to bear through any carnality. That is why, after we cleanse the Church, Satan runs to the world. See *WOES* page xx.

> *12:13 And when the dragon saw that he was cast unto the earth, he persecuted the woman which brought forth the man child.*

Satan's plan against God (part two)

Back to the Church... Satan realizes that the Elect, through Christ in us, have authority over him; therefore, he must do battle against them indirectly. In Rev. 17:14, we see that the Beast is behind the Harlot, sending forth her 'kings of the earth' against the Lamb. In this way, we know that his ultimate plan is to make the Harlot war against the Elect. To do this Satan must influence Christians with the blessing of certain religious leaders, just as he did through the Pharisees.

> *12:14 And to the woman were given two wings of [1]a **great eagle**, that she might fly into the wilderness, into her place, where she is nourished for a [3]time, and times, and half a time, from [2]the face of the serpent.*

The Elect **Eagles** bring the revelation of Christ-in-us to the Church to help nourish her with meat, instead of the milk she has been getting. The [1]**Eagles** (page v) encourage repentance, but we know that repentance can only come through a contrite heart. To help the Church remove her spots, God sends a Revelation that pierces hearts and makes carnality hurt (See Thunder 2). This produces the wilderness experience all Christians must face to possess the Glory of God. If they become overcomers, then they will stay away from the [2]transforming influence of worldliness (face of the serpent).

The Elect's ministry to the Church is only for the [3]first 3 ½ years (first dispensation). The **Eagles'** ministry will keep the Church out of the face of Satan, but any that stray from the life being offered will become unwilling instruments of the Beast…the Harlot. You may believe that everyone in the Church is after the Glory of God and desires to have a deeper revelation of Christ; if that were true, then the Harlot would never become a reality. Sadly, the real truth is that there are motivations and carnal leaders within the body that will be used of Satan.

There is a fundamental flaw in the Church that adds more carnality. In church leadership (not pastors), those most able to operate in this world (praise of man) are the ones who normally rise to the top. The truly separated Christ-like persons will be more focused on relationship with Christ and defer leadership to those who desire it. This is another way that Satan makes the Church more carnal. You can imagine as the sold out message of Christ-in-us is preached, leadership will reject it if it challenges their authority.

> *12:15 And the serpent cast out of his mouth water as a **flood** after the woman, that he might cause her to be [1]carried away of the **flood**.*

Many will not endure the wilderness, others may tire of the tribulation. Whatever the reason, they become susceptible to the lies of Satan. This is Satan's opportunity to entrench his influence within many Christians and religious leaders. He will cast forth a flood of 'tickling doctrines' and lies designed to soothe the tribulation associated with pursuing a deeper revelation of Christ.

This is where the end-time separation of Harlot and Bride begins. A flood of lies will penetrate the Church, securing Satan's place on the throne of all the carnal Christians in the Church. By choosing this world over Christ's, they are in effect fornicating with this world. Therefore, their marriage contract is void, and Christ will begin to focus on those who desire Him. It is here that we see the beginning of the separation of wheat and tares. It is the fulfillment of Christ preparing for himself a Bride without spot or blemish.

> *12:16 And the **earth** helped the woman, and the [1]earth opened her mouth, and swallowed up the flood which the dragon cast out of his mouth.*

BIRTH OF THE HARLOT IN THE CHURCH... a pact with the devil (earth)

It is tough for the Church who has gotten fat on blessing to face true tribulation. The die-to-self message is just too much for some Christians to hear. When God starts doing the things that cause Christians to be perfected through tribulation, many in the Church cry foul. They do not want to believe the truth of Christ-in-us; therefore, she (the Church) becomes susceptible to the lies.

The carnality in the Church becomes a safe refuge from the tribulation. This means that the Church swallows these lies as a thirsty man seeks water in the desert. The problem is that this is poisonous water. This is where God allows strong delusion to be sent; consequently, she will believe a lie because she will not believe the truth (2 Thes. 2:11-12). These are the lies that have found their home in the earth ([1]carnality) of the Church, AND Satan will find his home in the Church through this carnality. Refer back to the synagogue of Satan in the letters to the churches and see that it is among them.

Remember why Satan is doing this. He is after the Elect, not the Church (verse 4). Satan has no power over the Church or the Elect. But if he can get Christians to do his bidding, they will attack the Elect in the name of the Lord.

John 16:2

2 They shall put you out of the synagogues: yea, the time cometh, that whosoever killeth you will think that he doeth God service.

*12:17 And the dragon was wroth with the woman, and **went to make war with the** **remnant of her seed**, which keep the commandments of God, and have the testimony of Jesus Christ.*

The trap is sprung as the Church makes room for the Harlot, and now the Harlot will make war with the very ones that tried to save her. The Beast, now living through the carnality of the Harlot, will send the kings of the earth after the Elect. Satan realizes that his religious spirits (Pharisee spirits) are the only ones that can harm the Elect, but they must operate through religious leadership.

Parenthetical 3

The Beast

The Beast is from the antichrist spirit *(antichrist page xviii)* of lies and delusion with which Satan impregnated the 'earth' (carnality) in the heart of the Church. As the fire of the revelation of Jesus Christ, '**mountain burning**' (page xiii), falls into the sea (**sea** page xvi), the heart of the Church is pierced by perfecting truth. The Spirit of Lies by which she has been corrupted rises up and gives birth to the Beast, exposing Her true nature as the Harlot. The nature of this Beast is revealed whenever the antichrist characteristics of anger, strife, evil speaking, bitterness, judgment, etc. are present in an individual giving witness to the scripture, *"But those things which proceed out of the mouth come forth from the heart; and they defile the man."* (Matt. 15:18).

The Beast and the Harlot are very similar. The Beast is formed when the antichrist spirits, living in the carnality of the Church, increase to a level of manifestation. The Church, thus defiled by this manifestation, allows or even encourages the harlotry of carnal Christians. This is the atmosphere through which the Harlot church comes to life. This means that the Beast is the seed planted in the Church and when the seed is birthed, it brings forth the Harlot church. Vial Angel 1 (page 43) shows this as a picture of the Harlot riding on this Beast.

Satan is personally guiding the Beast and thus the Harlot, unleashing the fruit of such a union… religious spirits (the true antichrist). This is part of Satan's battle strategy to overcome the Lamb and convince Christians to attack the Truth. He will use these antichrist spirits in the Church to give birth to the Harlot church. All of this is in response to the birth of the Man-Child Elect. Therefore, the Harlot will empower false prophets who simulate the work of God and create an illusion of religiousness. To the world, the Harlot is as credible as the Elect.

The Beast will have an authority over the Elect until the 'appearing'. The carnal message will be so strong that to reject it will bring great tribulation to those who have not died to self. But what Satan means for ill, God uses for good. This tribulation brings people to a place of decision, bringing more sons into the kingdom and increasing His Glory until His appearing ultimately overcomes both the kings of the earth and false prophets. Once overcome, the kings of the earth repent and turn against the Harlot, eating her flesh (destroying her carnality) from the inside out.

Revelation Chapter 13

*13:1 And I stood upon the sand of the **sea**, and saw a beast rise up out of the sea, having [1]**seven heads** and [2]**ten horns**, and upon his horns [3]**ten crowns**, and upon his [4]**heads** the name of blasphemy.*

Seven Heads—*See page xvii,* **Ten Horns**—*See page xviii,* **Ten Crowns**—*Kings of judgment (**kings of the earth**, page x), Blasphemy—See page 44.*

The Beast judges the Harlot

Satan will be used to perfect the Church (refer to Vial Angel 1 to review the story of the Beast). That is the reason for the seven heads…Godly authority. The Beast that comes from the heart of the carnal Christians into the Church (page xvi) is allowed to rise up for the [1]divine purpose of bringing [2]judgment against the [3]Church (crowns=Christ's authority, 10=judgment), revealing the Beast's true [4]authority (blasphemy is its purpose). Christ can only be married to a spotless Bride. In the Jewish wedding of Jesus' day, the marriage contract takes place well before the ultimate consummation. Only when the friend of the Bridegroom declares the marriage consummated is it a true marriage. As the Beast rises up, it is evident that the Harlot (echoing in type the actions of Israel when they pursued false gods) has fornicated with this world and nullified her part in the marriage contract. The Church cannot consummate her union with Christ until He removes the Harlot.

The seven heads represent the Beast's divine authority, but that authority is for judgment (10). If the Beast is able to rise up in either a person or the Church, then its purpose is to <u>reveal its heart</u>. The ten crowns (which are excluded from the Vial Angel 1 description) represent how **kings of the earth** are used as part of this judgment. Moreover, the reference to the blasphemy on the head shows that while the authority is of God, the work is of Satan.

> **13:2** *And the beast which I saw was like unto a* **leopard***, and his feet were as the feet of a* **bear***, and his mouth as the mouth of a* **lion***: and the dragon gave him his power, and his seat, and great authority.*
>
> *The Beast's nature is revealed through its description...*

Leopard = *The Beast is the visible judgment of God. Read Hos. 13:2-7 to see that God is watching and judging as a leopard. These scriptures were written just to address this issue of disobedience. In Daniel, this same Beast is seen as having authority in the last time (See '4' page vii).*

Dan. 7:6

6   After this I beheld, and lo another, like a leopard, which had upon the back of it **four** wings of a fowl [*fowls speak of evil spirits*]; the beast had also **four heads; and dominion was given to it**.

Bear (feet) = *Power (crushing feet) of the Beast to get to the heart (crush/remove ribs) and take authority over much flesh.*

Dan. 7:5

5   And behold another beast, a second, like to a bear, and it raised up itself on one side, and it had three [*perfection*] **ribs in the mouth** of it between the teeth of it: and they said thus unto it, Arise, **devour much flesh**.

Lion (mouth) = *Sounds religious (roar of the lion), but it is revealed as a counterfeit (wings plucked out). In Daniel we see that it does not have God's heart as its source, but man's carnal heart.*

Dan. 7:4

4   The first was like a lion, and had **eagle's wings**: I beheld till the wings thereof were **plucked**, and it was lifted up from the earth, and made stand upon the feet as a man, and **a man's heart** was given to it.

    Satan gives it authority and a place to sit through the lies and carnal hearts of men.

> **13:3** *And I saw one of his heads as it were wounded to death; and his deadly wound was healed: and all the world wondered after the beast.*

The Beast originally had seven heads because it was appointed of God to judge hearts. But the mark of blasphemy seen on the heads reveals that it is no longer part of God's plan. The Elect will reveal the path of Satan operating through the earth (carnality) in the Church, exposing its carnal nature and thus wounding one head to death. The six heads remaining mark its carnal nature (six is the number of man) springing out of the heart of man (See Lion), not of God.

The Harlot is born because the Beast rises out of her heart, bearing witness of her fornication; because nothing so vile could be created in union with the Lord.

Scorned, she accepts authority from the Beast (rides it) and tries to conceal the Beast's carnality with her religious coverings. To those who cannot see with spiritual eyes, this Beast (antichrist authority) once again appears to be delivering a godly message (seven). In this way Satan has healed the wounded head by making the Beast look religious through the Harlot. The world now makes the Beast/Harlot an object of wonder and love. Why should it not? It is made in the image of the world.

> **13:4** *And they worshipped the dragon which gave power unto the beast: and they worshipped the beast, saying, Who is like unto the beast? who is able to make war with him?*

The worldliness now infusing the Harlot church is increased by a measure of wonder, enhancing its attractiveness to the world, and allowing Satan to be worshipped through his worldly message.

The power of man-made religion is already a force not easily confronted. Many man-made organizations will not be challenged on doctrine, intently believing they alone have spiritual truth. They focus on what makes them separate, and division is not of God.

> **13:5** *And there was given unto him a mouth speaking great things and blasphemies; and power was given unto him to continue* **forty and two** *[on page xiv]* **months***.*

The lies continue until Christ appears in a company of witnesses (Bride). This will take place forty-two months after tribulation begins (three-and-one-half years) or at the end of the first dispensation.

> **13:6** *And he opened his mouth in* **blasphemy against God***, to blaspheme his name, and his tabernacle, and* [1]**them that dwell in heaven***.*

The Elect will evoke much criticism and hatred. Christ prophesied that as the world hated Him, it would hate all those who are His and show forth His nature. Satan's true purpose is to destroy the [1]Elect; therefore, he uses the Harlot church to speak worldly things designed to destroy the true message of God (blasphemy, page 44).

> **13:7** *And it was given unto him to* **make war with the saints***, and to overcome them: and power was given him over all kindreds, and tongues, and nations.*

He has a certain authority over the redeemed and the Saints for the purposes of perfection; yet, he can only work through carnality. The Saints know that Jesus wants them to sacrifice their flesh, and Satan can only attack the parts of their lives that need to die anyway. Yet, this is not an easy path, and even many of the Saints will decide that the price is too high. With ear-tickling doctrines all around us, the temptation to give in to an easier path will be great. Since Satan will have power within the Church (See nation, kindred, etc. page xiii), the Saints who remain with her and accept such teachings will become the 'kings of the earth' (page x). Finding a Spirit filled, relationship-building, Christ-in-us body of believers to fellowship and worship with is critical to end-time ministry…not to mention our personal growth in Christ.

> **13:8** And all that **dwell upon the earth shall worship him**, whose names are not written in the book of life of the Lamb slain from the foundation of the world.

If you are carnal, then your name is not written in the Lamb's book of life (Rom. 8:6). This is hard to hear; thus, the worldly seek doctrines that tell people that they are all right when they are not. Carnality and Jesus do not go together. You cannot serve two masters (Matt. 6:24). Open your ears and listen. You may be saved and qualified; but unless there is a visible life of Christ revealed in you, you ARE carnal. If He is in you, then He will be seen. If He is not seen, can you be secure with your place in the book of Life?

> **13:9** If any man have an ear, let him hear.
> **Do You?**

Listen, listen, listen! This is about your eternal position with Christ. Please pull back the veil and look!

> **13:10** He that [1]leadeth into [2]captivity shall go into captivity: he that [4]killeth with the [3]sword must be killed with the sword. Here is the patience and the faith of the saints.

The Christ-in-us Message, Revealed in Revelation

[1]If you hope to lead people into a [2]surrendered life with Christ, then you must show that you are sold out (captive) to Him. If you plan on telling people the [3]truth of [4]the revelation of Christ, then it must no longer be you who lives (Gal. 2:20), but Christ who lives in you.

The real issue then is not what will you do in the end time, but what will Christ do through you? Christ does not need your natural strength. He desires you to have more of Him in you, so that He can minister to others through you.

Many ministers and leadership try to help others without first developing a deep relationship with Christ. Instead of trying to fix the world for God, the true patience of the Saints is seen when they turn their eyes inwardly and allow God to repair what sin has broken. In this way, the greater One in them can minister to others. If you want to minister as a Saint, then let Christ make you one! It is not a work of grace. It is the product of surrender and obedience to the LORD Jesus Christ.

> **13:11** And I beheld **another beast** coming up out of the earth; and he had two horns like a lamb, and he spake as a [1]dragon.

The "other beast" is the false religious witness (two = witness) of carnal worship. We saw this when the head of the Beast was healed (verse 3). This is where carnality takes on a religious authority for offensive purposes. As long as the Harlot shows forth carnality, the Beast will

have a religious covering (like a "lamb"). This is the true 'wolf in sheep's clothing'. It will now be hard for some to distinguish between the "gospel of the kingdom" and "another gospel" (2 Cor. 11:4) preached with evil intent. However, if you listen, you can hear that it is authored by [1]Satan, not Jesus Christ.

> **13:12** And he exerciseth all the power of the first beast before him, and causeth the earth and them which dwell therein to worship the first beast, whose [1]deadly wound was healed.

As the carnal religious message continues, we will see more and more religious spirits come forth. The progression is this: 1-Satan's lies touch the evil nature of our heart; 2-this allows the Beast to rise up and take authority in the worldly person and thus infect the Church; 3-the Beast in dominion finally becomes an accepted church doctrine, promoted to the world through false, misguided prophets.

[1]This is also a reminder of the fact that the Church is responsible for allowing the Beast's message through the Harlot.

> **13:13** And he doeth great wonders, so that he maketh fire come down from heaven on the earth in the sight of men,

'Fire from heaven' is used as a sign from God throughout the Bible. Elijah used this form of witness with the fifty men (2 Kings 1:10) and with the priest of Baal (I Kings 18:24). However, in Luke (see below) when the disciples wanted to use this form of witness (probably to impress others); Jesus accused them of being guided by a wrong spirit.

Luke 9:54-55
54   And when his disciples James and John saw this, they said, **Lord, wilt thou that we command fire to come down from heaven**, and consume them, even as Elias did?
55   But he turned, and **rebuked them**, and said, **Ye know not what manner of spirit ye are of.**

This verse is not really about anyone actually calling down literal fire. The word translated 'wonders' [Gr. semeion (say-mi'-on)] is usually translated 'sign'. "He does great signs so that men believe he is of God." Satan will cause the Harlot message to have a great witness - to the worldly. This may include miracles, financial blessings, or any other number of things that appeal to the natural mind. Whatever their signs they will not contain any power of Christ. Signs and wonders of the Saints will speak of the Glory of Christ and draw people to the revelation of Christ… you will know them by their fruit.

He is saying this very thing in verse 10 when He tells us that we must show forth Christ in everything we do. Some of the ministers of the Harlot appear to be very powerful men of God, able to do miracles, and hear directly from God. Closer examination however, reveals that their lives do not fully match their message. They are not in overt sin, but their speech, hobbies, desires, and ministries are worldly. This is a reflection of what we can expect from these false prophets. Check their fruit. Does it speak of the character of Christ (especially in 1 Cor. 13 'charity') or of antichrist? How much of Christ do you see?

Finally, there is one more sign - judgment. Is God for them (Goshen page viii)?

> **13:14** And **deceiveth them that dwell on the earth** by the means of those miracles which he had power to do in the [1]sight of the beast; saying to them that dwell on the earth, that they **should make an image to the beast**, which had the wound by a sword, and did live.

[1]Notice that the signs are only signs to those who operate with the Beast in them (dwell on the earth). 'Grace is all you need', 'You have a right to have a prosperous life full of the good things', and 'Need members? Make the Church more appealing (image)' are the messages of the false prophets who urge you to have both mammon and God.

> **13:15** And he had power to give life unto the image of the beast, that the image of the beast should both speak, and cause that as many as would not worship the image of the beast [1]should be killed.

Yes, there will be signs by which people are deceived because they are seeking the signs of man rather than those of God. The false prophets will promise all of the riches of this world if you follow after this carnal message (remember Satan's offer to Jesus). Yet, deeper than the promise of worldly prosperity is the lie that instills the belief that you can control your own life, operate from your own will, and still please God. It is a message that sanctions your choice of career, spouse, boyfriend, ministry, retirement, hobbies, etc.

The Harlot claims to be the true Church, and they believe they have the evidence to prove it. They believe the sold out believers forming the Bride are a bunch of fanatics. They believe their doctrines represent the only true word of God. [1]If you do not agree, they will kill you…which is the best part about them, because if there is something in you that needs to die, they will find it; you will be perfected as you take this message to the worldly.

> **13:16** And he causeth all, both small and great, rich and poor, free and bond, to receive a mark in their right hand, or in their [1]foreheads:

You will know them by their fruit. Those who buy into a carnal message show what is in them. Your [1]mind shows its carnality, and your [2]actions show it as well.

> **13:17** And that no man might buy or sell, save he that had the mark, or the name of the beast, or the number of his name.

Buy and sell are marketplace terms. You will find that doing business becomes increasingly more difficult as your relationship with Jesus Christ increases. During the end-time, it will take a real mark of carnality to ignore the urgency of the day and go about your business. Look at Jesus. How involved was He with the world's issues? If we manifest Him, He will be revealed in our lifestyle.

> **13:18** Here is wisdom. Let him that hath understanding count the number of the beast: for it is the number of a man; and his number is Six hundred threescore and six.
> **See 'mark of Beast' page xi.**
> **6…6…6, carnal…carnal…carnal. Three is the number of completion…COMPLETELY CARNAL.**

Parenthetical 4

The Bride/New Jerusalem

New Jerusalem is not a physical place; it is a place of spiritual relationship with Christ. The Angels of Rev. 21:9 declare that the New Jerusalem is the Bride, the Lamb's Wife. The distinctions between the New Jerusalem and the Bride are minimal, the most notable being that New Jerusalem is only for those members of the Bride who have received a robe of righteousness. To be a citizen of the New Jerusalem, you must be willing to lose yourself in service to Christ for others and to become complete through obedience to the body of Christ (hair page ix). This Parenthetical is about the path and character of those people.

The people of New Jerusalem, who have established a New Heaven and a New Earth in themselves through Christ, provide direct access for Christ to minister to the world. His presence is visible in their lives, which will

bring accountability that renders the world without excuse and forces all to choose whom they will serve. Those who have borne the sacrifice of self to be a part of the New Jerusalem are promised great reward. They will never see death or have any pain or sorrow. Through them God will restore creation to its original garden state and renew fellowship with His children.

Two thousand years ago the apostles laid the foundation of this city. The apostles represented a type of Christ's authority here on earth. The 144,000 will follow them as the apostolic authority for the end-time people and form the walls of New Jerusalem (figuratively speaking), providing access for all who will enter after them.

Revelation Chapter 21

> **21:1** And I saw a **new heaven and a new earth**: for the first heaven and the first earth were passed away; and there was **no more sea**.

The new heavens and new earth are those people who have allowed the kingdom of Heaven to pour out of their hearts, thereby bringing the kingdom of Heaven to earth.

These overcomers are the 'heavens' who form the New Jerusalem.

As Christ takes full dominion of their lives, a new heaven is formed in their hearts; their natural bodies become glorified bodies, as the new earth. We become a type of the Garden, a place in which heaven and earth are united. As He pours the spiritual realm from these earthen vessels, the profound presence of Christ also begins restoration to the earth (planet) and returns it to its original garden state. The curse is reversed.

Isaiah gives insight to this time and our transformation into the new heaven and earth…see 'Isaiah end time' page 89.

> **21:2** And I John saw the holy city, **New Jerusalem**, coming down from God out of heaven, prepared **as a bride adorned for her husband**.

Finally, this is the promise of Abraham fulfilled.
> *For he looked for a city which hath*
> *foundations, whose builder and*
> *maker is God. (Heb. 11:10)*

The Bride who becomes Wife is the New Jerusalem. It is not a literal city. It is born out of the ascension of the Saints in Christ. This ascension occurred back in Rev. 4:1 by those who heard the 'trumpet call'. The Angel refers to this city by saying "come see the lamb's Wife" (verse 9). This identifies another distinction of the citizens of the city - they must be married and consummated in relationship to the Lord to qualify - betrothed is not enough. They must ascend so that they can descend.

Rev. 3:12 declares that these 'overcomers' have the name of the city marked upon their foreheads. This corresponds to Rev. 7:1-3 where we see that these are the 144,000. To further illustrate the importance of these saints to the forming of this city, Rev. 21:17 states that the walls (framework) of the city measure 144 cubits. This symbolizes the role these people will take in forming the New Jerusalem.

The "marking" of the overcomers takes place at the very beginning of Revelation. That shows that we must choose now if we desire to be part of His marvelous end-time work.

Rev. 22:19 warns us that if we try to manipulate this revelation to take away the sting, we stand in jeopardy of losing our part of this city.

> **21:3** And I heard a great voice out of heaven saying, Behold, **the tabernacle of God is with men**, and he will dwell with them, and they shall be his people, and God himself shall be with them, and be their God.

When the Bride is indwelt by Christ during the parousia, then the kingdom of Heaven has come… "and His will be done here on earth as it is in heaven." He will rule with a rod of iron through us during the Millennium. In Isaiah, it says that we are so close to Him that even as we speak, He answers.

> **21:4** And God shall wipe away all tears from their eyes; and there shall be **no more death**, neither sorrow, nor crying, neither shall there be any more pain: **for the former things are passed away**.

This blessing is for those of the New Jerusalem and does not apply to others. Once the Elect have received the robe of righteousness (meaning they are now the New Jerusalem), then there is no more death for them. As Jesus said, some will not see death, but rather be changed in the twinkling of an eye. He also tells us in John 8:51 that if we walk righteously, then we will not see death. Receiving a glorified body gives us that ability to cross over death without entering in. When it is only the Lord who lives in us, then we will share His victory over death.

> **21:5** And he that sat upon the throne said, Behold, **I make all things new**. And he said unto me, Write: for these words are true and faithful.

He makes everything new, including creation. He will restore the Garden of Eden through us.

> **21:6** And he said unto me, It is done. I am Alpha and Omega, the beginning and the end. I will give unto him that is athirst of the **fountain of the water of life freely**.

The Word brought forth the Garden, and the Word will restore it. Once everything is restored and the final judgment is delivered, then Christ will be able to turn the kingdom over to the Father. This time the Father will have a family who will not leave or disobey Him.

> **21:7** He that overcometh **shall inherit all things**; and I will be his God, and he shall be my son.

The manifested sons of God will be joint heirs with Jesus and inherit all things. This inheritance is available today through Christ; all you have to do is die to live.

> **21:8** But the fearful, and unbelieving, and the abominable, and murderers, and whoremongers, and sorcerers, and idolaters, and all liars, shall **have their part** in the lake which burneth with fire and brimstone: which is the **second death**. *[on page xvi]*

Carnality in all forms will bring death, and spiritual death brings separation from God. "Have their part" means that this sin will be cast into the Lake of Fire together with all who will not release it. The second death will be at the White Throne Judgment.

21:9 And there came unto me one of the seven angels which had the seven vials full of the seven last plagues, and talked with me, saying, Come hither, I will shew thee the Bride, the Lamb's wife.

This verse shows that the description of New Jerusalem that follows is not the description of a physical city, but a spiritual description of the Wife of Jesus, those who are part of His appearing. The following verses should be spiritually discerned.

Jerusalem: A People He can Rule Through

*21:10 And he carried me away in the spirit **to a great and high mountain**, and shewed me that great city, the **holy Jerusalem**, descending [pouring] out of heaven from God,*

This is His people ascending to the 'great and high' mountain (mountain page xii), while God descends <u>out</u> of heaven to meet them. This is where the kingdom of Heaven pours out of the Elect's heart from God.

21:11 Having the glory of God: and her light was like unto a stone most precious, even like a jasper stone, clear as crystal;

Crystal means "without spots", so New Jerusalem is where the ones "without spots' dwell. Christ-in-us is the Glory. Look at Rev. 4:3, and you will see that 'jasper' is a type of Jesus on the throne. Jasper (page x) is a revelation about the visible Glory of this city, Christ-in-us.

Eph. 5:26-27

26 That he might sanctify and cleanse it with the washing of water by the word, [*The revelation of Christ-in-us*}

27 That he might present it to himself a glorious church, <u>not having spot, or wrinkle, or any such thing</u>; but that it should be holy and without blemish.

We see these spots removed in the parable of the 'wheat and tares' Matt. 13:36-43. Especially verse 43 where it says that when the tares are removed, the righteous will shine forth. For more on 'spots', see Jude 10, 12 and 16.

*21:12 And had a wall great and high, and had **twelve gates**, and at the gates **twelve angels**, and names written thereon, which are the names of the **twelve tribes** of the children of Israel:*

This is an interesting verse because it is not clear where the names are written. The names can be written on the gates or on the Angels; indeed, major translations vary. Perhaps the reason it is difficult to discern is that it may be both. After all, the gates and the Angels both represent the Portion of Jacob (page i), the 144,000, who have entered in the gates by obtaining the Pearl of great price. Here they are: the "ways" (gates), "message" (angels), and the "authority" (God's voice) of New Jerusalem.

21:13 On the east three gates; on the north three gates; on the south three gates; and on the west three gates.

Pearly gate, page xiv

Three represents completion). This city requires completion to enter. Look at the path as described by the 'gate Angels' (page 110). You are not required to be perfect, just complete in Christ. Jesus Christ must be your Savior and LORD. Many people may say, "Lord, Lord have we not called upon you and even done great things in your name?" They will not be able to enter because they have only confessed that He is Lord with their mouths and not their lives. The message that the 144,000 bring, Christ in you the hope of Glory, makes us all equal and makes access possible from any direction (unsaved, church leader, Buddhist, etc.).

*21:14 And the wall of the city had **twelve foundations**, and in them the names of the twelve apostles of the Lamb.*

The New Jerusalem began with the foundation that was laid by the apostles. Being sold out or dead to self (lamb) is what they promoted. As time went on and the <u>world</u> entered into the <u>Church</u>, then the mystery of godliness was replaced with a 'sinner's prayer' message of grace alone. The world loved this message; therefore, the number of professing Christians increased, but commitments decreased. The apostles supported the Christ-in-us message because it is their message. That is why the 144,000 are the apostolic part of the end-time.

*21:15 And he that talked with me had a **golden reed to measure the city**, and the gates thereof, and the wall thereof.*

We are to see if we qualify as part of the city. Gold represents divinity and speaks of being transformed by Christ through sanctification. Christ is the only ruler by which we can measure our lives.

*21:16 And the city lieth **foursquare**, and the length is as large as the breadth: and he measured the city with the reed, twelve thousand furlongs. The length and the breadth and the height of it are equal.*

The 'four' speaks of the end-time manifestation, while the equal sides tell us about the 144,000. Christ in the 144,000 is the Alpha and Omega of the city. Eph. 3:18 says that being rooted and grounded in love, we can know the 'height, depth, and breadth' of Christ which will enable us to be filled to all the fullness of God. The 144,000 will show that love and understanding.

21:17 And he measured the wall thereof, an hundred and forty and four cubits, according to the measure of a man, that is, of the angel.

The Elect 144,000 (angels) are the walls that keep the city together. One of the roles of the 144,000 is to provide headship within the appearing, so that the body of Christ will stay on track. Descriptions of angels operating from the throne room refer to these sold out, headless Saints of God.

Men form the 144,000; yet, men are shown as Angels. He is telling us that Angels (Angels page i) are men. However, not any man can be an Angel, but only those who have ascended to the high calling of God. That is why this study is so important. If you want to be able to minister from the throne room during this time, then you must begin now to ascend in relationship with Jesus Christ.

> **21:18** And the building of the wall of it was of **jasper**: and the **city was pure gold**, like unto clear glass.
>
> **Jasper, page x**

The 144,000, as the Bride without spot (clear), have manifested Christ-in-us (jasper) as Christ (gold) to the world. Just because the 144,000 initiate it does not mean that they are the only ones who are part of the appearing. They just help create the place (message of Christ) in which the rest of the Bride will meet. The first dispensation is about gathering His Elect into the Bride. For the most part, the city will be invisible while the Harlot is still in existence. This is the way it was two thousand years ago when the Church first began. To the outsiders and some insiders, the Christian movement was just a part of Judaism. After Jerusalem was destroyed, the Church came into its own.

> **21:19** And the foundations of the wall of the city were garnished with all manner of precious stones. The first foundation was jasper; the second, sapphire; the third, a chalcedony; the fourth, an emerald;
>
> **21:20** The fifth, sardonyx; the sixth, sardius; the seventh, chrysolyte; the eighth, beryl; the ninth, a topaz; the tenth, a chrysoprasus; the eleventh, a jacinth; the twelfth, an amethyst.

Apostolic Symbols

These are the meanings of the stones from the New Jerusalem. Their progression brings forth the revelation of Christ...

Jasper – *See page x. Used as a seal. He must break us to use us.*

Sapphire – *A stone for making Babylonian cylinder seals. The apostolic ones can seal those of Babylon or mark them as such. Then we break them through the tribulation of the message of Christ-in-us.*

Chalcedony – *Golden sand, speaking of the promise of God to Abraham for his children...a city whose author and builder was God. To operate in the authority of the apostle, the 144,000 must see themselves as the promise fulfilled.*

Emerald – *(page v) Highly prized gem, representing path to Christ-in-us. You must act as Him.*

Sardonyx – *Josephus says that the shoulder clasps of the ephod were sardonyxes. This is the stone that represents Jacob's portion (page i). This is where the names of the 12 tribes are written. You are of the tribe of Christ, the New Jerusalem.*

Sardius – *6th stone, 6 is number of man, this is the flesh colored stone. You must get past the flesh to enter life (7).*

> These first six stones show the progression that will bring the Christ Life into us. Six being the number of man also shows that these six stones will bring an end to our lives. The next four stones will take us on into the fullness... represented in the Throne Room [Calf, Man, Soaring Eagle, Lion]. Then the last two are the final manifestation of the Bride to Wife and thus having the Glorified body. We are then sealed with the mind of Christ.

1) Chrysolyte – *Yellow represents large amount of hay or stubble*

2) Beryl – *Light or yellow green represents visible life*

3) Topaz – *Rich green in color represents full life*

4) Chrysoprasus – *A precious stone, golden in color, representing divinity, Glory*

Jacinth – *(page x)*

Amethyst - *The Greek name speaks of being 'sober minded' and unable to be drunk (or deceived). The intoxication refers to the Harlot's wine. Nevertheless, the root word of amethyst is alpha, which is Christ. Therefore, amethyst speaks of the sober mind of Christ which all of the New Jerusalem aspire to.*

> **21:21** And the twelve gates were twelve **pearls** [on page xiv]; every several gate was of one pearl: and the street of the city was **pure gold**, as it were transparent glass.

The **gates of pearl** represent that pearl of great price in the parable of the kingdom, indicating you must sell out to enter. The number twelve represents apostolic authority, which we see as the foundation of Christ's kingdom. Once you enter, your walk (pure gold) will be ordered of God as a walk without spot (transparent) or blemish.

For more information on how to enter into New Jerusalem, see 'tribe' on page 110.

> **21:22** And I saw no temple therein: for the Lord God Almighty and the Lamb are the temple of it.

This is not about the outside, but the inside. It is not about sacrifice, but relationship. Surrender and obedience are not to be done in the natural, but in the Spirit. We no longer follow Him out of fear, nor do we try through natural strength to earn favors or to hold back judgment. We do not follow after Him to be seen of man, which is its own reward. Now we worship Him in Spirit and Truth through surrender and obedience, knowing that being in His perfect will brings His perfect presence. Laying down our life (lamb) ushers us into the presence of God, and His presence is our treasure. This is the true anointing of God. In His presence is fullness of joy.

> *21:23 And the city had **no need of the sun**, neither of the moon, to shine in it: for the glory of God did lighten it, and **the Lamb is the light thereof.***

You have no need of men to teach (lighten) you. For my anointing (Christ), which is in you, shall show you all things (1 John 2:27). There is no need for the natural once you enter the kingdom. Seek the kingdom first, and the natural will follow (Matt. 6:33). Letting go of this world is one of the hardest requirements for entering the kingdom. People believe that it is impossible to live as Christ lived. They prefer to reinterpret the words of Christ in a manner that justifies participation in worldliness or carnality (James 4:4). There is no other way. IF YOU WANT ALL THAT GOD HAS FOR YOU, YOU MUST LET THIS WORLD GO. If you give Christ permission to sanctify your heart and mind, He will then make all things new for you.

> *21:24 And **the nations of them which are saved** shall walk in the light of it: and the kings of the earth do bring their glory and honour into it.*

Rod of Iron... The rod stands for the word of correction given in love by the Elect. It is directly from God and should be heard as such. Obedience is the plumb line of the Millennium.

Ps. 2:8-12

8 Ask of me, and **I shall give thee the heathen for thine inheritance**, and **the uttermost parts of the earth for thy possession.**
9 **Thou shalt break them with a rod of iron**; thou shalt dash them in pieces like a potter's vessel.
10 Be wise now therefore, O ye kings: be instructed, ye judges of the earth.
11 Serve the LORD with fear, and rejoice with trembling.
12 **Kiss the Son**, lest he be angry, and ye perish from the way, when his wrath is kindled but a little. Blessed are all they that put their trust in him.

For almost a thousand years, the Elect will teach men the way of the Lord without the distractions from the lies of Satan. While this may seem good, it is hard to measure learning without a test. That is why, in fairness to the last generation, which was shortened from their promised 70 years, He allows a second chance at God's Glory with sufficient time to learn to walk in the kingdom. If these will die to self during the Millennium and allow Christ to be birthed in them, then they will become part of the Bride. Otherwise, they will have to wait for the 1000 years to end to get their robes of righteousness and risk the possibility that they could backslide or fail the end-of-Millennium test. This is a marvelous way for Christ to draw down the curtain of man.

> *21:25 And the **gates** of it shall not be shut at all by day: for there shall be no night there.*

Christ will be available to those ruled through His people. We stand as an open door through which men can still obtain the Glory of Christ. His people will no longer dwell in any form of darkness during the Millennium. The light of the gospel and the Glory of His presence will illuminate the world.

> *21:26 And they shall bring the **glory** and honour of the nations into it.*

Those ruled will still be able to die to self through obedience and become part of the Bride (thereby bringing Glory to Him). There will be no lies to confuse or deceive, so obedience will be the path to Christ's Glory. "And why call ye me, Lord, Lord, and do not the things which I say?" (Luke 6:46). By honoring Christ through His Elect, they follow the path of Glory.

> *21:27 And there shall in no wise enter into it any thing that defileth, neither whatsoever worketh abomination, or maketh a lie: but they which are written in the Lamb's book of life.*

The Elect are sin free; they walk in His presence. He is speaking of those who are part of the New Jerusalem. Therefore, this reveals that those ruled do not have Christ in them and still have sin that keeps them from becoming the Wife of the Lamb. If they possessed Christ's life, then they would have their names written in the book of life and be part of the New Jerusalem.

Parenthetical 5

ANGELS / 144,000 as Messengers

This Parenthetical is about the 'Angels' (holy messengers), the 144,000 apostolic Elect, who take the living revelation of Jesus Christ to the world. Because they have allowed God to judge and perfect them, they are truly dead to self and separated from this world. They are the voice of God bringing truth and accountability to the world, declaring that the tribulation and judgment are of God. As living examples of the revelation of Jesus Christ, they pour out the vials of His wrath, urging men to fear and glorify the one true God. If you desire to be a part of such an awesome calling, then let God perfect your heart (1Cor. 15:50). Christ has declared that no flesh will inherit the kingdom of Heaven.

Revelation Chapter 15 Prelude to Vials

*15:1 And I saw another **sign** in heaven, great and **marvellous**, **seven angels** having the seven last plagues; for in them is filled up the wrath of God.*

Read **marvelous sign,** on page xii. The Angels (the Elect) are the vessels which bring the end-time plagues. Plagues are the revelation that brings conviction and the opportunity for repentance.

*15:2 And I saw as it were a **sea of glass** mingled with fire: and them that had gotten the victory over the beast, and over his image, and over his mark, and over the number of his name, stand on the sea of glass, having the **harps** [on page x] of God.*

The relationship of the Elect with the Lord allows them to understand the language of God and to speak as His voice…they are truly Angels. Harps also represent victory over carnality. This is the victory referred to in Chapter 4 of those who have been perfected by the process of growing in Christ. Yet the time implied by verse 1 indicates that these are the 144,000, because the time of tribulation has not yet begun. The Vials are all full and ready for pouring. It is the pouring out of the Vials, the revelation of Christ, which brings the wrath of God.

These Angels have had their hearts judged (sea of glass) and their lives perfected by it (fire). Their spoken witness of the revelation is a harp (See Rev. 14:2) by which these messengers begin the time line of the judgment of God.

*15:3 And they sing the **song of Moses** the servant of God, and the song of the Lamb, saying, Great and marvelous are thy works, Lord God Almighty; just and true are thy ways, thou **King of saints**.*

He is the King of the Saints (Angels/144,000). The Angels are sold out to Lord Jesus, the Christ. Worshiping in Spirit and Truth, they are strong in their praise of God; they live and speak the message to the whole world.

From song of Moses
Exod. 15:2

2   The <u>LORD is my strength and song</u>, and he is become my salvation: he is my God, and I <u>will prepare him an habitation</u>; my father's God, and I will exalt him.

*15:4 Who shall not fear thee, O Lord, and glorify thy name? for thou only art holy: for all nations shall come and worship before thee; for thy [1]**judgments** are made manifest.*

[1]Angels are the 'manifest judgments'; their lives are convicting agents for God. They speak boldly of Him. They know His ways and purposes. As men observe the lives of the Elect and their favor with God, they will be without excuse. The worship and reverence of Christ by the Elect will pierce any heart that is open to Him.

*15:5 And after that I looked, and, behold, the temple of the **tabernacle of the testimony in heaven was opened**:*

The 144,000 reveal the spiritual place of God to the world. Christ's presence within them opens heaven for the world, and they see the reality of Eph. 6:12 "For we wrestle not against flesh and blood, but against principalities, against powers, against the rulers of the darkness of this world, against spiritual wickedness in high places." They confront the natural with the supernatural, and they disclose that the natural is only there to reveal the spiritual.

This is the kingdom of Heaven, where Christ's message originates. It is the holy place revealed to the world by our relationship with Jesus. It was in the Holy of Holies that man could meet God face to face. Christ-in-us represents that same place; now men can see the true testimony being lived by His Elect. The 144,000 are that peculiar people who have no fear of man nor lust for the world. The world will see a victorious Christ (not a defeated church) and a Church made up of people who measure themselves against Christ, not the world.

*15:6 And the seven angels came out of the temple, having the seven plagues, **clothed in pure and white linen**, and having their breasts girded with golden girdles.*

These are the garments worn by the high priest when he goes to inquire of God. The Angels will have the most intimate relationship with God possible. God's voice will direct them through a face to face relationship. We anticipate that many, if not all, will have direct face to face encounters with Christ.

When they come forward to speak the Revelation to the Church and then to the world, they will be agents directly from God's presence. As with Moses, men will see the Glory of Christ on the Angels' faces and be convicted by it.

15:7 And one of the four beasts gave unto the seven angels seven golden vials full of the wrath of God, who liveth for ever and ever.

The Soaring Eagles (page v) are the ones who give the seven Vials, showing the relationship between the Eagles and the Angels. In Rev. 8:13 the translators even use the word Angel for Eagle. The Eagles soar in the heavens and seldom touch this earth.

*15:8 And the temple was filled with smoke from the glory of God, and from his power; and **no man was able to enter into the temple**, till the seven plagues of the seven angels were fulfilled.*

"No MAN can enter the temple," means that victory over carnality is necessary to qualify as an Angel. Angels must be subject to the seven plagues which bring perfection by destroying the antichrist breeding areas within the heart.

By the time the last plague is poured out (Vial seven page 82), you will be an Eagle able to ascend to the throne of God.

Parenthetical 6

Time to Start

This parenthetical tells us the story of those for whom the 'little book' has been opened. The 'seven Thunders' is the full revelation of Jesus Christ. They are sealed until each of the seven messages delivered by the Angels could be fully understood in the Spirit and 'opened' (made part of the life of) by each individual elected to bring this revelation forward. To be fully able to declare the new understanding this message brings, Christ must first be revealed through us. We must become a living message, embodying the testimony of the 'two witnesses' portrayed in Chapter 11; they suffer and endure to the end to bring this end-time message to the world.

Revelation Chapter 10

> *10:1 And I saw another mighty angel come down from [1]heaven, **clothed with a [2]cloud**: and a [3]**rainbow** was upon his head, and his face was as it were the [4]**sun**, and his feet as [5]pillars of fire:*

Does this description of Christ coming on a cloud support the rapture theology? No, it reads "clothed with a cloud." This is a picture of Christ coming to earth IN the Glory of a "cloud" of witnesses. This is really a description of the end-time Angels, portrayed in the full Glory of Christ. [1]They will be operating from 'heaven', meaning they are spiritually guided by Christ. They may even cross back and forth through the veil that separates the heavenlies. [2]They will be part of a great, unified, sold out body of believers, showing forth the appearing (parousia page 12) of Christ. They are sold out to the [3]promise of (page xv) a Christ Life, which becomes their only focus. [4]The intimacy of their personal relationship with Christ shows forth His Glory. [5]They go forth as Eagles from the kingdom of Heaven to perfect the world with the message of Christ's Glory.

> *10:2 And he had in his hand a **little book open**: and he set his right foot upon the **sea**, and his left foot on the **earth**,*

They will take the revelation first to the Church (sea) and then to the inhabitants of the world. Remember that they have feet of fire, meaning that they will bring perfecting fire to the earth.

> *10:3 And cried with a loud voice, as when a **lion** roareth: and when he had cried, **seven thunders** uttered their voices.*

They will speak in the authority of Christ as a living witness of the revelation. Only those who can speak with the authority of the 'lion' (Christ-in-us) can utter the thunders (page xix) to others.

The Thunders Sound the End of Time

> *10:4 And when the seven thunders had uttered their voices, I was about to write: and I heard a voice from heaven saying unto me, **Seal up those things** which the seven thunders uttered, and write them not.*

John was ready to go. He knew what we know and was ready to write what you are reading, but the time had not yet come. Verse 6 says that not until there are no more generations or time between the opening of the book and the dispensing of the book will the book (as 1:1 states) be given to a particular generation, and they will see these things take place. Therefore, John is told not to reveal or explain these thunders...Praise God, we now can roar them out for all to hear.

The good news is found in Dan. 12:4 where this same scene is played out and Daniel is told to seal the book. However, it also says that at the end-time the book shall be opened. Then men will go forth in the wisdom of God.

> *10:5 And the angel which I saw stand upon the sea and upon the earth **lifted up his hand to heaven**,*

This is the recruitment station for the end-time army of God. Christ Himself swears you in.

> *10:6 And sware by him that liveth for ever and ever, who created heaven, and the things that therein are, and the earth, and the things that therein are, and the sea, and the things which are therein, that there should be **time no longer**:*

The NIV translates "time no longer" as "there will be no more delay." NOW is the time!

Are you prepared to take God seriously? Can you see your place in the plan of God? Has this study stirred your soul? Can you return to waiting for the next thing to befall your life, thinking that most of your life is chance and meaningless? Are you ready to be part of the army of God, people with purpose, and a generation in which the prophets have longed to see for six thousand years? Do you want to be a part of that victorious Church without spot or blemish? Does your spirit leap at the idea of perhaps millions or billions coming into a relationship with Christ?

If yes is the answer to the last question, then maybe IT IS TIME to let go and LET GOD transform your life!

> **10:7** But in the days of the voice of the seventh angel, when he shall begin to sound, the **mystery of God should be finished,** as he hath declared to his servants the prophets.

By this time, you understand the full message of Revelation. You have unlocked the 7th Seal and understand all the seven Trumpets. The final Trumpet is sounding in your life (page 79), and the kingdoms of your life are now His. Christ is revealed in you, and the mystery of God will be finished through the tribulation your sold out desire for Christ brings. Now, you are an angel in the army of God, accountable for your measure of Glory in the resurrection.

Prophets take the message…as holy Messengers. Read verse 11 to reveal what the prophets are to do and verse 3 to reveal how they are to do it!!!

The Angelic Plan

What Christ is trying to tell us is simple. The reason that the mystery, Christ-in-us the hope of Glory, is now quickened to this generation of Saints is so that Christ can open the book. The revelation of the mystery did not come just to help people have sold out personal relationships with Christ - that has been happening as long as there have been people in love with Jesus. The mystery has been revealed today in a generation hand-picked by Him, so that corporately they might comprehend this truth by faith, and He could open the book. Then with the book opened to a generation, a way is prepared for His Angels to become better manifested. Once the Angels (144,000 sealed) are manifest, then a way can be prepared for His appearing. Finally, with His appearing, a way can be made to harvest the earth! What a wonderful plan!

> **10:8** And the voice which I heard from heaven spake unto me again, and said, **Go and take the little book** which is open in the hand of the angel which standeth upon the sea and upon the earth.

Now that we are sworn in (Rev. 10:5), we are told to get our weapon and our operational manual. The word, through the revelation of Jesus Christ, is sharper than any two-edged sword. This sword will discern the true intent of soul and spirit.

This is a call to take hold of this revelation. The little book is now being opened, even as you read this. Can you feel destiny's moment as Christ is saying "Behold the Bridegroom, go out to meet Him?"

> **10:9** And I went unto the angel, and said unto him, Give me the little book. And he said unto me, **Take it, and eat it up**; and it shall make thy belly bitter, but it shall be in thy mouth sweet as honey.

A Shot of Truth for all His Army… Before you prophesy the book, Jesus wants you to count the cost. A revelation of Christ is at first sweet to speak, but digesting it in your life will require laying down your life. That is a bitter pill to swallow. You will be crushed of all pride and self-righteousness. You are broken to slivers so that you can manifest the life of Christ. He is giving you knowledge, in order that you will make the commitment necessary for Him to complete His work in you and to make you an Angel.

> **10:10** And I took the little book out of the angel's hand, and ate it up; and it was in my mouth sweet as honey: and as soon as I had eaten it, my belly was bitter.

NO pain, NO gain… If you accept the call of God, you can expect the result to be as He has promised, "in this world you will have tribulation, but be of good cheer I have overcome the world." He can overcome the world in you, if you let Him.

Many say that they want all of Christ in their lives. However, when the test and trials of His perfecting occur they seem to forget that, "all things work together for good to those who love God and are CALLED according to His purposes."

> **10:11** And he said unto me, Thou must **prophesy** again before many peoples, and nations, and tongues, and kings.

We are given the charge: take His message to the battle front! What a wonderful promise: endure to the end and we can be a prophet of God with the greatest revelation in the history of man, the revelation of Jesus Christ. Our first assignment is to take the message to God's people, thus they have the opportunity to repent and receive afresh the truth that can set them free. This is just what the apostles did two thousand years ago, going first to the synagogues then to the gentiles. Now, the message is taken first to the Church (page xiii), and next to the inhabitants of the earth.

Parenthetical 7

Two witnesses in the 144,000

The Woman with child (Rev. 12:1) is the first sign indicating the start of the tribulation. The Man-Child who is delivered of the woman is the 144,000, the Elect Angels, or 'holy messengers' who speak and LIVE Christ; they declare His revelation to the world. What makes them who they are? This Parenthetical shows us more about the fullness of their witness.

We begin with a rod (Christ's measuring stick) by which we are asked to determine if we **measure up** to the qualifications set for those who would be the spiritual temples of Christ. The Elect will have to live and breathe Jesus Christ. They will rule with a "rod of iron", gathering together to perfect each other…as iron sharpening iron. They will become the 'two witnesses' to the world: Spirit and Truth.

The presence of Christ in them allows the Elect to show forth Christ, which translated means 'anointed of God'. In Zec. 4:14, the two witnesses are called the anointed ones. As His anointed ones, God will deal roughly with those who speak against or physically harm them. They will be a stone of stumbling that calls forth the carnality in those with whom they come into contention. This is how Jesus revealed the hearts of the Sadducees and Pharisees. The area in which someone can be stumbled is the area in which they must die. That is the power of the witnesses. They reveal Christ, and anyone who comes face to face with Christ will be transformed. In reality, these Elect are so sold out to Christ that they become living judgments, bringing wrath to the earth (carnality).

Power to Die

The Elect manifest the anointed presence of Christ. This is not so that they can call down fire from heaven (Luke 9:54), but so they can have the power to die. They want to die to this world (the crushing) so that they might be a witness to this world. The Beast, which rises up in the world, will have authority over them and kill them. However, in the same way that Christ died to bring victory, the Elect "love not their lives unto death" to help bring freedom to those imprisoned by this world. They will let the Beast rise up in others and run all over them, in order to show the real freedom of Christ's love. This then will reveal the Beast in others and help them see their own sin…just like Judas.

They are not going to defend themselves; they only want to share the truth in love to those who have been deceived. Doctrine will not convince the "kings of the earth" of their waywardness; only the nature of Christ will pierce their hearts. When the Elect do not respond in the flesh to the attacks, they show forth the Lord's death. Those who are worldly will believe that they have defeated these fanatics, but those with a heart after God will see power in the Elect's death. No matter how hard they try, the kings of the

earth will not be able to deny the presence of Christ. They will not be able to bury and forget the self-sacrifice of the Saints, which they know is of Christ.

As the **two witnesses** (Spirit and Truth in the Elect) continue to die, the Bride will come into the fullness and rise in power and Glory. This will allow Christ to defeat the **kings of the earth** with the brightness of His 'appearing' (2 Thes. 2:8). In this way, the two witnesses will have accomplished their ordained task: to bring forth His 'parousia" (appearing). The Lamb's Wife will lead the way out of Babylon into the glorious presence of Christ.

Matt. 24:14

14 And this **gospel of the kingdom** shall be preached in all the world **for a witness** unto all nations; and **then shall the end come**. [or end-time]

John 5:36

36 But I have **greater witness** than that of John: for the works which the Father hath given me to finish, the same **works that I do, bear witness of me**, that the Father hath sent me.

Rev. 11:1-13

> **11:1** And there was given me a reed like unto a **rod**: and the angel stood, saying, Rise, and **measure the temple of God,** and the **altar**, and them that worship therein.

This is the rod used to measure those who are of the Firstfruits who go into the Church.

MEASURE Greek 'metreo'
1) To measure, to measure out or to measure off
   a) any space or distance with a measurer's reed or rule
   b) metaphorically, to judge according to any rule or standard, to estimate.

We are the temples and we must qualify as a place for Christ to dwell. 1 Cor. 3:16 says, "Know ye not that ye are the temple of God…" He is looking for true worshipers who desire His fullness and are willing to endure the iron sharpening iron for the sake of completion. The 'altar' is a reference to the self-sacrifice of this calling as well as to the dying to self which brings the Glory of Christ.

This is really the first step in becoming the two witnesses. There should be equal measures of Spirit and Truth in our lives. If we are just all spirit then there are no roots and if we are all truth then there is no power of Christ' love for the world to see.

> **11:2** But the **court which is without the temple leave out**, and measure it not; for it is given unto the Gentiles: and the **holy city** shall they tread under foot [1]**forty and two months.**

The outer court was not a place God ordained for worship or sacrifice; it was not in the original plans, literally or spiritually. True worshipers are not in the outer court. That is where the unclean gentiles were allowed to go; and here, it represents the place in which carnal worship takes place. Worldliness will keep you out of the New Jerusalem, and today, it is keeping many out of that face to face relationship with Christ. Only those focused on their spiritual relationship with Christ can come into His presence; the rest are blind.

At the end of **forty-two** (on page xiv) months, there will not be an outer court, the Harlot will be removed and a new standard of the Bride will be in place. The first forty-two months of the Revelation are focused on a Bride without spot, the "holy city" into being. The New Jerusalem will not have a place for the unclean because carnality will not be tolerated among the true worshipers of God…Spirit and Truth.

The Two Witnesses
(also see Commentary 1 page 113)

> *11:3 And I will give* ~~power~~ *[inserted] unto my* **two witnesses** *[on page xix], and they shall* **prophesy** *a thousand two hundred and threescore days, clothed in sackcloth.*

The better translation should be: and I will give (of myself) to my two witnesses so that they can prophesy. This is Christ in us opening the book to us and then letting the revelation of Christ humble us (sackcloth), so that we can become the **two witnesses** of God. He is giving of Himself, Spirit and Truth, to establish these **two witnesses** that they may impart the revelation of Christ.

> *11:4 These are the two olive trees, and the two* **candlesticks** *[on page iv] standing before the* **God of the earth.**

This is a poor translation. The lord of the earth is not God, but Satan. The term for God in this verse is 'kurios', and it is just a title. It is used mainly of the Lord but not always; and since we are told this god is "of the earth", we can be sure that this is not Jesus. This may seem like a small point, but it defines the target of the witnesses. We must go back to the Old Testament to understand these symbols. For a detailed look at the two witnesses, see Commentary 1, 'The Two Witnesses', page 113.

> *11:5 And if any man will [desire] hurt them, fire proceedeth out of their mouth, and devoureth their enemies: and if any man will hurt them,* **he must in this manner be killed.**

As these witnesses go to the Church and people reject the revelation of Christ, they will face the perfecting fire of God. It is not that these Elect will literally try to harm anyone; it is their witness that promotes carnal death. These are God's anointed, and their words ring with the power and truth of God.

This also shows that the things which offend carnal men and which lead them to attack the Witnesses become their areas of perfecting. For example, if they try to hinder by their doctrines, then their doctrines will kill them (die to self).

> *11:6 These have* **power to shut heaven***, that it rain not in the days of their prophecy: and have power over* **waters** *to turn them to* **blood***, and to smite the earth with all plagues, as often as they will.*

Heavens are Christians; in this case, they are Christians without water (spirit). These are the ones who do not have Christ in them. The witnesses bring perfection by showing these Christians what it is that they do not have. The Elect will cause a draught in Christians, who do not have Christ in them, by bringing them into accountability. They cannot justify a lack of relationship with Jesus Christ even with all their "religious" activity. As the witnesses gather into a unified voice (**many waters** see page xi), it brings life (blood) and tribulation (plagues) wherever they go.

1 Chr. 16:20-22

20	And when they went from nation to nation, and from one kingdom to another people;
21	He suffered no man to do them wrong: yea, he reproved kings for their sakes,
22	Saying, **Touch not mine anointed**, and **do my prophets no harm**.

Their power is to make the word life and to afflict carnality through their witness.

The Gathering is Complete…
(…they are ready to die)

> *11:7 [1]**And when they shall have finished their testimony***, the Beast that ascendeth out of the bottomless pit shall make war against them, and shall overcome them, and kill them.*

A better translation would be (Greek—kai hotan teleo autos marturia), [1]"Even while they perform their witness…" This takes us back to the beginning of the first dispensation. As the Harlot forms, she sends forth the kings of the earth to do battle with the Saints. If there is any carnality left in the Witnesses, then it will be killed here. This is also a witness for the Church. Our power now is in death. As Jesus said in John 10:17, "He will lay down His life that He may take it up again." We will let ourselves be overcome and die completely to self so that we can show the 'kings of the earth' who they are truly against…Christ in us. As we offer ourselves as sheep, it provides the path of Love that brings in many.

> *11:8 And their [1]**dead** bodies shall [2]**lie in the street** of the great city, which spiritually is called Sodom and Egypt, where also our Lord was crucified.*

Our [1]dying to self is a [2]witness to the worldliness (Egypt - see verse 4) of the Harlot. She will rise up against the Elect, and this is the place in which they will die. As we try to perfect the Church and bring truth to her, the Harlot will kill us. This is a death with victory; because when the kings come out to do battle (Vial Angel 1, Rev. 17:14), they will be overcome by Christ in us.

> **11:9** And they of the [1]**people and kindreds and tongues and nations** [on page xiii] shall see their dead bodies **three days and an half**, and shall not suffer their dead bodies to be put in graves.

The [1]Harlot cannot get rid of us; the more they try to put dirt in our faces, the more they see Jesus. They try to bury us in the **earth**, but no amount of their carnality can hide Christ's Glory. In other words, they try to ascribe selfish motives to our witness, yet the lies cannot stick. This shows that we minister through our death for the first dispensation. They just cannot fight against Christ, and many will turn on the harlotry of the Church and try to devour the Harlot for being the deceiver of their lives.

> **11:10** And they that **dwell upon the earth** shall rejoice over them, and make merry, and shall send gifts one to another; because these two prophets tormented them that dwelt on the earth.

In Jesus' day, the enemies of Jesus thought that they had power over Him and His witnesses. John 19:11 says that they only thought that they had power over Him. God was in control then, and He is in control today.

To the worldly, the Elect will not seem to have any real power; their power is only in their surrendered life. If truth witnessed has no affect on them, then there is virtually no authority over those who make earth (carnality) their home. They will just ignore them and make merry at their expense. They will honor (Greek implies gifts or sacrifice for honoring) each other, as men tend to do. They will consider these witnesses to lack the proper credentials and ask, "why would God speak through such as this"?

The 144,000 Finish Gathering the Bride (power comes)

> **11:11** And after [1]three days and an half the Spirit of life from God entered into them, and

> [2]**they stood upon their feet**; and great fear fell upon them which saw them.

Now, we come to the end of the first [1]three and one-half years, the time in which <u>power</u> comes to the Elect. Spiritual life and power come in the form of a glorified body. They will be [2]seen as having the power of God because of the robe of righteousness. This is the apostolic power of the Elect revealed again to the world. Since God is now our witness, then our message must be God given. This is a terrible realization for those who love their lives and can no longer hide behind false 'religious' man-made doctrines.

> **11:12** And they heard a great voice from heaven saying unto them, Come up hither. And they **ascended up to heaven in a cloud**; and <u>their enemies beheld</u> them.

Just as Jesus took His Elect up on a high mountain and was transfigured before them, the Elect will ascend and be transformed into the Wife of the Lamb. In Rev. 21:10 the angel takes John up on a high mountain to see the Wife of the Lamb, and this verse is revealing the same thing.

God's voice goes before His army (Joel Ch. 2). These witnesses will ascend spiritually as a body of believers. This ascension takes their witness before the world. The New Jerusalem is now seen; the marriage supper of the Lamb is about to take place. Every knee will bow and every tongue will confess that Jesus Christ is Lord, whether they accept Him or not.

> **11:13** And the same hour was there a **great earthquake**, and the **tenth** part of the city fell, and in the earthquake were slain of men seven thousand: and the remnant were affrighted, and gave [1]**glory to the God** of heaven.

This is the great perfecting of the harvest 'woes' (**woes** page xx). This is the time when the Wife of the Lamb in her [1]Glorious wedding robe is completed; but as you can see, some did not make the final cut. That is enough to frighten anyone.

Parenthetical 8

The Corporate Nature of the 144,000

Christ always promoted a corporate fellowship in His ministry. His work was conducted in the context of a close fellowship with the twelve apostles to the degree that even when Judas was excluded from the group, lots were drawn to ensure that he was replaced and the original twelve restored. He sent His disciples out two by two; and even Paul was always accompanied on his missionary trips. Being in unity of Spirit and Truth as a corporate body brings a Godly presence. It is the pattern established by Christ for the 144,000; therefore, it is an essential part of His manifestation.

Worshiping together in unity (verse 3) brings forth increasingly more of Christ in the individual and creates a path of perfection that will help us stay before the throne (Verse 5, also see 'fall before the throne', page vii). There are numerous references to covering and unity in the Old Testament end-time prophecies (Joel Ch. 2). Being of one heart and mind with each other allows the power of God to increase in the individual members of the body. Revelation indicates that corporate accountability is vital to the Elect army of God. "Being killed even as you were" (Rev. 6:11) is a reference to the dual role of dying to self as you assist others with the process. We need Christ in our brothers and sisters to see the things in us that need to die. This iron sharpening iron in love edifies the body and takes us into the fullness of Christ. To be part of the 144,000, you will have to be joined with a body that is collectively seeking after His appearing.

Revelation Chapter 14...
The 144,000 are Revealed

> **14:1** And I looked, and, lo, a Lamb stood on the mount Zion, and **with him an hundred forty and four thousand**, having his Father's name written in their [1]foreheads.

This is Christ and His Elect on Mount Zion representing the New Jerusalem. In the study of the New Jerusalem (on page 97), you will discover that the walls are 144 cubits. This show the relationship to the New Jerusalem...they are the defining walls. The Lamb opened the book, and the 144,000 are with the Lamb. They are [1]sold out and marked with the Glory of God.

The 144,000 of Hebrews
Heb. 12:22-29

22	But ye are come unto mount Zion and unto the city of the living God, the heavenly Jerusalem, and to an innumerable company of angels,
	Christ will gather His 144,000 (See Rev. 14:1 and they are the angels), which begin raising the New Jerusalem. These are a 'Firstfruits' company of people. The New Jerusalem is a fulfillment of the corporate nature of the Elect. They need to gather as an "innumerable" group. Innumerable speaks of being lost in the group and not seen as an individual. In other words, you cannot number them because they are as one through many.
23	To the general assembly and church of the firstborn, which are written in heaven, and to God the Judge of all, and to the spirits of just men made perfect,
	Firstfruit means the first of the harvest, the tithe portion that is God's. The 144,000 are God's possession (pages vi, i on this people). He will create the Bride Church from this group because they submit themselves willingly to the fire in order that their spirit would be spotless, perfect before God. Again the "general assembly" is the focus on corporate gathering and appearing.
24	And to Jesus the mediator of the new covenant, and to the blood of sprinkling, that speaketh better things than that of Abel.
	Abel's sacrifice denoted 'believe/faith', which is the focus of most of the churches today. The problem with faith alone is that it does not speak of true sanctification through self-sacrifice. Faith alone may be able to keep people in fellowship with God, but it is our sacrificial relationships that builds
	Christ-like maturity. Abel gave a portion; the Elect give it ALL. *'In Zion', Christ speaks to His people and helps them die to themselves, which brings more of His presence (which is perfection). According to James, faith (without 'perfecting' works) is dead being alone and is unacceptable. To whom much is given, much is required; today, that plumb line is in Christ. Christ living in you is the only way to qualify. The Angels of Zion must become accountable to Christ and to each other.*
25	See that ye refuse not him that speaketh. For if they escaped not who refused him that spake on earth, much more shall not we escape, if we turn away from him that speaketh from heaven:
	Those to whom He has spoken will not be able to turn their backs on the high calling, which is revealed in their hearts through this small book. The Truth will speak to them from now on. They will never be able to ignore what they have always known...that there was something more. They were chosen from the foundation of the earth to be an angel, a good news messenger to the world.
26	Whose voice then shook the earth: but now he hath promised, saying, Yet once more I shake not the earth only, but also heaven.
	He came not only to shake the earth (tribulation), but He came to clear the heavens in us. He will clear out the 'air' of the principalities and powers that have plagued us. Christ in us will clear out the garden and make a new heaven and earth. See 'New Heavens and Earth' page 98.
27	And this word, Yet once more, signifieth the removing of those things that are shaken, as of things that are made, that those things which cannot be shaken may remain.
	Perfection through tribulation is the Lord's way. Let Satan come at us; he can only touch those things that are temporal or carnal. We want those ungodly things in our lives to be shaken, so that we can make more room for those things of God (that will remain). To stand on Mount Zion with God is to stand on the immovable foundation of Christ.
28	Wherefore we receiving a kingdom which cannot be moved, let us have grace, whereby we may serve God acceptably with reverence and godly fear:
	Kingdom living awaits those who accept the tribulation that brings forth Christ. If we stand with Him, then we will enter the New Jerusalem. Once we have entered with our robes of righteousness, then we will not be moved again from our position in Christ. In type, if we are an 'Eagle' in Christ, we will never have to worry about losing that weight of Glory.
29	For our God is a consuming fire.
	Immovable because...It is no longer we who live, but Christ who lives through us. We have been through the fire and have come out as pure gold. He will possess the possession: dwell in His habitation and marry His betrothed.

There is no better place to dwell than on Mount Zion as the Bride of Christ.

> **14:2** And I heard a voice from heaven, as the voice of many waters, and as the voice of a

great thunder: and I heard the voice of harpers harping with their harps:

The 144,000 speak with the unified Revelation voice of God. They speak in one accord, with the authority of God (harps page x). This is the voice that Hebrews just referred to, as coming from heaven. We are the heavens who allow God to speak to the world in the [1]authority of Christ (thunders page xix).

> **14:3** *And they sung as it were a* **new song** *[on page xiii] [1]before the throne, and before the four beasts, and the elders: and no man could learn that song but the hundred and forty and four thousand, which were redeemed from the earth.*

[1]Sold-out worship of our Lord through the lives we live and the revelation of Christ we profess. This is more than a song; it is an attitude of the heart. It is the Joy of the Lord found in the revelation of Christ. It will bring such a profound change of character, that it is an unmistakable work of God; therefore the message of wrath and deliverance will be both sweet and bitter. Their psalm will be sweet to those who see the love and bitter to those who see only wrath and miss the delivering hand of God at work.

> **14:4** *These are they which were not defiled with women; for they are* **virgins** *[on page xix]. These are they which [1]follow the Lamb whithersoever he goeth. These were redeemed from among men, being the Firstfruits unto God and to the Lamb.*

This scripture is the best definition of what it means to be sold out. The 144,000 desire nothing but Christ and His will for their life. They are the true chosen generation of God.

Paul, knowing better than anyone the revelation of God, tells of his desire to get his generation married to Christ (New Jerusalem), thus hastening the appearing of the Bride. Paul says, "For I am jealous over you with godly jealousy: for I have espoused you to one husband, that I may present you as a chaste virgin to Christ (2 Cor. 11:2)." However, he goes on to say, "But I fear, lest by any means, as the serpent beguiled Eve through his subtlety, so your minds should be corrupted from the simplicity that is in Christ" (verse 3). Being corrupted by Satan's lies was the only hindrance that prevented them from being the generation which would be able to enter. They were not ready to hear the simplicity of the revelation of Christ. Satan has beguiled Christians for 2000 years robbing them of ears to hear.

This verse tells us that a generation is on the scene that will keep their garments spotless and provide a path through which others will be able to enter.

> **14:5** *And in* <u>their mouth was found no guile</u>: *for they are without fault before the throne of God.*

Only those in whom Christ is manifest can be blameless. See Zeph. 3:12-20

Parenthetical 9

The Gathering of the 144,000

In the Parenthetical of "The Harlot" page 90, we see the dragon stand over the woman to devour the Man child as soon as he is born. That Man Child is the 144,000 birthed out of the Church. As we have learned in the Parenthetical "The Corporate Nature of the Elect" (on page 107), the **gathering** of the 144,000 is critical to their spiritual growth. In this Parenthetical we will also see that this gathering is what sets loose the four winds of tribulation, held back until the 144,000 can be assembled for their ministry. The process of the gathering is described in Rev. 7:2 in which we are told that the Angels will ascend through the east (**east** page v). They will have the seal (Christ) of God (2 Tim. 2:19-21 below) upon them. This means that they are sold out and are pressing on to the high calling of God in Christ Jesus. These people are the tithe of God, the Firstfruits of Christ, and the true tribe of Israel who is reaped first for God's purposes. He wants to perfect them, so they can be used as His vessels to show forth the true Messiah to the world. They will bring great tribulation and per-

fection (verse 11) to the Church (verse 9) by showing the Lamb on His throne in us (verse 10).

Those who hear the Trumpet call and are chosen to be one of the 144,000 vessels of honor will die through great tribulation (verse 14). Before any go forth into their ministry, they must personally unlock all of the Seals of Revelation and endure the pouring out of all seven Vials of wrath upon their earth. This is the only way to be separated from the world and to be able to abide continually in the throne room of the Most High God (verses 15-16). The reward for enduring this tribulation until the end will be a perpetual dwelling place in the blessed presence of the Lord, where He supplies all needs and removes all pain. This is the true REST that awaits the Elect who will lay down their lives, so that Christ can live through them.

2 Tim. 2:19-21 Are you worthy to be sealed?

19   Nevertheless the foundation of God standeth sure, <u>having this seal</u>, The Lord knoweth them that are his. And, Let every one that nameth the name of Christ <u>depart from iniquity</u>.

20 But in a great house there are not only <u>vessels of gold and of silver</u>, but also of wood and of earth; and **some to honour, and some to dishonour.**

21 If a man therefore purge himself from these, he shall be a vessel unto honour, sanctified, and <u>meet for the master's use</u>, and prepared unto every good work.

It is God's right to honor whom He will honor, but He bases it on our willingness to enter into his process of sanctification. The 144,000 dedicate themselves to the high calling, willing to have themselves purged of all iniquity.

Revelation Chapter 7

Nothing can happen until the 144,000 are gathered

> *7:1 And after these things I saw four angels standing on the four corners of the earth, **holding the four winds of the earth,** that the wind should not blow on the earth, nor on the sea, nor on any tree.*

Before we see the events of the Seven Thunders begin, the gathering of the 144,000 must take place. This Elect company of Saints are the apostles and prophets who will usher in the tribulation time. They have already faced their personal tribulations, vials, seals, etc. in advance of this time and are prepared as spotless Saints. They are the prophetic vessels in which the Glory of God will speak to the world.

Wind represents spirit or spiritual tribulation, and four represents the last times (4 page vii). In Dan. 7:2 when these four winds are allowed to blow, the Beast rises up, signifying the beginning of the tribulation. God has ordained a specific moment in time for the tribulation to begin: at about the half-hour of the 7th Seal.

II Thes. 2:7-8

7 For the <u>mystery of lawlessness is already at work</u>; only He who now restrains will do so until He is taken out of the way.

8 And then **the lawless one will be revealed,** whom the Lord will consume with the breath of His mouth and destroy with the brightness of His ~~coming~~ [*appearing/parousia page 12*].
Not only will the Beast be revealed but so also will the glorious appearing of Christ-in-us as the Bride. The two-witnesses (Spirit and Truth) will destroy the Beast.

> *7:2 And I saw another angel ascending from the east, ¹<u>having the seal of the living God</u>: and he cried with a loud voice to the four angels, to whom it was given to hurt the earth and the sea,*

The four angels are the end-time Elijah company ¹messengers who prepare a way for the apostles and prophets to come. These are the initial revelators who gather the 144,000. This is the same ministry of John the Baptist, who was also called Elijah. 'Ascending from the east' represents the spiritual ascension of this group as they enter (east) into the presence of Christ. These end-time messengers will by their message 'hurt' carnality wherever it is, especially in the heart (sea) of the Church.

> *7:3 Saying, Hurt not the **earth**, neither the **sea**, nor the **trees**, till we have sealed the servants of our God in their foreheads.*

There is a time of preparation before the time of tribulation. The Elect must be ready before this Revelation goes to the world. They must walk out the book of Revelation in their hearts before they can be counted worthy of this calling (7th Seal, page 78). The 144,000 must first be sealed by God through Spirit and Truth (the Parenthetical 'Two Witnesses' page 105). God will place His name on them, labeling them as a peculiar people, sold out for Christ. (See how they become His City in Rev. 3:12.)

> *7:4 And I heard the number of them which were sealed: and there were sealed **an hundred and forty and four thousand** of all the tribes of the children of Israel.*

The definitions associated with the names of **The tribes** represent a path through the Gate to become the **portion of Jacob** *on page xv.* These persons are not of natural Israel. This is a spiritual book, and these are members of true Israel (the true vine). The order in which their names are given gives us a wonderful path to follow into the fullness.

The names of the tribes of Israel are written on the angels who are at the gates. We have already established that the 144,000 is the portion of Jacob (which is Christ's inheritance). Christ wants to gather sons into the kingdom for the Father. This Firstfruits company of angels has entered into the kingdom of Heaven (now seen as New Jerusalem) by coming through the gates. The names of the tribes describe a path that they (we) must follow to enter through the 'Pearl of great price' into the city.

Heb. 2:10

10 For it became him, for whom are all things, and by whom are all things, in **bringing many sons unto glory**, to make the captain of their salvation perfect through sufferings.

Christ came through the lineage of the tribes in the natural, and He is our pattern Son. We can follow His example to ascend spiritually through the lineage of the tribes to become a manifest son. Watch the progression of the spiritual walk as it is defined through the meanings of the tribal names as they are given in Thayer's definitions.

> *7:5 Of the tribe of Juda were sealed twelve thousand. Of the tribe of Reuben were sealed twelve thousand. Of the tribe of Gad were sealed twelve thousand.*
>
> ***These are also the names written on the gate angels:***
> -¹<u>Judah</u> = He shall be praised, [Ps. 48:1]
> ²<u>Reuben</u> = behold a son [Rev. 12:5],
> ³<u>Gad</u> = a troop [Joel 2:11],
>
> *7:6 Of the tribe of Aser were sealed twelve thousand. Of the tribe of Nephthalim were*

sealed twelve thousand. Of the tribe of Manasses were sealed twelve thousand.

[4] **Asher** =blessed [Rev. 1:3],
[5] **Naphhali** = my struggle or wrestling [Eph. 6:12],
[6] **Manasseh**=causing to forget [Phil. 3:13-15],

7:7 Of the tribe of Simeon were sealed twelve thousand. Of the tribe of Levi were sealed twelve thousand. Of the tribe of Issachar were sealed twelve thousand.

[7] **Simeon** = hearkening [Ps. 103:20-22],
[8] **Levi** = a joining [Jer. 50:4-5],
[9] **Issachar** = reward [Rev. 22:12],

7:8 Of the tribe of Zabulon were sealed twelve thousand. Of the tribe of Joseph were sealed twelve thousand. Of the tribe of Benjamin were sealed twelve thousand.

[10] **Zebulun** = dwelling, habitation [Zac. 2:10-13],
[11] **Joseph** = may He add or gather [Eph. 1:9-10],
[12] **Benjamin** = son of the right hand [Col. 3:1-4].

THE WAY OF THE TRIBES

Refer back to the previous scriptures as we show that the meaning of the tribes' names will lead us into the fullness of Christ.

As we [1]praise Him with our life, we become recognized as a [2]son but not yet a joint heir. We [3]gather together and become [4]blessed. To obtain more blessing, we let [5]iron sharpen iron; thereby, [6]we lose our old life and its carnality. His [7]voice of correction (iron) within the body [8]joins us together through the single purpose of revealing more of Christ in us, [9]which is our treasure. As He increases in us, His [10]presence is seen through us; consequently, the world can see and desire "He who is working within us." Therefore, as we [11]gather more sons into the glory of His presence, we are made perfect through sufferings (Heb. 2:10 above), and are manifested as a [12]son of the kingdom. Now, as a joint heir, we are His wife, the New Jerusalem.

The 144,000 Begin New Jerusalem

7:9 [1]After this I beheld, and, lo, a great multitude, which no man could number, of all [2]nations, and kindreds, and people, and tongues, stood before the throne, and before the Lamb, clothed with white robes, and palms in their hands;

[1]After the four winds blow tribulation into the Church, they begin to separate those who have been redeemed from the [2]Harlot. They are to receive the robes that signify them as members of the New Jerusalem in the second dispensation.

7:10 And cried with a loud voice, saying, Salvation to our God which sitteth upon the throne, and unto the Lamb.

7:11 And all the angels stood round about the throne, and about the elders and the four beasts, and fell before the throne on their faces, and worshipped God,

Except for the first century church, there has never been so great an emphasis on relationship and growth (elders fall down page vii). The gathering represents a time of great spiritual growth. It takes a lot of dying to see the 144,000 come forth, and even more as they gather the Bride.

7:12 Saying, Amen: Blessing, and glory, and wisdom, and thanksgiving, and honour, and power, and might, be unto our God for ever and ever. Amen.

These are the beginnings of rewards for the Elect. As you die, more of Christ is yours (blessing, Glory, wisdom, thanksgiving, honor, power, and might). These are the fruit of the seven spirits of God or the fullness of Christ (7 spirits page xvii).

7:13 And one of the elders answered, saying unto me, What are these which are arrayed in white robes [robe of righteousness] and whence came they?

Citizens of New Jerusalem

7:14 And I said unto him, Sir, thou knowest. And he said to me, These are they which came out of great tribulation, and have washed their robes, and made them white in the blood of the [1]Lamb.

The 144,000 have allowed all the spiritual perfection of the revelation of Christ to slay them. They are [1]dead to self and entered into the fullness of Christ. The longer you wait, the less chance you have of being part of this end-time army of God.

7:15 Therefore are they before the throne of God, and serve him day and night in his temple: and he that sitteth on the throne shall dwell among them.

Those in the fullness of Christ are always in the presence of the Lord. No wonder they are so anointed.

As the Wife of the Lamb, we can have a face to face relationship reserved for lovers. Going and coming, He is with us. That is why during the Millennium, we are ruling with a rod of iron. We speak with the authority of God in the same way that Moses did.

7:16 They shall hunger no more, neither thirst any more; neither shall the sun light on them, nor any heat.

All natural needs are eliminated in our glorified bodies, but the deeper spiritual meaning must be seen. Those in the fullness of Christ will no longer hunger and thirst for righteousness, because they are already full of Christ. The sun (natural light) represents the worldly glory that tempts and tests Christians; however, the 144,000 will not be tempted with the natural. Neither will there be any more tribulation (heat) in their life for Satan has no place in them.

> *7:17* For the Lamb which is in the **midst of the throne** shall feed them, and shall lead them unto living fountains of waters: and God shall wipe away all tears from their eyes.

He is in complete control of the lives of the Saints. He will be their all in all.

Parenthetical 10

The Heart of God...the Elect

This Parenthetical describes the spiritual relationship of the 'heart of God' manifested in the Elect of the New Jerusalem, as it is recorded in the last chapter of the book of Revelation. The pure water that will run from the throne of God will pour out from the heart of the Elect as pure spiritual truth and life. Those who follow this pure revelation of Christ and tap into its Life will be fruitful and healthy. Not only will they be healthy in the natural sense, but they will be spiritually healthy; they will be cured from the curse of sin, and always able to bear fruit.

The sold out followers of Christ will see Him face to face (verse 4), and this will produce Glory that the entire world will see (verse 5). These Elect messengers show, by their much anointed lives, that they have Truth. As Jesus said, "Believe me for my work's sake." Truth reveals truth; so when the Glory begins to be seen in the lives of the Elect, all will be accountable to walk after what has been revealed. Those who do will see the things written in this book take place in their lives and in the world as well.

> If you have read this and your spirit soars at the idea that you could be part of the greatest move of God since Christ walked the earth, then let the pastors of Hope of Glory Ministries know. We are dedicated to joining in spirit with those who love His appearing.
> www.hopeofglory.us or vtanner@kohm.net

Revelation Chapter 22

> *22:1* And he shewed me a pure **river of water** of life, **clear as crystal**, proceeding out of the throne of God and of the Lamb.

The throne of the kingdom of Heaven is in us; therefore, the revelatory Word will run purely in and through us from now on. The Bride will be without spot or blemish to show forth the love of the Lamb.

> *22:2* In the midst of the street of it, and on either side of the river, was there the **tree** of life, which bare twelve manner of **fruits**, and yielded her fruit every month: and the leaves of the tree were for the healing of the nations.

Our way (road) will be a path of Life (tree of life), and we will be fruitful trees of the Spirit from which others can eat. In contrast to the first garden, there will be no more trees of 'good and evil', only the tree of life. This scripture is very much like Jer. 17. Our blessed life is a mark of the presence of Christ; this is hope for many. The revelation of Christ will be healing for the nations.

> *22:3* And there shall be no more curse: but the throne of God and of the Lamb shall be in it; and his servants shall serve him:

As the curse goes away, the kingdom flows out of us, and the planet is restored. The land cursed by sin is returned to its original Garden state by the manifestation of the sons of God.

> *22:4* And they shall see his face; and his name shall be in their [1]foreheads.

We are [1]sold out, and He will be visible to us.

> *22:5* And there shall be no night there; and they need no candle, neither light of the sun; for the Lord God giveth them light: and they shall reign for ever and ever.

The Glory is established in us; there is nothing more to perfect. The lies of the Beast and the false prophets have been eliminated, and Satan is locked up or cast out. Notice that we will continue to rule. The White Throne Judgment is an all-inclusive judgment, from which none will escape. This verse speaks of a time after the White Throne Judgment and suggests apparently there are many more plans for God's Saints, even after the end.

> *22:6* And he said unto me, These sayings are faithful and true: and the Lord God of the holy prophets sent his angel to **shew unto his servants the things which must shortly be done.**

This verse in the last chapter of Revelation echoes the message in the first (Rev. 1:1): all that we have heard and learned is true. It is our hope that if you have ears to hear, by now you, too, should realize the truth in this message. If this has happened and you have now finished the book, you can be sure that the Revelation time line has begun in you.

Supplement II Commentaries

These Commentaries are similar to the Parentheticals, but they are subject studies rather than chapter studies. They are designed to provide added background to the types and doctrines associated with the study of Revelation

Commentary 1

The Two Witnesses

The two witnesses of Revelation are normally portrayed as two persons who are given certain powers to 'witness' against the antichrist and his plans. However, line upon line study of the scripture suggests a better interpretation of the "two witnesses" of Revelation. We will see that the two witnesses is a condition of the heart: an empowerment of 'Spirit and Truth' that will enable the revelation of Christ to go forward in power to all the nations.

> **Isa. 43:9-10**
> 9   All the nations gather together and the peoples assemble. Which of them foretold this and proclaimed to us the former things? Let them bring in their witnesses to prove they were right, so that others may hear and say, "It is true."
> 10   "You are my witnesses," declares the LORD, "and my servant whom I have chosen, so that you may know and believe me and understand that I am he. Before me no god was formed, (NIV)

The focus of this study will be on how the Elect obtains the two witnesses, or how "having the two witnesses" reveals Christ. We will use both Old and New Testament verses to show the foundation of the terms associated with Chapter 11. We will cover only the first four verses of Chapter 11 in this Commentary. The remainder of Chapter 11 relates to the part the two witnesses play in Revelation events and is discussed in Parenthetical 7, 'Two Witnesses in the 144,000', on page 105. While this Commentary focuses on how the believer spiritually obtains the two witnesses, the Parenthetical discusses their place in Revelation.

Measure the Temple
Rev. 11:1-4

11:1** And there was given me a reed like unto a rod: and the angel stood, saying, Rise, and **measure the temple of God, and the altar, and them that worship therein.

Greek metreo –b) metaphorically, to judge according to any rule or standard, to estimate.
John is told in Rev. 11:1, to measure the temple of God, the altar, and those who worship therein. As the following scriptures indicate, we are the temples of God. To measure these temples is to

judge according to the rule or standard given in the Word of God, to determine if they meet the requirements necessary for a dwelling place for Christ.

> **1 Cor. 3:16**
> 16   Know ye not that **ye are the temple of God,** and that the Spirit of God dwelleth in you?
>
> ### The call to purify the temple
> **2 Cor. 6:14-18**
> 14   Be ye not unequally yoked together with unbelievers: for **what fellowship hath righteousness with unrighteousness**? and what communion hath light with darkness?
> 15   And what concord hath Christ with Belial? or what part hath he that believeth with an infidel?
> *If we claim to be the temple of God, then we should not accept anything unholy in the temple. If there is unrighteousness in us, then we are brought into question as to whether or not we are the temples of God. This is not to condemn us about our lack of perfection; instead it is to motivate us to the fulfillment of the promise in Rom. 8:1. There is no condemnation if we "walk not after the flesh but the Spirit." What makes the Elect the chosen of God is their unwillingness to settle for less of Christ.*
> 16   And what agreement **hath the temple of God with idols? for ye are the temple of the living God**; as God hath said, I will dwell in them, and walk in them; and I will be their God, and they shall be my people.
> 17   **Wherefore come out from among them,** and be ye separate, saith the Lord, and **touch not the unclean thing**; and I will receive you,
> 18   And will be a Father unto you, and ye shall <u>be my sons</u> and daughters, saith the Lord Almighty.

***11:2** But the court which is without the temple leave out, and measure it not; for it is given unto the Gentiles: and the holy city shall they tread under foot **forty and two** months.*

The gentiles are those well meaning but misguided persons who worry over worldly things. They view the world through natural eyes. These are the carnal immature Christians placing value on natural instead of spiritual events. Satan can distract these outer court Christians with almost any form of offence. Therefore, they can never get past the natural and go on to the inner court temple of the heart; this prevents them from judging the temple to determine if it is the dwelling place of the Spirit of Christ or the spirit of antichrist.

These carnal Christians will not be able to see the heart issues that bring forth the fullness of Christ; therefore, there is no reason to dispute or debate with those who do not have ears to hear. The revelation of Christ is for those who are seeking that 'inner' relationship with Christ.

11:3 And I will give ~~power~~ unto my **two witnesses**, and they shall prophesy a thousand two hundred and threescore days, clothed in sackcloth.

The conjunction 'And' in verse 3 connects the information in this verse to the "measuring of the temple." "After we measure the temple within, He will give…"

The revelation in verse 3 is about something being given, by the "measuring of the temple", to the two witnesses, which enables them to prophesy for three-and-one-half years. The measuring of the temple also brings humility (sackcloth) which makes those measured worthy to receive what the Lord wants to give.

Who are the two witnesses, and what will be given…

11:4 These are the **two olive trees**, and the **two candlesticks** standing before the God of the earth.

In verse 4 we see that the two witnesses are the two OLIVE TREES, AND THE TWO CANDLESTICKS. Zechariah 4:1-14 will give us insight into the nature of these two witnesses.

THE LAMPSTAND / CANDLE-STICK (verse Rev. 11:4 explained)

To fully explain the olive trees and the candlesticks, we must look to Zechariah and Haggai. In these verses we will see that measuring the temple is to look for the presence of Christ. He is the oil (spirit) and the light (truth) of the menorah. Christ-in-us is the fullness of the two witnesses.

Zec. 4:2-14

Zec. 4:2	And said unto me, What seest thou? And I said, I have looked, and **behold a candlestick all of gold**, with a bowl upon the top of it, and his seven lamps thereon, and seven pipes to the seven lamps, which are upon the top thereof:
Zec. 4:3	And *two olive trees* by it, one upon the right side of the bowl, and the other upon the left side thereof.

In verses 2 and 3 a description in 'type' is given of the two witnesses (a lampstand or menorah). There is one main candlestick with a bowl on top

and three branches coming out from both sides. These branches are the two olive trees and the two candlesticks.

Zec. 4:4	So I answered and spake to the angel that talked with me, saying, What are these, my lord?
Zec. 4:5	Then the angel that talked with me answered and said unto me, Knowest thou not what these be? And I said, No, my lord.
Zec. 4:6a	Then he answered and spake unto me, saying, This is the **word of the LORD unto Zerubbabel**, saying…

Zerubbabel *means begotten in Babylon. He was a type of Christ or the Son of man. He led Israel out of the Babylonian captivity to build the temple and altar. This is a wonderful picture for us to see. Christ wants to lead us out of Babylon to build the temple and the altar within us.*

Lampstand/candlestick [on page iv] *represents the visible witness of God (Christ in us).*

The golden lampstand has the true vine (Christ) and the branches (us). Together they form a light (witness) to the world. The Spirit of Christ and the spoken revelation of Christ-in-us are Spirit and Truth.

In Zec. 4:4-6 the angel reveals the two fig trees and the two candlesticks. WE SEE THAT THEY ARE THE WORD OF THE LORD UNTO ZERUBBABEL. In this case, the word given to Zerubbabel is in Hag. 1:1-7.

The Word to Zerubbabel

Revelation 11:1 commands us to measure the temple. Why are we given such a personal command? What does measuring the temple have to do with the two witnesses? Why is it that the two witnesses seem to appear only as part of Revelation? The word to Zerubbabel gives us some insight as to what God is really asking us to do. Therefore, before we continue with verse 6 to 14 of Zechariah, we must divert into Hag. 1:1-8 to answer this question.

Hag. 1:1-8	
1	In the second year of Darius the king, in the sixth month, in the first day of the month, came the word of the LORD **by Haggai the prophet unto Zerubbabel** the son of Shealtiel, governor of Judah, and to Joshua the son of Josedech, the high priest, saying,
2	Thus speaketh the LORD of hosts, saying, This people say, The time is not come, the time that the LORD's house should be built.
3	Then came the word of the LORD by Haggai the prophet, saying,
4	Is it time for you, O ye, to dwell in your cieled [*paneled*] houses, and **this house lie waste**?
5	Now therefore thus saith the LORD of hosts; Consider your ways.
	The first part of the word to Zerubbabel tells us that the people of the Lord are living in their comfortable homes when God's temple lies in waste. This sounds like lazy Christians, fat on faith without works, seeing no need to make greater room in their lives for Christ.

	The message yesterday and today is that God wants His people to consider their ways. They are comfortable with their lives; yet they are not right before God. They are content with their 'Sunday/Wednesday' Jesus, and will not hear of the need for a sold out relationship. We see in verse 6 (below) that this state of comfort is a lie, and they should not be deceived.
6	Ye have sown much, and bring in little; ye eat, but ye have not enough; ye drink, but ye are not filled with drink; ye clothe you, but there is none warm; and he that earneth wages earneth wages to put it into a bag with holes.
	These people feel that they have favor with God even though their lives visibly contradict that fact. All of these things speak of a lack of Christ in their lives. No matter how hard they work, it never works out. If Christ is in you, He will be evident in your life.
7	Thus saith the LORD of hosts; Consider your ways.
	The Lord says consider your fruit, and do not hide behind your "religion".
8	Go up to the mountain, and bring [1]wood, and build the house; and I will take pleasure in it, and I will be glorified, saith the LORD.
	The word [1]wood (Greek `ets is the same word for 'trees' page xix.) stands for people. Isa. 61:3 "To appoint unto them that mourn in Zion, to give unto them beauty for ashes, the oil of joy for mourning, the garment of praise for the spirit of heaviness; that they might be called TREES of righteousness, the planting of the LORD, that he might be glorified." These people in Isaiah are willing to be chastened and perfected, so that they can be "of the Lord" and His Glory can appear.
	The second part of the word of the Lord to Zerubbabel (and the people of the Lord) is to complete the building of the temple. To accomplish this, you will let Him "measure you" and build you into a habitation of God. Therefore, be willing to be chastened of the Lord, and focus on the spiritual not the natural.
	How can this be accomplished? Let's go back to Zechariah 4:6 where we left off…

Now we know that "to measure the temple" is to make (become) a home for the two witnesses. So who are the two witnesses?

Back to Zechariah…

Zec. 4:6b Then he answered and spake unto me, saying, This is the **WORD** of the LORD unto Zerubbabel, saying, Not by might, nor by power, but by my **SPIRIT**, saith the LORD of hosts.

The building of the temple (measuring up) is by the Spirit of the Lord. This is the second witness. The first witness is the word (truth). Therefore, we see the two witnesses as SPIRIT AND TRUTH. As we let go and let God have His way in our lives, He will build us into a holy habitation. Dying to self is the process by which we let go of those things that are not of God and allow more of the Spirit of Christ to dwell in us.

In verse 6 we see that the witness will not be by might, nor power. Today, we tend to look for the spectacular; we want to see some "fire from heaven." Yet, the Word tells us that our true witness is "loving not their lives unto death" (Rev. 12:11). This is how life in the 'holy place' differs from that in the 'outer court'. Outer-court ministries are usually dead because they do not believe that there is a deeper place to go in their relationship with Jesus Christ (the most holy place). On the other hand, some try to spruce up the outer court with spectacular spiritual gifts. Indeed, the Holy Spirit wants them to taste of what is ahead, but these gifts are designed to motivate people toward Jesus (in the most holy place). The Holy Spirit wants them to partake of the Giver, not the gift, to answer Christ's call to measure the temple, and to move out of the outer court and into the inner chamber of His dwelling place.

Yet, we will not be able to please God and see the temple (relationship) built by our might or power. Our works are as filthy rags. All we can hope for is (Phil. 4:13) to be able to do all things "through Christ". Dying is our part; Christ will provide the Life.

Christ-in-us the Master Builder

We know that God wants us to build the temple by measuring it, so how is that accomplished? The outer court is the place of the Holy Spirit. He was given to us as an 'earnest' or down payment of the full inheritance of Christ. As it says in Eph. 3:16 (page 24), the Holy Spirit is trying to strengthen the inner place (our heart) in order that Christ can dwell there.

People often ask about the distinction between the role of the Holy Spirit and the Spirit of Christ. The enemy has robbed the Church of the great revelation of Christ-in-us by persuading men to reduce the triune Godhead into two persons, Father and Son. When they refer to the Holy Spirit, they do not see Him as a separate entity; but instead, they see Him as a spirit form of Christ or the Father. They stumble over the scriptures about Christ in us. By not seeing this distinction and understanding the nature of the "kingdom", they may fail to see that Christ is the bearer of Life. The Holy Spirit is the comforter and teacher until we come into that Life. The Spirit of Christ is the omnipresent form of Christ; He is the only one who can build the temple.

God has created a perfect plan in which each member of the Trinity performs a perfect role. They are not interchangeable: the Holy Spirit did not die on the cross nor is the Son greater than the Father. Once we see this plan, we can walk in victory. The Holy Spirit leads us into the outer court and helps us prepare the place for the temple. Christ comes and builds the temple with a throne in our hearts to dwell upon. Christ is the bearer of Life, and in Him is Life. When the temple has been prepared by the Holy Spirit and Christ has Lordship of our lives, the Life of God can operate in us; His presence transforms us "face to face."

Zec. 4:7 Who art thou, **O great mountain**? before Zerubbabel thou shalt become a plain: and he shall bring forth **the headstone** thereof with shoutings, crying, Grace, grace unto it.

The great mountain brought low
Luke 3:4-6

4 As it is written in the book of the words of Esaias the prophet, saying, The voice of one crying in the wilderness, Prepare ye the way of the Lord, make his paths straight.

5 Every valley shall be filled, and **every mountain and hill shall be brought low**; and the crooked shall be made straight, and the rough ways shall be made smooth;

6 And all flesh shall see the salvation of God.

See mountain page xii. When the great mountains (representing carnal religion) no longer obstruct the flow of God's presence (plain), then we shall see Christ. Christ then being manifest (headstone) in the temple will allow all flesh to see God.

Matt. 21:42-44

42 Jesus saith unto them, Did ye never read in the scriptures, The stone which the **builders** rejected, the same is become the head of the corner: this is the Lord's doing, and it is marvellous in our eyes?

'Builders' represented the Hebrew leadership of Jesus' time and the Church leadership of today. Any time the shepherds are not faithful to follow God's design and choose instead to build their own mountains, the Lord steps in. To study this further, take time to read Ezekiel Chapter 34. Watch as the Lord declares that if the shepherds will not do it, then He will. That is what Christ-in-us is all about.

43 Therefore say I unto you, The kingdom of God shall be taken from you, and given to a nation bringing forth the fruits thereof.

44 And whosoever shall fall on this stone shall be broken: but on whomsoever it shall fall, it will grind him to powder.

The ultimate end to carnal leadership is a carnal church (Parenthetical "The Harlot" page 90). The candlestick is then removed from the Harlot and given to the Elect as the Bride Church.

Zec. 4:8 Moreover the word of the LORD came unto me, saying,

Zec. 4:9 The hands of Zerubbabel have laid the foundation of this house; his hands shall also finish it; and thou shalt know that the LORD of hosts hath sent me unto you.

Christ began the building of the temple in us and He will finish it. John 14:3-18 makes this clear: "He goes to prepare a place for us." Some believe that this is a far-off place; yet, in these scriptures, Jesus points out that the place is where He is. Then in verse 18 of John 14, He says that He will come to us. This only makes sense when we see Christ-in-us as the answer.

He wants a place prepared _in us_ so that He can come to us.

Zec. 4:10 For who hath despised the day of **small things**? for they shall rejoice, and shall see the **plummet** in the hand of Zerubbabel with those **seven**; they are the **eyes** of the LORD, which run to and fro through the whole earth.

Small means insignificant. The word 'things' was added. Plummet represents the plumb line, measuring ruler, way to see if something is straight or measures up.

Seven eyes represents the 'seven spirits of Christ or His fullness'. See page xvii.

This is a wonderful picture. Christ is clearing out of our lives the things inhibiting the fullness. The process goes like this: First, the Holy Spirit prepares the place in our heart through our surrender and obedience. Second, Christ dwells in that place and starts building us as a holy habitation. Third, He begins the process in which we die to self; this leads to the fullness of Christ's presence. This process is one step at a time (small things). The fullness is what we are supposed to be striving to obtain. In Eph., Chapters 3 and 4, the fullness is only obtained through the mystery of Christ-in-us, the hope of Glory.

Zec. 4:11 Then answered I, and said unto him, What are these **two olive trees** upon the right side of the **candlestick** and upon the left side thereof?

Zec. 4:12 And I answered again, and said unto him, What be these two olive branches which through the two golden pipes empty the **golden oil** [anointing] out of themselves?

Zec. 4:13 And he answered me and said, Knowest thou not what these be? And I said, No, my lord.

Zec. 4:14 Then said he, These ~~are~~ the two anointed ~~ones~~, that stand by the LORD of the whole earth.

The words used to translate the 'anointed ones' are descriptive of Spirit and Truth, not two people. A study of Zec. 4:14 shows a change in the translation. There is no 'are' or 'ones', instead 'ben' and 'yitshar' are used to translate to 'anointed'. These two words are 'anointed one' and 'anointing oil' respectively, seen as the anointing of Christ-in-us. Therefore, Zechariah reveals that the "anointing" in the life of the Elect is a witness of the presence of the "anointed one". The two then are not the number of persons, but the number of internal witnesses; Christ-in-us is being revealed through us.

Vs. 11-14 show us the two witnesses functioning in relationship to Christ (the anointed one); this is showing how the golden oil (the anointing, spirit) is flowing to the branches (us). The anointing then is able to fulfill the Word of the Lord, which is to build the temple in each person who desires the life of Christ in them.

Commentary 2

The righteous shall never be removed: but the wicked shall not inhabit the earth (Prov. 10:30)

The Rapture

Where did it originate?

Despite the current widespread belief of many, it can be shown that rapture theology is not rooted in Church history. The foundation of the rapture **theory** is only about two hundred years old. Emmanuel Lacunza, a Jesuit priest, published a book that first introduced the idea of a pre-tribulation rapture in 1812. Prior to that, only Morgan Edwards in 1788 published anything that can be loosely construed as relating to an end time rapture.

> **From The Origin of the Pre-tribulation Rapture, by John Bray[1], a southern Baptist Evangelist and author.**
>
> Though many believe and teach this Pre-tribulation Rapture theory, they erroneously do so. Neither Jesus, Paul, Peter, John, nor any of the other writers of the Bible taught this. Neither did the early Church fathers, nor any others for many hundreds of years.
>
> Did you know that NONE of this was ever taught prior to 1812 (later amended to 1788), and that all forms of Pre-tribulation rapture teaching were developed since that date? I mean by this that NO New Testament rapture writer taught a Pre-tribulation rapture, NONE of the early church fathers taught it. No Catholic Church creed taught it, NO Protestant Church creed nor Reformer taught it. No other group or person ever published such teachings before 1812 (amended to 1788).

Dispute over the rapture is not new with this study; many well-established denominations and groups go on record against this theory. The real problem with the belief in a pre-tribulation rapture is that it lulls us into complacency and distracts us from preparing for an end time *harvest*. The parable of the tares (Matt. 13:24-43) clearly shows that the **wheat and the tares must grow together** until the harvest (later described as the end of the world (Matt. 13:39). In this parable, the first thing to be done in the harvest is to **"remove the wicked from the righteous"**, not the righteous from the wicked! If all of God's children remain until the wicked are removed, there would be no need for a rapture of the Church.

Rapture means "snatching away"; and according to those who believe in this doctrine, the Church will be

---

[1] The Origin of the Pre-tribulation Rapture Teaching, by John L. Bray. The address of Evangelist Bray is PO Box 90129, Lakeland, Florida, 33804, USA, and his phone is (863)858-6625.

snatched away by Jesus Christ's coming. The snatching away of the Church is the foundation of this belief, although there is still division about when, who, and how many will be taken. Some believe that the Church will leave before a tribulation time, thus they are described as 'pre-trib'. Others think this event will take place in the middle of the period of tribulation, and still others believe it will be at the end of tribulation. This is not the only area of division; some rapture doctrines believe that only the worthy believers will be taken away. Others believe that there are two partial raptures with multiple variations on when and who. Who is right? How can there be so much division on one single issue?

The scriptures do not seem to support any single rapture doctrine; therefore, men keep adding and changing doctrinal positions to accommodate the contradictions. There is an alarming trend taking place in which fictional accounts of the end-time events are becoming established as doctrine; these doctrines are believed because of their cultural acceptance, not their scriptural soundness. To counter that trend, let's look at the scriptures related to the 'rapture' and see what rightly dividing them shows us.

JUST WHO IS LEAVING?

Matt. 24:36-44 is a passage of scripture commonly associated with the rapture. There can be no doubt in Verse 39 that these scriptures are to be associated with the "coming" of the Lord. It is also clear that someone in these scriptures is being 'snatched away'. The question is who is leaving? The people who are leaving in verses 40 and 41 are to be compared to the ones leaving in verse 39; and thus knowing who is leaving in 39 is critical. Some like to try and interpret verse 39 as a rapture verse with Noah and his family being swept away to safety, meaning we would want to be one of the ones taken in verse 40 and 41. Yet, Luke 17:27 makes it clear that it was those who "knew not" who were taken away. In this scripture it shows that the wicked were taken away (or destroyed) from out of the midst of the others. "They did eat, they drank, they married wives, they were given in marriage, until the day that Noah entered into the ark, and the flood came, **and destroyed them all.**"

As in the days of Noah
Matt. 24:36-44
36   But of that day and hour knoweth no man, no, not the angels of heaven, but my Father only.

37	But as the days of Noe were, so shall also the **coming of the Son of man be.**
38	For as in the days that were before the flood they were eating and drinking, marrying and giving in marriage, until the day that Noe entered into the ark,
39	And knew not until the flood came, and took them all away; **so shall also the coming the Son of man be.**
40	Then shall two be in the field; the one shall be taken, and the other left.
41	Two women shall be grinding at the mill; the **one shall be taken**, and the other left.
42	Watch therefore: for ye know not what hour your Lord doth come.
43	But know this, that if the goodman of the house had known in what watch the thief would come, he would have watched, and would not have suffered his house to be broken up.
44	Therefore be ye also ready: for in such an hour as ye think not the Son of man cometh.

According to this scripture, you do not want to be one of the ones taken. They were the ones so busy with this world that they failed to see the signs of the end-time coming. They were taken by surprise when the door was shut. It was Noah and those in the Ark who were left here on the earth! This shows a **REVERSE RAPTURE**, a rapture whereby the wicked are removed at His appearing. There are other places in which Jesus speaks of the evil ones being removed at His coming. Let's look further back in Matthew at the parable of the tares.

The Wicked Removed

The parable of the tares gives us a wonderful picture of the Church age, starting with the planting of the Church and ending with the spotless Bride Church (verse 43). It is also a classic example of the wicked being removed. This parable shows that both the wicked and the good grow together UNTIL "the end of the world." The key word is "until", pointing out that both the wicked and the good stay together until the wicked are removed.

Matt. 13:24-30	
24	Another parable put he forth unto them, saying, The kingdom of heaven is likened unto a man which sowed good seed in his field:
25	But while[1] men slept, his enemy came and sowed tares among the wheat, and went his way.
30	**Let both grow together until the harvest: and in the time of *harvest* I will say to the reapers, Gather ye together <u>FIRST</u> the tares, and bind them in bundles to burn them: but gather the wheat into my barn.**

The first thing is to remove the wicked...that is the reverse of the rapture!!

Tares explained by Jesus	
Matt. 13:36-43	
36	Then Jesus sent the multitude away, and went into the house: and his disciples came unto him, saying, Declare unto us the parable of the tares of the field.
37	He answered and said unto them, He that soweth the good seed is the Son of man;

38	**The field is the world; the good seed are the children of the kingdom; but the tares are the children of the wicked one;**
39	The enemy that sowed them is the devil; **the *harvest* is the <u>end of the world</u>**; and the reapers are the angels.
40	As therefore the tares are gathered and burned in the fire; so shall it be in the end of this world.
41	**The Son of man shall send forth his angels, and they shall gather out of his kingdom all things that offend, and them which do iniquity;**
42	And shall cast them into a furnace of fire: there shall be wailing and gnashing of teeth.
43	<u>**Then shall the righteous shine forth as the sun in the kingdom of their Father. Who hath ears to hear, let him hear**</u>.

Notice that the reason for the wicked being removed is so that the righteous can shine. This is the Bride Church coming into being. There is the same picture of her in Rev. 21:11. Study of this parable plainly demonstrates that God's intent is not to remove the Church from out of the earth, but to remove the wicked so that the Church can be perfected (without spot or blemish).

The "**FIRST**" thing that the angel does is to <u>remove the tares</u>. For this scripture to support the rapture, it would have to read: "first, I will <u>remove my wheat</u> from among the tares." These scriptures contradict the rapture doctrine, which has the "good" - not the evil - being snatched away.

Several other scriptures support the removal of evil from good. Not far from the parable of the 'tares' in Matt. 13:47-50, we read about the parable of "the net". In this parable two kinds of fish are caught and gathered; and again, the wicked are separated from the righteous. "So shall it be at the **end of the world**: the angels shall come forth, and <u>sever the wicked from among the just</u>," (Matt. 13:49). In the parable of the "ten virgins", the same thing happens as the five foolish virgins are turned away. In each of these parables, it is the wicked or foolish that are sent or cast away from the good and righteous.

As you can see, these scriptures bring into question some of the popular beliefs that support the notion of a rapture. However, please do not fail to see the wonderful truth that is also being expressed in these scriptures. Remember that Christ wants a Bride without spot or blemish. As you know, a little leaven leaveth the whole lump, and it only takes one bad apple to spoil the bushel. **These scriptures point to the first truth of Revelation 1:1: Christ is coming to prepare for Himself a Bride. He will start by purifying His church, removing the wicked from among her so that she will be spotless** (Read Jude 1:4-12 particularly, verse 12).

Before his Bride can be ready for the love feast, everyone who is of Christ will be changed. Until this occurs, until the Elect have had all of the Revelation finished in them, the tribulation cannot even begin.

Rev. 10:7 says, "But in the days of the voice of the seventh angel, when he shall begin to sound, the mystery of God should be finished," This is speaking of the last trump when everyone who has been made **complete** (page 124) will get a **robe of righteousness**. Paul knew of this and wrote of it to the Corinthians.

1 Cor. 15:51-53	
51	Behold, I shew you a mystery; **We** shall not all sleep, **but we shall all be changed**,
52	In a moment, in the twinkling of an eye, ***at the last trump***: for the trumpet shall sound, and the dead shall be raised incorruptible, **and** we shall be changed.
53	For this corruptible must put on incorruption, and this mortal must put on immortality.

Many use this verse to support the rapture, but notice that it takes place at the last trump. Paul uses the pronoun "we", demonstrating that he expected to be part of this event, which gives no room for a rapture, either before or during the tribulation. This is describing the robes of righteousness that everyone who endures to the end will receive. Even those who are asleep in Jesus will rise to be part of the Millennium.

THE FOUNDATION OF THE RAPTURE DOCTRINE

First and Second Thessalonians

These verses in Thessalonians provide the backbone to all rapture doctrine. Rightly divide these, and you will be forced to conclude that, in actuality, they do nothing to support such a doctrine.

Paul taught in some detail about the end-time to the churches to which he traveled (2 Thes. 2:5). However, not all that he taught was understood (much the same way as today). Such as was the case with the Church in Thessalonica. Even though he taught them in person, many questions still remained after he left. First Thessalonians was written as a response to these questions and concerns. However, Paul's answers were cryptic and hard for them to understand. They got so confused that they began to believe that the Day of the Lord had already come to pass (2 Thes. 2:2). Paul admitted to "troubling" readers; therefore, he sought to clear up all misunderstandings with a final explanation in a second letter to the Thessalonians written in plain language. First Thessalonians should be studied in conjunction with Second Thessalonians to ensure proper understanding of Paul's position. Unfortunately, few people go on to Second Thessalonians to resolve the questions that occur during the study of Chapter Four of the first book. Today, many scholars take advantage of the cryptic language in Chapter Four to build their case for their particular doctrine, but they fail to justify their position in light of Paul's further exposition on this subject in Second Thessalonians.

4:14-17 …The Snatching Away?

This is the most quoted verse for rapture theologians. It is actually the verse from which the concept of the rapture comes. There is no actual word 'rapture' used in the Bible, rather rapture is Latin for "caught up", which is harpazo (har-pad'-zo) in the Greek; it is from a derivative of Strong's # 138; 'to seize'.

1 Thes. 4:14-16	
14	For if we believe that Jesus died and rose again, even so them also which sleep in Jesus will God bring

with him.

15	For this we say unto you by the word of the Lord, that we which are alive and remain unto the coming of the Lord shall not prevent (precede) them which are asleep.
16	For the Lord himself shall descend **from heaven with[in] a **shout**, with[in] the voice of the **archangel**, and with[in] the **trump** of God: and the **dead in Christ shall rise first**:

Paul was not trying to deliver a doctrinal treatise on end-time events in I Thes. 4:13 when he wrote "I would not have you ignorant concerning them which are asleep (dead), that ye sorrow not…" Paul was only trying to comfort his readers by answering their concerns that their loved ones would be together with them after the events described as the Lord's appearing (verse 15). Yet, the confusion he caused the Thessalonians by his statements in Chapter Four was perhaps less than that caused by these same three verses which are being scripturally interpreted as justification for the rapture theology. The problems with using these scriptures to support the rapture may be difficult to be perceived by the casual reader, but our purposes in this study are to read the Word LINE UPON LINE.

Eliminating the Confusion of 1st Thessalonians Chapter 4

- 'Dead in Christ' and 'asleep in Jesus' represent two different peoples.

God brings one group with Him (verse 14); the other rises up (verse 16). For clarity we define 'the **dead** in Christ' on page iv as those who have 'died to self'. Seeing the **dead** as the Elect resolves this issue.

- His return is "IN OR WITHIN" a shout, voice of an archangel, trump of God.

The meaning of the Greek word 'en' in verse 16 is translated 'with'; yet, 'en' is about position IN or within something, not separated from it. The focus is not that He will come when these things happen, but IN these things; thus, it must be figurative. For example, "He will rule *with* a rod of iron"; 'Rod of iron' is meant to be a visual type. It is not saying He will use a rod to rule; but instead, it describes the way He will rule. He does not want you to see these verses literally, and so He uses 'en' to say 'in this way', meaning He will come in the form of a shout, voice, etc. Later, we will see how He does "come" IN a SHOUT.

- Use of air (Greek 'aer') is the wrong translation.

The Greek word 'Aer' is not the place where clouds exist (verse 17). 'Aer' to the Greeks is the lower denser air, even below the height of a bird's nest. Therefore, this too should be seen figuratively.

'Ouranous' would be the literal word for the level of air in which clouds exist. Paul was just using figurative language to convey his point. In Second Thessalonians he uses plain language to remove confusion.

- The place we meet Him is where we will be with Him forever.

Verse 17 says, "**and so shall we be with the Lord forever.**" This means that 'in like manner or place', we will dwell with the Lord. A literal interpretation of this scripture would have the body of Christ sitting around on literal clouds for eternity. So the place of 'aer' must be different from the place in which the literal clouds exist.

Now, let's study these scriptures line for line and see what he IS saying instead of what he is not saying.

1Thes. 4:15-17

Be sure you have read the two commentaries '**Dead in Christ**' (on page 124) and the '**Garden**' (on page 122) and fully understand these terms. Let's take a closer look at 1 Thes. 4:15-17 to gain insight into the confusion associated with the rapture. As stated earlier, these three scriptures provide the backbone to the rapture. Try to withhold all judgment until we study 2 Thessalonians, where it will begin to be clear what Paul is trying to say.

---

15 *For this we say unto you by the word of the Lord, that we which are alive ~~and~~ [added word]* **remain** *unto the ~~coming~~ [appearing] of the Lord shall not prevent[1] (precede) them which are asleep.*

The phrase used here and in verse 17 reads, "we who are alive remain"; (Gk. Perileipo) is poorly translated. The ancient Greek meaning of 'remain' is not "sticking around", but being held over to be part of something to come. It would better read, "we who are still alive, are chosen to be part of the appearing..." (parousia' see page 12).

Paul thought that the appearing was going to happen during his generation. He was explaining that first there must be an appearing, but this appearing would not give "those still" alive a head start on being with Jesus. He was just assuring the readers those physically dead would not be [1]PRECEDED TO OR PREVENTED FROM COMING to the place of meeting.

---

16 ~~For~~ *[first] the Lord himself shall descend ***from heaven with[in] a* **shout**, *with[in] the voice of the* **archangel**, *and with[in] the* **trump** *of God: and the* **dead in Christ** *shall rise first:*

The appearing must take place before we meet in the 'air' (next verse). The Commentary 'Garden' explains this on page 122.

This verse gives insight into how Jesus Christ will appear (shout, archangel, and trump). These are described throughout this study, but the essence is this: the way He descends is the way He will appear. The Lord will appear: (Greek-'en', translates 'in') IN a shout, IN an archangel's declaration, and IN a trumped revelation. The **dead in Christ** represent those In whom He will appear.

17 *Then we which are alive and remain shall* **be caught up** *together with them in the* [1]**clouds***, to meet the Lord in the* [2]**air***: and so shall we ever be with the Lord.*

THEN... (when verse 16 is over) we will all come to the meeting place at the same time. The vehicle to the meeting place is the [1] clouds (on page iv). The actual destination is called the 'air'.

[2]This translation of the word air (Gr.- aer) means lower, denser (no more than 20 feet) air. This is not the air (Gr.- ouranos), which is the upper air where clouds and lightning exist. Paul purposely used the wrong 'air'. He would have used 'ouranos' if he had wanted us to take him literally. So what other idea is Paul trying to convey? There is only one other place in the New Testament where 'aer' is not used literally...

> **Eph. 2:2**
> 2   Wherein in time past ye walked according to the course of this world, according to the <u>prince of the power of the air</u>[1], the spirit that now worketh in the children of disobedience:

This shows that 'aer'[1] can be used for the spiritual realm (2[ed] heaven) in which Satan now lives (not for long!). This makes verse 17 more understandable; we will meet in the 2nd heaven after we ascend in **Glory**. *Refer to the commentary on the Garden 122.*

Second Thessalonians...It all comes out

In II Thes. 2:2 we see that the "troubled" ones he speaks to in this section are those who misunderstood First Thessalonians. They thought the Day of the Lord had already come. If Paul had been writing about the rapture as it is traditionally conceived, would it not be difficult to "miss" that event?

Follow along as we study each verse within the proper context. Open your heart and ears, and watch how Paul clarifies his previous letter.

II Thes. 1:7-2:14

7   *And to you who are troubled rest with us, when the Lord Jesus shall be revealed from heaven with his mighty angels,*

He is trying to comfort those who are troubled and to explain the misunderstandings. Paul is describing Jesus Christ appearing with His mighty holy messengers (Elect) and is letting them know that it has not yet taken place. He is also implying that they all will soon be a part of this event, if they are worthy (1:11).

8   *In* **flaming fire taking vengeance on them** *that know not God, and that obey not the gospel of our Lord Jesus Christ:*

He is not coming to take the Church out, but to bring vengeance. He is coming as the righteous judge to make war. "And I saw heaven opened, and behold a white horse; and he that sat upon him was called Faithful and True, and in righteousness he doth judge and make war." (Rev. 19:11) His appearing is Judgment...declaring a serious 'last call' to the world. **Fire** *(page vi) is the* *perfecting nature of this last call for those who repent.*

Notice that there are two groups: disobedient ones and unbelievers. His appearing will be to cleanse the Church (disobedient) and convict the world (unbelievers).

9 *Who shall be punished with **everlasting destruction** from the presence of the Lord, and from the glory of his power;*

God is serious about this day of His appearing. He wants everyone to know that this is not a game.

10 *When he **shall come to be glorified IN his saints**, and to be admired in all them that believe (because our testimony among you was believed) in that day.*

This destruction will occur at His appearing when His Glory shines through us for all to see. He is coming to judge and make war "when He shall be glorified in" us. We are the vehicles that bring His judgment.

11 *Wherefore also we pray always for you, that our God would **count you worthy** of this calling, and fulfil all the good pleasure of his goodness, and the work of faith with power:*

This 'appearing' is something to desire personally. Paul makes it clear that we are to strive to be counted worthy to have that Glory revealed in us. This is why a rapture doctrine can be dangerous; people refuse to get ready, so they can be worthy of His appearing.

12 *That the name of our Lord Jesus Christ may be **glorified in you**, and ye in him, according to the grace of our God and the Lord Jesus Christ.*

Christ-in-us the hope of GLORY is how we can get ready. Twice (1:10, 12) Paul makes sure the readers understand about Christ 'appearing' in them. He is repeating himself to make sure that this time they understand. Do you understand, and will you get ready for His appearing?

CHAPTER 2

1 *Now we **beseech you**, brethren, by the ~~coming~~[1] (**appearing**) of our Lord Jesus Christ, and by our **gathering** together[2] unto him,*

Here in verse 1 and 2 He is begging them to understand and desire to be part of the appearing, pointing to the two events described in the earlier letter: His appearing[1] (1 Thes. 4:16) and the gathering[2] (verse 4:17). Paul sees these as two events, and so do we. First, He appears (as Christ-in-us); then when all is accomplished through His appearing, we will gather in the Garden forever.

2 *That ye be not soon shaken in mind, or be troubled, neither by spirit, nor by word, nor by letter as from us, as that the day of Christ is at hand.*

He is telling them that they have not missed anything because ...

3 *Let no man deceive you by any means: **for that day shall not come**, except there come a falling away first, and that man of sin be revealed, the son of perdition;*

The day is not come because the man of sin has not been revealed (Satan). This is the spirit of antichrist which will be revealed as the spots in our love feast. It is that spirit which sits on the throne of our heart and declares itself (or ourselves) to be as God. Verse 10 shows that this revealing of the antichrist spirits is an internal appearing as is Christ-in-us. The special nature of this day declares that no longer will antichrist spirits be hidden; men will be accountable. This is when we will see the 666 that marks those who are controlled by carnality; it will be a different type of appearing.

4 *Who opposeth and exalteth himself above all that is called God, or that is worshipped; so that he as God sitteth in the temple of God, shewing himself that he is God.*

Many traditional end-time scholars will try to tell you this is about Israel building a temple on the Temple Mount, and that the antichrist will ultimately sit on a throne in that building. This verse is not to be interpreted literally to mean that a "son of Satan" rebuilds the temple in Jerusalem, sits on a big chair and says, "Hey look I am God"! I Cor. 3:16 tells us <u>we</u> are the temple of God, and Satan wants to take it over and misguide us.

5 *Remember ye not, that, when I was yet with you, I told you these things?*

6 *And now ye know what withholdeth that he might be **revealed in his time**.*

The Holy Spirit is restraining by convicting Christians' hearts, but soon He will let Christians follow after their hearts. If they are evil, then Satan will be revealed in them; and if Christ is in them then Glory will be seen. So in reality there will be two appearings, Christ in His servants and Satan in his.

7 *For the **mystery of iniquity** doth already work: only he who now letteth will let, until he be taken out of the way.*

There are two mysteries: Godliness (Christ-in-us Col. 1:26, 27) and iniquity. Satan was already busy trying to exalt himself two thousand years ago. 1 John 2:18 says there are many antichrists at work, and that they are spirits.

8 *And then shall that Wicked be revealed, whom the Lord shall consume with the spirit of his mouth, and shall destroy with the **brightness of his** ~~coming~~ [appearing]:*

This is how he will be defeated and cleaned out of the 'aer'. The Revelation will consume him, and Christ's Glory will destroy him for all time. In a practical sense, we will see that the Bride will

show such a Christ like glorious life that it will make all men accountable to whom they serve.

---

9 ~~Even him~~, *(added text) whose* ~~coming~~ *[appearing] is after the working of Satan with all power and signs and lying wonders,*

This is not about a person (the "even him" is not in original text). He is speaking about the spirit of antichrist which will appear in carnal worshipers. The next verse confirms that this is not about a person appearing, but a spirit appearing in people.

---

10 *And with all deceivableness of unrighteousness* **in them that perish;** *because they received not the love of the truth, that they might be saved.*

The spirit of antichrist is working and thus appearing in these people. This is about the spirit of antichrist appearing in the deceived and thereby marking them as perishing. They did not believe the revelation of Christ; consequently, the truth cannot set them free.

---

11 *And for this cause God shall send them strong delusion, that they should believe a lie:*

They will be turned over to their own lusts and will be sent a spirit of strong delusion. It is this spirit of antichrist, which comes on those who will not believe. This also ties in with the earlier

verse 6 in which we saw a restraining taking place to keep the antichrist spirits at bay until God was ready. Now, we can see why the whole process will accelerate during the tribulation time; God's mercy will be replaced with judgment.

---

12 *That they all might be damned who believed not the truth, but had pleasure in unrighteousness.*

Unbelievers are defined as those who have pleasure in unrighteousness. They will be damned.

---

13 *But we are bound to give thanks alway to God for you, brethren beloved of the Lord, because God hath from the beginning chosen you to salvation through sanctification of the Spirit and belief of the truth:*

14 *Whereunto he called you by our gospel, to the* **obtaining of the glory** *of our Lord Jesus Christ.*

WE ARE ALL CALLED TO OBTAIN GLORY…Christ-in-us, the hope of Glory.

Paul spoke in clear, direct terms here in second Thessalonians. There should be little doubt about the rapture. There is not even a hint of such a thing here in this second book. It is about Judgment Day…The Day of the Lord!

Commentary 3

The Garden and the 3 Heavens

In the beginning, God created a perfect Garden in which He could fellowship with His children. After Adam and Eve disobeyed God and fell from His grace, they were driven out of the Garden; consequently, they could not eat of the 'tree of life' and live forever. Cherubim (Angelic beings) and a flaming sword were put in place to keep them from reentering (Gen. 3:23) and stealing this fruit. However, just because man sinned and was cast out of the Garden does not change the fact that it was created perfectly and is still part of God's design for his family. Acts 3:21 promises restoration of creation, and we can assume that it is God's desire to have His garden returned to its original state.

The Garden is not physically visible, which lends credence to the belief that it resides in a place of spirit. Yet Ezekiel, Isaiah, and Joel have all prophesized that the Garden shall yet appear. In Rom. 8:19-21 we hear that all of creation groans for restoration to its perfect condition, free from the "bondage of decay", something that is promised when the "sons of God" are made manifest. When "the righteous shine forth as the sun in the kingdom of their Father" (Matt. 13:43) and sin (wickedness) is removed, then the way to the Garden will be opened again. This can

be linked to our study of the Rapture in which God, in the end-time, will remove the wicked by His Angels (holy messengers). Joel describes these holy messengers in Chapter 2 as a mighty army who has the "Garden of Eden" before them. They are the Bride of Christ who will lead the way back to the Garden.

The restoration of the earth to its pre-fallen condition has been expected since before the time of Christ. Many believed that this would only happen when God removed "carnality" from the earth. That is exactly what the book of Revelation teaches; God is coming to destroy the earth (carnality), then we all will meet the Lord back in the 'Garden' and "so shall we ever be with the Lord."   Amen

Meeting in the Garden… the Second Heaven

In 1 Thes. 4:14 Paul is trying to console believers about their misunderstanding regarding loved ones who have passed away (asleep). He comforts them by telling them that God will bring those 'asleep' with Him when He comes. In addition, he reveals that we "who are alive at the appearing" will not precede those who are 'asleep' into the 'air', which we define as a spiritual place known as the second heaven. Jesus will descend from the third heaven to meet with both those alive and asleep in the second heaven (Garden of Eden).

> **2 Cor. 12:2**
> 2   I knew a man in Christ above fourteen years ago, (whether in the body, I cannot tell; or whether out of the body, I cannot tell: God knoweth;) such an one caught **up to the third heaven**.

Let me explain more about these heavens. In 2 Cor. 12:2-4 Paul says he knows of a person who has been to the third heaven and another person who has been to the second heaven called 'paradise'. We know that 'paradise' (Gr. – paradeisos) is the Garden because Rev. 2:7 says the tree of life is in paradise. This is the same tree that is in the Garden of Eden (Gen. 3:24). We also know that if there is a "third" heaven, there must be at least three heavens. The third heaven is where the throne room is. This is where God the Father sits with Jesus on His right hand. We call the Garden the second Heaven because it is the place where God descended to be with Adam.

Only those of the Kingdom of Heaven can meet in the Garden

In John 14:2 & 3 Jesus tells us that there is a place for us in the Father's house, and He is going to prepare it for us and receive us there. In John 16:13-16 and 17:21-24, the secret of what Jesus is revealing comes to light. These verses describe the basic truth of Christ in us. Unfortunately, there is not enough room in this study to detail all of the scriptures that show that Jesus is in the Father and the Father is in Him; and that to have Jesus Christ in us is to have access to the Father. But to be one with the Son and be received[2] by Him, we must first receive the Lord's 'Glory' (Spirit of Christ) from the Holy Spirit. The path through that Glory (**clouds** iv) is a path that we can follow to Him, a path that starts in the first heaven.

> **The Way to the First Heaven**
> **John 14:2-4**
> 2   In my Father's house are many mansions: if it were not so, I would have told you. I go to prepare a place for you.
>
> *This word 'mansions' is the same Greek word found in verse 23 of that same chapter. This place is in you and the Son and the Father will come and live in your 'mansion/abode' when love has been perfected in you.*
>
> 3   And if I go and prepare a place for you, I [1]**will come** again, and [2]**receive you** unto myself; that where I am, there ye may be also.
> 4   And whither I go ye know, and the way ye know.

The first heaven is the kingdom of Heaven which is created in us when we surrender to Jesus as Lord and King. If we surrender and die-to-self, then we can receive the Spirit of Christ into the prepared throne 'room' of our hearts; thus the kingdom of Heaven is born. This kingdom is in existence as long as the Lord has dominion in our lives. In Rev. 17:12 we see kings (believers) who do not have a kingdom yet. They have not yet chosen to surrender their wills to the Lord, thus the Beast rules them. For greater scriptural support, look into Eph. 3:16-17, and notice how the Holy Spirit must prepare us before Christ can dwell in us. Just being a Christian is not enough to have the kingdom of Heaven within you. We must allow the Holy Spirit to finish His work before the throne room can be occupied.

When Jesus is on the throne of our hearts, He can receive us to Himself. This means that we can operate **IN** Him, and He can operate through us. He has received us to Himself so "that where He is we can be." This verse in Corinthians shows us that the man who went to the third heaven went "in Christ". This not only means that he was a Christian, but it also shows that "in Christ" he was a new creature. With the kingdom of Heaven and its King now living in us, we can dwell in the heavens; and He can come to the earth.

When this natural body passes away, we just slip out of this world and into the only place where we still remain, that is with Jesus. In addition, we can choose to walk by faith (which is heavenly vision) and not by sight, and dwell with the Lord right now. If we do, we will let the Glory of the Lord shine through us as a witness to the world. This is the way He will come again to the earth for the end-day "appearing".

First the Garden must be cleaned out

If you will remember, Satan was never cast out of the Garden (Gen. 3:13). He is still there as the 'prince of the power' (Eph. 2:2) of the air (Gr. – *aer*). If we are to dwell with the Lord in the Garden, then it stands to reason that Christ would want Satan out before He moves in. Satan has lost the victory to Jesus; but he is still in the Garden, being kept alive by the 'children of disobedience' (Eph. 2:2). How? He is feeding off their carnality.

Every time we open up our **heart** to the carnal bestial nature, Satan gets strength from our spirit. We do not mean to feed the Beast, but we do. He slips back into the Garden within us (kingdom of Heaven) and offers us a little bad fruit; as a result, he feeds off our spirit through our flesh. This happens every time we seek our 'will' instead of Christ.

> **Rev. 17:12-13**
> 12   And the ten horns which thou sawest are ten **kings**, which **have received no kingdom** as yet; but receive power as kings one hour with the beast.
> 13   These have one mind, and shall **give their power and strength unto the beast**.

*In Gen. 3:13 Satan was cursed to eat nothing but the dust of the **earth** or carnality. Jesus' victory plan is to starve the rascal out. He is coming to bring judgment to the earth. Carnality then is the target of Christ's coming. He wants to destroy it for the last time, so that Satan can never again slither around peddling bad fruit.*

Commentary 4

The Dead in Christ

Many people throughout the ages have been 'dead in Christ'; they choose to die to the life of self, so that Christ might live through them. Yet, there is a group of these people who have a special role in end-time events. Rom. 8:19 calls them the manifest 'sons of God'. These are the servants referred to in Rev. 1:1, for whom Christ opens the book. They are the Firstfruits company, who are called the 144,000 in Rev.14:4 (page i) and reveal Christ to the Church and the World. They are the ones who will show the world that dying to self is the process by which Christ-in-us can be revealed.

Colossians 3:1 and 3 show that we are to be dead NOW, in the present. It also supports restoration to the Garden and having access to the third heaven, because we are told to seek things in heaven. Yet, the most important thing it says for us is that if we are dead in Christ, then we can be part of the Lord's appearing.

We are "dead" if we are Christ's
Col. 3:1, 3-4
1   If ye then be **risen with Christ**, seek those things which are above, where Christ sitteth on the right hand of God.
3   **FOR YE ARE DEAD**, and your life is hid with Christ in God.
4   When Christ, who is our life, shall appear, then shall **ye also appear with him in Glory**.

In I Cor. 15:20 Paul tells us that Christ rose from the dead and is the Firstfruits of the risen. In verse 15:22 below, we are told that we are made alive when we are in Christ (which echoes verse 3 of Col. 3 above), and the 'dead in Christ' are the Firstfruits of the resurrection. What a wonderful picture we have of receiving our resurrection NOW. This also reveals the resurrection that will finally enable the Elect of John 8:52 to step over the grave. Jesus says that they will not even have to taste of death. John 11:25 tells us the reason: Jesus is their Resurrection.

The "dead" in Christ are Christ's Firstfruits
1 Cor. 15:20-23
20   But now is Christ risen from the dead, and become the **firstfruits** of them that slept.
21   For since by man came death, by man came also the resurrection of the dead.
22   For as in Adam all die even so in Christ shall all be made alive.
23   But every man in his own order. Christ, the **firstfruits**; *afterward they that are Christ's at his coming*.
There are three groups in the Greek: 1) Christ, 2) Firstfruits, and 3) those that are His at His coming.

This is that group which will manifest the resurrection without going to the grave. These are Firstfruits selected to be the 144,000, who have totally abandoned their own wills to follow the Lord wherever He takes them. They are not spotted with the carnality of this world (virgins); the Harlot has no hold on them, and they have been redeemed from the **earth**. These are the Elect, dead in Christ, Firstfruits Company of 144,000. They are the tithe (redeemed) of the Lord, and their role is to lead the way. In 1 Thes. 4:16 they are the "dead in Christ" who rise up first during the time of His appearing.

The Firstfruits are the 144,000
Rev. 14:3-4
3   And they sung as it were a new song before the throne, and before the four beasts, and the elders: and no man could learn that song but **the hundred and forty and four thousand**, which were redeemed from the earth.
4   These are they which were not defiled with women; for they are virgins. These **are they which follow the Lamb whithersoever he goeth**. These were redeemed from among men, BEING THE **FIRSTFRUITS** unto God and to the Lamb.

Therefore, the dead in Christ are become the Firstfruits and will manifest as the 144,000, who then step over the grave (having been made alive in the fullness of Christ).

Commentary 5

Complete vs. Perfect

See also 'Robe of Righteousness' on page xvi and 'completion' on page iv.

Completion and perfection (the fullness) are two different but important conditions of the Christ' life that are frequently confused and require clarification. As you have already seen, we achieve the fullness as we realize different levels of fruit-bearing (Glory) associated with our level of dying to self. This perfecting process represents the greater measure of Christ operating through us because there is less of us to constrain Him. **Calf, man**, and **flying-eagle** are associated with these levels of Christ's Glory. Yet, if this was all there was to our maturing in Christ, then we would only focus on dying to self and have no need to knit together as the Bride of Christ. However, there is a quick work that God is revealing in this eleventh hour.

Jesus Christ will provide a way for those who have not fully matured (eagles) to receive the promise of the **robe of righteousness**. This process will come through their complete surrender to the apostles and prophets who will guide the Bride into the harvest. In this way, those who would never have time to mature, due to the lateness of the hour, will be able to obtain the promise with the rest of the Saints.

This study has taught us much about dying-to-self and having the Spirit of Jesus increased in us. However, being filled to the fullness does not necessarily mean that we are complete in Christ. Look at Hebrews, and see that even Jesus was not complete until he was put to the test of obedience.

Heb. 2:10	
10	For it became him, for whom are all things, and by whom are all things, in bringing many sons unto glory, to **make the captain of their salvation** ~~perfect~~ [complete] **through sufferings**.
	We know that Jesus Christ had the fullness of the Spirit (Col. 1:19); yet, He was not complete. That completeness came through suffering (tribulation), but how?
Heb. 5:8-9	
8	Though he were a Son, yet **learned he** <u>obedience</u> by the things which he suffered;
9	And being made perfect, he became the author of eternal salvation unto all them that obey him;
	It was through obedience that He was made complete. If you search the scriptures, you will see that obedience is what God is trying to teach all of us. "How can you say you love me if you do not the things I say"? Enoch walked with God and then he was not (Gen. 5:24). He was complete and God took him.

*Perfection is victory over carnality (a **flying eagle**), a victory we know Christ has always had.* So perfection would be that state in which we manifest all of Christ and none of us. However, just because a person is perfect (or in the fullness of Christ) does not mean that they have everything God wants them to have. Even Christ as the pattern Son needed to learn obedience, and thus we do as well. If God has a specific plan for every person to fulfill, even those operating in the fullness are not complete until they walk out that plan through obedience. However, the good news for this generation is that they do not have to obtain perfection in Christ to become 'complete'. Completion

comes as we lose ourselves to the will of the Lord and cease to have a will of our own. This might sound like perfection, but perfection is won as Christ-in-us obtains victory over the spots that bind us. Therefore, 'perfection' comes through testings, trials, and tribulations, while completion comes through a **total** surrender of our will.

Enoch went to be with the Lord before the grave, signifying that he was one of the few in the Old Testament who must have been on the verge of completion. He finished his course and did all that God had for Him. It was said about Enoch that "he walked with God"; thus he lived a life in step with God, pleasing the Father in all that he did. In this way, God led Enoch through everything He desired for Enoch, 'completing' Enoch before the years ordained for his life. If we lose ourselves in Christ and walk solely after the perfect will of the Father, then we too shall obtain completion.

In the last generation, understanding completion is very important; because the 'robes of righteousness' (page xvi) or 'glorified bodies' will be given to those who are complete in Christ. In other words, when we learn to stay in step with Christ, then we will be 'complete' in Christ (which will allow us to step over the grave)!

John 8:51	
51	Verily, verily, I say unto you, If a man <u>keep</u> my saying, he shall never see death.

"Keeping" Jesus' sayings is more than a list of dos and don'ts; it is a life totally after Christ. The bad news for us is that it is our nature to stray and lose focus. We are easily preoccupied with the things of this world (including self-guided ministry). We need a way to constrain ourselves and provide barriers that keep us on track with God's plan. This way can only be found in the Corporate Body of Christ. It is under the direction of the Apostles and Prophets and the love and commitment of the brethren, that we can stay on a path of completion. Joel Chapter 2 shows a people marching in lines; these lines represent the iron that sharpens iron which keeps us on track. We need our brethren to help keep us focused; **therefore, we need the body of Christ to be made complete**.

This brings new focus to our die-to-self (perfection) message. Dying to the carnality (spots) in our life is good; but by itself it will not help direct our path. God is showing each of us that the body of Christ is critical to our walk with Christ. If we take His body for granted or feel we are independent of it, then we will never obtain all that God has for us. Yet, we still need victory over the carnality in us; because the fewer the spots the easier it is for the body to constrain us. This is how completion and perfection work hand in hand.

Commentary 6
The 'Sea'...Heart of the Church

The symbol of water in the book of Revelation has two meanings depending on the term and context used. If it is a named source of water, such as a sea or a river, then it speaks of peoples and their issues. If the word used is 'waters', then it speaks more of the common doctrine or 'word' that links a group together. In Revelation we see that the people and the message are one and the same; people will live what they speak (commentary 'two witnesses'). The waters, as they refer to a type of people, can be either of the Lord or of the Beast; yet, they both speak of the commonality of a group. Perhaps the most significant of these 'bodies' of water is the sea, because it is the birthplace of the Beast in Revelation. To understand this term is to understand the foundation of the Beast. Traditionalists like to believe that this is a literal sea, such as the Mediterranean; this is why they think an antichrist is going to come from Iran or Iraq. However, the scriptures in Revelation show us something different.

Rev. 17:15

15	Then the angel said to me, "The **waters** you saw, where the prostitute sits, are **peoples, multitudes, nations and languages**. (NIV)

The Harlot sits on, or is supported by water. This water is defined as carnal Christians in the Church. Therefore people in the Church who are like-minded with the Beast give authority (support) to the Harlot. What mind is that...?

Rev. 17:3

3	Then the angel carried me away in the Spirit into a desert. There I saw a **woman sitting on a scarlet beast** that was covered with blasphemous names and had seven heads and ten horns. (NIV)

This verse establishes that it is the Beast that supports the Harlot. The Harlot sits on the waters (or carnal Christians of the Church) in 17:15 and on the Beast in 17:3; therefore, the Beast and the waters are one and the same. They are revealed in a multi-faceted aspect which gives a greater depth of truth much in the same way that Jesus is revealed as the Word, the Way, and the Truth. The peoples of like-mind in 17:15 are like-minded in their carnality, and it is the carnality in these people that brings life to the Harlot. The image of the **Beast** describes the spiritual aspect of what unites these people and provides the source of support for the Harlot: it is their beastlike carnality.

Rev. 13:1

1	And the dragon stood on the shore of the sea. And I saw a **beast coming out of the sea.** He had ten horns and seven heads, with ten crowns on his horns, and on each head a blasphemous name. (NIV)

The Beast originates from the sea. We know that carnality is an issue of the heart; therefore, we can define the 'sea' as the heart of the carnal Christians who birth the Beast, which gives rise to the Harlot. Mark 7:21-23 tells us that it is what comes out of the heart that defiles us. This **Beast** is defined on page ii as persons with spots or blemishes, which defile the body of Christ.

If you connect this with the 'mountain burning' going into the sea (*page xiii*), then it is easy to see that as this 'perfecting' Revelation (**mountain burning**) touches the **heart of the carnal church (sea)**, it causes the Beast, hidden under the surface, to rise in 13:1. The Psalms also portray the Lord's plans to deliver His people from this carnality in the Church.

Ps. 68:21-22

21 But God shall wound the head of his enemies [the serpent], and the hairy scalp of such a one as goeth on still in his trespasses.

He will remove the covering (hairy scalp, see hair ix) of those who continue to trespass. Those of the 'sea' count on the carnal Harlot message to be their covering for sin.

*22 The Lord said, I will bring again from Bashan, I will **bring my people again from the depths of the sea**:*

God wants His people to be redeemed from their carnal hearts and the harlotry in the Church. Bashan means fruitful or plentiful. Bashan was the land that attracted the half tribe of Manasseh away from their appointed place in the promised land. This is a type of the Sea. The heart of carnal Christians is worldly minded because they seek after their own natural desires. This will be revealed when they refuse to accept their appointed place in the sold out Bride.

Commentary 7

The Fullness of Salvation...the Saving of the Soul

SOUL LIFE THOSE UNDER THE ALTAR

The three parts of the Human being 1Thes. 5:23
23   And the very God of peace <u>sanctify you wholly</u>; and I pray God your whole **spirit** and **soul** and **body** be preserved blameless unto the ~~coming~~ [appearing/parousia] of our Lord Jesus Christ.

There are three parts to the Human Being...a mind, a body, and a spirit. The **mind** defines who we are. Psychology calls this the psyche. The Greek word is psuche (psookhay'), which is translated **SOUL** in the Bible. The soul is where our will, thoughts, and self-image reside. "As a man thinketh so is he."

The second part of the 'human being' is the **body**. Paul calls it "our members" and speaks of its sinful influence on the soul. The body is also the home for base 'natural' desires. These desires of the flesh (Rom. 8:13) are what some people refer to as "animal" desires (sex, fear, dominance, etc.), because they seem to be evident in animals as well as humans. Nevertheless, it is certain that the body is more than skin and bones; it also contains ungodly spirits and spiritual desires.

The heart (see below) is the home for the third part of the 'human being'...the **spirit**. The spirit is our 'spiritual self' created in the image of God. Even though our spirit is in the image of God, it does not mean we are godly. It only means that we have the capacity to know right from wrong (Gen 3:22). After redemption, the Holy Spirit will reveal sin and godliness.

Our hearts (**bottomless pit** on page iii) also contain the gateways to heaven and/or hell. If our gatekeeper (mind) shuts off God, then evil will rise up out of hell and dwell in our members (Rom. 1:28, 8:5). However, if our mind embraces God, the Holy Spirit will move in and help guard our heart from intrusion.

Easton's Bible Dictionary "the **Heart**" Author: Easton, M. G.
According to the Bible, the heart is the center not only of spiritual activity, but of all the operations of human life. "Heart" and "soul" are often used interchangeably (Deut. 6:5; 26:16; compare Matt. 22:37; Mark 12:30, 33), but this is not generally the case.
The heart is the "<u>home of the personal life</u>," and hence a man is designated, according to his heart, wise (I Kin. 3:12, etc.), pure (Ps. 24:4; Matt. 5:8, etc.), upright and righteous (Gen. 20:5, 6; Ps. 11:2; 78:72), pious and good (Luke 8:15), etc. In these and such passages the word "soul" could not be substituted for "heart."
The heart is also the **seat of the conscience** (Rom. 2:15). It is naturally wicked (Gen. 8:21), and hence it con-

taminates the whole life and character (Matt. 12:34; 15:18; compare Eccl. 8:11; Ps. 73:7). Hence, the heart must be changed, regenerated (Ezek. 36:26; 11:19; Ps. 51:10-14), before a man can willingly obey God.

The ***process of salvation begins in the heart*** by the believing reception of the testimony of God, while the rejection of that testimony hardens the heart (Ps. 95:8; Prov. 28:14; 2 Chr. 36:13). "Hardness of heart evidences itself by light views of sin; partial acknowledgment and confession of it; pride and conceit; ingratitude; unconcern about the word and ordinances of God; inattention to divine providences; stifling convictions of conscience; shunning reproof; presumption, and general ignorance of divine things."

Stopping the Battle Within

Rom. 7:23
23   But I see another law in my members, **warring against the law of my mind**, <u>and bringing me into captivity to the law of sin which is in my members.</u>

Paul explains what happens after we are redeemed, and the Holy Spirit comes to live in us. The Holy Spirit starts revealing the sin that is in our lives. He shows us that this sin makes us an enemy of God. Our "carnal" minds, prior to the Holy Spirit, were in agreement with our bodies and allowed the pursuit of sin (Rom. 8:7). The real revelation of the Holy Spirit is that we are unable to stop sinning because of our sinful state (Rom. 7:15). Paul realizes that even though he "delights after the law (way) of God in his spirit-man", he is still **captive to the sin in his body**. A mental decision for Christ is not good enough. We cannot change the nature of our flesh, no matter how hard we try. That is why the "law is weak" (Rom. 8:3) through the flesh. Christ needs to reign over our minds (soul) to set us free from sin (Rom. 8:2). Reigning over our sinful and self-willed mind will **transform it into the mind of Christ**. However, Christ must be IN you to transform you.

2 Cor. 3:17-18
17   Now the Lord is that Spirit: and where the Spirit of the Lord is, **there is liberty**.
18   But we all, with <u>open face beholding as in a glass the glory of the Lord</u>, **are changed into the same image** from glory to glory, even as by the Spirit of the Lord.

Before Christ can live in us, our "inner man" must gain strength through the Holy Spirit (Eph. 3:16-17). This is so our mind will **go beyond just agreement with the Spirit, and instead it will submit to the Spirit of Christ**. Yet, how can we strengthen our spirit-man when there is a war going on inside of us? The Holy Spirit needs things of the Spirit to strengthen the Spirit. Fleshly things take away from the things of the Spirit.

The biggest obstacle to having the Spirit strengthened is the accuser of the brethren, Satan. He will try to defeat you with lies of your unworthiness. Paul cried, "oh wretched man that I am" (Rom. 8:24) when he realized that he was unworthy. Nevertheless, praise God, Paul saw through the lies. He saw that it was not Paul sinning, but it was the sin in him doing its natural thing. Romans Chapter 8 starts with the revelation of worthiness: remove the "sin consciousness" by walking after the Spirit of Christ. "There is no more condemnation to those who are in Jesus and **walk after the Spirit**" (Rom. 8:1). **"Sin is under the Blood of Jesus Christ"!**

Rom. 8:5-6

5   For they that are after the flesh do mind the things of the flesh; **but they that are after the Spirit mind the things of the Spirit.**

6   For to be **carnally minded is death**; but to be **spiritually minded is life and peace.**

Sanctification begins as we occupy our time and mind with the things of God. Verse 6 gives us the persuasive reasons for filling our mind with the Spirit. However, just doing spiritual things is not enough to transform our mind into the mind of Christ. Pride could be part of such a walk. Therefore, surrender and obedience need to be part of our

spiritual walk because they are enemies of pride. Obedience comes as we obey Christ and follow after Him.

Rom. 6:13

13   Neither yield ye your members as instruments of unrighteousness unto sin: but **yield yourselves unto God**, as those that are alive from the dead, and your members as instruments of righteousness unto God.

When we start adding works to our walk (James 2:20), then we are putting "feet" to our faith. Faith that follows God into action is faith that can save. Eph. 3:17 says that **faith** is the means by which Christ can dwell in our heart. To empower such faith we need to listen to our hearts (Holy Spirit) and draw from the strength that is in our spirit man; this brings our mind (filled with the Spirit) into agreement with the Spirit-man (and the Holy Spirit).

People with minds full of the Spirit will bow their 'will' to Christ and make Him Lord of all. With their minds (soul) in total agreement with their spirits, Christ will sit upon His throne. With Christ on HIS throne, He can defeat the sin in our members. Christ's glorious life will then pour into OUR SOUL. **Thus, living souls are persons totally sold out to Christ** (Rom. 12:2).

Dying-to-self makes us risen with Him...TO THE SAVING OF OUR SOUL (Heb. 10:38, 39).

Commentary 8

THE MYSTERY OF GOD

CHRIST APPEARING IN US...THE MYSTERY REVEALED

The <u>key</u> that unlocks this <u>mystery</u> and the <u>mystery</u> that unlocks the <u>book</u>

The book of Revelation is about the revelation of Jesus Christ (a revelation that Jesus himself could give to His servants, Rev. 1:1). To receive the revelation is to open the book. **It is NOT the study of the book that brings the revelation; it is the receiving of the revelation from Christ, which unlocks the truths of the book.** To receive the revelation is to have Christ quicken the truth to you through eyes to see and ears to hear. However, Christ must be in dominion or birthed in you, so that He can quicken this truth to you. If you believe that Christ is in every believer, then you are probably wondering why we would call Christ-in-us "the mystery now revealed." This is a question that will be discussed in more detail as we proceed. For now, just be open to the possibility that what you know about Christ-in-us may be far short of what is really meant by Col. 1:25; there is a revelation of Christ' manifesting in

us that is uncommon to today's Christian knowledge and experience.

The person of Jesus Christ 'in us' shows us "the things that must shortly come to pass." It is **Christ** living in us which opens the book to understanding. This is not an issue of belief in Christ or salvation by grace. It is an issue of Christ living in and taking control of the life of a submissive believer. Let us go back to the beginning of Revelation and review what is written about this mystery. Verse 1 says, "*The revelation of Jesus Christ which God <u>gave unto him</u>, to show unto his servants things which must shortly come to pass; and he sent and signified it by his angel unto his servant John.*" Literally...the revelation of Jesus Christ was given <u>to Jesus</u> enabling Him to personally give it to those whom He calls **servants (slaves of Christ).**

If it takes Christ to open the book, Christ must be empowered through us. The birthing of Christ in a believer

---

SERVANT *Gr. doulos (doo'-los)
--a slave (literal or figurative, involuntary or voluntary; frequently, in a qualified sense of subjection or subserviency).*

---

by the Holy Spirit enables Christ to be manifested <u>in</u> and <u>through</u> the life of that believer. Manifesting Christ, however, is not easy. Paul said to the Galatians, "My little children, of whom I **travail in birth** again until Christ be formed in you (Gal. 4:19)." He was speaking to Christians who experienced great difficulty submitting their will sufficiently to allow Christ to be birthed in them. We must diligently seek after Christ. Blessed are those who hunger and thirst after righteousness.

In Gal. 4:19, Eph. 3:16-17, Rom. 8:9, etc., we see references to Christ being formed in believers after they are already justified by the blood of Christ. Most would agree that the Holy Spirit is born in the believer at the point of profession in Jesus Christ, so this later manifestation must be recognized as a separate operation of the Spirit (Life page xi). Rom. 8:9-10 refers to this later manifestation as the Spirit of Christ, which is the omnipresent form of Jesus Christ. Look at the Christ-in-us study for more information and scriptural support.

The need for Christians to have the Spirit of Christ manifest as a separate work in their life is what makes this revelation so important today. Spoon-fed on grace alone, Christians do not want to recognize God's true desire for a family of sons; nor have they felt compelled to meet His requirement to die to self so that His Son can live through them. Paul preached this message two thousand years ago, but it did not take hold. It is a hard message to hear, even today. Christ says, "if you want life, you must lose your life." Most Christians TODAY do not understand or operate at this level of truth. How can they when there is no visible pattern to follow?

This Revelation needs to be demonstrated through the actions of a living example. That is why it was hard for the Galatians and other first century believers to adhere to the truth after their mentors died. Without the visible witness of the living Christ in the lives of the disciples, the teachings of the world began to infiltrate the Church, veiling the truth until the Saints of God could once again hear and obey. If you watch the progression of the Church from the first century until now, you will see God's hand leading His remnant back to the truth. In the last 100 years, we have seen the Church mature to a level that finally provides His remnant with good spiritual ground in which to prosper. The fullness of the age of the Gentiles is now here. The time of the chosen generation is upon us.

The scriptures show Christ-IN-us

In Matt. 25:1-13, Jesus tells the story of ten bridesmaids who are eagerly awaiting the return of the bridegroom. Yet only the five who had the oil (representing the anointing of Christ) in their lamps (in them) were allowed into the bridal chamber. The door was locked to the others; and Christ, the bridegroom, would not let them enter. All were waiting for Christ's return; but only those who had Christ in them actually became His Bride. John 15:1-6 further amplifies the difference in relationship between being "in Christ" and having Christ abiding in you This passage clearly states that there are three possible types of relationships to have with Christ; but only one is acceptable.

The True Vine

> **Is He IN YOU?**
> **John 15:1-6**
> 1   I am the true vine, and my Father is the husbandman.
> 2   Every branch ¹⁾ **in me** that beareth not fruit he taketh away: and every branch that beareth fruit, he purgeth it, that it may bring forth more fruit.
> 3   Now ye are clean through the word which I have spoken unto you.
> 4   Abide in me, and I in you. As the **branch cannot bear fruit of itself**, except it abide in the vine; no more can ye, except ye abide in me.
> 5   I am the vine, ye are the branches: He that ²⁾ **abideth in me, and I in him**, the same bringeth forth much fruit: for without me ye can do nothing.
> 6   If a man ³⁾ abide not in me, he is cast forth as a branch, and is withered; and men gather them, and cast them into the fire, and they are burned.

Having Jesus Christ as your Lord is more than having Him as you Savior. This scripture helps us see the difference. We can "abide in" Him (1) and bear no fruit (v.2) and be taken away; or we can abide in him *and* Him in us (2) and bring forth much fruit; or we can "abide not" in Him "(3) and be cast forth. Many are "in Him"; yet do they have Him in them; that is the crucial difference that Paul calls the mystery of godliness (Col. 1:25-28). It is through the manifestation of this great mystery in the lives of believers that a generation will come into the knowledge of the truth.

The Mystery of God (Col. 1:25-26)[1]

The mystery of Godliness in Col. 1:25 is designed to fulfill[2] the word of God; thus it must play an important part in the book of Revelation because Revelation is the fulfillment to all the scriptures. Since Christ is the only one who can loose or open the book, then having Christ-in-them is the way that the last generation of Saints can unlock endtime events. Furthermore Rev. 1:1 tells us that no other generation but the last generation will be able to see the events of Revelation come to pass. Those eyes to see come from Christ-in-them. This concept is supported here in Col. 1:26, which also states that it has been hidden from 'generations' past. Thus, Christ becomes the eyes and keys to Revelation. However, the people referred to here in Colossians are not the last generation, so how does this relate to us? Notice, 1:26 does not say that Paul's generation received the mystery, just the Saints of His day. That is important to understand if you are to see the last generation as the first 'generation' to fully receive the mystery, and thus open the Revelation.

> **The Mystery of God**
> [1]**Col. 1:25-27**
> 25   Whereof I am made a minister, according to the dispensation of God which is **given to me** for you, **to fulfil[2] the word of God**;
> 26   Even the mystery which hath been hid from ages and from generations[3], but now is made manifest <u>to his saints</u>:

27 To whom God would make known what is the riches of the glory of this mystery among the Gentiles; which is <u>Christ-in-you, the hope of glory</u>:

Notice that this mystery is specifically given to his **"Saints"** to **"fulfill"** or complete the **"Word of God"**. In verse 26 we see that God purposely hid this mystery from all generations except the one ordained to receive it. Paul received this great revelation (Galatians Chapters 1 and 2) and took it to the gentiles. Yet only a few of the Saints of his time heard it and had it quickened in them. Most who heard the message were led away from the truth by religious legalism. Paul properly thought that because some Saints were given and walked in this mystery that his was the generation of manifest sons. He even promised the 'foolish Galatians' that he would travail through birth **again** until Christ be formed in them; but study of Galatians reveals that he was never successful. What happened to most of the Church of that time and of subsequent generations is that they vainly focused on developing a relationship through legalism rather than developing a relationship to God through Christ. They allowed pride and the world into their thinking and theology and left out the mystery. God in His infinite wisdom knew that it would take the dedication of the Saints to see Christ birthed in a people, and that this generation would only come in the fullness of time. Today is that time, and Christ-in-us is a revelation that must again be given by Christ to His Saints to fulfill the plan of God. Unlike in times past, a full generation will come into this truth and thereby make a way for Christ to appear to the world. They will not only see the events of Revelation take place; they will be a critical part of those events!

Look at just a few of Paul's writings and see them in a new light. These scriptures are not about acting like Jesus, living according to His principles, or even having the Holy Spirit IN you. They are about Christ-IN-you. Refer back to "the true Vine" on page four as a reminder that the Bible clearly states that it is not enough to be in Christ, He <u>must</u> be IN you.

The Mystery Revealed in Scripture

2 Cor. 4:7 But we have this treasure [Christ] **IN** earthen vessels, ***that*** <u>the excellency of the power may be of God, and not of us</u>.

Gal. 1:16 To **reveal** his Son **IN** me, ***that*** I might <u>preach</u> him among the heathen; immediately I conferred not with flesh and blood:

1 Tim. 1:16 Howbeit for this cause I obtained mercy, ***that* IN** me first Jesus Christ might shew forth all longsuffering, ***for*** <u>a pattern</u>

<u>to them</u> which should hereafter believe on him to life everlasting.

Gal. 2:20 I am crucified with Christ: nevertheless I live; yet not I, but <u>Christ liveth **IN** me</u>: and the life which I now live in the flesh <u>I live by the faith</u> **of** the Son of God, who loved me, and gave himself for me.

2 Cor. 13:5 Examine yourselves to see whether you are in the faith; test yourselves. Do you not realize that <u>Christ Jesus is **IN** you</u>-- ***unless***, of course, you ***fail the test***? (NIV)

Rom. 8:10 And **if** Christ be **IN** you, the body is dead because of sin; but the <u>Spirit is life</u> *because of* righteousness.

II Thes. 1:11-12 Wherefore also we pray always for you, that our God would count ***you worthy of this calling***, and fulfil all the good pleasure of his goodness, and the work of faith with power:

12 That the name of our Lord Jesus Christ may be **glorified <u>IN you</u>, <u>and ye in him</u>**, according to the grace of our God and the Lord Jesus Christ.

Rom. 8:18 For I reckon that the sufferings of this present time are not worthy to be compared with ***the glory*** [Christ] which shall be revealed <u>**IN** us</u>.

II Thes. 1:10 ***<u>When he shall come to be glorified IN his saints</u>***, and to be admired in all them that believe (because our testimony among you was believed) in that day.

Rom. 8:17 And if children, then heirs; heirs of God, and joint-heirs with Christ; *if so be that we suffer with him*, that we may be also **glorified together**.

There are many more scriptures that echo the same message: *it is not about believing in Christ, it is about **receiving Him**.* There is a great difference between Christ living in you and you being a Christian. Living under the banner of Christian sounds good in concept and may even result in good works, depending on your heart. Nevertheless, it is still your carnal mind, the very thing that is an enemy of God, which you are depending on to guide you and dictate your actions. Yet, if you surrender and totally submit your carnal mind and body to Christ's authority, He can live His life 'perfectly' through you. These scriptures show that when Christ is revealed through you, it is He that is glorified and not you. "And I, if I be lifted up from the earth, will draw all men unto me" (John 12:32)

Reference Notes

Reference Notes

The 144,000

These are the chosen servants of Christ, who are the first to receive the revelation of Christ and the first to have that Revelation lived out in them. As Christ's Firstfruits possessed people, they are the first to receive their coats of righteousness and become His Bride "without spot or wrinkle". They are "risen up" before Revelation and are to be the angels of revelation. They are the tithe of God, His portion. See 'Angels' (page 101), see 'Firstfruits' (page vi), and 'Portion of Jacob' (on page xv).

ABADDON/ APOLLYON

9:11	And they had a **king** over them, which is the angel of the **bottomless pit**, whose name in the Hebrew tongue is **Abaddon**, but in the Greek tongue hath his name **Apollyon**.

Abaddon or Apollyon means the Destroyer, a title often given to Satan. Yet, does this mean that the function he performs here is outside of the plan of God. Like many of us know, if Satan can attack some part of our life, then it is a part outside of God. Indeed in Ex. 12:23 we see that the 'destroyer' was an instrument of God's purposes to judge Egypt (a type of worldliness).

Exod. 12:23	
23	For the _LORD_ **will pass through to smite the Egyptians**; and when he seeth the blood upon the lintel, and on the two side posts, the Lord will pass over the door, and will not suffer **the DESTROYER** to come in unto your houses **to smite** you.
	This makes it very clear that the LORD will pass through "to smite". Yet, He goes on to say that the destroyer is the instrument of this destruction. It is not uncommon to see God use the enemies of His people as instruments of their perfection.

Also...

Jer. 4:7-8	
7	The lion has come up from his thicket, and **the DESTROYER of nations is on his way**. He has gone forth from his place to make your land desolate. Your cities will be laid waste, without inhabitant.
8	For this, clothe yourself with sackcloth, lament and wail. **For the fierce anger of the LORD has not turned back from us.** (NKJ)

In Rev. 9:11 John uses the term 'angel' to describe Apollyon. Since angel is a title John uses exclusively in a positive way, we must assume that there is a spiritual message here and not just a natural description. This angel seems to compare to the angels of Rev. 9:1 and 20:1 "And I saw an angel come down from heaven, having the **key of the bottomless pit** and a great chain in his hand." He comes from heaven and 'has' the keys necessary to open the pit. He opens the pit and has full authority over whom and what comes out. He even gives direction not to hurt God's people, which shows that the work he does here is under approval of God. Apollyon speaks more of the nature of the work that the locusts perform; a work that destroys those things not of God. Satan therefore becomes an instrument of God's end-time deliverance.

ANGELS / HOLY MESSENGERS
(ALSO PARENTHETICAL ON PAGE 101)

The word in Greek for Angel means messenger (angelic plan page 104) In our case it represents those who keep, teach, and dispense the truth of the book of Revelation. They are the Eagles (flying eagles - page v). God will use those who have ascended in Him as Eagles to be dispensers of this message. They begin as the 144,000 (Parenthetical of Angels page 101) who have lived out the Seals, Vials, etc. before the beginning of the first dispensation. They have ascended and are able to operate out of the throne room.

Rev. 22:8-9 and 8:13	
8	And I John saw these things, and heard them. And when I had heard and seen, I **fell down to worship before the feet of the** **angel** which shewed me these things.
9	Then saith he unto me, See thou do it not: for **I am thy fellowservant, and of thy brethren the prophets**, _and of them which keep the sayings of this book_: worship God.
	Can it be any clearer? The angels of revelation are brethren prophets who are obedient to take this message to the world. Just in case you need more proof, look at 8:13...
8:13	And I beheld, and heard an ~~angel~~ [Eagle] flying through the midst of heaven, saying with a loud voice, **Woe, woe, woe,** [on page xx] to the inhabiters of the earth by reason of the other voices of the trumpet of the three angels, which are yet to sound!
	The word used here for angel is not 'aggelos', but 'aetos', which means "Eagle". Imagine how hard it must have been for the translators to ascertain how Eagles would be shouting "woe, woe, woe." **Eagles are, however, the angels that bring this message.**

Armageddon

Armageddon is the place of final decision. It has as its origin, 'periecho' and 'epicheo'. Look at their definitions below to see the meaning of this misunderstood word. God will SURROUND YOU (Gr. Periecho) giving you no place to run, then He WILL POUR OUT (Gr. Epicheo) His presence on you to force a decision about Christ.

Periecho -to surround, to encompass
a) to contain: used of the subject-matter (contents) of a writing
b) to take possession of, to seize
Epicheo (ep-ee-kheh'-o);-- to pour upon: -- pour in.

Armageddon is also "Har Meggiddon" or 'hill' of the city 'Megiddon'. Zec. 12:11 spoke of this place where the people will mourn because they will see the Lord and many will finally repent when they understand that they have pierced Him. However, those who still will not repent and *are against the Lord will be destroyed. Many call this place, the place of final "decision"; because this is the last chance to choose Him.*

Joel 3:13-14
13 Put ye in the sickle, for the *harvest* is ripe: come, get you down; for the press is full, the fats overflow; for their wickedness is great.
14 **Multitudes, multitudes in the VALLEY OF DECISION**: for the day of the LORD is near in the valley of decision.

BABYLON

Babylon represents the 'captivity' that sin and worldliness bring the children of disobedience. It also represents the punishment God directs at those who refuse to repent of this sin.

Babylon is a Harlot gone into full perdition. Remember that God allowed Babylon to take His people captive because of the evil they did in His sight. He sent prophets to warn them; yet, they would not repent. Therefore, He gathered these rejecters into Babylon. God does this same thing in 'type' during the tribulation; worldly Christians who do not repent will be gathered spiritually in Babylon. Moreover, it will be there that the wrath of God will be most severe. This is not necessarily a physical place, but a condition of the heart. It is a heart so hardened to the revelation of Christ that they are all but hopeless. That is why the tribulation must be so great upon them in the end, so that something can break their hearts. But all that have eyes to see will see the mark of the Beast upon these rejecters

*Babylon/worldliness causes the Church to fall from her spiritual place and become the Harlot. Then as more and more of the "**kings of the earth**" repent and become the Elect, then the only thing left in the Harlot is the world; therefore, Babylon is the distilled essence of a rejecting people. God no longer sees those who do not bear fruit (John 15:2) as the Body of Christ, any more than Israel is seen as His chosen people. He rejected those of Israel, because they would not accept the truth of His Son; and He will reject the carnal Church because they refuse the truth.*

BALANCES

Balances represent judgment, see Dan. 5: 27 on page 51, "TEKEL; Thou art weighed in the balances, and art found wanting." "Balances" weigh out our true motives and show forth our true nature. Our heart and our actions must <u>balance out</u>. If not, then our own works will judge the condition of our heart.

BARLEY

Barley represents the Elect Company who is perfected through adversity and judgment. Barley matures better in adversity. It was called winter wheat. It also represents the voluntary tribulation necessary to remove the "marring" or defilement of the Harlot. Without this, they would not be able to receive a robe of righteousness this side of the grave.

BARLEY

Barley was also used as an offering for those who had been defiled by a Harlot or those who had practiced harlotry (See Hos. 3:2, Num. 5:15, and Ezekiel 13:19). Barley was offered to the Lord to remove the defilement. In Seal 3 barley represents those wanting to go on into perfection (3 parts). However, to be part of the Elect, you must not be defiled by the Harlot; therefore, we have to see 'adversity' as the offering we must pay to remove any defilement from the Harlot. Barley matures best in adverse conditions.

Barley removed defilement
Rev. 14:4
4 These are they which were **not defiled with women**; for they are virgins. These are they which follow the Lamb whithersoever he goeth. These were redeemed from among men, being the **Firstfruits** [Elect] unto God and to the Lamb.

BEAST Scarlet colored

The Beast represents carnality within the redeemed or a 'will' other than God's will. The use of the word Beast indicates that this is a heart issue, which has bite. It is more than just a sin nature; it is a nature that attacks the will of God. It may look and sound religious, but Satan directs it, supported by selfish desires...pride, lust, deception, etc.

The Beast nature

(the definition of Beast is taken from verse 12)

2 Pet. 2:9-13 The Beast defined in scripture
9 then the Lord knows how to deliver the godly out of temptations and to reserve the unjust under punishment for the **day of judgment**,
10 and especially those who **walk according to the flesh** in the lust of uncleanness and despise authority. They are presumptuous, **self-willed**. They are not afraid to speak evil of dignitaries,
11 whereas angels, who are greater in power and might, do not bring a reviling accusation against them before the Lord.
12 But these, like **natural brute <u>BEASTS</u>** made to be caught and destroyed, speak evil of the things they do not understand, and will utterly **perish in their own corruption**,
13 and will receive the wages of unrighteousness, as those who count it pleasure to carouse in the daytime. **They are <u>spots and blemishes</u>, carousing in their own deceptions while they feast with you**, (NKJ)

Verse 9 shows that this scripture is to be associated with the Day of Judgment, when the unjust will come into wrath. In verse 10 we see that these 'beasts' walk after the flesh (See Rom. 8:5, 6), which is defined as self-will. The rest of these verses define these beasts as spots and blemishes, the very thing that will not be in the Bride.

> **Jude 1:12**
> 12 These are **spots in your feasts of charity**, when they feast with you, feeding themselves without fear: **clouds they are without water**, carried about of winds; trees whose fruit withereth, without fruit, twice dead, plucked up by the roots;

Make no mistake, these beasts are carnal Christians. 'Clouds without water' is a reference to being a witness (cloud of witnesses) without spirit, without the 'latter rain' associated with the Spirit of the Lord.

BLOOD (SEE ALSO 'LIFE')

The life is in the Blood. Blood is a reference to 'life', either eternal life or redemptive life (See below on page xi).

BLOOD OF DEAD MAN

This is pure Christ's life, life of those dead to self... the fullness of Christ. See Life page xi, the Eternal Life of God. (Blood=life, dead man=Elect through Christ-in-them)

BOTTOMLESS PIT

[GREEK - ABUSSOS (AB'-US-SOS)]

The bottomless pit is a type for the "heart". In reality, it is our gateway to the spiritual realm. "The kingdom of Heaven is within you," and "It is what comes out of a man that defiles him" are two scriptures that speak of a way to the spiritual realm within us. We call this the 'heart'. We are dealing with "heart" issues and not monsters from Hell. Since this term is covered with traditional dark veils, look only at the scriptures, not unsupported concepts.

In New Testament times, the secular use of this word did not carry today's dark connotations. It was a variation on a word used (Gr. buthos/us) to describe depth. In its strictest use, it declared a depth so deep only God could discern it. As a variation to this, it was used to denote the place of the dead (both the good and bad). All of the dark connotations stem from the dark misunderstandings given by the Church in the Middle Ages. Artists depicted the "deep" (bottomless pit) as a horrible place due to their misunderstandings associated with the imagery in Revelation. The definition footnoted below gives insight into secular use of this word.

> **Ps. 64:6** They **search out iniquities**; they accomplish a diligent search: both the inward thought of every one of them, **AND THE HEART, IS DEEP**.
> **Abussos** – 'deep' is sometimes rendered as 'a very deep hole'; in other instances, it thought to be 'a hole without a bottom' or 'the deepest hole in the earth.' *Greek-English Lexicon of the New Testament* [2]

Outside of Revelation there are only two other places in the New Testament in which this word is used: Luke 8:31 and Rom. 10:7.

---

[2]Louw, Johannes P. and Nida, Eugene A., *Greek-English Lexicon of the New Testament based on Semantic Domains*, (New York: United Bible Societies) 1988, 1989.

> **Luke 8:31**
> 31 And they besought him that he would not command them to go out into the **deep**.
>
> **Rom. 10:7**
> 7 Or, Who shall descend into the **deep**? (That is, to bring up Christ again from the dead.)
> 8 But what saith it? The word is nigh thee, **even in thy mouth, and in thy heart**: that is, the word of faith, which we preach;
> 9 That if thou shalt confess with thy mouth the Lord Jesus, and shalt **believe in thine heart** that God hath raised him from the dead, thou shalt be saved.

Both are translated 'deep' and have the significance of being a 'way' to the spiritual realm. In Luke the demons did not want to go back that way, but rather they pleaded to go by way of death. In Romans, it is the place of the dead (neither good nor bad). Romans enlightens us by stating that the heart is the correct place to look for the bottomless pit.

The **bottomless pit** *is the gateway in our heart from which we can be defiled (Mat. 12:34, 15:11) **or** receive eternal life. It is the place where the real battle is taking place (Rom. 7:23).*

> **John 4:11, 14**
> 11 The woman saith unto him, Sir, thou hast nothing to draw with, and the **well is deep**: from whence then hast thou that living water?
> 14 But whosoever drinketh of the water that I shall give him shall never thirst; but the water that I shall give him **shall be in him a well of water springing up into everlasting life**.

BREASTPLATES

This term represents 'breastplates' of righteousness (Eph. 6:14). Breastplates speak of the deeper truth about the "robes" of righteousness... iron sharpens iron. Being sharpened means that we help kill each other through relationship (See seal two). Breastplates (robes of righteousness) are part of the full armor of God" for all who submit one to another (Eph. 6:14). As our iron is sharpened, we walk in agreement with others; thereby, we complete our walk with God. In Joel Chapter 2, this is symbolized by well-defined columns in which the Elect march. This is where others provide the walls that keep us straight.

BRIMSTONE

This is bad judgment, just like the smell of brimstone. It speaks of the opposite of...

> **Ezek. 20:41** I will accept you **with your sweet savour**, when I bring you out from the people, and gather you out of the countries wherein ye have been scattered; and I will be sanctified in you before the heathen .

Brimstone is a form of final judgment. Brimstone judgment is final judgment. "Ten" represents judgment, but it is a precursor to deliverance. Brimstone, on the other hand, is the type of judgment that Sodom and Gomorrah received (Gen. 19:24)...FINAL. However, final judgment can be good as a deterrent to eternal separation. The **lake of fire** *and* **brimstone** *speak of final judgment that brings eternal separation. It is the fear of that final outcome that should perfect (* **fire** *) our hearts. This is what is unique about the* **fire** *and* **brimstone** *judgment. The fear of that* *judgment can bring repentance; while in the other judgments, the actual penalty must fall before repentance comes.*

CANDLESTICKS (SEE ALSO *LAMPSTANDS*)

The candlesticks are the holders of God's light; i.e. the representatives of Christ here in the earth. Christ chooses who this should be. This should be the Church but it will switch to the Bride as the Bride appears. She is more of who Christ is and therefore a better witness of Him. The bigger problem with this term is that the lamps and lampstand speak of the fullness of Christ in us. It is close to the same thing, but with more of a personal heart issue than a corporate manifestation. (Rev. 2:5 says, "Remember therefore from whence thou art fallen, and repent, and do the first works; or else I will come unto thee quickly, and will remove thy candlestick out of his place, except thou repent.")

CARNAL CHURCH

This church loves the things of men more than the things of God. They are led by pride and position more than Spirit and Truth. From the heart of this church, the **Beast** *will rise. (Also, see* **Kindred, and tongue, and people, and nation** *(page xiii) as well as* **sea,** *or* **Harlot***).*

CLOUDS

Clouds represent the Glory of God and the vehicle through which He is coming.

Throughout Exodus He appears in a cloud. In Revelation He is clothed in clouds. God appeared in a cloud over the mercy seat and in Solomon's temple. Heb. 12:1 says that we are surrounded with a great cloud of witnesses. Clouds are a place of His appearing. Luke 9:34 "While he thus spake, there came a cloud, and overshadowed them: and they feared <u>as they entered into the cloud.</u>*" Here we see people caught up in a cloud and not going anywhere. (Erchomai on page 12)*

COMPLETION (FOR A BETTER EXPLANATION, *SEE COMMENTARY ON PAGE 124.*)

To be complete in Christ is to be obedient to the point that it is no longer us seen, but Christ. Obedience is the key to completion because we must walk in His perfect will for us. This is how Jesus acted with the father. He said that He never said a word or did a deed that was not shown Him by the Father. John 14:9 tells us that to see Jesus was to see the Father. This is unlike perfection or fruit bearing; here the focus is on surrendering. In 'perfecting', the spots are shown; and we die to them (surrender) by letting Christ have dominion over them. In 'completion', we learn to walk as Christ.

CUP

This is the Cup of wrath, the measure of sin, that when full brings wrath. It is also the dispenser, which brings the wrath. She cannot complain because she is receiving what she has prepared.

Rev. 14:10	
10	The same shall drink of the <u>wine of the wrath</u> of God, which is poured out without mixture into the **cup of his indignation**; and he shall be tormented with fire

and brimstone in the presence of the holy angels, and in the presence of the Lamb:

Rev. 16:19	
19	And the great city was divided into three parts, and the cities of the nations fell: and great Babylon came in remembrance before God, to give unto her the **cup of the wine of the fierceness of his wrath**.

Rev. 18:6	
6	Reward her even as she rewarded you, and double unto her double according to her works: in the **cup** which she hath filled fill to her double.

DARKEN

Darken means the dimming or removal of Glory light through judgment. Darkened does not mean that the light of God is dimmed; rather there are fewer "lights" because they were separated through judgment.

The following verse shows why they were separated... they shamed the Glory of God in them by not shining forth as a witness. This is similar to the parable of the talents. In that parable the fellow who buried what God gave him and did not multiply it was punished by having what he was given taken away; thus he was also separated from his fellow servants (Matt. 25:14-30). In the parable of the 'talents', the servant who had only one was called wicked because he knew what His Master wanted, and he refused. That is the same point being made in the following scripture in Romans. They knew God and what He expected from them; therefore, they are "without excuse". The reason God separates them from His servants is so they will not confuse those seeking to know Him.

Rom. 1:20-21	
20	For the **invisible things** of him from the creation of the world are **clearly seen**, being understood by the things that are made, even his eternal power and Godhead; so that they are without excuse:
21	Because that, *when they knew God, they glorified him not as God*, neither were thankful; but became vain in their imaginations, and their foolish **HEART WAS DARKENED.**

DAY

Day represents a time of light, a time when the revelation of Christ is understood and accepted.

DEAD IN CHRIST (SEE ALSO 'FIRSTFRUITS' AND THE COMMENTARY 'DEAD IN CHRIST')

This phrase is used to define those who have died to this world, not in a physical sense but a spiritual sense. They are not perfect, just surrendered to the 'master's' hand. They are "SOLD OUT" to Jesus.

Paul says that "it is no longer I that live but Christ that lives in me." He also said that he dies daily. Col. 3:1-4 shows the 'dead in Christ' is a position in Christ that is to be obtained. Being dead in Christ is to be SOLD OUT to Christ. It also means that Christ is your Lord and has birthed His Spirit in you. The focus of this phrase is "It is no longer we who live, but Christ-in-us that lives." He has control and we are "beheaded" to the world.

DRUNK

Drunken means confused in the spirit, and is normally associated with spiritual hypocrisy.

> **Jer. 51:7** Babylon hath been a golden cup in the Lord's hand that made all the **earth** <u>drunken</u>: the nations have drunken of her wine; **therefore, the nations are mad**.

EAGLES

Eagles are the highest of the three beasts who minister around the Lion in Chapter Four of Revelation. These are the 100 fold overcomers, sold out believers who operate in the fullness of Christ. They are separated from this world and constantly minister to the Lamb. They are even referred to as Angels (on page i) in Rev. 8:14.

EARTH

The earth represents carnality: 'self-will' independent from God's will. It is also a term that means a fleshly earthy nature, the carnal mind with its lust. Carnality is what the Lord is coming to conquer; it was also what caused man to fall from the Garden. It is defined in Rom. 8 as the enemy of God; understandably, it keeps us from Him. Therefore, carnality must be conquered before Christ can be revealed in us.

> **1 Cor. 15:47-48 (also see Rm. 8:5-7)**
> 47 The first man is of the **earth, earthy**: the second man is the Lord from heaven.
> 48 As is the **earthy, such are they also that are earthy**: and as is the heavenly, such are they also that are heavenly.

*Earth is the spot on our garments, the ugliness that keeps the Bride from putting on her wedding dress. Christ will come to judge and destroy the 'earth' wherever it exists. If carnality exists in us, then we better get rid of it or face the tribulation that is destined for the earth. Since carnality exists in the Church, then He will judge the Church and separate the Bride from the Harlot. This is the time when the '***dead in Christ***' appear or "rise first". They are the sold out believers whom Christ will indwell, as He did in Paul. Their Glory, or His appearing, will destroy the wickedness of carnality. "And then shall that Wicked be revealed, whom the Lord shall consume with the Spirit of his mouth, and shall destroy with the brightness of his coming:" II Thes. 2:8. **Christ comes and prepares for Himself a spotless body (no carnality), which will be the vessel for His corporate appearing.***

GREAT EARTHQUAKE

This is 'the shaking' that brings separation through tribulation. It is a form of purification. Shake things up and only that which is attached to the solid Rock of Jesus Christ will remain.

> **Heb. 12:27-29**
> 27 And this word, Yet once more [*implied shaking*], signifieth the **removing of those things that are shaken** [*not of God*], as of things that are [*man*]made, that those things which cannot be shaken may remain.

> 28 Wherefore we receiving a **kingdom which cannot be moved**, let us have grace, whereby we may serve God acceptably with reverence and godly fear:
> 29 For our God is a **consuming fire**.
>
> *As we see in verse 28, we are to have a kingdom that cannot be shaken. Our foundation is to be in Christ, the solid Rock. If you are always up and down in your relationship with Christ, then maybe you have built your relationship with Him on a sandy foundation.*

> **Amos 9:13**
> 13 Behold, the days come, saith the LORD, *that the plowman shall overtake the reaper, and the treader of grapes him that soweth seed*; and the mountains shall drop sweet wine, and all the hills shall melt.

The wrath is so great, results will be immediate...
Matt. 24:21-22

> 21 For then shall be **great tribulation**, such as was not since the beginning of the world to this time, no, nor ever shall be.
> 22 And except those days should be shortened, there should no flesh be saved [Greek-sozo]: but for the **Elect's sake those days shall be shortened**.
>
> *A better translation, based upon an intense study of the Greek, gives greater insight into this scripture...if the days were not shortened, (as with the reaper catching up with the sower), then men could not be saved (Greek-sozo). Dying must be accelerated, or time would run out for most people.*

EAST

We enter the temple from the east which spiritually represents 'ENTERING IN' or the way of transformation through spiritual ascension. The temple represents a pattern of how we walk out our relationship with Christ, and we begin that walk through the Eastern Gate.

EMERALD

Emeralds are highly prized stones. If we seek Jesus, as we seek the treasures of this world, we will see His Glory manifested in our lives. The promise of His Glory will come only when He is highly sought after and prized. In Rev. 21:11 the description of the Bride says she is called "like unto a stone most precious." Therefore, those who diligently seek Him will become the Bride.

EVERLASTING GOSPEL

Fearing God and giving Him Glory through Christ-in-you is the hope of that Glory. Showing the full revelation of Christ by the gospel you live gives God the greatest Glory. Revealing Christ declares your fear and reverence of God.

> **Col. 1:27**
> 27 To whom God would make known what is the riches of the glory of this <u>mystery</u> among the Gentiles; <u>which is Christ-in-you, the hope of glory</u>:

EYES (FLAME OF FIRE)

Jesus is the only one described with 'eyes that are a flame of fire'. The first place we see this description of Him is in Rev. 1:14, where Jesus is described as the righteous judge. The judge would need eyes that reveal the truth for the sake of perfection (fire). Therefore, these 'eyes as a flame of fire' are the revealing nature of Christ-in-us. To die-to-self we must have the spots revealed and then cleaned; this is what Christ living in us does. Without Him to show us our faults through the glorious face of His presence, then we would never be perfected. Our heart is evil without Christ on the throne, so it would be impossible to see past our evil hearts if it were not for Him.

FEET OF BRASS

In Rev. 1:15, this description is given to Jesus Christ when He is manifested in a body of people. This description is right after His description of 'eyes of fire'. The two terms are related. The brass feet are purified through the **fire** *in 1:15, symbolizing the walk that becomes perfected through the cleansing power of Christ-in-us.*

This walk helps us become 'complete' in Jesus. (See commentary 'Complete vs. Perfect' on page 124 to understand this walk of completion.) Through the constraining and the perfecting power of Christ-in-us, we will begin to walk in the footsteps of Jesus.

FIRE

Fire is the perfecting power of God. This tribulation shows forth those things that are of God. This occurs because anything that is not of God will perish (wood, hay, and stubble) and gold is all that is left.

1 Cor. 3:14-15	
14	If any man's work abide which he hath built thereupon, he shall receive a reward.
15	If any man's work **shall be burned**, he shall suffer loss: **but he himself shall be saved; yet so as by fire**.

FIRSTFRUITS (SEE *ALSO COMMENTARY 'DEAD IN CHRIST'*)

The term 'Firstfruits' comes from the harvest and stands for the tithe of the harvest given to the Lord. There is to be a great Harvest *of God in the end-time, and the Firstfruits are a group of people (the 144,000) who are the first return of the harvest. God has chosen this group of the Elect to bring the message to the Church and the world. The 144,000 Firstfruits company is to be compared to the Apostles (144,000 divided by the 12 = 12,000, which is called the portion of Jacob). For full clarity see: 'Angels' page 101; '144,000' page i; and 'Portion of Jacob' page xv.*

James 1:18	
18	Of his own will <u>begat he us</u> with the word of truth, **that** we should be a **kind of Firstfruits** of his creatures.

1 Cor. 15:20, 23	
20	But now is Christ risen from the dead, and become the **firstfruits** of them that slept.
23	But every man in his own order: [1]Christ *the* [2]firstfruits; afterward they that are [3]Christ's at his ~~coming~~ appearing ['parousia', see page 12].
	He chose them and quickened the Revelation to them so they could be the apostolic beginning for the book of Revelation. According to verse 15:23, the Firstfruits are the first to rise during the end-time resurrection ([1] Christ was first 2000 years ago).

The glorified body, robe of righteousness (on page xvi), signifies the resurrection. As you study the resurrection, you will see that you receive the glorified body (robe of righteousness) as you are made complete in Christ. Since you are complete and there is no other will in you but the Lord's, then you will be given your inheritance, which is a glorified body. This is how you are a part of the resurrection, and it will happen to a generation without going to the grave.

The order of resurrection or stepping over the grave is: first, [1]Christ (He has already done it); second the [2]Firstfruits of Christ (Christ made manifest in His 144,000), then finally those who are part of His appearing [3]. This last group is all the others who became completed, but they are not part of the initial 144,000; they are the fruit of the Firstfruits.

Rom. 8:23	
23	And not only they, but ourselves also, which have the **firstfruits of the Spirit**, even we ourselves groan within ourselves, waiting for the **adoption, to wit, the redemption of our body**.
	This verse connects the 'robe of righteousness to the Firstfruits. We get a glorified body and are recognized as the manifest sons of God.

FLOOD

A flood is made of water, and water is a type of words. A mass of <u>destructive lies</u> sent to separate the Harlot and the Church.

FOUNTAINS OF WATERS

*People of the Church… the SOURCES for the heart-of-the-Church (***sea***) are its people. These are the people and the issues that comprise and affect the makeup of the Church's heart. Fountains are the individuals and 'rivers' are the Church bodies; all flow together to the sea.*

*The secular and historical use of 'fountains', (Greek 'pege' {pay-gay'}) denotes it as a '***source'***, not only in a literal sense but in a figurative sense also. A well can be a fountain.*

FOUR AND TWENTY ELDERS

The twenty-four elders represent a peace offering to God. This number is seen several times in the Old Testament, but it nearly always relates to peace. In Revelation this number of elders represents the sacrifice of our will to be at peace with God (this is not propitiation). This is not about salvation; rather it is about the full will of God. As long as there is carnality in us, then there is a part of us who is at war with God. Paul saw this in Rom. 7. We must offer up this carnality for the sake of peace and perfection. If we are willing to make this offering, then we will be part of the 'Lamb slain', and thereby visible to the world. This is the 'appearing' of the Lamb slain for the world to see. The elders falling down shows the sacrifice they make, as well as the sacrifice they become. The thrones and crowns are what they give (personal authority and self-rule) to Christ to be part of the Elect. This sacrifice is for the sake of others, not themselves. They want the world to see Jesus, not them.

The following verses from the Old Testament show that sacrifice must be made to have peace with God. Christ became the ultimate peace offering to replace the one we see in Num. 7:88. Yet, when disobedience took place even though the peace offering was made, another sacrifice was required. This is showing us that even though Jesus made the ultimate sacrifice for the remission of sin, there are still offerings necessary when disobedience is still in place. In Num. 25:9 the price paid was large… 24,000 people. Today, a carnal church and carnal Christians have put us back in a place of disobedience. God therefore demands an offering for peace. THE OFFERING HE DEMANDS IS…OUR WILL. The elders (a type of our will) represent the sacrifice we must make so that Christ can be on the throne. God has waited two thousand years to have a generation who will offer up a true spiritual peace offering, so that His will has dominion in this world.

FOUR AND TWENTY in the Old Testament

Num. 7:88

88 And all the oxen for the sacrifice of the **peace** offerings were <u>twenty and four bullocks</u>…

Num. 25:9-12

9 And those that died in the plague were <u>**twenty and four thousand**</u>.

10 And the LORD spake unto Moses, saying,

11 Phinehas, the son of Eleazar, the son of Aaron the priest, hath turned my wrath away from the children of Israel, while he was zealous for my sake among them, that I consumed not the children of Israel in my jealousy.

12 Wherefore say, Behold, I give unto him my [1]**covenant of peace**:

Also in Chr. 27:1-15 we see that the peacekeepers of the army set over Israel each month was twenty and four thousand.

<u>Corporate revealing</u> – In Chronicles 27 we read of a military division of peace keepers (24,000) who stood watch over Israel. This division is a type of the watchmen who the Elect represent in Revelation. They will sacrifice themselves so that others can have peace. We are to become a living sacrifice so that others will be able to enter in just as did the apostles. We must become a peace offering for the Lord, or the world will not see how to escape His wrath. This is the four and twenty seats (thrones) and elders (wisdom) that must bow down to the will of Christ. **The Elect are the [1]covenant of peace.**

FOUR AND TWENTY ELDERS FALL DOWN

Any time the elders fall down, man (either personal or corporate) has ascended. Falling down is a mark of ascending because their (or our) 'will' has been bowed to His. You will see this in several places in Revelation, and all should be associated with growth in Christ.

Every time we see the elders fall down, we have surrendered our will to Him. This brings more lightning and thundering to continue His sanctifying work in us. The process goes on and on until we are in the fullness, or we decide to stop pressing forward because we think the cost is too great. Some will be distracted and not reach the full-

ness (moon, stars, etc.). Rev. 8:5 adds earthquakes to the thunderings and lightnings; and Rev. 11:19 adds earthquakes and hail. This shows that God is going to continue to motivate us onward, trying not to let us stop. If we do stop, it is an act of disobedience.

FOURTH PART OR 4

Any use of 'four' or 'fourth' is about the end-time because the last watch is the fourth watch, and we are in the last watch of man-kind. Therefore, four Angels would represent the angels of the end-time. The book of Daniel uses 'fourth' to mean the last kingdom and beast, which are references to the last days.

*The reference to the fourth part is not a percentage of the world population or geography. Instead, it is a reference to the **last watch** of the world. In Matt. 14:25 during the fourth (last) watch, Jesus came walking on the sea (see the symbolism) to the disciples.*

FROGS

Frogs represent JUDGMENT, as do the plagues of Egypt (locust, hail, etc.); yet, each different type gives us greater insight into judgment. The frogs of Revelation represent the lying spirits of the Beast (come out of mouth). They do miracles or present signs that appeal to the carnally minded. In addition, the imagery shows us that the lies they tell will be so obvious that you will have to be blind to ignore them or their source. Therefore, the thrust of the 'frogs' is the accountability we are under to see with spiritual eyes, not self-centered carnal eyes.

GARDEN (FOR MORE INFORMATION SEE THE COMMENTARY ON THE GARDEN ON PAGE 122)

The garden represents the second heaven, a place in the spiritual realm that will be the "new heaven and earth." It is also the restoration of the sin-laden earth to its original Garden of Eden state. It also represents a spiritual place referred to as the air (Greek – aer), where Satan still has his principalities and powers, and God has His Paradise.

*The Garden is where Adam and Eve were living before the fall. After the fall, they were driven out of the Garden so that they could not eat of the 'tree of life' and live forever. Satan, however, seems to have remained. Cherubims (Angelic beings) and a flaming sword were put in place to keep them from reentering (Gen. 3:23) and stealing this fruit. The symbolism of this story is hard to dismiss. [**You can only reenter (eastern gate) the Garden through the flaming sword (truth that perfects) and by the Angelic beast (those with Christ in them)**].*

GLORY

Glory is the radiant presence of something. There are two glories, God's and ours. Ours must diminish before His can increase. In most places Glory is Christ-in-us being seen (Col. 1:25, John 17:10); but in some, it is carnality shining forth.

<table>
<tr><td colspan="2">TWO GLORIES: OURS AND CHRIST'S
1 Cor. 15:40</td></tr>
<tr><td>40</td><td>There are also celestial [heavenly] bodies, and bodies terrestrial [earthy]: but the glory of the celestial is one, and the glory of the terrestrial is another.</td></tr>
<tr><td colspan="2" align="center">CHRIST IN US SHOWING HIS GLORY
Rom. 8:18</td></tr>
<tr><td>18</td><td>For I reckon that the sufferings of this present time are not worthy to be compared with the glory which shall be revealed in us.</td></tr>
<tr><td colspan="2" align="center">OUR GLORY WILL FADE
1 Pet. 1:24</td></tr>
<tr><td>24</td><td>For all flesh is as grass, and all the glory of man as the flower of grass. The grass withereth, and the flower thereof falleth away:</td></tr>
</table>

GOD'S RADIANT GLORY –

In Revelation the bodies that emanate Glory are usually represented as 'heavenly' bodies. Sun, moon, and stars are examples of the bodies that emanate Glory. Matt. 13:43 and 17:2 all declare these bodies as God's Glory. In addition, these same bodies can represent either personal or corporate Glory. The sun, for example, in Christ's kingdom represents the Eagle, which is the highest degree of Glory a person can obtain. Yet the sun could also represent the highest corporate Glory (the Bride), as in Matt. 13:43. Stars, too, could be either personal or corporate. They are the babes in Christ individually or 'Holy Messengers' corporately. In any of these examples, Glory is the reflection of the source.

MAN'S CARNAL GLORY –

In the second dispensation, the great 'appearing' of Christ brings God's Glory to the world to pale man's glory. Nevertheless, what is man's glory? Like God's Glory, **the highest form of natural glory** is the <u>sun</u>. It represents man's greatest accomplishments from the tower of Babel to Wall Street. All of these are designed to make men proud of their achievements. This is how Satan distracts man from God's Glory. This kind of Glory sounds like: "Get a good education to obtain this world's treasures", "get a good job and make lots of money", or "power is the true mark of a man." Even in the Church, this kind of glory exists, and no one seems to mind. These mindsets and others like them become the strength guiding people's lives and giving them reasons to live. However, God will change all of that as His Glory increases in the Church.

The second level of man's glory is the moon; it rules over the night. The moon represents the lust of the flesh that guides our evil desires and hides us from God's Glory. John 3:19 says, "And this is the condemnation, that light is come into the world, and men loved darkness rather than light, because their deeds were evil." *The moon enables us to walk in darkness; therefore, this verse reveals that the moon is our evil lust. Nevertheless, when God's Glory shines into the darkness the moon will turn to blood (life).*

Jesus will catch them unaware in the nakedness of their glory which cannot cover them.

<table>
<tr><td colspan="2">1Thes. 5:2-5</td></tr>
<tr><td>2</td><td>For yourselves know perfectly that the day of the Lord so cometh as a thief in the night.</td></tr>
<tr><td></td><td>He will rob them of their "glory" because they are of the night.</td></tr>
<tr><td>3</td><td>For when they shall say, Peace and safety; then sudden destruction cometh upon them, as travail upon a woman with child; and they shall not escape.</td></tr>
<tr><td></td><td>The tribulation will overcome them and rob them of this world's covering.</td></tr>
<tr><td>4</td><td>But ye, brethren, are not in darkness, that that day should overtake you as a thief.</td></tr>
<tr><td></td><td>This robbing is only for those who choose to walk in darkness.</td></tr>
<tr><td>5</td><td>Ye are all the children of light, and the children of the day: we are not of the night, nor of darkness.</td></tr>
</table>

Lastly, the stars represent those who profess religion, but are carnally minded (Rom. 8:6-7). Do not confuse these with carnal Christians. Carnal Christians are deceived, but at least they desire some sort of relationship with God. These 'stars' have no interest in serving God. Their minds are full of the flesh. They are only socially involved with Christianity. In some cases, they are just hedging their bets, involved only enough to say they are involved. They draw their strength from earthly glory (sun and moon). It is not until God touches this world by wrath that they even take notice of what God is doing. Their eyes are so full of the world during the first dispensation that they are unaffected by the "Bride" and the revelation of Christ.

GOSHEN '*HILL CITY*'

Goshen is a type of the New Jerusalem, the protected dwelling place of God's people...Bride Church. In the Old Testament Goshen is where the children of Israel lived while in Egypt.

<table>
<tr><td colspan="2">Exod. 8:22-23, 9:26</td></tr>
<tr><td>22</td><td>And I will sever in that day the land of Goshen, in which my people dwell, that no swarms of flies shall be there; <u>to the end thou mayest know that I am the LORD in the midst of the earth.</u></td></tr>
<tr><td>23</td><td>And <u>I will put a division between my people and thy people:</u> tomorrow shall this <u>sign</u> be.</td></tr>
<tr><td>9:26</td><td><u>Only in the land of Goshen, where the children of Israel were, was there no hail</u> [judgment].</td></tr>
<tr><td></td><td>Egypt is a type of the world, we are children of Israel, and the flies are evil spirits. The Bride will be the visible declaration that "the Lord [is now] in the midst of the earth" Matt. 5:14. We are to be cities on a hill...light to the world.</td></tr>
</table>

GRASS

Grass represents the life of man, temporal... as well as the works founded on personal strength. Grass fades and so will the part of our life that is carnal (stubble)...

<table>
<tr><td colspan="2">Isa. 64:6</td></tr>
<tr><td>6</td><td>But we are all as an unclean thing, and all our righteousnesses are as filthy rags; and we all do fade as a leaf; and our iniquities, like the wind, have taken us away.</td></tr>
<tr><td colspan="2">1 Pet. 1:24</td></tr>
</table>

24	For **all flesh is as grass**, and all the glory of man as the flower of grass. The **grass withereth**, and the flower thereof falleth away

Grass is a type used in Revelation to declare what is of man. If it is of 'us', then it shall be burned in the fire of perfection…

1 Cor. 3:13-15	
13	**Every man's work shall be made manifest**: for the day shall declare it, because it shall be revealed by fire; and the **fire shall try every man's work** of what sort it is.
14	If any man's work abide which he hath built thereupon, he shall receive a reward.
15	If any man's work shall be burned, he shall suffer loss: but he himself shall be saved; yet so as by fire.

Using grass in conjunction with "green" focuses on the part of our "efforts" that speak of Life. Green represents life; even though they are works of men, they are "well intentioned" and have some life in them.

GREEN

Green is life. (See **trees** *and the reference to Jeremiah.)*

HAIL

Personal Judgment *from heaven should not to be confused with the Great Hail in Thunder 6. This judgment is meant to perfect us by making unGodly things hard to retain. God is forcing you to listen to the truth.*

Isa. 28:17	
17	Judgment also will *I lay to the line, and righteousness to the plummet:* and the **hail** shall sweep away the refuge of lies, and the waters shall overflow the hiding place.

Great HAIL

Hail represents the judgment of man. This is a different judgment from that mentioned in Thunder 1. That judgment was personal for perfection. This is the 'Great' Judgment, the last judgment as far as the inhabitants of the earth are concerned. 'Great' in Greek is 'megas', and that means big, enormous. This is the time of reckoning. If you are not saved by this point, then the next thing you will see is the White Throne Judgment (where the eternal separation awaits).

HAIR

Hair is the corporate covering of Christ through obedience and surrender to His body. Covering means that we are accountable to someone or something. The hair is a reference to the accountability that a woman has to the man. In Revelation this means that the Bride is accountable to Christ. For the individual Christian who wants to be conformed to the image of Christ, then accountability to the corporate Bride is the way, especially since we know that she walks after her husband Christ. There will be no private works; we are a corporate appearing.

1 Cor. 11:15	
15	But if a woman have long hair, it is a glory to her: for her hair is **given her for a covering**.

This is in type; the hair is to be associated with the covering that Christ gives to those who become His Wife.

1 Cor. 11:8-10	
8	For the man [Christ] is not of the woman [Wife]; but the woman of the man.
9	Neither was the man created for the woman; but the woman for the man.
10	For this cause ought the **woman to have power on her head because of the angels**.

Her 'hair' represents the power of the headship and not the individual. In our case, it is the whole body.

HARLOT / GREAT WHORE (SEE PARENTHETICAL 'THE BEAST' PAGE 94)

The Harlot represents the carnal Christians who reject Christ. They love the things of this world more than the things of God. Look at these scriptures and see those who have a form of Godliness but no power. They may even study the scriptures and learn many doctrines, but the truth eludes them because of their PRIDE.

The Harlot	
2 Tim. 3:1-7	
1	This know also, that in the last days perilous times shall come.
2	For men shall be lovers of their own selves, covetous, boasters, proud, blasphemers, disobedient to parents, unthankful, unholy,
3	Without natural affection, trucebreakers, false accusers, incontinent, fierce, despisers of those that are good,
4	Traitors, **heady, highminded, lovers of pleasures more than lovers of God;**
5	**Having a form of godliness, but denying the power** thereof: from such turn away.
6	For of this sort are they which creep into houses, and lead captive silly women laden with sins, led away with divers lusts,
7	**Ever learning, and never able to come to the knowledge of the truth.**

In the same way that Israel played the harlot with other gods, the Christians will play the harlot with this world. God is not enough to her; her converts become men pleasers and pleasure seekers! They reject the sold out message of Christ and run from the chastening of God. This type of Christian focuses on a 'form of Godliness' but will deny the power of a risen Christ Life. In Rev. 12:16 the Harlot makes a pact with the earth and receives the antichrist's lies to stop the tribulation that the Eagles cause her. Receiving the worldly lies of Satan is a form of spiritual fornication because Satan is in those lies.

The Harlot is the designation given Christians who reject the 144,000's message of Life. See the Parenthetical "The Harlot" (page 90). The Beast then rises up out of her heart to reveal the true nature of carnal Christians, as a spiritual Harlot. Once the Harlot is formed, Satan has an influence in the Church (many waters), so that he can do battle with the Elect.

HARPS

'Harps' represent the Revelation voice of God given to those who have received the revelation (See Rev. 5:8). In Joel 2:11 we see that the Lord's voice goes before (Greek 'paniyn' = in their face) His army.

HORSES

These are vehicles for the Lord; the Elect in whom He will take this message to the world.

> **Zec. 1:8-10**
> 8   I saw by night, and behold a man riding upon a red horse, and he stood among the myrtle trees that were in the bottom; and behind him were there red horses, speckled, and white.
> 9   Then said I, O my lord, **what are these**? And the angel that talked with me said unto me, I will shew thee what these be.
> 10   And the man that stood among the myrtle trees answered and said, **These are they whom the LORD hath sent to walk to and fro through the earth**.
> *These are the different horses, not the rider. The rider rides on those "walking" to and fro.*

White Horse – the Firstfruits Elect ones in whom He can bring the message to the Church.

Red Horse – those who bring the life of Christ to the Church.

Black Horse – those who bring doom and destruction to the carnal church. In Zec. 6:6 they are associated with the North Country. In Jer. 50:9 the North Country is what will come against Babylon to destroy her.

Pale Horse – those who bring Death to those of the last watch. These are the Eagles who will bring Christ's life to those ready to die-to-self.

INHABITANTS OF THE EARTH

These have never accepted Jesus as Savior, and they are the focus of the second dispensation.

ISLANDS *SEE ALSO 'MOUNTAINS'*

Islands are even more separated than mountains. They surround themselves in doctrine (water) just to be separate.

JACINTH

Jacinth represents the Glory of the last generation. Jacinth is only mentioned in Revelation. It is the 11th foundation holding up the wall of New Jerusalem (wall' represents the Elect 144,000). Eleven appears as a number to represent the last generation or a final chance for God's Glory. This is shown in the parable of the vineyard (Matt. 20:6-9). It is also shown in the people of Zech. 1:7-11 who go to and fro throughout the earth in the end-time. Jacinth is to show us that the Glory which is on us will bring life to those in the dark.

JASPER

This stone is used as a seal. Jasper represents the seal that must be broken in our heart (die-to-self); it can only be broken if we seek after Christ. It is also a type of the Bride.

KEY

*A KEY is an item or means to open something. Note that Jesus Christ is the possessor of the keys to the pit (Rev. 20:1 and 1:18). Christ descends out of Heaven to rise with power over the heart (**bottomless pit** iii).*

KINGS OF THE EARTH

Kings of the earth are redeemed, but they serve mammon instead of God. They take their authority from the world. They have not received their kingdom; Christ is not yet manifest in them. They have received Jesus as their Savior, but He is not the Lord of their lives... living in them.

> **Rev. 17:12**
> 12   And the ten horns which thou sawest are ten **kings, which have received no kingdom** as yet; but receive **power as kings one hour with the Beast**.

KINGS & PRIESTS

These are part of the Melchizedek order, of which we are a part through Christ in us. We will be kings and priests in the house of our Father and rule here on earth.

> **Rev. 5:10**
> 10   **And have made us** <u>kings and priests</u> **to our God; and we shall reign on the earth."(NKJ)**
> **Heb. 7:1-3**
> 1   For this Melchisedec, king of Salem [peace], priest of the most high God, who met Abraham returning from the slaughter of the kings, and blessed him;
> 2   To whom also Abraham gave a tenth part of all; first being by interpretation **King of righteousness**, and after that also King of Salem, which is, **King of peace**;
> 3   Without father, without mother, without descent, having neither beginning of days, nor end of life; but made like unto the Son of God; abideth a priest continually.

LABOURS *(GR. KOPOS)*

Labours are defined in Strong's Dictionary as a beating, trouble, intense labor united with trouble and toil.

This is the thing from which we must rest. The Lord will do the work. This is the entering of our rest.

LAMB (SLAIN)

The Lamb represents Christ-in-us when we are dead to self. Chapter Four of Revelation makes it clear that the one who is sitting on the throne is Christ Himself. In verse 11, He is called Lord and is the only one worthy to receive all power and Glory. Yet, the 'Lamb slain' takes the book from the Christ on the throne. It sounds as if Christ is taking the book from Christ, and, indeed, He is. It is Christ in a humble, dead-to-self vessel reaching out and receiving the revelation. The Lamb therefore represents Christ-in-us.

LAKE OF FIRE AND BRIMSTONE (SEE SECOND DEATH *ON PAGE XVI AND* BRIMSTONE *ON PAGE III*)

This speaks of the final separation from God. It is called the lake of 'fire and brimstone'; the fear of eternal separation from God (judgment) will bring the perfecting power of God (fire). This means that the fire and the brimstone are on this side of the lake and are meant to make people repent before it is too late. It is called the second death because there is no more resurrection from it.

LAMPSTANDS (CANDLESTICKS)

Lampstand represents the witness of Christ…those who represent Him in this world. *You could say that it is the one carrying the light of God to the world. In the Old Testament, it was Adam, Noah, Abraham, Abraham's children (Israel). In the New Testament, it was Jesus, the disciples, the Church, and finally, it will be the Bride. When He threatens to remove the candlestick (Rev. 2:5), He is saying that they will no longer have His authority or witness.*

Rev. 1:20	
20	"The mystery of the seven stars which you saw in My right hand, and the seven **golden lampstands**: The seven stars are the Angels of the seven Churches, and the **lampstands which you saw are the seven Churches.**
Rev. 2:5	
5	Remember therefore from whence thou art fallen, and repent, and do the first works; or **else I will come unto thee quickly, and will remove thy candlestick out of his place, except thou repent.**

LIFE (SEE *COMMENTARY 'LIFE' ON PAGE 128*)

LOCUSTS …THE ARMY OF GOD

Locusts represent part of God's army that emerges in Glory, meaning they wear their spiritual Robes of Righteousness. Harvest begins with the locusts coming forth to sting but not to kill. They are to torment or bring tribulation to the inhabitants of the earth. They are the Wife of the Lamb sent to eat the natural glory of this world.

Joel Chapter 2 shows the stages of the locust. This is how the Bride Church will become the appearing. This also corresponds to the four beasts of the throne room. The first three are the Elect in their stages of growth in Christ (calf, man, eagle). The last is the appearing of Christ, just like the Lion on the throne in Chapter Four of Revelation.

Joel 1:4	
14	That which the **palmerworm** hath left hath the **locust** eaten; and that which the locust hath left hath the **cankerworm** eaten; and that which the cankerworm hath left hath the **caterpillar** eaten.

Palmerworm	**Calf** stage w/o wings…*immature*
Locust	**Man** young adults w/wings, (swarm-becomes part of the body…*mature*)
Cankerworm	**Eagle** *fully mature*, devours flesh…like an eagle
Caterpillar	**Christ' Body** final stage (THE APPEARING), *comes as a cloud*, destroys all in path…Jesus in a cloud of witnesses

Locusts are given POWER as Scorpions. You need to see this power as the ability to influence, not just to perform miracles. The result of the power is redemption through the witness of Jesus Christ. This power is spiritual

power; however, they will show great signs and wonders, except theirs will not be "lying" wonders.

POWER AS SCORPIONS
POWER… *"as the scorpions of the earth have power"*, to *"torment as the torment of a scorpion"*, and as *"tail like scorpions…sting in their tail."* This represents quick, powerful, and deadly wrath. This wrath will quickly prepare the way for death to this world and Life from Christ.
Scorpion… is a generic term for about a dozen species which inhabit the Holy Land. The poison is in the sting at the end of the tail. **The scorpion is an emblem of torture and wrath.** Some of the species in southern Palestine are six inches long. Unger's dictionary © [3]

MANY WATERS

Many waters mean 'many people declaring one doctrine': in some cases, the Harlot's doctrine; and in others, the Bride's. The focus is not on the doctrine, but on the "commonality" they have.

Rev. 17:15	And he saith unto me, The **waters which thou sawest**, where the whore sitteth, are **peoples, and multitudes, and nations, and tongues.**

Reference to the Harlot, she sits on many waters	
Jer. 51:13	
13	O thou that dwellest upon **many waters**, abundant in treasures, thine end is come, and the measure of thy covetousness. [worldliness]
Isa. 17:11-12	
11	In the day you will make your plant to grow, and in the morning you will make your seed to flourish; but the *harvest* will be a heap of ruins in the day of grief and desperate sorrow.
12	**Woe to the multitude of many people who make a noise like the roar of the seas,** and to the rushing of nations that make a rushing like the rushing of mighty waters! (NKJ)

SEE ALSO the description of **Sea**

MARK OF BEAST

It is the number of a man (13:17-18) = 666. The number 666 is a figurative number. **Six** *is the number of man (carnality).* **Three** *is the number of completion; therefore, three sixes represent "COMPLETELY CARNAL". This is a spiritual mark to show those sold out to the carnal/worldly message. These are the hypocrites who make the world* **drunk** *(confused) with the Church.*

The scriptures below describe two groups that share a common bond of carnality. The first group (II Thes. 2:11-14) is sold out to the carnal message (666). They openly love this world and make no excuses about it. These are men who have become lovers of pleasure more than lovers of God (see below). They may become Saints of God, but the mark of carnality will always be present.

Carnal and loving it	
II Thes. 2:11-14	
11	And for this cause **God shall send them strong delusion,** that they <u>should believe a lie</u>:

---

[3] Ungers dictionary © 1988 The Moody Bible Institute of Chicago. All rights reserved

12	That they all might be damned **who believed not the truth**, but had <u>pleasure in unrighteousness</u>. (worldliness)
13	But we are bound to give thanks always to God for you, brethren beloved of the Lord, because God hath from the beginning chosen you to salvation through sanctification of the Spirit and belief of the truth:
14	Whereunto **he called you by our gospel, to the <u>obtaining of the glory</u>** of our Lord Jesus Christ.

The second group (II Tim.3: 1-5) <u>*loves the image of carnality;*</u> *they lust after the "good life". They play around with the world and refuse to die to it. They are not as obvious to spot. They rationalize their lack of commitment to the Lord by grace. They trod the Lord underfoot by indulging self.*

Carnal and denying it
II Tim. 3:1-5
1   This know also, that in the last days perilous times shall come.
2   For men shall be **lovers of their own selves**, covetous, boasters, proud, blasphemers, disobedient to parents, unthankful, unholy,
3   Without natural affection, trucebreakers, false accusers, incontinent, fierce, despisers of those that are good,
4   Traitors, heady, highminded, **lovers of pleasures more than lovers of God;**
5   Having a **form of godliness**, but denying the power thereof: from such turn away.

Verse 5 shows that this is the carnal Church which has a "form" of godliness - not the unredeemed.

The Christ-in-us message will mark the earth in those who are thus minded. The Glory revealed by the sold out life of the Holy Messengers will provide the spiritual mechanism that reveals the earth. We, the Vials, will become an offense to all who love the world. These are the true antichrists.

The most disturbing fact about this group is that once they have "sold" their inheritance for this pottage (world), they will never be completely restored. They may repent and become Saints, but they will never obtain the full measure of God's plan and Glory for their life. They will not rule with Christ during the Millennium, but they will have to go the way of the grave.

THOSE WHO ARE MARKED BY BEING "LOVERS OF THIS WORLD MORE THAN GOD"
Heb. 12:15-17
15   looking diligently lest anyone fall short of the grace of God; lest any root of bitterness springing up cause trouble, and by this many become defiled;
16   lest there be any fornicator or profane person like **Esau**, who **for one morsel of food sold his birthright**.
17   For you know that afterward, <u>**when he wanted to inherit the blessing, he was rejected, for he found no place for repentance, though he sought it diligently with tears.**</u>(NKJ)

MARRIAGE SUPPER OF THE LAMB (SEE GREAT SUPPER)

MARVELOUS SIGNS

There are three 'marvelous signs' in Revelation (Rev. 12:1, 12:3, and 15:1). Since three is the number of completion, then this is the complete sign that God will give (in three parts) to confirm His plan for the Elect. The three marvelous signs in the book of Revelation are the woman, 12:1, the dragon, 12:3, and the Angels. These are the "signs" that God has given to the Elect to confirm the truth and purposes of Revelation.

Jesus told us to discern the times through signs (Matt. 16:3). The first sign we see is the pregnant woman. This is the time in which the Elect will begin to emerge from the traditional church. The second sign we see is Satan trying to stumble the Elect before they can be birthed into a gathering. This is a time when great tribulation comes against those sold out to Christ. Friends, pastors, and family members (Matt. 10:36) will all try to make you more "reasonable" about your "religion". Finally, the last sign we see is the Elect gathering as the holy messengers of God. They will separate themselves from the pull of this world and rise up as 'soaring Eagles'. The love of Christ will put purpose into their lives. They will be a people with a mission (Joel Ch. 2).

MERCHANTS

These are carnal man-made denominations who profit from the Lord's body. They are more impressed with numbers and programs than with the heart of the people. The word in Greek for merchant is 'megistanes' which means great men or lords within a royal court. These 'merchants' are the leaders of carnal denominations and ministries. They care more for the size of their ministries than for the sheep themselves. They will even deceive to achieve their ends, and they believe that they are justified in their position.

MOON (SEE ALSO 'GLORY' AND 'SUN')

The moon is the second in the resurrection **Glory** *of Christ, or the glory of the night. Moon, when used with Christ, represents that second stage of growth in which His Elect have overcome the lust of the night. When used in conjunction with the glory of the world, it represents the base lusts that guide our lives (immorality, sensuality, etc.).*

MOUNTAINS (See also 'great MOUNTAIN BURNING WITH FIRE')

Mountains are places or organizations that make up the Church. The right kind of worship brings us to God. The wrong kind of worship is an empty, carnal worship meant to show forth religion more than God. In the Old Testament, it meant both: a place to meet God or a 'high place' of worship, which is a counterfeit and an insult to God.

1) Mountains can stand for the place in which we meet God, such as a **great mountain**. *Much of the Revelation is about a face to face relationship with Christ, and 'great*

Mountains' speak of the need for that relationship. 2) Mountains can also speak of independent religious organizations... Babylon is made of such places. That is why Revelation speaks of mountains being removed or cast down.

Zec. 4:7-9	
7	Who art thou, **O great mountain**? before Zerubbabel thou shalt become a plain: and he shall bring forth the headstone thereof with shoutings, crying, **Grace, grace unto it**.
	This mound of rubbish represents the old religious (Babylon) system and organizations that will be brought low. However, God will bring forth a new temple (e.g. Bride) from the ashes of the old
8	Moreover the word of the LORD came unto me, saying,
9	The hands of Zerubbabel have laid the foundation of this house; his hands shall also finish it; and thou shalt know that the LORD of hosts hath sent me unto you.
	God may use a man (Zerubbabel), but the accomplishment is His (grace). His Bride will sweep away the old refuge and build a new temple (New Jerusalem).

Great MOUNTAIN BURNING WITH FIRE
(SEE *ALSO* 'MOUNTAINS')

*The Great Mountain burning represents a perfecting personal revelation of Christ, with all of the heavenly experiences that come from a face to face encounter with Christ. It is an encounter similar to the one Moses had with the burning bush on 'his' mountain top experience. Christians who experience this type of relationship stand in stark contrast to social Christians, who tend to wonder what all the fuss is about. They are deprived from a full Christ Life. This 'revelation of Christ' (**great mountain**) will cause the Church to come into judgment (e.g. perfecting FIRE). In other words, as these sold out messengers share their revelation of Christ (See "voice out of the fire" below), judgment will come into the hearts of those whom they touch.*

Deut. 5:23-25	
23	And it came to pass, when ye heard the voice out of the midst of the darkness, (for the mountain did burn with fire,) that ye <u>came near unto me</u>, even all the heads of your tribes, and your elders;
24	And ye said, Behold, the LORD our God hath shewed us his glory and his greatness, and we have heard his voice out of the midst of the fire: we have seen this day that God doth talk with man, and he liveth.
25	Now therefore why should we die? for this great fire will consume us: if we hear the voice of the LORD our God any more, then we shall die.

NATION, AND KINDRED, AND TONGUE, AND PEOPLE

*This is the carnal, worldly Church populace. They are in contrast to the unredeemed "inhabitants of the earth" and the Elect. The names used in conjunction with each other give insight to the common nature of these **many waters** that the Harlot sits on.*

Kindred = Jacob's descendents in the Old Testament, today God's representatives... **CHRISTIANS**...

> GREEK 'PHULE' - all the persons descending from one of the twelve sons of the patriarch Jacob.
> *God's representatives or witnesses to world...i.e. Christians.*
> *These people are part of the Church, yet they are bound by greater ties than their ties to Christ. The following definitions show these bonds and why they are considered the **Many Waters** that the **Harlot** rides on.*

Tongue = **SPEAKING THE SAME THING**...Bound by **DOCTRINE**

> GREEK 'GLOSSA' - a tongue; the language or dialect used by a particular people distinguishes them from that of other nations.
> *Groups bound by common doctrine. Although this separates each group, it gives each person a false sense of being right and part of the right group. Pride brought the judgment of languages at the tower of Babel. It is still represented by the worship of diverse doctrines within the Church. Christ is not the author of division..."a house divided..."*

People = Those who gather together like a **DENOMINATION**...Bound by **DENOMINATIONISM**

> GREEK LAOS - a people, people group, tribe, nation, all those who are of the same stock and language
> *Once they gather under the banner of a doctrine, the next step is denominational separation. People can be more devout loving their church and its doctrines than loving Christ.*

Nation = The **CALLED** but not the Chosen...Bound by **PRIDE**

> GREEK ETHNOS - Paul uses the term for Gentile (non-Jewish) Christians.
> *Ethnos is the root of 'ethnic' which is the pride of one's heritage. This term is used to show that although they are worshipers (like the Gentile believers), they are not the chosen. This term was used in the Old Testament to mean 'those not worshiping the true God'. Combine Old and New Testament meanings and we see a type of the prideful believer worshiping the wrong things...things of self...i.e. carnality.*

NEW SONG

*"And he hath put a **new song** in my mouth, even praise unto our God: many shall see it [the song sung], and fear, and shall trust in the LORD" This is the revelation of Christ coming in power through the 144,000 to declare deliverance to the earth. The 'rod' that both comforts and corrects.*

'New Song' represents Christ-in-us singing a song of deliverance and victory to the "heathen" (See below). This is a love song manifested in the hearts of the 144,000 for the deliverance of His children from the earth.

Revelation says that only the **144,000** can learn and sing this song, this is because they operate in the fullness. The world does not perceive them as the singers but sees Christ singing directly to them. That is what makes it a love song from the throne of God. It is a song, which tells of the wrath to come; a wrath for His people who have become His enemies (the Harlot); and yet, He still pursues them. He still loves them and will do what it takes to win them back. In Isaiah 42:10-25 we read about the 'new song' in which the Lord rises up _as a_ "mighty man" bringing judgment against His own. This "mighty man" is the **Man-Child** of Revelation who will go down to the **'sea'** (heart of the carnal Christians) to declare the judgment of God against the carnality in the Church. They sing this song before the altar in intercession for those needing deliverance from this Harlot…"come out from among her", they cry.

Ps. 40:3-4	
3	And he hath put a **new song** in my mouth, even praise unto our God: **many shall see it, and fear**, and shall trust in the LORD.
4	Blessed is that man that maketh the LORD his trust, and respecteth not the proud, nor such as turn aside to lies.
Ps. 96:1-3	
1	O sing unto the LORD a **new song**: sing unto the LORD, all the earth.
2	Sing unto the LORD, bless his name; shew forth his salvation from day to day.
3	Declare his **glory among the heathen, his wonders among all people**.
Ps. 98:1-2	
1	O sing unto the LORD a **new song**; for he hath done marvellous things: his right hand, and his holy arm, **hath gotten him the victory.**
2	**The LORD hath made known his salvation: his righteousness hath he openly shewed in the sight of the heathen.**

NICOLAITANS

(Nicolaitans in Greek means "destruction of people"). Nicolaitans are a sect mentioned in Rev. 2:6, 15. These are worldly self-righteous Christians, who are forward towards others. They are worse than just sinful Christians; this group tries to get others involved with their sins. They even try to convince others that they are not sinning. They destroy the people by getting them away from a Christ-centered relationship. They worship the image of this world and try to bring that image into the Church; instead of just backsliding, they justify their sin as religion.

Scripture tells us these Nicolaitans were charged with holding the error of Balaam. They cast a stumbling block in front of the ekklesia of God by upholding the liberty of eating things sacrificed to idols, as well as committing fornication.

NUMBERS AND THEIR MEANING

-Two

Two is the number of witnesses. Heb. 6:18 says, "That by two immutable things, in which it was impossible for God to lie…" And He sent the disciples out by twos to establish the witness. Also "in the mouth of two witnesses, a thing is established."

-Three

Three is the number for God. God is complete in one. God chooses to reveal Himself in THREE.

I Jn. 5:7	
7	For there are **three** that bear record in heaven, the Father, the Word, and the Holy Ghost: and **these three are one**.

Three can also be used to mean completion. As God is COMPLETE in three; it is both His number and His understanding in which three completes Him and everything.

-FOUR (SEE FOURTH PART)

-FORTY-TWO

Forty-two is the number of his appearing in us, the witnesses. Jesus appeared to the world for 42 months in His natural body, and then He was glorified. Also it took 42 generations from Abraham until He appeared. In Revelation it will take forty-two months before His 'parousia' to the world.

From Abraham to Jesus = 42 generations	
Matt. 1:17	
17	So all the generations from Abraham to David are **fourteen** generations; and from David until the carrying away into Babylon are **fourteen** generations; and from the carrying away into Babylon unto Christ are **fourteen** generations.

-FIVE

Five is the number of Grace.

-SIX

Six is the number of Man or carnality.

-SEVEN

Seven is the number of Godly perfection.

-Ten

Ten is the number of tribulation and judgment – The ten plagues of Egypt, ten Commandments, and Dan. 1:11-15 are examples of the ways in which God has used ten to bring tribulation/judgment, so that His Glory can be revealed.

PEARLY GATE

The pearly gate is the gate into the New Jerusalem or the way into the completion necessary for the robe of righteousness. One way that a person can be sold out is to become submissive to the body of Christ, and the 144,000 will pro-

vide a "wall" to constrain the citizens of the
New Jerusalem into Holiness. See "complete vs.
perfect" on page 124. Yet, the most obvious
type is 'the pearl of great price'… we must sell
out to enter New Jerusalem.

Matt 13:45-46	
45	Again, the kingdom of heaven is like unto a merchant man, seeking goodly pearls:
	This is a Christian seeking for more.
46	Who, when he had found one pearl of great price, went and sold all that he had, and bought it.
	When he gets the revelation of Christ-in-us, he lays down his life to gain Christ's life.

PEOPLES OF REVELATION

The three groups of people in Revelation:

1) **Those who have died to self and have Christ in them: [Elect (page 112), <u>Angels</u> (page 101), <u>Overcomers</u>, 144,000, etc.].**

2) **Those who are qualified through the blood of Jesus to be part of group one but have not yet manifested His life. They have not died to self or made Jesus their Lord and King. (<u>kings of the earth</u>,** *page x***.) They dwell in or on the earth (*on page 43*).**

3) **People who have never accepted Jesus at any level are <u>inhabitants of the earth</u>, on page x.**

PORTION OF JACOB

The twelve tribes mentioned in Rev. 7:5-8 are God's chosen Elect or the portion of Jacob. The portion of Jacob is Christ' inheritance, the fruit of His labors (Firstfruits). The 12 tribes of people are the inheritance of Jacob. They represent God's <u>promise</u> to Abraham fulfilled. You remember that Abraham was looking for two promises. The first was a promise to find a city whose founder and builder was God (New Jerusalem). The second was that His descendants would be as the sands of the sea. In reality, they are both accomplished in the "portion of Jacob", because the remnant of the twelve tribes (spiritual Israel) represents the Elect forming the New Jerusalem… a city of peoples. In Rev. 7:5-8 we see a path through the meanings of the names. This path leads to the New Jerusalem.

The 144,000 will be the tribe of Firstfruits, the tithe of Christ's ministry, here on earth. You can say it this way: the 144,000 are the fruit of the labor of Jesus while He was on earth. This is not all of the harvest, just the Firstfruits. They are the Firstfruits for God or the return on the seeds planted by Jesus… the tithe.

These verses show that the 12 tribes really are not from modern Israel, but are a type of God's Firstfruits for the end-time. All of God's work sown into Israel and the early church is now returning a 'tithe' back to God. He gives this tithe to His Son for His kingdom.

Deut. 32:9	
9	For the **LORD'S portion is His people**; <u>Jacob</u> is the place of His inheritance. (NKJ)
Jer. 51:18-19	

18	They are vanity, a work of delusion: in the time of their visitation they shall perish. *[end-time rejecters]*
19	**The portion of Jacob** is not like these; for [1]**he** is the former of all things; and (Israel) *[added word not implied]* [2]<u>is the tribe of his inheritance</u>: Jehovah of hosts is his name. (ASV)

[1]Christ in a Firstfruits company of people is the new portions or tribes of Jacob. As a 'Firstfruits company', Christ-in-us represents the tribes of His own inheritance. He made us His tribe by being in us, "He[1]… [2]is the tribe of His inheritance." Since there is no subject for this second phrase, the translators added Israel. Israel is NOT the tribe spoken of here and is not even implied in the original. The last phrase tells us who the inheritance is… "Jehovah is his name." The translators could not see how God could make and be His own tribe. Christ-in-us is the answer.

Luke 1:32-33	
32	He shall be great, and shall be called the Son of the Highest: and the [1]<u>Lord God shall give unto him the throne of his father David</u>:
33	And he shall <u>reign over the house of Jacob</u> for ever; and of his kingdom there shall be no end.

Look at what the Lord is telling us in Gal. 3:28-29.
1 – Christ's people are His portion. Christ's inheritance is His people and it began with Jacob. God has always wanted sons in the kingdom.
2 – Christ will be the King of the Portion of Jacob. That is exactly what makes the 144,000 the Lord's; they follow Him wherever He goes. He is their King.

Gal. 3:28-29	
28	There is neither Jew nor Greek, there is neither bond nor free, there is neither male nor female: **for ye are all one in Christ Jesus**.
29	**And if ye be Christ's, <u>then are ye Abraham's seed, and heirs according to the [1]promise.</u>**

So, what is the [1]promise? Christ is the promise. He is the sum of all the promises of Abraham and anyone who is His can partake of this promise. There is no greater promise. So why argue about the dead promises given to a nation that God divorced? The Church became the new Wife and eligible for the promises that were given His ex-wife. Jer. 3:8 says, "And I saw, when for all the causes whereby backsliding Israel committed adultery I had put her away, and given her a bill of divorce; …" Also see Lev 21:14 on the prophecy about the Lord not marrying a divorced woman.

RAINBOW / BOW

Bow represents the 'bow' of God, which is the rainbow. The rainbow was a promise or a covenant with God; therefore, Jesus' bow represents a promise or covenant with God. He will no longer declare war on all of mankind. The heart of the promise is that He will not destroy mankind and His creation. Therefore, even though we see Jesus coming to conquer, it is not to destroy, but redeem. The 'bow' He brings is a promise of a Glory cloud. It was in the clouds that He placed His bow. Therefore, He will defeat carnality with a "hope of Glory".

Gal. 3:14 [*The promise is the Spirit received...Christ-in-us*]
14   That the blessing of Abraham might come on the Gentiles through Jesus Christ; that we might receive the **promise** of the **Spirit** through faith. [Christ's Spirit is implied, see Eph. 3:16-17.]

RIVERS

Similar to **fountains**, these are organizations that are filled with carnality, thereby adding to the **Sea** of Carnality. In the natural, fountains form rivers, and rivers feed the sea. This means that rivers are the organizations and local bodies that gather '**fountains**' [vi]. See also Vial 3 to see that these are people.

ROBE OF RIGHTEOUSNESS

Stepping over the grave

1 Cor. 15:53-54 At the Last Trump
53   For this corruptible must put on incorruption, and this mortal must put on immortality.
54   So when this **corruptible shall have put on incorruption**, and this mortal shall have put on immortality, then shall be brought to pass the saying that is written, **Death is swallowed up in victory.**
When the last trump has sounded in our life, then the final victory will have happened; Christ will have "reigned until death is his footstool." This is not about rapture; it is about the robes of righteousness or the 'parousia' of Christ in an individual. We know that this is about stepping over the grave with our eternal robes of righteousness because death is defeated. This is either an individual issue or it must take place at the white throne, because there will be 'death' occurring all the way to the end of the Millennium. Remember that Revelation is the revealing of Christ.

We are qualified to receive a robe through the righteous acts of the Saints (showing forth Christ in all we do). The Robe is also the 'better resurrection' because it is the 'glorified body'. It is given to those who died to this world completely. Once given, it establishes our weight of Glory for all time. This is the <u>GLORIFIED BODY.</u>

Isa. 61:10-11
10   I will greatly rejoice in the LORD, my soul shall be joyful in my God; for he hath clothed me with the garments of salvation, he hath **covered me with the robe of righteousness**, <u>as</u> a **bridegroom** decketh himself with ornaments, and as a **bride** adorneth herself with her jewels.
11   For as the earth bringeth forth her bud, and <u>as the garden causeth the things that are sown in it to</u> ¹spring forth; so the Lord GOD will cause righteousness and praise to spring forth before all the nations.

We get to wear 'Christ' to harvest the world. The robe is Christ in us ¹revealed in all we do and say.

SARDINE

Sardine is a stone of dark red color. It speaks of the precious blood which provides the grace that unlocks His Glory.

SEA (*SEE commentary on page 126*)

The 'sea' represents the heart of the carnality in the Church (carnal church populace); it is the place from which the Beast rises. It is also the general worldly nature of much of the Church. When we hear "going to the sea" or "traversing the sea", it is speaking of ministry to the carnality in the Church.

Hab. 3:7-8
7   I saw the tents of Cushan in affliction: and the curtains of the land of Midian did tremble.
Cushan means "their blackness" and Midian means "strife". These are the issues of the heart that invite the "Beast". The Beast comes out of the sea in 13:1, but how did it get there? These passages give us the clue. The blackness and strife in man's heart made a perfect home for the Beast to mature.
8   Was the LORD displeased against the **rivers**? was thine anger against the rivers? Was thy wrath against the **sea**, that thou didst ride upon thine horses and thy chariots of salvation?
*Notice that the Lord is against all the sources of the sea, as well as the sea itself (**Rivers** above). If **rivers** and **sea** are not some form of mankind, then these verses just do not make sense. God is not angry at His creation; it is the disobedient hearts of mankind that bring His wrath. The horses and chariots are the Revelation horsemen and Joel's chariots, God's instruments of wrath.*

SEA OF GLASS

This is God's mirror action. This is Christ's intimate presence, which reveals the spots of our heart (**sea**). Crystal means without spot. Look into the presence of the one 'without spots' to see our own. This is the perfecting fire of Christ-in-us.

SEAT OF THE BEAST

His authority is in the riches and pleasures of this world and our desire to be like God (carnality).

1 Tim. 6:9-10
9   But they that will be rich fall into temptation and a snare, and into many foolish and hurtful lusts, which drown men in **destruction and perdition**.
10   For the **love of money is the <u>root</u> of <u>all</u> evil**: which while some coveted after, they have erred from the faith, and pierced themselves through with many sorrows.

The carnal mind is the enemy of God. Satan sets himself on the throne of our hearts because we want to be as God and make our own decisions.

SECOND DEATH

The second death is the eternal separation from God for those who reject the life of Christ. It is also called the **Lake of fire and brimstone** (on page x).

SEVEN EYES

Seven is the number of perfection, and eyes represent perception and wisdom. Eyes also represent what we are 'focused' on (see below); therefore, seven eyes refers to focusing on God's perfection. Focusing on God's perfection is described in detail in the **seven spirits of God**. *Read the definition for the* **Seven Lamps** *below.*

"In the Bible the eye is often described symbolically. "Evil eye" (Matt. 20:15) describes envy; "bountiful eye" (Prov. 22:9) refers to generosity; "wanton eyes" (Is. 3:16) mean pride; "eyes full of adultery" (2 Pet. 2:14) are symbolic of lust; "the lust of eyes" (1 John 2:16) means earthly temptation; and "the desire of your eyes" (Ezek. 24:16) refers to a loved one. "The apple [pupil] of His eye" (Deut. 32:10, Zec. . 2:8) referred to the nation of Israel implying its special place in God's plan. (from Nelson's Illustrated (Bible Dictionary Copyright (C) 1986, Thomas Nelson Publishers[4])

SEVEN LAMPS or THE SEVEN SPIRITS OF GOD

– or **Seven eyes**. *This is the fullness of Christ, the lack of carnality. If all the lamps were burning brightly, then we would be in the fullness of Christ (See below). The seven spirits show us the areas of our heart that need work. All three terms (7 lamps, 7 eyes, 7 spirits of the Lord) mean the same thing. They tell us that the only way into the fullness of God is through the perfecting work of Christ-in-us. Christ will show us the areas in which we need to die. Combine all three terms, and we see (eyes) the true extent of God's Glory (lamps) shining in our lives; this is the level of Christ-in-us. The fire represents the perfecting work of this revelation. (See also Zec. 4:10.)*

THE FULLNESS OF CHRIST
Eph. 4:12-13
12   For the **perfecting of the saints**, for the work of the ministry, for the edifying of the body of Christ:
13   Till we all come in the unity of the faith, and of the knowledge of the Son of God, unto a perfect man, unto the measure of the stature of **the fulness of Christ**:

Is. 11:1-2 THE SEVEN SPIRITS (love, wisdom, understanding, counsel, might, knowledge, fear of Lord)
1   And there shall come forth a rod out of the stem of Jesse, and a Branch shall grow out of his roots:
2   And the spirit of the [1]LORD (**God's love**) shall rest upon him, the spirit of [2]**wisdom** and [3]**understanding**, the spirit of [4]**counsel** and [5]**might**, the spirit of [6]**knowledge** and of the [7]**fear-of-the-LORD**;

SEVEN HEADS

God's authority – 'seven' is the number of godly perfection; 'heads' are interpreted as authority.

SEVEN MOUNTAINS *SEE ALSO 'MOUNTAINS'*

The seven mountains are the Church organizations that support the Harlot. The Harlot sits on: 1) the **beast**, 2) **many waters**, 3) Seven Mountains. These three descriptions of what support the Harlot give insight into just how such*

harlotry exists in the Church. The only option for God is to remove these spots through tribulation.*

These organizations promote forms of religion that can keep us from a relationship with Christ. Luke 23:30 and Rev. 6:15-16 show how these things will be used to hide us from God and prevent a direct encounter with Christ, allowing us to be justified by religion rather than relationship. But Rev. 6:20 promises that they will be removed and, if they are your covering, then you will be naked before God.

SEVEN STARS

These are those who will declare this revelation to the Church, and then to the world. They are defined in Rev. 1:20 as the Holy Angels (Messengers) to the Church.

SEVEN THUNDERS

The Seven Thunders are the revelation truths of Christ that have been sealed until the last generation of the Elect could manifest the mystery of Godliness (Christ in them). Christ then opens the seals and reveals these Thunders through His holy prophets and apostles.

Revelation 10:3, 4
3   and cried with a loud voice, as when a lion roars. When he cried out, seven thunders uttered their voices.
4   Now when the seven thunders uttered their voices, I was about to write; but I heard a voice from heaven saying to me, "**Seal up the things** which the seven thunders uttered, and do not write them."

John says he is about to explain what he was hearing, but he is told not to explain what was being revealed; therefore, the Thunders are sealed until...

Revelation 10:7
7   but in the days of the sounding of the seventh angel, when he is about to sound, the mystery of God would be finished, as He declared to His servants the prophets.

Here, we are told that just before the angels sound these thunders to the world, that first these Thunders will be open to His servants and prophets of that generation. This is exactly what Rev. 1:1 tells us; the revelation of Christ will show His servants the things that will shortly come to pass.

SHIPS

*These are programs that make up the Church organization; they are more 'pride' than Christ. These are the vehicles by which commerce is done in the heart (**sea**) of the Church.*

Isa. 43:14
14   Thus saith the LORD, your redeemer, the Holy One of Israel; For your sake I have sent to Babylon, and have brought down all their nobles, and the Chaldeans, whose ~~cry~~ [pride] is in the ships.

The things that engender religious pride really have no business in the Church. They are similar to those things that Jesus removed from the temple with a whip. This is how the Beast rides into the Church: man's programs, man's religious idols, man's pride of life, etc.

[4] from Nelson's Illustrated Bible Dictionary Copyright (C) 1986, Thomas Nelson Publishers

SIT ON EARTH

*This is anyone who gets his or her peace and rest from the **earth**. They do not want to change their lives. These people definitely do not want to trade their lives for the Lord's life. They are content with letting carnality stay in their lives and resent anyone who tries to remove it. This is a heart issue. Redeemed or not, they have found THEIR lives.*

SMOKE (SEE GLORY ON PAGE VII)

Smoke represents Glory: pillar of smoke, smoke on the mountain, etc., all speak of His presence.

Great STAR/MORNING STAR (Spirit of Christ)

Christ is the Morning Star (Rev. 22:16). Stars are defined in Rev. 1:20 as the Angels (holy messengers). Christ is the great Holy Messenger, and Christ-in-us makes us Holy messengers.

*This is Christ as the Morning Star in trumpet 3 (Rev. 22:16). He comes to the Elect (Rev. 2:28) to shine forth through them, bringing judgment to the sources of the heart (**sea**). In other words, this revealing is a perfecting presence (burning lamp) that perfects the very source of the Sea [(rivers (churches) and fountains (Christians)].*

SUN (SEE ALSO 'STARS' AND 'MOON' AND 'GLORY')

The sun represents the greatest glory in whatever context it is used. If it is the better resurrection, then it is the eagles; and if it is about the Corporate Body, then it is the Bride Church (See Matt: 13.43). If it is about carnality or worldliness, then it is about the dragon.

The sun, as a heavenly body, can be His glorious body of people (the Bride), or the "natural light" of this world. However, the key to understanding any of the three heavenly bodies (sun, moon, or stars) is glory.

All Kinds of Glory
1 Cor. 15:40-42
40   There are also **celestial bodies**, and bodies **terrestrial**: but **the glory of the celestial is one, and the glory of the terrestrial is another**.
41   There is one glory of the sun, and another glory of the moon, and another glory of the stars: *for one star differeth from another star in glory*.
42   *So also is the resurrection* of the dead. It is sown in corruption; it is raised in incorruption:

Great SUPPER

This is the final time of tribulation when we glean the harvest. The Eagles will play a major part in this final squeeze of the winepress.

STARS (SEE ALSO 'GREAT STAR/MORNING STAR' / 'GLORY' / 'SUN')

Stars can be the third level of resurrection Glory, or they can be the Christians who are really of the night. As far as the message of Revelation, Stars are defined in Rev. 1:20 as the Angels or holy messengers. This is because any amount of Christ-in-us makes us a messenger.

SWORD

(TWO EDGED) (SEE ALSO THE TWO WITNESSES)

The sword is the revelation of the two witnesses. This means that it should be heeded because it both speaks and shows the revelation of Christ. Those who bring the Revelation (two-edged truth) will both live and speak the same message. See Revelation 2:16 and 19:15.

SYNAGOGUE OF SATAN / SPIRIT OF ANTICHRIST

*This is a lying spirit sent forth from Satan to infiltrate the Church and give birth to the Harlot. It will rise in those who promote a life independent of Christ. The spirit that is anti-Christ will also promote doctrines of men; it promotes the belief that Christians do not need anyone else to advance spiritually, and they should be responsible for dictating what is right for them. In other words, they can have it their own way; they can sit on the throne and guide their own lives. They can be as God! These are worldly Christians (See **Nicolaitans**) who worship this world while claiming to be Christians (For more information, see summary of the Parenthetical on the Beast page 94.)*

TEETH

*Teeth are the devouring work of Christ appearing through us. His presence eats the flesh. (See **Locust**)*

TEN HORNS = TEN (NUMBER OF JUDGMENT), HORNS (TYPE OF CLEMENCY)

These are the ones who God uses to bring judgment to the whore. They are unknowing instruments of God's plan.

Horns of Clemency
The projections of the altar of burnt offering (Ex. 27:2) and of the altar of incense (Ex. 30:2) at their **four** corners were called "horns." By laying hold of these horns on the altar of burnt offering, <u>a person found safety</u> (I Kin. 1:50; 2:28) <u>if his alleged offense was accidental</u> (Ex. 21:14). Unger's dictionary ©[5]

Horns represent the heart of the 10 kings who are with the Harlot at first, but who turn on her when they realize that she misled them. They wanted to serve God, but pride blinded their eyes until the Lamb lifted the veil.

THREE MEASURES OF

The completeness or fullness

THIRD DAY

The 'third day' is the contemporary term used to describe the 'appearing of Christ' in a body of people. It specifically looks to the third millennial day (day as a thousand years) since Christ' birth. In the same way that Christ rose on the morning of the 'third' day, He will rise again in the hearts of His Elect to bring forth resurrection life into this world. It also compares to the Day of the Lord or the seventh millennial day since creation. They are one and the same day, but with focus on the resurrection and not so much on the ultimate reign of Christ.

---

[5] from Ungers dictionary © 1988 The Moody Bible Institute of Chicago. All rights reserved

THIRD PART

The 'third part' is God's part. Three is the number for God (also 'three' on page xiv). The 'third part' is to be interpreted as the redeemable part. In the same way that spots reveal what is NOT of God, the 'third part' is the part that will be recognized as His. This has to do with any 'part' that stands the test of fire is His.

Zec. 13:9	
9	And I will bring the **third part through the fire**, and will refine them as silver is refined, and will try them as gold is tried: they shall call on my name, and I will hear them: I will say, **It is my people**: and they shall say, The LORD is my God.

THUNDERINGS

Thunder is God's voice of authority being heard. It comes with His presence and increases with the number of voices that are speaking in one accord. (See 14:2 & 19:6) In Ex. 20:13 the thunder showed that God was on the mountain. It is also a revelatory voice for those who have ears to hear; a revelation of God's desire.

TREES

Trees represent men. These are the ones who stand up to chastening and choose to be pruned of/for God. These are willing to be visible instruments of pruning. Jeremiah 17 shows this to be an act of trust. It we trust God, then "all things work together for our good."

Jer. 17:7-8	
7	Blessed is the man that **trusteth** in the LORD, and whose hope the LORD is.
8	For he **shall be as a tree** planted by the waters, and that spreadeth out her roots by the river, and shall not see when heat cometh, but her leaf shall be **green**; ...

If people do not see that they need to have their lives pruned, then they do not qualify as the trees that move on into completion (third part). **Isaiah 61:3** says, "To appoint unto **them that mourn in Zion** *[i.e. pruned]*, to give unto them *(1)* beauty for ashes, *(2)* the oil of joy for mourning, *(3)*the garment of praise for the spirit of heaviness; **that** they **might be called trees of righteousness**, the planting of the LORD, **that he might be glorified**." [Notice the '3' benefits to completion as a tree!]

TRIBULATION

Tribulation is chastening of the Lord, for purposes of perfecting (removing the flesh) and for the revelation of Christ (Glory to be seen). As a result, we can dwell in the kingdom of Heaven. It is not to be shunned, but embraced as a way to reveal Christ.

Rom. 8:18	
18	For I reckon that the **sufferings** of this present time are not worthy to be compared with the **glory** which shall be **revealed in us**.

TRUMPET

The trumpet is the revelation or revealing voice of Christ. (See REV. 4:1.)In Thunder 6, the trumpet represents the revelation of that particular segment. In other places it represents the message being shouted out to the world like the trumpet that sounded to declare the 'feast of tabernacles'.

TWO WITNESSES
(SEE ' THE TWO WITNESSES ON PAGE 113'.)

The **two** witnesses represent Spirit and Truth. It is the living and speaking of the revelation of Christ-in-us. We witness with both our mouth and our walk. Today, many declare Christ with their mouths, but they do not show Him in their walks. That is to be expected, because you cannot show what you do not have. If Christ is IN you, then the fruit of your walk will show this. The Church has allowed too long the hypocrisy of just one witness. He wants us to worship Him in Spirit and Truth... true worshipers.

John 4:23-24	
23	But the hour cometh, and now is, when the **true worshippers** shall worship the Father **in spirit and in truth**: for the Father seeketh such to worship him.
24	God is a Spirit: and they that worship him **must worship him in spirit and in truth**.

The prophets of Rev. 10:7, 11 are only able to prophesy in the fullness of the two witnesses...Spirit and Truth. This means that they have digested the little book, and now they live it as well as speak it. The sackcloth represents the affliction that is necessary to qualify for the fullness of the two witnesses. In Phil. 3:10 we see that the sufferings, represented as the sackcloth, bring resurrection power, defined as Glory.

VOICES (SEE MANY WATERS)

Voices are the corporate revelatory voice of Christ. Waters represent people (Rev. 17:15); so when we hear 'voices of many waters', the connection shows us that voices represent the revelation spoken by a corporate body of believers.

VIRGINS

'Virgins' are those who have not soiled themselves with the Harlot by selling out to the world while claiming to be a Christian. All the 144,000 are virgins by this definition. We know this by verse Rev. 14:4. Any who have received Satan's mark of carnality will not rule with Christ. They will be passed over for the robe of righteousness as well.

2 Cor. 11:1-3	
1	Would to God ye could bear with me a little in my folly: and indeed bear with me.
2	For I am jealous over you with godly jealousy: for I have espoused you to one husband, that I may **present you as a chaste virgin to Christ**.
3	But I fear, lest by any means, as the **serpent beguiled Eve** through **his subtilty**, so your minds should be corrupted from the simplicity that is in Christ.

WHEAT

Chosen, or Redeemed. (SEE parable of Tares).

WHORE (SEE *HARLOT*)

WINE

Spirit(ual) - Many times it speaks of evil when given in the context of worldliness, but it means peace and joy when the Lord is the subject. Remember, there are two spirits contending for your soul: Christ and antichrist.

Eph. 5:18-19
18   And be not drunk with wine, wherein is <u>excess</u>; but be **filled with the Spirit**;
19   Speaking to yourselves in psalms and hymns and **spiritual** songs, singing and making melody in your heart to the Lord;

In Revelation when it speaks of being 'drunk with wine', it means that hypocrisy is involved. In the case of the Harlot, the world is confused by her stated relationship with Christ, yet she acts un-Christ like. The carnal Christians in the Church indulge in the enticing things of this world confusing people about what is really important. Christ should be all that is important…that is the simplicity of Christ (2 Cor. 11:3). All else is vanity.

THE WOMAN

The Woman is the Church.

The book of Revelation is about washing or cleansing the woman to make her a wife worthy of Christ. Christ has only one Wife, so neither Israel nor the Harlot can make claim to Him; they broke the (betrothal) marriage contract.

THE WIFE
Eph. 5:23-27
23   For the husband is the head of the **wife**, even as **Christ is the head of the church**: and he is the saviour of the body.
24   Therefore as the **church is subject unto Christ**, so let the **wives** be to their own husbands in every thing.
25   Husbands, love your wives, even as Christ also loved the church, and gave himself for it;
26   **That he might sanctify and cleanse it with the washing of water by the word,**
27   **That he might present it to himself a glorious church, not having spot, or wrinkle**, or any such thing; but that it should be holy and without blemish.

The woman bringing forth the true Wife
Rev. 12:5
5   She (the woman) bore a male Child (the remnant) who was to rule all nations with a rod of iron. And

her Child was caught up to God and His throne. (spiritually)

The Church gives access to the Beast/Harlot
Matt. 13:33
33   Another parable spake he unto them; The kingdom of heaven is like unto leaven (the leaven of the Pharisees…A religious spirit), **which a woman took**, and hid in three measures of meal, till the whole was leavened

WORMWOOD (SEE *ALSO 'MORNING STAR'*)

Wormwood means 'bitter waters'. Wormwood is the perfecting presence of Christ through His Elect that make 'bitter waters' (e.g. offending truth). Anything that is not of Christ will be bitter. The Day of the Lord is here and nothing is important but seeking Him. Worldly things that were acceptable will become unacceptable to those who desire Christ. Look how easily we accept doctrines of wealth and prosperity when the Lord instead speaks of suffering and tribulation. Why do we do so much contrary to the full revelation of the gospel…the salt has lost its savor? The truth is a bitter pill to swallow for those who love their lives. The bitter waters are the salt that returns to His body.

WOE

Woe is a state of intense hardship or distress - 'disaster, horror.'

The term 'woe' reveals the extreme hardship that will come against the world. This word in the Greek speaks of disaster, which is what the world faces during the second three-and-one half years. This is Christ's last chance to bring mankind to the Father. In the first dispensation, most of the tribulation is spiritual; but during Thunder 4, things change. The inhabitants of the earth tend to respond only to the natural; therefore, expect to see worldwide trouble. That is one of the reasons that the Bride must become endowed with power, with the full witness of Christ-in-us. When the world starts looking for answers, Christ will be there to minister to them. Moreover, they will be looking for help from world economic depression, natural disasters, maybe even unhindered demonic activity. Only God knows His plan for the world; yet we will be spared, and this will show God's favor.

God did this before when He brought wrath to a people; yet he spared His own. This was a testimony to the Egyptians (a type of the world) that God was with the seed of Abraham.

REVELATION SCRIPTURE INDEX